Praise for *No Gods, No Masters, N*

"Broad in scope, generously ecumenical in outlook, bold in its attempt to tease apart the many threads and tensions of anarchism, this collection defies borders and category. These illuminating explorations in pan-anarchism provide a much-needed antidote to the myopic characterizations that bedevil the red and black. As Trotsky should have said, you may not be interested in anarchism, but anarchism is interested in you."
—Sasha Lilley, author of *Capital and Its Discontents* and *Catastrophism*

"This wonderful collection challenges the privileging of Europe as the original and natural laboratory in which anti-statist ideas developed as well as the belief that anarchism and communism could not intersect in fruitful ways. Drawing on non-Western locations (from Latin America, the Middle East, North Africa, and South Asia) its authors demonstrate how anti-authoritarian movements engaged with both local and global currents to construct a new emancipatory politics—proving that anarchy and anarchism have always been global."
—Barry Carr, La Trobe University

"Anarchism is back. This magnificent collection of essays coincides with an awakening of interest in global anarchism. *No Gods, No Masters, No Peripheries* succeeds admirably in what it sets out to do, providing an important service to those interested in important but neglected anarchist contributions to politics, art, and theory. A quirky, exciting, and imaginative collection, *No Gods, No Masters, No Peripheries* is bound to become a cornerstone of reference for activists and academics."
—Andrej Grubačić, associate professor and department chair, Anthropology and Social Change, California Institute of Integral Studies

"Ranging from Kabylie to Oakland, Cairo to Peru, and across the uneven span of a century and a half, these essays register an ongoing and collective effort to de-provincialise our image of anarchism—a movement long buried in cliché and caricature by friends and enemies alike. In these pages, the reader will encounter some of the ways in which the dreams of the dead might dispel the nightmares that continue to plague the brains of the living."
—Alberto Toscano, reader in critical theory, Department of Sociology, Goldsmiths, University of London

NO GODS, NO MASTERS, NO PERIPHERIES: GLOBAL ANARCHISMS

Edited by Barry Maxwell
and Raymond Craib

ICM
THE INSTITUTE FOR COMPARATIVE MODERNITIES

PM

No Gods, No Masters, No Peripheries: Global Anarchisms
Edited by Barry Maxwell and Raymond Craib

ISBN: 978-1-62963-098-4

Library of Congress Control Number: 2015930884

Cover by John Yates/Stealworks
Interior design by briandesign

10 9 8 7 6 5 4 3 2 1

PM Press
PO Box 23912
Oakland, CA 94623
www.pmpress.org

Printed in the USA by the Employee Owners of Thomson-Shore in Dexter, Michigan.
www.thomsonshore.com

CONTENTS

BLACK, RED, AND GREY: ANARCHISM, COMMUNISM, AND POLITICAL THEORY

All theory is grey. —the Devil

ACKNOWLEDGMENTS

We deeply thank all of the contributors to this volume, who collectively and patiently bore the long process of getting this book together.

And we thank these folks, too:

All of the speakers at the September 2012 ICM conference "No Gods, No Masters, No Peripheries," and the conference presenters not included in this book: Banu Bargu, Iain Boal, Glen Coulthard, Andrej Grubačić, and Jolene Rickard. The conference website can be found at http://www.icm.arts.cornell.edu/conference_2012/index.html. Audio and video recordings of the conference sessions are available at http://www.icm.arts.cornell.edu/video_archive_conference_2012.html.

The array of cosponsors at Cornell who helped the conference happen (a deep breath): the Africana Studies and Research Center, the American Indian Program, the American Studies Program, the Atkinson Center for a Sustainable Future, the Department of Comparative Literature, the Department of Development Sociology, the Department of English, the Feminist, Gender & Sexuality Studies Program, the Department of Government, the Department of History, the Department of History of Art and Visual Studies, the Institute for German Cultural Studies, the Latin American Studies Program, the Latino Studies Program, the Near Eastern Studies Program, the Department of Romance Studies, the Rose Goldsen Lecture Series, and the Society for the Humanities.

Those who contributed new work to this volume: Silvia Rivera Cusicanqui and Barry Maxwell.

G. Peter Jemison (Heron Clan, Seneca Nation) for the prayer that began the conference.

All of the people who attended the conference, some from faraway places. We should have argued more, no?

The chairs of the conference panels: Barry Carr, Eric Cheyfitz, Sasha Lilley, Barry Maxwell, Satya Mohanty, and Mechthild Nagel.

Jolene Rickard, for permission to use an image from her installation "Fight for the Line" (2012).

Ramez Elias, for the proverb quoted in the Afterword, and for the conference website and poster design.

Molly Kerker, former ICM program coordinator, for helping to organize every aspect of the conference, including a large, loud dinner for the hungry, thirsty thinkers.

Mary Anne Grady Flores and the crew at La Cocina Latina for great food.

Alexis Boyce, ICM program coordinator, for scrupulous and knowledgeable editing of the entire manuscript, for hitting just the right notes of encouragement as we moved toward final assembly, and for corresponding with the contributors, some of whom, like the editors, benefitted from well-timed reminders. What a pleasure it has been to work with Alexis.

All of the members of the ICM: Iftikhar Dadi, Salah Hassan, Fouad Makki, Natalie Melas, Viranjini Munasinghe, and Sunn Shelley Wong (particular thanks to Shelley for the cover photograph—the "light writing").

Barry Carr, Andrej Grubačić, Sasha Lilley, and Alberto Toscano for some good words at the right time.

And last but definitely not least, Ramsey "Rock on" Kanaan and everyone at PM Press, as well as John Yates at Stealworks for the great cover.

A FOREWORD

Raymond Craib

> There is not even a thought, or an invention, which is not common property, born of the past and the present.
>
> —Kropotkin, *The Conquest of Bread*

Collectively, the essays in this volume are undisciplined, exploratory, and wide-ranging.[*] It is, in one sense then, a collection in the subjunctive—purposely so. Neither this volume, nor the gathering out of which it derives, were designed to make declarations or establish orthodoxies but instead to explore—across geographic, temporal, and disciplinary limits—the pasts, presents, and futures of anarchism. This volume arose from a gathering held on Cayuga Nation land in upstate New York currently occupied by Cornell University. The people who assembled came together to present work, discuss, and argue about anarchism, the Left, and the world. More specifically, they came together to think through the geographies and temporalities of anti-statist and anti-capitalist movements. The gathering's intellectual starting point—as well as this book's midpoint, evidenced by Bahia Shehab's remarkable work—was one word: NO. No gods and no masters. No orthodoxies and no hierarchies. And, most emphatically, no centers and no peripheries, neither geographical (i.e., Eurocentrism) nor political (anarchist theory and practice as marginal, epiphenomenal, untheorized, and utopian).[1]

---

* I am grateful to Geoffroy de Laforcade, Barry Maxwell, Kyle Harvey, Ernesto Bassi, Ryan Edwards, Barry Carr, and Josh Savala for their comments on earlier drafts.

1 The point here is not to cast anarchism as negation. Rather, "no" serves as the starting point from which to think through implicit affirmatives.

To start with the latter: one aim of our gathering was to reexamine the historical and contemporary relationships between anarchism and other currents of the Left without starting from the position of sectarian difference (for example, Marxism *versus* anarchism). This is not to ignore the disputes that exist, and have existed, within the broad, contentious, and polysemic tradition of socialism, nor is it a breezy call for some cheerful reconciliation or synthesis of its varieties. Rather, our intent is to undermine the facile definitions and teleologies that catalog, rank, and oppose them, often ahistorically, in the imaginary of the Left. Why? For one, the categories and orthodoxies in which we tend to incarcerate concepts and commitments are constantly being constructed, broken, reworked, and reconstituted.[2] As Bruno Bosteels notes in his essay, perhaps heterodoxies precede orthodoxies. What is certain is that they need to be historicized. Moreover, differences and disputes *within* putatively Marxist, anarchist, and related movements—for example over the use of violence (sometimes invoked as a form of vanguardism) or participation in politics (seen as reformist, statist, or both)—often blur the boundaries between those movements, calling into question the very categories by which we name them.[3] The task then is to historicize anarchism—and, as a number of authors in this collection remind us, communism—without fetishizing genealogies and lineages.[4] Contributors to this volume—across a range

2 For excellent discussions, see Ruth Kinna and Alex Prichard, "Introduction," in Alex Prichard, Ruth Kinna, Saku Pinta, and David Berry, eds., *Libertarian Socialism: Politics in Black and Red* (London: Palgrave Macmillan, 2012), who use the language of "broken" and "reworked," and Andrej Grubačić, "The Anarchist Moment," in Jacob Blumenfield, Chiara Boticci, and Simon Critchley, eds., *The Anarchist Turn* (London: Pluto Press, 2013).

3 I draw these two examples here from contemporary anarchism in the "Chilean region," where anarchism has been particularly important in recent years. See Hugo Cristian Fernández, *Irrumpe la Capucha: Qué quieren los anarquistas en el Chile de hoy?* (OceanSur, 2014); Felipe del Solar and Andrés Pérez, *Anarquistas: Presencia libertaria en Chile* (Santiago: RIL, 2008); and Víctor Muñoz Cortés, *Sin Dios ni Patrones: Historia, Diversidad y Conflictos del anarquismo en la región chilena* (Valparaíso: Mar y Tierra, 2014). But such issues, among a multitude of others, are part of the discussions within anarchism more broadly. Ruth Kinna points out, for example, that some "anarchists saw Colin Ward's views as inherently reformist and liberal," a point that Ward did not contest as he did not see "anarchy in action" and "revolutionary anarchism" as necessarily mutually exclusive. See Matthew Wilson and Ruth Kinna, "Key Terms," in Kinna, ed., *The Continuum Companion to Anarchism* (London: Continuum, 2012), 352. See also James C. Scott's recent *Two Cheers for Anarchism* (Princeton, NJ: Princeton University Press, 2012) which, to my mind, resonates with many of Ward's perspectives. See also Andrej Grubačić and David Graeber, "Anarchism, or the Revolutionary Movement of the Twenty-First Century" (2004). For a useful overview of figures associated with critiques within Marxism, see David Renton, *Dissident Marxism: Past Voices for Present Times* (London: Zed Books, 2004). I am especially indebted to Geoffroy de Laforcade for his comments here.

4 On the issue of genealogy, see David Graeber, *Fragments of an Anarchist Anthropology* (Chicago: Prickly Paradigm Press, 2004), but also cf. Kinna and Prichard, "Introduction."

of disciplines—look at how anarchism has been theorized, practiced, and lived in particular places and moments; how the insurgent Left could appear, and in fact was, much more ecumenical and dynamic than frequently portrayed; and how such capaciousness might in fact be a hallmark of anarchist practice, of prefigurative politics and nonhierarchical organizing.[5] Numerous authors have sought in varied ways to give voice to this capacious Left: from Fernando Tarrida del Mármol's "anarquismo sin adjetivos" (anarchism without adjectives) and Colin Ward's anarchy in action to, more recently, Ilham Khuri-Makdisi's recuperation of the "multiplicity of Lefts" in the eastern Mediterranean and Staughton Lynd's and Andrej Grubačić's "Haymarket Synthesis."[6] The authors in this volume, rather than "looking for anarchism," as Maia Ramnath has nicely put it, examine the Left with an eye toward "affinities." They recognize how the label "anarchism" can at times obscure more than it reveals, and thereby refuse the demand and implication of any "-ism."[7]

Another goal of the collection is to counter the lingering diffusionist (and implicitly Eurocentric) perspectives that can characterize work on ideas and movements. The diffusionist line—anarchism (and many other "-isms") was in areas outside of Europe an import and a script to be mimicked—has faced in recent years the challenge of research that reveals anarchism in its plural origins and sheer multiplicity of local variants.[8] At

5 For a recent collection in precisely this vein, see Prichard et al., *Libertarian Socialism*.

6 On Tarrida del Mármol, see Benedict Anderson, *The Age of Globalization: Anarchists and the Anticolonial Imagination* (London and New York: Verso, 2013); Colin Ward, *Anarchy in Action* (Freedom Press, 1982) and Ward, *Anarchism: A Very Short Introduction* (London: Oxford University Press, 2004); Ilham Khuri-Makdisi, *The Eastern Mediterranean in the Making of Global Radicalism, 1860–1914* (Berkeley: University of California Press, 2009); and Staughton Lynd and Andrej Grubačić, *Wobblies and Zapatistas: Conversations on Anarchism, Marxism and Radical History* (Oakland: PM Press, 2008).

7 Ramnath, *Decolonizing Anarchism: An Antiauthoritarian History of India's Liberation Struggle* (Oakland: AK Press, 2012), 5–6; on obscuring and revealing, see George Ciccariello-Maher, "An Anarchism That Is Not Anarchism: Notes toward a Critique of Anarchist Imperialism," in Jimmy Casas Klausen and James Martel, eds., *How Not to Be Governed: Readings and Interpretations from a Critical Anarchist Left* (Lanham, MD: Lexington Books, 2011). See also James Scott, who notes that "anarchist principles are active in the aspirations and political action of people who have never heard of anarchism or anarchist philosophy." Scott, *Two Cheers for Anarchism*, xii. On refusing the "-ism," see Gavin Arnall's essay in this volume.

8 Sho Kinishi, *Anarchist Modernity: Cooperatism and Japanese-Russian Intellectual Relations in Modern Japan* (Cambridge, MA: Harvard University Press, 2013); Lucien van der Walt and Steven Hirsch, eds., *Anarchism and Syndicalism in the Colonial and Postcolonial World, 1870–1940* (Leiden: Brill, 2010); Khuri-Makdisi, *The Eastern Mediterranean*; Ramnath, *Decolonizing Anarchism*; Geoffroy de Laforcade and Kirwin Shaffer, eds., *In Defiance of Boundaries: Anarchism in Latin American History* (Gainesville: University of Florida Press, forthcoming); Constance Bantman and Bert Altena, eds., *Reassessing the Transnational Turn: Scales of Analysis in Anarchist and Syndicalist Studies* (London: Routledge, 2014); Sam Mbah and I.E. Igariwey, *African Anarchism* (Tucson: See Sharp Press, 1997); Grubačić,

one level it has faced the implicit challenge of work that understands anarchism as a form of "strategic positioning" and "deliberate statelessness" going back at least two millenia.[9] This is an anarchism defined in part by the forms of social and political relations which existed in communities—acephaly, fluidity, horizontality—that both preceded and arose out of capitalism, industrialization, and the modern nation-state. As such, the question of Europe or "the West" is irrelevant. The relevant map is, instead, topographical (spaces of refuge, flight, and friction, be they hills, mountains, swamps, or jungles) and the relevant unit of causation is the state. Such communities are not of the past. As James Scott has eloquently made the case, state discourses have an enormous amount invested in locating self-governing peoples either as outside of time or as backward holdovers from a previous era, but in fact such forms of social organization not only exist in constant relation to a broader world of trade and power but are also all too frequently responses to (rather than mere precursors of) the destabilizing effects of state expansion, capitalist encroachment, or both.[10]

In contrast to works that have explored forms of anarchist practice over a broad swath of time, others have sought to historicize anarchism more specifically by situating it in the context of nineteenth-century industrialization, capitalism, and the efforts by working men and women

---

"The Anarchist Moment"; Jason Adams, *Non-Western Anarchisms: Rethinking the Global Text* (Johannesburg: Zabalaza Books, n.d.); and Raymond Craib, *The Cry of the Renegade: Subversive Santiago, 1920* (New York: Oxford University Press, forthcoming).

9 See, for example, Pierre Clastres, *Society Against the State: Essays in Political Anthropology* (New York: Zone Books, 1989, rpt. ed.) and James C. Scott, *The Art of Not Being Governed: An Anarchist History of Upland Southeast Asia* (New Haven, CT: Yale University Press, 2009), from which the quoted text is taken. Scott's work has long had an anarchist sensibility to it. See, for example, *Weapons of the Weak: Everyday Forms of Peasant Resistance in Southeast Asia* (New Haven, CT: Yale University Press, 1985), *Seeing Like a State: How Certain Schemes to Improve the Human Condition Have Failed* (New Haven, CT: Yale University Press, 1998), and *Two Cheers for Anarchism*.

10 Scott, *The Art of Not Being Governed*, passim; Clastres, *Society Against the State*; Roseberry and O'Brien, eds., *Golden Ages, Dark Ages: Imagining the Past in Anthropology and History* (Berkeley: University of California Press, 1997); and Scott's trenchant critique of Jared Diamond's *The World Until Yesterday* in *London Review of Books* 35, no. 22 (November 2013): 13–15. The classic and deeply problematic perspective of locating peoples on a kind of civilizational timeline determined by state functions or capitalist relations continues, most obviously of all in Cold War modernization theoretics that have been reworked to fit an era of dramatic land grabbing, forcible privatization, and geopiracy, all in the name of spreading (diffusing) notions of democracy ideologically defined as "free markets." See, among others, Greg Grandin, *Empire's Workshop: Latin America, the United States, and the Rise of the New Imperialism* (New York: Metropolitan Books, 2007); Joel Wainwright, *Geopiracy: Oaxaca, Militant Empiricism and Geographical Thought* (New York: Palgrave Macmillan 2012); Naomi Klein, *The Shock Doctrine: The Rise of Disaster Capitalism* (New York: Metropolitan Books, 2007); Fred Pearce, *The Land Grabbers: The New Fight over Who Owns the Earth* (Boston: Beacon Press, 2013); and the "Forum on Global Land Grabbing," *Journal of Peasant Studies* 38, no. 2 (2011): 217–47.

to respond to the exploitative foundations of such systems. There is significant value to precisely such historicizations, not least of which is the emphasis on the socialist underpinnings of classical anarchism as well as the avoidance of lumping all forms of anti-statist politics together.[11] But at the same time in this work the rest of the world—so prominent in the "deliberate statelessness" literature—vanishes or survives only as a hazy outline on Europe's horizon. The destiny of communities—cities, towns, countries, labor unions, worker federations—in the "global south" is to be derivative, places of practice awaiting the arrival of theory from without. We should grant them historical agency beyond that of being recipients of imported paradigms or, as Sartre might have put it, "political illiterates." As many of the essays in this volume attest, ideas about the world—and, in this case, their anarchism—were not disembodied imports, another manufactured good delivered as part of a relation of unequal exchange, but a broad set of principles put to work in, and also created from, the specificities, the particularities, of the structural realities of the towns, cities, and regions within which people worked and lived.

Little surprise state officials deployed the language of diffusion (recast as "infection") as part of a broader "prose of counterinsurgency" that cast anarchism as a "misplaced idea" or a foreign ideology to be brutally extirpated from the ranks of labor and the halls of universities through mass expulsions, imprisonment, and assassinations.[12] The point to stress here

11 See especially Michael Schmidt and Lucien van der Walt, *Black Flame: The Revolutionary Class Politics of Anarchism and Syndicalism* (Oakland: AK Press, 2009), esp. "Defining Anarchism: Socialism from Below," and Mark Bray, *Translating Anarchy: The Anarchism of Occupy Wall Street* (Winchester: Zero Books, 2013), esp. 54–60, and Carl Levy, "Social Histories of Anarchism," in *Journal for the Study of Radicalism* 4, no. 2 (Fall 2010): 1–44 for vigorous and thoughtful assessments.

12 Ranajit Guha, "The Prose of Counterinsurgency," in Guha and Spivak, eds., *Selected Subaltern Studies* (New York: Oxford University Press, 1985), and Roberto Schwarz, *Misplaced Ideas: Essays on Brazilian Culture* (London: Verso, 1992). It is essential to recognize just how prevalent such assertions were and remain. Marxism was to the Cold War what anarchism was to the turn of the twentieth century. Military dictatorships in Chile, Argentina, and Brazil in the 1960s and '70s would repeatedly declare that Marxism was an alien ideology. The U.S. government in 1954 would declare that any Marxist government—even if popularly elected—in Latin America would constitute an "invasion" of the Western Hemisphere. Such claims persist. The Mexican government's first response to the Zapatista uprising in 1994 was to accuse a shadowy group of unidentified "outside agitators" of stirring up what it presumed to be an otherwise passive and content indian population. Needless to say, this was not the case and for a discussion of indigenous anarchism among the Zapatistas, see Klein in this volume. Crucial here is that the rhetoric of the "misplaced" idea was not limited to the Right: it is also a language or vocabulary that provides grist for the anti-imperialist mill, whether in Brazil, Chile, or Mexico. This was the very tension Brazilian intellectual Roberto Schwarz sought to explore, using the notion of the misplaced idea as a means to critique the suggestion that if "peripheral" countries such as Brazil were to finally shrug off the European imports in which they purportedly decked themselves, they would

is that anarchism was not a foreign ideology, of course, but neither was it a domestic one. The response to claims of "foreignness" should not by default be nationalist (although I will return to this issue shortly). Rather, it is the very antinomy of "foreign/domestic"—the very binary of importation and autochthony—that needs to be understood as historically determined, linked to the formation of the nation-state, capitalism, and an unequal international division of intellectual labor and legitimation.[13]

The political philosophies and practices, including anarchism, that emerged from Europe, as well as elsewhere, did so in a context that was already part of an imperial, transnational context.[14] The French Revolution proved pivotal for nineteenth-century revolutionary traditions but so too did the Haitian Revolution, which itself dramatically shaped the contours of French political and intellectual life.[15] Given that industrial forms of discipline, labor organization, and production—not to mention policing—were first tested in colonies, in the Caribbean and elsewhere, before being "imported back" to the metropole, exactly where should we locate the point of origin?[16] Big-'A' anarchism was shaped undoubtedly by indus-

---

discover their true essence. For Schwarz, this was the nationalist trap which both the Left and the Right seemed unwilling or unable to avoid. Moreover, it missed the key point that "Brazilian culture" was both product and producer of European culture (akin to the relationship of unequal exchange that was necessary for Europe's industrialization). Schwarz went even further, arguing that Brazilian authenticity was precisely the very application of "improper" names and concepts and ideas to a reality in which they *purportedly* did not fit. The deeply unequal reality of the international division of intellectual labor means that a place such as Brazil could be, in fact, authentic in its *apparent* inauthenticity. For a discussion in the context of Chilean intellectual history, see Bernardo Subercaseaux, *Historia de las ideas y de la cultura en Chile (vol. 3): El centenario y las vanguardias* (Santiago: Editorial Universitaria, 2004). I am indebted to the discussion of Schwarz's work in Elías José Paltí's fine essay "The Problem of 'Misplaced Ideas,'" *Journal of the History of Ideas* 67 (2006): 149–79, and that of Neil Larsen, *Determinations: Essays on Theory, Narrative and Nation in the Americas* (London: Verso, 2001) and Larsen, *Reading North by South: On Latin American Literature, Culture and Politics* (Minneapolis: University of Minnesota Press, 1995).

13 See the first part of the volume in the essays of Rivera Cusicanqui, Klein, and Ramnath as well as in those of Hurley and Porter. On historical determination, see Larsen, *Determinations*, esp. "The 'Hybrid' Fallacy or Culture and the Question of Historical Necessity," and more broadly, Dipesh Chakrabarty, *Provincializing Europe: Postcolonial Thought and Historical Difference* (Princeton, NJ: Princeton University Press, 2007).

14 In particular here see Sho Konishi, "Reopening the 'Opening of Japan': A Russian-Japanese Revolutionary Encounter and the Vision of Anarchist Progress," *American Historical Review* 112, no. 1 (February 2007); and Ramanth, *Decolonizing Anarchism*.

15 See Susan Buck-Morss, *Hegel, Haiti and Universal History* (Pittsburgh: University of Pittsburgh Press, 2009); Michel-Rolph Trouillot, *Silencing the Past: Power and the Production of History* (Boston: Beacon Press, 1997); and Nick Nesbitt, *Universal Emancipation: The Haitian Revolution and the Radical Enlightenment* (Charlottesville: University of Virginia Press, 2008).

16 See, for example, Stefan Palmie, *Wizards and Scientists: Explorations in Afro-Cuban Modernity and Tradition* (Durham: Duke University Press, 2002) and Sidney Mintz,

trialization and capitalism in parts of Europe but it is worth recalling that it was a relentlessly aristocratic, feudal, and agrarian Russia out of which came Bakunin and Kropotkin, with the latter's perspectives informed in important ways by Japanese commoners and intellectuals.[17]

Even where "Europe" ends and begins is geographically unsettled when looking from the perspective of indigenous peoples who bore the brunt of settler colonization.[18] One of colonialism's most insidious consequences was precisely that colonized and formerly colonized peoples had little choice but to participate in some form of dialogue with the metropole and its epistemological foundations, a fact nowhere better expressed than in the continuing struggles of indigenous peoples in various parts of the globe who are forced to conform to evidentiary and analytical criteria, determined by the interests of states and capital, often at odds with their own. This is why this collection begins, purposefully, with an invocation from Taiaiake Alfred and with indigenous anarchisms. And this is why the conference itself opened with a prayer from G. Peter Jemison (Heron Clan) of the Seneca Nation. From the beginning, gods and nations were in attendance, which is in part the point: in particular contexts—continuing colonial contexts, for example—gods and nations may not be *necessarily* ontologically antithetical to anti-statist and anti-capitalist politics.[19] They may at points constitute a means, perhaps one of the few means, through which to organize against exploitation, colonial occupation, and dispossession. All the more reason to be cautious about reproducing a "sterile formalism" that favors purity over context and potentially recolonizes decolonial and anti-colonial politics.[20] In which case, perhaps nineteenth- and twentieth-century anarchists, wherever they resided, were—in their emphasis on the world as their home, in their peripatetic as well as sedentary radicalism, in the fact that anarchist perspectives were articulated and reinvented across geographical and cultural boundaries, in their

---

Sweetness and Power: The Place of Sugar in Modern History (New York: Penguin, 1986, rpt. ed.). Miranda Frances Spieler, in *Empire and Underworld: Captivity in French Guiana* (Cambridge, MA: Harvard University Press, 2012), has argued for situating French Guiana directly in the center of France. The results are mixed but the effort is quite suggestive.

17 Konishi, "Reopening" and *Anarchist Modernity*.

18 On neo-Europes, see Alfred Crosby, *The Columbian Exchange: Biological and Cultural Consequences of 1492* (Westport, CT: Greenwood, 1973); Gregory Cushman, *Guano and the Opening of the Pacific World: A Global Ecological History* (New York: Cambridge University Press, 2013); and Scott, *The Art of Not Being Governed*.

19 See, for good examples of the point, Anderson, *The Age of Globalization*; Ciccariello-Maher, "An Anarchism That Is Not Anarchism"; and Ramnath, *Decolonizing Anarchism*.

20 Ciccarielllo-Maher, "An Anarchism That Is Not Anarchism," 38; Ramnath, *Decolonizing Anarchism* as well as Ramnath in this volume. See also Michael Löwy, *The War of Gods: Religion and Politics in Latin America* (London and New York: Verso, 1996).

anti-colonial politics, in their fraught but occasional fusion of cosmopolitan and indigenous perspectives, and in their visions of a common humanity—some of our most visionary postcolonial theorists.[21]

Anarchist currents are ubiquitous and, as with most currents, points of origin and proprietary rights are difficult to determine. As they should be: there is no immaculate conception. Ideas arise out of specific material contexts, to be sure, but the latter have all too frequently been subsumed by origin stories rooted in the falsified geographies of the nation-state or the metageographies of continents. (As if "Europe," to take one example, were not itself an ideological formation with its own uneven development, its own 'internal' colonial processes, and its own peripheries and centers.)[22] Geography becomes genealogy; ideas become property. But property is the problem.

So let us conclude not with property, but with poetry. As a number of the essays in this volume stress, culture and the imagination—poetry in the broadest sense—should not be, and has not been, removed from the struggle. This is as it should be: "Poetry" is arguably *nothing but* the free act and the anarchic apex. And it is assuredly inseparable from the futures—the *real* futures—that have flooded anarchism's anti-amnesiac politics.[23] The properties of poetry are such that it can not remain on the margin.

No gods, no masters, no peripheries.

---

21 For a volume which highlights anti-colonial and anti-imperialist anarchisms, see van der Walt and Hirsch, eds., *Anarchism and Syndicalism in the Colonial and Postcolonial World*. The editors emphasize these issues in the preface to the paperback edition. See also Anderson, *The Age of Globalization*. For a study of postcolonialism that pays close attention to anti-colonial politics over the twentieth century, see Robert Young, *Postcolonialism: An Historical Introduction* (Oxford: Wiley-Blackwell, 2001).

22 Liberalism, for example, is hardly self-explanatory and cannot be reduced to a "European" phenomenon: it meant one thing in parts of France, another in England, and something else in Russia, just as it acquired different contextual meanings in the United States and Brazil. Emilia Viotti da Costa, "Liberalism: Theory and Practice," in Viotti da Costa, *The Brazilian Empire: Myths and Histories* (Raleigh: University of North Carolina Press, 2000). Brazilian education theorist Paulo Freire remarked that it was in Boston, while in exile, that he came to understand "third-world" as a political rather than geographic category. See Freire, *The Politics of Education: Culture, Power and Liberation* (Westport, CT: Greenwood, 1985), 139–40.

23 See the essays by Linebaugh, Maxwell, Rosemont, and Shehab in this volume.

“Fight for the Line,” Jolene Rickard (2012)

LEARNING FROM INDIGENOUS EXPERIENCE: ANARCHISM AND INDIGENEITY

Is there a Native philosophical alternative? And what might one achieve by standing against the further entrenchment of institutions modeled on the state?

Taiaiake Alfred

THE CH'IXI IDENTITY OF A MESTIZO: REGARDING AN ANARCHIST MANIFESTO OF 1929

Silvia Rivera Cusicanqui

The document I will analyze here, *La Voz del Campesino*, is a notable example of the particularities of anarchist thought and action in Bolivia before the Chaco War (1932–1935).* Its author, the mechanic Luis Cusicanqui, was one of the most creative and persevering libertarian ideologues of La Paz. Together with anarchist seamstress Domitila Pareja, he gave life to the group La Antorcha (The Torch) that existed in La Paz from the early 1920s. In 1927 Cusicanqui became part of the Local Worker Federation (FOL) and became their general secretary in 1940, when the libertarians had already suffered the buffeting of state repression, forced recruitment, and the corporatist policies of cooptation and neutralization by the postwar governments of David Toro and Germán Busch. For her part, Domitila did not live to see the founding of the FOL, dying of tuberculosis in La Paz at twenty-six years of age.[1]

Cusicanqui's trajectory does not seem to have been an exception. In the anarchist archive that survives, we find texts of philosophical and doctrinal reflection, journalistic chronicles, essays, and plays. Like Cusicanqui,

* A very preliminary version of this paper was presented at the Fifth Encounter of Bolivian Studies of the Altiplano Region in June 1988. Picking it up again after so many years (in 2011), I have added a deeper theoretical reflection about the insurgent potential of *mestizaje* (lo ch'ixi), which was not entirely clear when I wrote it the first time. In contrast with the pessimistic and solitary tone of my first diagnoses of mestizaje, the ideas I have elaborated here emerge from the rich interaction in/with the activist group Colectivo Ch'ixi, which since 2008 has undertaken research projects and publications that express, theoretically and aesthetically, that fundamental notion. The essay was originally titled *La identidad ch'ixi de un mestizo: En torno a* La Voz del Campesino, *manifiesto anarquista de 1929* and is here translated by Molly Geidel.

1 In the video *Voces de Libertad*, to whose script I contributed substantially, there appears a fictionalized figure of this anarchist seamstress, although she is represented as a chola and not as a *birlocha*.

many men and women of the cholo/a urban working class linked manual labor with a broad humanistic self-education and the daily work of agitation and propaganda. They wrote philosophy and dabbled in essays and the theater without ceasing to work in their respective manual jobs or becoming armchair ideologues or politicians. Rather, their political philosophy and critical writing were closely intertwined with their daily work of manual labor and solidarity organizing. They were determined in their desire to reveal the arrogance and arbitrariness of the *misti* (now we would say *q'ara*), elite, with its lack of authentic culture and its illegitimate hold on wealth and power. The continuity between the colonial oppressor and the bourgeois oligarchy nurtured the memory of suffering and violence, and denoted a *qhipnayra* sense of historical time.[2] In these brief notes I will try to elucidate these aspects of the history and thought of the La Paz anarchist movement, considering this singular text and the personal seal of its author in the context of the intense mass participation of the cholo and indigenous populations of the hills of La Paz and El Alto.

I

Even though we do not know the exact context that surrounded the manifesto's diffusion, recent research by historian Roberto Choque (2009) shows that *La Voz del Campesino* had widespread distribution in the countryside, in rural regions, and among the urban artisan cholo class, bearer of the labor energy that gave life to the city. The La Paz anarchists' verbal and written style, which combines a Spanish full of archaisms and distortions with a metaphorical and politicized Aymara, resembles a *ch'ixi* fabric interwoven with their reflections and experiences. This is a dialect that threads its doctrine through the twisting crosshatch of *castimillano* (Aymara-inflected) Spanish: an intercultural lingua franca that permitted the anarchists to adapt and re-create libertarian and indigenous metaphors through a dense testimonial fabric.

La Voz del Campesino is directed at the countryside and written in the first person. In this we see the first contradiction, since the author wrote it in the city rather than the country. Is this a calculated gesture, a paternalist approximation of the reality of an Aymara free communies and *hacienda colonos* by an urban mestizo artisan in an attempt at demagoguery or impersonation?[3] Or was the document really written by an Indian, in which case it is only the urban anarchist translation of an Indian's thought? As any middle-class vanguardist or rearguard Indianist could

2 *Qhipnayra* is the Aymara sense of continuity or simultaneity between the past and the future (see below).

3 An example of this type of discourse can be seen in Reyeros's *El Pongueaje,* written in the same period.

affirm, seeing the color of his skin next to Domitila's: you just have to see his face to know he is an Indian! But things are never so simple. Because of his education, because of the imbrication of two languages that permanently battled in his brain, because of his family trajectory, Cusicanqui was what we would call a *ch'ixi* mestizo, an Indian spotted with white, transculturated in an agonizing, ambivalent, and unruly manner.

Throughout the manifesto, the "I" and the "we"—more frequently the first person plural—refers to *the Indian*, even though a few times he uses the word "peasant." The title, rather than denoting the real content of the text, actually obscures it. In the subtitle the identification is clearer, but it moves along an oppositional path; this reads: "our challenge to the great *mistes* of the State . . ." *Miste, misti,* State = *misti*; a term that denotes caste. It means we, the Indians, face our enemies, the *mistis* and the State.

It is worth clarifying that in the 1920s the term "peasant" did not carry the ideological *khumunta*[4] it was later given during the era of revolutionary nationalism of the post-Chaco period. Between the *misti* classes it was simply a term used as a euphemistic synonym for Indian—which is largely the way it continues to be used today—perhaps due to the shame of the elites who, faced with these others, realized their own position in such an ostensibly colonial relationship. In any case, it is likely that such shame weighed on them as a hidden motivation for the post-1952 official incorporation of the term, and for the *khumunta* or linguistic servitude the term has carried from that point forward.

But Cusicanqui does not speak or construct his sentences like a "*misti*." Within him the two languages live and intertwine, as two categorical ways of defining reality. His use of the term "peasant" seems to have a rationalizing and ordering sense. It speaks of an attempt at precision, one made clear by its context. For example, when he says "*comunarios* peasants of the hacienda" he refers to Indians (*comunarios*), workers of the land (peasants), subject to the dominion of a patron or landowner. Indian would be the broadest generic identification, which would obviate the need to provide skin-color or differentiations in location or labor activity. "Peasant," on the other hand, alludes to the Indians of the countryside, in contrast with the Indians of the city, and refers specifically to those who live and work in communities that are free or controlled by the hacienda. The same is true when he speaks of herders in an exemplary ch'ixi construction:

> The animal herders enter and at the end of the year all the animals the poor peasant possesses will be captured.

4 Burden, or heavyweight carried in the back, in Aymara [translator's note].

Here the word "peasant" is accompanied by "poor" in a paternalistic sense. When he talks about the "Indian," however, the resignation and the everyday nature of the oppression that go along with his use of "peasant" disappear. He chooses the term "Indian" at the moment he presents the heroic features of subjects in action:

> More than a hundred thirty years ago we came from suffering the cruelest slavery imaginable to the republican moment that offered us independence, costing us Indian blood and lives to free us from the Spanish yoke that made us wail during more than 400 years, or four centuries.

The colonial horizon, including the decades of republican life, condenses into a present of vivid oppression shared by dwellers of the Andean altiplano and the cities in their territory.

> The creoles in pants insult us, whip in hand—woman, man, child, ancient, how they enslave us. What will we say of the doctors, lawyers, and other Kellkeris?[5] Oh! Those are the worst thieves and outlaws who rob us with the Law in hand; and, if we say something, they beat us and for good measure, send us to jail for ten years, and during all this, throw out our woman and children, and top it off with the burning of our houses, and we are chased with the bullets of those men so honorably enlightened.

Apart from the burning of the houses—which alludes to a habitual practice employed by those "so honorably enlightened" to expand their haciendas—the "Indian workers" in the cities suffered identical abuses (see THOA 1984, Mamani 1991, Rivera 1992). As Cusicanqui notes:

> This year the thing has taken on a more anguished tone. With the motive of threatening war with Paraguay, numerous *Indian workers* rebelled against a conflict that they guessed was intentionally provoked by capitalists and politicians. The consequence is the repression in Oruro, Cochabamba, and Potosí, with some *indigenous communists* shot by Siles' executioners, and others made prisoners: Cusicanqui, confined at the foot of the majestic Illimani, in the corner of Cohoni, and M.O. Quispe, detained in Yungas.[6]

---

5 Spanish-influenced spelling of the Aymara word *qilqiri,* meaning clerk or scribe.

6 My emphasis. Report sent by Luis Cusicanqui to the editors of the Uruguayan anarchist magazine *El Hombre* (Montevideo, October 1, 1929) under the pseudonym "Aymara Indian." In this document he takes note of the government's repressive actions, motivated by the diffusion of *Voz del Campesino,* which caused his confinement to Cohoni. We should note that when he speaks of "indigenous communists," he refers to libertarian communism.

The inclusivity of Cusicanqui's community-in-rebellion alludes not only to colonial oppression abstracted as a memory, but also to real connections between La Paz artisans and Indian communities: one is deported to Cohoni—where his comrade had relatives and lands—and the other to the coca-farming zone of the Yungas. This wide territorial circulation had, however, a nucleus: the city of La Paz. It also had a doctrinary head: the libertarian communists. They formed an exclusive but inclusive *nanaka* ("we"), which is universal and particular at the same time, and which proposes an "avant-garde" identity of Indian libertarians, mutually contaminated in the process of anti-colonial struggle.

II

The grammatical structure of Aymara recognizes two types of first person plural: the inclusive "we" (*jiwasa*), and the exclusive "we" (*nanaka*). The first can also have a plural form (*jiwasanaka*). *Jiwasa* refers to situations in which the subject includes the interlocutor, and in plural includes everyone. *Nanaka* alludes to a "we" that excludes the interlocutor. The collective identity attributed throughout the text to the urban artisan class includes the indigenous community-members, but also speaks from a distinctly urban location. The context of this act of communication is one of emergency. The increasingly radical mobilizations of the Andean communities and of the multihued sectors of urban *cholos* intertwined their struggles, until they were pushed together to the precipice of a war that cost Bolivia fifty thousand victims, most of them coming from rural communities and urban popular neighborhoods.

Another distinctive mark of the Spanish Cusicanqui employs is his use of time. Written three years before the war, his long memorial of aggravation expresses an anticipatory conscience that continually builds bridges between the future and the past (*qhipnayra*). His denunciation is the subjective expression of this dual movement in which two collectivities unite and separate facing a common oppressor: the *misti* State, whose modes of power are degradation, disdain, and contempt, from which even the most qualified artisan and the most lettered Indian cannot escape. The interpellatory force of anarchism's egalitarian and anti-state doctrine derives from the shared experience of those motley, oppressed collectivities who "ride between two worlds" and traverse multiple borders.[7] History, remote or recent, thus articulates a long anti-fiscal communitarian memory with the exclusions and violence of the present. But this does not imply that Andean communities were perceived as ideally anarchist,

---

7 This is an allusion to the volume of the same name from Chukyawu, *The Aymara Face of La Paz* (CIPCA, 1987), by Albó, Greaves, and Sandoval [editor's note].

or "societies against the State" as theorized by Clastres (1974). The Andean communities had previously possessed their own state, which had been beheaded and dispossessed of its structure of leadership and meaning. In the republican era, this reality had been obscured, and it was precisely the most iconic emblem of citizenship that revealed the critical potential of that erasure. As Cusicanqui writes:

> The Identity card, what does it do for us Indians? Since we are beasts of burden and nothing more. . . . Why do we now pay twenty centavos for a box of matches? Since now we find ourselves without warm clothing, without bread, and now without light, and we see ourselves reduced to returning to the primitive era, so-called by our governors and legislators. Why do you, the civilized, force us to return to savagery?

This passage presents a complex traverse between *nanaka* and *jiwasa*, first person plural and fourth person singular, and between colloquial and formal forms of Spanish.[8] The nanaka questions the State, and the negation of the other is transformed into an affirmation of the self through the memory of that very alterity. "Was it the work of our civilization?" Here he refers to a distant past in which there was no slavery, although there was "civilization" (and the State). The box of matches refers to the mercantile-capitalist present, to the sale of labor power to obtain clothing, light, and bread (the typical urban food). The central point, however, comes in the conclusion, written in an "enlightened" tone, perhaps to make more intelligible the prosaic truth it conveys: that the civilized leaders make the present archaic, returning not only Indians to the colonial past, but themselves as well. The *mistis* and *q'aras* who degrade and enslave are the most archaic, as they don't debate with argument, but simply murder.

In this way, it becomes clear that Cusicanqui's broader identity, the one that challenges "the mistis and their state," is his identity as an Indian. This identification produces the most heartfelt words of the manifesto: "Take heed, my Indian brothers of the American race, that bloodshed will be the sign of the revolution that will topple this vile society, a thousand times cursed." This moral indignation, the creative rage of the text, emerges from such broad identification (*jiwasanaka*), now not only with his brothers of the Altiplano, but rather with the whole "American race," that which battled for centuries against European colonizers, Indians of the country and the city identified as collective subjects. But this "long-term memory" is always tied to the denunciation of the modern republican

---

8 The fourth person singular is roughly equivalent to the obviate grammatical person, which is often rendered in English by "one."

paradox, which makes citizens of the Indians only in order to continue by other means pillaging their lands and exploiting their labor. The lettered circles of the anarchist movement, as much as the *caciques-apoderados* movement led by Santos Marka T'ula, forcefully perceived the parodic and twisted character of the republic's laws, labeling them "illegitimate, criminal" and "cynical."[9]

Here we see a new overlap between anarchist doctrine and the experience of Aymara communities: a vision of the law as a fictional and deceitful discourse, of judicial power as a tentacle of the State, and of official language as a duplicitous and immoral plot. This melds the doctrinaire notion of the existence of a moral law embodied by individual freedom with the action of the Aymara *caciques-apoderados* movement, which also approached the linguistic and ethical contradictions of colonialism as a battle against an other who is *pä chuyma*, or two-faced.

With this in mind, let us return to the chronological order of the document, which blends episodes of communal rural resistance and mobilizations of urban artisans into a single sequence. For example, it describes the "recent" event of the 1920 assassination of Prudencio Callisaya at the orders of the powerful hacendado of Guaqui, Benedicto Goytia, ". . . and the recent events of Cochabamba, Potosí, and Sucre, and the martyr of Guaqui, it is clearly soldiers who have fractured the limbs of our brother Prudencio Callisaya. Like savage fiends, you soldiers have no right to call yourselves civilized, you are barbarous criminals of the twentieth century, mutilators and destroyers of humanity."

Relatives of Prudencio Callisaya, in the trial they held for many years against the landowner Benedicto Goytia, denounced that Callisaya's body was not dismembered; rather, he was "found" hanged by his own rope. The fracturing of his limbs that Cusicanqui notes thus most likely refers to a longer memory: the dismemberment of Tupak Katari. Events throughout the narrative occur with this kind of apparent temporal disorder. Is this about imprecision or irrelevant lapses? Clearly not. The image of the indigenous martyr is reactivated in the body of any victim assassinated by the colonial powers: through each death, the social body of the oppressed is again fractured.

Beyond this, however, this "long" memory had been reactivated more recently in a meeting between Cusicanqui and Santos Marka T'ula, in

9 See THOA, El Indio Santos Marka T'ula, cacique principal de los ayllus de Qallapa y apoderado general de las comunidades originarios de la República; Silvia Rivera Cusicanqui, "Pedimos la revisión general de límites: un episodio de incomunicación de castas en el movimiento de caciques apoderados de los Andes bolivianos" in Segundo Moreno and Frank Salomón, *Reproducción y transformación en los Andes, Siglos XVI–XX* (Quito: Abya Yala, 1991).

the city of La Paz in 1928.[10] The philosophy of *La Voz del Campesino* was strongly influenced by this direct contact between the libertarian leaders and the indigenous authorities, resulting in a worldview that, in the case of Cusicanqui, is rooted in previous experiences and convictions. Not only the writing style—which reveals the influence of his native tongue—but also the chronological disruption of the document allows us to think in a logic of *quipnayra*, an indigenous way of perceiving time and expressing it in writing.

In this sense, the rage is timeless. As in all ethics, the judgment that emerges from this event projects through time as a historical moral and caution. Reading the judgment for the murder of Prudencio Callisaya, it is shocking to verify that, after he died hanging in the Guaqui barracks at the orders of Colonel Julio Sanjinés—son-in-law of Benedicto Goytia, one of the largest landholders of the Altiplano—his relatives discovered the crime and initiated a long trial that ended in frustration. At various moments in the process they demonstrated the treachery and premeditation of the assassination. Three times they went through arduous autopsy procedures, and even appealed to the Superior District Court with irrefutable proof. But it was all in vain, as Sanjinés and Goytia were never touched by the complicit and corrupt justice, which their caste had created to assume a republican appearance.[11]

Cusicanqui's solidarity with Callisaya is fraternal, almost familial. He mourns his murdered brother. Other phrases also reveal genealogical ties, which clarify the inclusive identity Cusicanqui assumes:

> We are martyrs forever, fresh are the wounds you opened with our ancestors.
>
> Why would we help carry out the cynical laws called income taxes, since our ancestors left us common lands and now we find ourselves reduced to true slavery, was that the work of our civilization?

The past here represents civilization and respect, dignity and community, but also the regression and stagnation occasioned by colonialism, which invaded and disrupted the historical autonomy of Amerindian societies. As such, the amalgam between the anarchist doctrine and the experience of oppression becomes still more evident. The Indian/victim frequently associated in the text with the "peasant" alludes to a particularist

10 The cacique leader approached the FOL in search of solidarity and support for the communal cause, according to accounts by his comrades Teodoro Peñaloza, Max Mendoza, and Lisandro Rodas in a testimony collected at the beginning of the 1980s and published in the *Boletín Historia Oral,* no. 1, THOA, La Paz 1986.

11 This case was consulted in the Archive of La Paz, UMSA, Superior District Court, 1920.

and exclusive identity. It is that which, chained to the yoke of oppression, would be seen to force them to regress toward a low and humiliated subjectivity. Faced with this moral regression, only the dream of future emancipation would provide access to a universal subject-position.

Later, the text nevertheless alludes to an alliance with "poor mestizos"; those who, in contrast to "the *mistis* and their State," would be possible interlocutors in the emancipatory project. To whom is this phrase directed? Is it to other comrades, artisans or anarchists like Cusicanqui; those more Westernized, who considered the Indian an impediment to social progress?[12] The threatening tone of the text tells us that the anti-colonial Indian identification seems to prevail over any doctrinal considerations:

> Take heed Indian brothers of the American race, the bloodshed is a warning of the revolution that will topple this vile society, a thousand times cursed, and the "mistes," who have bought and assassinated our caciques. Blood must spill like before because we are tired of the present domination, we know this and we know very well the Vampires of the dominant state and its dirty tricks, that if the poor mestizo does not lead us to liberation, we Indians will make torrents of blood flow in America Bolivia.

It is not possible to delve more deeply into this point, because the manifesto—and the project it embodies—is ideologically constructed by the logic of opposition as a source of identity. It tells us little, explicitly, about the characteristics of the future society that would be born after this bloodshed. Undoubtedly this metaphor is a resource of the last instance, a threat that is incredible but real, since it is framed as legitimate self-defense:

> Now we ask ourselves: where are the rights of the people? What do the Governing men call the people? We are Indians contained in the Andean steppes of America by the exclusive work of our oppressors. The Bolivian Indian has his hypocritical sympathizers in the upper-classes and the clergy, but only while they secretly plan our complete disappearance from civilization, supplying us with laws of the gallows.

There is a citizenship claim inscribed in this invective against the colonial double standard of the oligarchy. The paradox of oppression in

12 Anarchists of this type also existed, in Bolivia and elsewhere, but there was also Ezequiel Urviola in Puno, and the itinerant Paulino Aguilar, leader of Regional Indigenous Workers' Federation of Peru until his deportation by the government of Leguía in 1928. Private archive of Luis Cusicanqui, Tambo Colectivo archive, La Paz.

a liberal state consists of what fallaciously appeals to the recognition of the rights of all—as workers and as citizens—but in practice denies even the humanity of oppressed populations.

In this and other documents we glimpse an image of a broad and inclusive society in which there would be no more (colonized) Indians but rather human beings, equal in their rights as workers and free to construct their own destiny. But would there be space here for the recognition of cultural and linguistic diversity of the society? If we take into account the permanent effort of the anarchist ideologues to connect lived experiences with the doctrine taken from classic texts, we would find a possible image in the idea of a "federative" society. A manifesto launched by the FOL in 1938 puts it this way:

> In politics, there should be broad governmental decentralization, beneath a federative system respecting the independence and autonomy of every last village and citizen, free expression of thought, and of the press: the diversity of thought, tendencies, and affinities would make possible the evolution of science and art.[13]

For Luis Cusicanqui, anarchist and Indian, the desired emancipation would not be embodied by a unique focal point or in a strict program. It would be expressed in the ordinary and extraordinary actions of concrete collectives, in the joint action of workers and manual laborers—indigenous artisans and farmers—for whom anarchism would be the most fitting expression of universality. It is a libertarian and indigenous philosophy that, decades afterward, would find expression in the slogan launched by the Zapatista movement of Chiapas: "one world in which many worlds fit."

13 "1886—May 1—1938," Manifesto of the Local Workers' Federation, Tambo Colectivo archive, La Paz.

THE ZAPATISTA MOVEMENT: BLENDING INDIGENOUS TRADITIONS WITH REVOLUTIONARY PRAXIS

Hilary Klein

When the founders of the Ejército Zapatista de Liberación Nacional (Zapatista Army of National Liberation, EZLN) went to the mountains of Chiapas, Mexico, to form a guerrilla nucleus in 1983, this small group of Marxists encountered, and began to interact with, a campesino movement with deep roots in Mayan culture and a history of indigenous resistance. Their willingness to learn from the indigenous communities of Chiapas and to adapt their revolutionary model and philosophy helped to transform the EZLN into one of the most interesting and closely analyzed social movements of the late twentieth century.

Although it did not emerge directly from an anarchist tradition, the EZLN's unique blend of radical traditions resulted in it having much in common with an anarchist philosophy: a critique of the state, a commitment to horizontal institutions and participatory decision-making, working collectively, and a focus on social transformation rather than attempting to seize state power. At the same time, other revolutionary traditions that helped birth Zapatismo, including Marxism-Leninism, are still present in the EZLN, and its hierarchical military structure coexists with its more democratic civilian institutions.

With its project of indigenous autonomy, the Zapatista movement has demonstrated that it is possible to build alternative institutions based on indigenous philosophy and culture while also incorporating revolutionary elements. Zapatista territory, in the highlands and jungle regions of eastern Chiapas, has a functioning autonomous government, economy, and health and education infrastructure.

Based on the author's years of experience living in Chiapas and working in Zapatista communities, and using testimony from members of the Zapatista support base, this essay will examine the ways that the

Zapatista movement combines indigenous traditions with revolutionary praxis to offer a fascinating model for building alternatives to the state and challenging state power from below.

The Historical Roots of the EZLN

The EZLN is an insurgent army and grassroots social movement fighting for land and indigenous rights in the southern Mexican state of Chiapas. Since its brief armed uprising in January 1994, the EZLN has been known more for its peaceful mobilizations, dialogue with civil society, and construction of indigenous autonomy. The EZLN is named for Emiliano Zapata, a hero of the Mexican Revolution, and takes up his rallying cry of *Tierra y Libertad* (land and freedom). The EZLN has also set forth a broad set of demands around issues of justice and democracy.

January 2014 marked the twentieth anniversary of the Zapatista uprising and thirty years since the formation of the EZLN as a clandestine organization. Over the past three decades, the impact of the Zapatista movement can be seen at the local, national, and international level. The Zapatista construction of indigenous autonomy has meant that rural villages in Chiapas have gained access to rudimentary health care and education, which they previously lacked; autonomous village and regional governments established by the Zapatistas permit these communities to exercise self-determination; and economic cooperatives organize the production of goods and generate resources which are invested back into the communities.

At the national level, the EZLN signed the San Andrés Accords with the Mexican government in 1996, which recognized indigenous rights and promised indigenous autonomy. (Celebrated at the time, the San Andrés Accords were never implemented by the Mexican government.) The Zapatista movement arguably helped bring an end to seventy years of one-party rule in Mexico, when the Partido Revolucionario Institucional (Institutional Revolutionary Party, or PRI), which had monopolized state power since the Mexican Revolution, lost the presidential elections in 2000.

Around the world, the Zapatistas catalyzed a wave of solidarity with their struggle and inspired a generation of young activists to organize for social justice in other contexts. The repercussions of the Zapatista movement at the international level may be difficult to measure but should not be underestimated. International gatherings organized by the EZLN nourished the burgeoning global justice movement. Events inspired or influenced by the Zapatistas include the World Social Forum—an annual global forum for grassroots activists and organizations—and demonstrations against global capitalism, such as the protests against the World Trade

Organization (WTO) in Seattle in 1999. Evo Morales, a socialist and the first indigenous president of Bolivia, has often referred to the Zapatistas in his speeches and writings.[1] With its ideological critique of neoliberalism and its internal emphasis on participatory democracy, the EZLN was also a precursor to the Occupy and "We Are the 99%" movements that emerged almost two decades after the Zapatista uprising. Perhaps most importantly, after the fall of the Berlin Wall and with pundits declaring the definitive triumph of free market capitalism, the EZLN provided the world with a vision of what the next wave of revolutionary social movements might look like.[2]

The story of the Zapatista rebellion begins with the Spanish conquest of the Americas. Colonialism brought to Chiapas not only the economic subjugation of indigenous peoples and the concentration of land and wealth in the hands of a few, European-descended families, but also a deep and enduring racism. The roots of indigenous resistance go back as far as these structural inequities. The history of the ELZN also grows out of the legacy of the Mexican Revolution. The vastly unequal distribution of wealth and political power during the dictatorship of Porfirio Díaz helped spark the Mexican Revolution of 1910. Díaz was overthrown in 1911 but the Mexican Revolution developed into a protracted civil war that lasted until 1920. The promise of agrarian reform, institutionalized in the Mexican Constitution of 1917, was not realized in most of Mexico until the administration of President Lázaro Cárdenas (1934–1940).

But Cárdenas's reforms, and the Mexican Revolution as a whole, were slow to reach Chiapas and unevenly implemented. As Neil Harvey put it, "the [Mexican] revolution in Chiapas was essentially about who would control access to Indian land, labor, and production."[3] In the decades leading up to the Zapatista uprising, much of the land and wealth of Chiapas continued to be concentrated in the hands of a small number of mestizo families. Many indigenous peasants who now make up the Zapatista support base lived and worked on *fincas* themselves, or remember stories told to them by their parents and grandparents. (*Fincas*—or *haciendas* as they were also called in other parts of the Americas—were extensive and largely self-sufficient estates that trapped indigenous labor-

---

1 For example, on January 22, 2006, Evo Morales closed his inauguration speech by saying, "I will fulfill my commitment, as Subcomandante Marcos says, to lead by obeying the people; I will lead Bolivia by obeying the Bolivian people." From: "Mandaré obedeciendo al pueblo boliviano," *Prensa de Frente*, January 22, 2006, accessed December 27, 2013, http://www.prensadefrente.org/pdfb2/index.php/a/2006/01/22/p1006.

2 See, for example, Francis Fukuyama, "The End of History?," *The National Interest* 16 (Summer 1989): 3–18.

3 Neil Harvey, *The Chiapas Rebellion: The Struggle for Land and Democracy* (Durham and London: Duke University Press, 1998), 52.

ers through debt peonage, often from generation to generation.) These peasants describe violence and exploitation that sound like they might have taken place in previous centuries but happened just a few decades ago.

Chiapas became part of Mexico in 1824 but it took Mexico's federal government many decades to fully integrate Chiapas and other distant states. Throughout the twentieth century, Chiapas continued to function as an internal colony in many ways, with its natural resources extracted and sent to central and northern Mexico. Chiapas is rich in natural resources such as land, oil, natural gas, and water, yet it is one of the poorest states in Mexico. It produces more than half of Mexico's hydroelectric power, yet in 1990, a few years before the Zapatista uprising, almost half of its own population did not have electricity.[4] More than a decade after the uprising, over two-thirds of its population still had no access to clean drinking water.[5] Chiapas has one of the largest indigenous populations in Mexico, and some of the highest rates of malnutrition, maternal mortality, and illiteracy. All of these indicators of marginalization are highest in eastern Chiapas, where the indigenous population is most concentrated.

The Development of Zapatismo

The more recent roots of the Zapatista movement lie in the second half of the twentieth century. The 1960s and '70s were a time of social unrest and vibrant social movements around the world, including in Mexico. In the 1970s, Chiapas saw a surge of peasant organizations fighting for land reform and other agrarian demands. Maoist students and organizers, believing that peasants would be a key sector in the overthrow of the capitalist state, traveled to Chiapas from other parts of Mexico and helped build some of these organizations.

The campesino movement also counted on support from the Catholic Church. In 1962, Vatican II expressed a "preferential option for the poor" and liberation theology became a locus for grassroots mobilization. The Diocese of San Cristóbal de las Casas, led by Bishop Samuel Ruiz García, contributed to the politicization and leadership development of the indigenous communities of Chiapas. Many indigenous deacons and catechists trained by the Diocese, who Christopher Gunderson has termed "organic indigenous campesino intellectuals," went on to become militants and

4 George Collier, *Basta! Land and the Zapatista Rebellion in Chiapas* (Oakland: Food First Books, 1994), 17.

5 Physicians for Human Rights, *Excluded People, Eroded Communities: Realizing the Right to Health in Chiapas, Mexico* (El Colegio de la Frontera Sur, Centro de Capacitación en Ecología y Salud para Campesinos-Defensoría del Derecho a la Salud, 2006), 12.

leaders of the EZLN.[6] Thousands of indigenous men and women were not only instructed in the catechism, but taught to read and write, encouraged to analyze their social, political, and economic reality, and encouraged to speak up against injustice. The Indigenous Congress of 1974, organized by the Diocese, brought together over a thousand Tzeltal, Tzotzil, Tojolabal, and Chol delegates and is often pointed to as a pivotal moment when indigenous groups began to voice their own solutions to the problems they faced.

By the late 1970s, the Fuerzas de Liberación Nacional (National Liberation Forces, or FLN) the political-military organization that founded the EZLN, had begun organizing in some indigenous villages of Chiapas. The FLN, founded in 1969 in the northern Mexican city of Monterrey, was a clandestine Marxist organization with a revolutionary nationalism inspired by the Cuban and Nicaraguan revolutions and made up primarily of leftist intellectuals and students. In 1983, the FLN founded the EZLN as a guerrilla nucleus in the mountains of Chiapas. As Gloria Muñoz Ramírez describes it, "On November 17th, 1983, a small group of indigenous people and mestizos set up camp in the Lacandón Jungle. Under cover of a black flag with a five-pointed red star, they formally founded the Zapatista Army of National Liberation. And they began an unlikely adventure."[7] When it created the EZLN, the FLN was guided by Che Guevara's "foco theory" that a small band of guerrillas, without close ties to the masses and not necessarily participating in their struggles, could launch small-scale guerrilla warfare and thus spark a broader popular uprising.

Those first members of the EZLN, however, encountered a different reality from what they had expected, including a culture shock from contact with the indigenous communities of Chiapas, many of whom were already deeply engaged in grassroots social movements. What allowed for the creation of Zapatismo—and one factor that led the EZLN to become such a successful organization—was the willingness of the core leadership to adapt its revolutionary model. The ELZN's leaders did not abandon their critique of capitalism or their commitment to national liberation, but they were able to reshape their political philosophy and strategy according to the material reality and historical context of rural Chiapas, including the relationship between Chiapas and the federal government, the history of the PRI in rural Mexico and, later on, their interaction with Mexican civil society. And, rather than maintaining a

6 Christopher Gunderson, "The Provocative Cocktail: Intellectual Origins of the Zapatista Uprising" (PhD dissertation, City University of New York, 2013), 266.

7 Gloria Muñoz Ramírez, *The Fire and the Word: A History of the Zapatista Movement*, trans. Laura Carlsen with Alejandro Reyes Arias (San Francisco: City Lights Books, 2008), 47.

rigid ideology, they were open to learning from, and incorporating, the diversity of worldviews and wealth of political practices represented in the indigenous communities, the Maoist-influenced peasant organizations, and the Diocese of San Cristóbal, all already present in Chiapas.

Subcomandante Marcos, the military leader and poetic spokesperson of the EZLN, described this process in an interview with French sociologist Yvon Le Bot:

> Zapatismo was not Marxism-Leninism, but it also was Marxism-Leninism. It wasn't the Marxism of the university, it wasn't the Marxism of concrete analysis, it wasn't the history of Mexico, it wasn't fundamentalist and millennialist indigenous thought, it wasn't indigenous resistance: it was a mix of all this, a cocktail that was mixed in the mountains and that crystallized in the fighting force of the EZLN, that is to say among the regular troops. The regular troops, the insurgents, us, Major Mario, Captain Maribel, Major Ana Maria, those that had spent all this time in the mountains, we are the final product of this collision of cultures. And all the *compañeros* of the [Clandestine Revolutionary Indigenous] Committee that had spent the most time, like Tacho, David, Zebedeo, *compañeros* that were there from the start, who had been in the Zapatista Army of National Liberation for ten, twelve years, and who by their work were the leaders of the movement, began to produce their own definition of what Zapatismo is.[8]

Marcos has often referred to the fluid and dynamic interactions between these two cultures, and the figure of Viejo Antonio (Old Antonio) highlights this relationship. Marcos talks about Viejo Antonio as a critical link between the guerrillas training in the mountains and the indigenous villages that would become the EZLN's civilian support base and transform it into a broad social movement. Speaking to Le Bot, Marcos said:

> The first community we took in 1985—or, I should say, that first community that we entered as Zapatistas—was Viejo Antonio's community. He acted as a kind of translator, explaining to us what we were and what we should do . . . At the same time we are going through an internal process of change regarding Zapatismo. It is Viejo Antonio who serves as a bridge so that the guerrillas in the mountains arrive in the communities. His final contribution was to make the Zapatistas understand the specificity of the indigenous

8 Yvon Le Bot, *El sueño zapatista: Entrevistas con el subcomandante Marcos, el mayor Moisés y el comandante Tacho, del Ejército Zapatista de Liberación Nacional* (Barcelona: Plaza y Janés, 1997), 198–201.

> question in the mountains of southern Mexico. . . . In the end, this is the tool that Marcos appropriates to join the indigenous world with the urban world. Viejo Antonio is the one who contributed the indigenous elements to the Zapatista discourse that we present to the outside. I am a plagiarist.[9]

Described by Marcos as a Tzeltal elder whom he met in 1983 and who died of tuberculosis in 1994, Viejo Antonio is also believed to be an amalgam of indigenous elders, representing the collective voice of indigenous communities. In Marcos's writing, Viejo Antonio becomes something of an alter ego for Marcos, who uses Viejo Antonio's fables and stories to explain how the indigenous communities and their worldview shaped the Zapatista movement.

There are other elements of Zapatismo that represent an evolution from the FLN's original political philosophy but do not stem solely from the insurgents' relationship to the indigenous communities—for example, the focus on social transformation rather than attempting to seize state power. When it rose up in arms in 1994, the EZLN's intention was to take state power. The Zapatistas' First Declaration from the Lacandon Jungle was a declaration of war against the Mexican government and included orders to the EZLN's fighting forces to "advance to the capital of the country, overcoming the Mexican federal army."[10]

This perspective changed quickly. Although the EZLN had been preparing for an armed insurrection for over a decade, the Zapatista uprising lasted only a few days. Another culture clash ensued, this time with Mexican civil society. Within the first few days of January 1994, while fighting was still raging in Ocosingo and the Mexican military was bombing the hills around San Cristóbal and the jungles of Chiapas, solidarity with the Zapatista movement began to build. While people who mobilized in Mexico and around the world were overwhelmingly sympathetic toward the root causes of the Zapatista uprising, there was also a call from Mexican civil society for both sides to put down their weapons and negotiate a peaceful solution. The EZLN chose to accept this call. "We do what the people ask," said Major Ana María, one of the military leaders of the EZLN. "The people have asked that we try this way, and we are going to try. We are going to try, because we don't like to kill and we don't like to make war. So we decided to sit down and negotiate, to see

9 Ibid., 154–55.
10 First Declaration from the Lacandon Jungle, January 1, 1994, http://flag.blackened.net/revolt/mexico/ezln/ezlnwa.html.

what will come out of it. But if things are not resolved this way, we will have to continue."[11]

Although the EZLN did eventually sign a peace treaty with the Mexican government, the San Andrés Accords on Indigenous Rights and Culture were never implemented. As it became evident that negotiations with the Mexican government would be fruitless, the more productive dialogue with national and international civil society became an increasingly important component of Zapatismo. The EZLN has become well known for organizing national and international *encuentros*, or gatherings, spaces for different sectors of society who have been negatively impacted by global capitalism to come together to share ideas and form alliances. The philosophy of Zapatismo became less focused on seizing state power and more focused on the need to push the state aside and create space for civil society to flourish. In Antonio Gramsci's terms, the EZLN's strategy evolved from a "war of movements," challenging state power through armed struggle, to a "war of positions," contesting the moral and intellectual leadership of Mexico's ruling class.

Another element of Zapatismo, stemming from the political and historical context of rural Chiapas, is the EZLN's critique of the state. Initially the party of the Mexican Revolution, the PRI became a kind of dictatorship, a one-party monopoly of power in Mexico for over seventy years. The PRI developed an extensive system of patronage, its political machine distributing government positions and other benefits to key sectors in exchange for their support. The PRI's network of patron-client relationships was particularly strong in Mexico's rural areas. Individual peasants received jobs, food, shelter, and other types of assistance in exchange for their votes. When necessary to maintain social control, the PRI also resorted to electoral fraud, corruption, bribery, and repression. For decades, the PRI effectively coopted any social movement that seriously threatened the status quo.

This history led the Zapatistas to an additional critique of the state: their deep mistrust of political parties and their belief that real social change will not be achieved through the electoral arena. And because of the history of cooptation, "resistance" for the Zapatistas means refusing to participate in any government program or receive any governmental assistance. Since social welfare programs are often used to reward political support and to manipulate and divide communities, the Zapatistas maintain that accepting government hand-outs has a higher price than doing

11 Interview with Major Ana María of the EZLN, February 28, 1994, http://flag.blackened.net/revolt/mexico/ezln/interview_annmaria_feb94.html.

without them, and this is one factor that led the Zapatistas to develop their own autonomous institutions.

The Zapatista Project of Indigenous Autonomy

> Autonomy means we want to govern ourselves. We have the right to do so and to do it according to our traditional customs.
>
> —Margarita, a Zapatista woman from the Tzeltal community of Morelia[12]

Once it became clear that the Mexican government had no intention of implementing the San Andrés Accords, the EZLN decided to put indigenous autonomy into place on its own terms. As with the evolution of Zapatismo as a political philosophy, we also see the blending of indigenous customs and revolutionary praxis within the Zapatista project of indigenous autonomy. Structures for participatory decision-making are integrated into Zapatista autonomous governments, for example. Working collectively is fundamental to the Zapatista economic cooperatives. And the Zapatista autonomous health care system has incorporated indigenous practices and recuperated traditional knowledge that was in danger of being lost. The Zapatista movement has also reinforced a sense of pride in an indigenous identity and elevated the question of indigenous rights to one of increased national importance.

Geographically, Zapatista territory covers much of eastern Chiapas and includes the highlands region, the northern zone, and the canyons that run eastward into the Lacandon Jungle. The Zapatistas have organized approximately forty autonomous municipalities, each made up of anywhere from fifteen to seventy-five villages. There are five regional centers, called *caracoles.* (*Caracol* means snail shell in Spanish. The name *caracol* connotes the conch shell that the Mayans traditionally used to call a meeting. The spiral figure of the snail shell also represents dialogue, central to the Zapatista project.)

Zapatista territory is not "liberated territory" in the traditional sense where a guerrilla army has complete control over a certain geographical area. The Mexican military has an intense presence throughout Zapatista territory and many of the villages are made up of non-Zapatistas as well as Zapatistas. There are clear boundaries of Zapatista territory, however, and this is meaningful because in this small corner of the world, the Zapatistas

12 Margarita, interview by author, tape recording, Morelia, Chiapas, Mexico, February 18, 2001. Some names in this book are women's real names, some are pseudonyms that Zapatistas chose for themselves, and some are invented names. Some of the testimony in this book is collective testimony, meaning it was gathered during a women's assembly.

are experimenting with their own government, alternative education and health care infrastructure, and an economic system based on cooperation, solidarity, and relationships of equality.

Autonomous Government

Zapatista territory has its own autonomous government, parallel to but completely separate from the Mexican government. The autonomous governments are founded on the principle of *mandar obedeciendo* (to lead by obeying). There is a sign at the entrance of each *caracol* that announces: "*Está usted en territorio rebelde zapatista. Aquí manda el pueblo y el gobierno obedece.*" (You are in rebel Zapatista territory. Here the people lead and the government obeys.)

Each municipality has an autonomous council and several commissions, including health, education, land, production, and culture. Each of the five *caracoles* has a *Junta de Buen Gobierno* (Good Government Council), which oversees all the projects in their region, administers funds, and receives visitors to Zapatista territory. The Good Government Councils are also widely recognized for their role in resolving individual and community disputes. It is common for non-Zapatistas to take their disputes to the Zapatista structures because they recognize that they will find real justice there, as opposed to the corrupt state justice system.

"The authorities don't make decisions on their own," said Otelina, a young Zapatista woman from the Tzeltal community of La Garrucha. "They have to listen to everyone and take into consideration what the people want. The [Mexican] government does whatever it wants to. Our indigenous authorities lead but they lead by obeying."[13] The concept of *mandar obedeciendo* consciously draws upon many elements of traditional indigenous structures and seeks to implement a system of direct democracy, where all voices are heard in community decision-making and everyone can and should participate in community affairs. Some elements of governance that embody this principle and predate the Zapatistas include the community assembly, the system of *cargos* (positions of leadership or authority), a belief that all people are capable of governing, and the permanent *consulta* (a process of consultation with the people).

Community assemblies have historically been an important institution in Mayan villages but were not inherently democratic. Assemblies became considerably more deliberative and participatory under the influence of the Catholic Diocese and Maoist organizations in the 1970s. The

13 From an interview with the author, originally published in: Hilary Klein and Gustavo Castro, "Women and Indigenous Autonomy," CIEPAC (Centra de Investigaciones Económicas y Políticas de Acción Comunitaria) Bulletin *Chiapas al Día* 242, May 10, 2001.

Zapatistas hold regular local and regional assemblies. Assemblies are held in any available communal space: the church, the school, or in an open-air structure with a thatched roof and wooden benches. Discussions can be long, because everyone has the right to speak until an agreement is reached, and decisions are made by an informal process of consensus. Each community assembly, attended by all adult members of the village, makes local decisions and chooses local authorities. The regional assembly, made up of all the local authorities in that region, makes decisions about anything that affects the whole region and chooses the members of the autonomous government. Assemblies can also remove someone from their position of authority at any time.

Cargos are the structure of traditional indigenous authorities. To hold a *cargo*, or a position of authority, is a way to offer service to one's community. The Spanish word *cargo* also means a weight or a burden, and the verb *cargar* means "to carry," so to have a *cargo* is like shouldering a burden or carrying your share of the weight. While it is a position of power, it implies financial sacrifice rather than being a path to wealth. Historically, anyone holding a *cargo* was expected to sponsor religious festivals, which depleted any wealth he had managed to accumulate. By accepting a *cargo*, one gained prestige but became impoverished. On the other hand, the *cargo* system tends to concentrate power in the hands of wealthier community members since they are the ones best able to absorb their high costs.

Many aspects of this system have been continued by the Zapatistas. "We don't go out and campaign like the politicians of the bad government," said Citlali, a member of the Good Government Council from La Garrucha. "The people elect the person who they think will do the best job. We are very clear that we, as authorities, are providing a service to our communities and we are not thinking about receiving any kind of salary."[14] As was the case for traditional Mayan authorities, being chosen as a member of the autonomous government is seen as a hardship as well as an honor. Many Zapatista authorities are impoverished by absorbing the costs associated with being an authority, and it requires being away from home for days, sometimes weeks at a time. Zapatista authorities gain prestige and are highly respected by their community members, but they are also closely scrutinized by their peers and are subject, at times, to heavy criticism.

The Zapatistas' Good Government Councils are based on the belief that all people are capable of governing. Members of the Good Government

14 Testimony from the Third Gathering between the Zapatista People and the Peoples of the World "Comandanta Ramona and the Zapatistas," La Garrucha, Chiapas, Mexico, December 29–31, 2007.

Councils are elected for one three-year term. Each Good Government Council is made up of rotating members of the autonomous councils from that region. For example, there might be four groups, each group made up of representatives from the autonomous municipalities in that region. The four groups might take turns spending one week each in the *caracol* and, while there, they form the Good Government Council. When the following group arrives, the previous group alerts them to any recent decisions and pending issues. The Zapatistas explain that this system works because they believe that all members of the community have the capacity to govern and that, not only does it prevent the concentration of power in a few hands, it also promotes transparency and reduces any risk of corruption.

Finally, a *consulta* is something like a popular referendum except that it is carried out by discussion, rather than voting. Through the process of *consultas*, people participate directly in decision-making in a regular and ongoing fashion. *Consultas* are used internally by the Zapatistas when an important decision needs to be discussed not only in the regional assembly, but also in every community. The EZLN's decision to go to war with the Mexican government is the most frequently cited example, but a number of other proposals or decisions made by the highest echelons of Zapatista leadership have been taken to the support base communities and discussed in each village.

Women's Participation in the Zapatista Movement

> The Zapatista movement has opened our eyes and opened our hearts. In the past, women didn't participate, but today there are Zapatista women insurgents and Comandantes. Things have changed and now there is hope and freedom in our lives.
>
> —Zapatista women from the region of Morelia[15]

The Zapatistas draw on elements of traditional indigenous governance but recognize the need to incorporate their own beliefs and practices as well. Since traditional indigenous governments have historically been dominated by men, strong leadership from Zapatista women and the aspiration to have equal gender representation at all levels of the autonomous government are clear examples of this balance.

Women's participation in the EZLN has helped shape the Zapatista movement, which has, in turn, opened new spaces for women and led to dramatic changes in their lives. It is difficult to appreciate the enormity of

15 Regional women's gathering, handwritten transcription, Morelia, Chiapas, Mexico, June 9–10, 2001.

the changes women have experienced, however, without understanding women's starting point. Centuries of violence and discrimination against women serve as a backdrop for the striking changes that have taken place in Zapatista communities. Before the Zapatista uprising, women in the indigenous villages of Chiapas had limited control over their own lives. They often married young and against their will, and it was common for women to have a dozen children or more. Girls were not allowed to study. According to Eugenia, an education promoter, "The only right we had [as girls] was to take care of our younger brothers and sisters and work in the house. That's why our mothers and grandmothers don't know how to read and write."[16] Domestic violence was generally considered acceptable behavior, and women could not leave the house without permission from their fathers or husbands. The gendered division of labor meant that women were expected to work in the home, do the cooking and cleaning, take care of the children, and carry firewood and water, while the men worked in the fields. Women worked long hours, from early in the morning until late at night.

There was also a strict and gendered division between public and private spaces. There are certain phrases that you are likely to hear from women in Zapatista communities. "*Siempre nos decían que las mujeres no tenemos derechos.*" (We were always told that women didn't have any rights.) "*No nos tomaban en cuenta.*" (Women were never taken into consideration.) "*Antes las mujeres no participaban.*" (Before, women did not participate.) These phrases and their frequent repetition communicate the overall lack of women's voices in public spaces of power and decision-making.

Zapatista women achieved, especially in the years just before and after the 1994 uprising, social changes that often take generations to unfold. Transformations in women's lives include the right to decide whom to marry and when, and how many children to have. There has been a notable reduction in alcohol consumption and domestic violence. Women have much greater access to health care and education and are exercising their right to participate in public affairs.

Zapatista women from the region of Morelia explained, "Now we know that men and women have the same rights. Before, women didn't participate, but now they do. Because of this struggle, we felt encouraged to go out and start participating more. We have the freedom to participate in meetings and gatherings. In community and regional assemblies we participate side by side with the men. We also have the right to hold any

16 Testimony from the Third Gathering between the Zapatista People and the Peoples of the World "Comandanta Ramona and the Zapatistas," La Garrucha, Chiapas, Mexico, December 29–31, 2007.

position within our organization. Without women's participation, there cannot be equality."[17]

The EZLN's commitment to equality within its own ranks is upheld in the Women's Revolutionary Law: "Women, regardless of their race, creed, color or political affiliation, have the right to participate in the revolutionary struggle in any way that their desire and capacity determine."[18] And while there is still a long ways to go before achieving true gender equality, Zapatista leaders—men and women—conduct ongoing political education to remind people of women's rights and to encourage the Zapatista communities to choose more women authorities at all levels of the organization.

For Zapatista women, indigenous autonomy also means fighting to recover, maintain, and defend indigenous traditions while simultaneously looking at their own culture with a critical eye and rejecting the cultural practices that oppress them as women. Within their own communities, Zapatista women are engaged in an ongoing, collective process of analyzing which customs they want to hold on to and challenging the ones they want to let go of or change. Speaking to the Mexican Congress in 2001, Comandanta Ester said: "We know which of our customs and traditions are good and which ones are bad. The bad ones are when women are beaten, bought and sold, forced to marry even when they don't want to, not allowed to participate in the assemblies, and not able to leave their homes. . . . We want to be recognized in our ways of dressing, of speaking, of governing, of organizing, of praying, of healing; our tradition of working collectively, of respecting the earth and our understanding of life, that we are all part of nature."[19] The EZLN contributes to this dialogue by acknowledging that culture is dynamic, not static. This evaluation of their own practices contributes to an indigenous culture based on ancient customs but open to change.

Autonomous Health Care and Education

The rural indigenous villages of Chiapas historically faced appalling health conditions and extremely limited access to health care. Many communities did not have schools, and those that did found government schools to be lacking in quality and detrimental to their culture. In both cases, the Zapatistas committed to building their own health and education

17 Regional women's gathering, handwritten transcription, Morelia, Chiapas, Mexico, June 9–10, 2001.

18 The Women's Revolutionary Law was first published in *El Despertador Mexicano*, Órgano Informativo del EZLN, México, no. 1, December 1993. The text of the law can be found at: http://palabra.ezln.org.mx/comunicados/1994/1993_12_g.htm.

19 Comandanta Ester's complete speech can be found at http://palabra.ezln.org.mx/comunicados/2001/2001_03_28_a.htm.

infrastructure based largely on indigenous culture and traditions but also guided by the revolutionary perspective of the ELZN.

Health Care

> The indigenous communities in resistance chose to fight for life and not wait for the death to which the government had condemned us. The people in these forgotten places decided to confront our health problems on our own.
>
> —Magali, a midwife from La Realidad[20]

Many of the indigenous villages are far from the nearest city and historically had no access to doctors or health clinics. In the state capital of Tuxtla Gutierrez there is one doctor for every 397 inhabitants whereas, in the municipalities where indigenous people make up more than 70 percent of the population, there is only one doctor for every 25,000 inhabitants.[21] Arnulfo, a member of the Autonomous Health Commission in La Garrucha, explained: "One of the difficulties we had was getting the patients to a hospital in an emergency. Back then, there was no road here, and the government never helped us. We had to carry the patient for several hours to the road."[22]

One of the first steps in organizing the autonomous infrastructure was for each community to choose its own health promoters. These promoters are expected to serve and be accountable to the community. At the regional level, a Health Commission began to oversee the progress of autonomous health care and to develop local as well as regional infrastructure.

The autonomous health care system initially focused primarily on Western medicine. The first generation of health promoters was mostly young men and women and they were trained by visiting doctors. With time, however, Zapatista health care began to incorporate traditional practices such as the use of medicinal plants, and traditional healers like *parteras* (midwives) and *hueseros* (bone-setters). This was a gradual and sometimes challenging process; a long history of racism meant that indigenous communities had been taught to mistrust their own cultural

---

20 Testimony from the Third Gathering between the Zapatista People and the Peoples of the World "Comandanta Ramona and the Zapatistas," La Garrucha, Chiapas, Mexico, December 29–31, 2007.

21 Hilary Klein and Gustavo Castro, "Health and Indigenous Autonomy," CIEPAC (Centro de Investigaciones Económicas y Políticas de Acción Comunitaria) Bulletin *Chiapas al Día* 228, January 17, 2001.

22 From an interview with the author, originally published in Klein and Castro, "Health and Indigenous Autonomy."

heritage and much traditional knowledge had already been lost. According to Arnulfo:

> We decided to resist the entire governmental system not only because we didn't have any medicine but also to take advantage of our knowledge about medicinal plants, to learn from the wisdom of our elders. For example, the elders, they know how to cure tuberculosis and snake bites. This knowledge was of great use to our parents and grandparents. We want to rescue this knowledge before it is lost forever. It has always been here but for a long time no one gave it any importance. But now we have won much more respect for medicinal plants. Many people have starting using them again. In fact, medicinal plants is where we have seen the most progress.[23]

An area of traditional medicine that has seen much greater continuity is midwifery. According to a study done by Physicians for Human Rights, almost nine out of ten rural indigenous women in Chiapas give birth in their homes and almost three quarters of them give birth with the assistance of a midwife.[24] Josefa is an older Tzeltal woman from the community of La Garrucha. Having no front teeth has never stopped Josefa from laughing, and her irreverent sense of humor is contagious. She is one of two traditional midwives in her community.

> I learned to be a midwife completely on my own. That's how all of us who are older learned; before, there were no courses to learn. The knowledge just came to me in my dreams. All the older midwives say the same thing. We receive this capacity like a gift from God. The first child that I received was my own granddaughter. At first I just tried to see how it would go, and then again and again. I have now received fifty-five babies and, thank God, not one has died. Now I'm not afraid anymore. We do this work to serve our community, we don't ask for anything in return.[25]

Integrating traditional midwives into the autonomous health care system has been a mutually beneficial process. Younger midwives have much to learn from their elders, and institutionalizing this knowledge means it's more likely to be handed down to future generations. The traditional midwives benefit from access to certain resources and the support that comes with being part of the Zapatista health care system.

---

23 Ibid.
24 Physicians for Human Rights, *Excluded People, Eroded Communities*, 26–28.
25 From an interview with the author, originally published in Klein and Castro, "Health and Indigenous Autonomy."

An increased focus on women's health is one of the innovations being made by the Zapatista project of autonomy. "Now there are women health promoters and that's important because sometimes with men we feel too embarrassed to talk to them about our health problems," said a group of Zapatista women from the Morelia region. "But with a woman, we can speak more comfortably."[26] Chiapas has historically suffered from extremely high rates of maternal mortality, and the autonomous health care system has worked hard to change this. "We provide prenatal care during the pregnancy," said Elvia, a health promoter from Oventic. "We also do home visits to women with high risk pregnancies. In the central clinic and some of the micro-clinics, we are also attending births."[27]

The autonomous health care system faces some real limitations. Because no one is paid for community service, health promoters sometimes find it difficult to sustain the work over long periods of time. When a health promoter steps down, the experience they accumulated is lost, and the new health promoter must learn the relevant skills and knowledge, a process made more challenging by the fact that few adults in Zapatista communities have more than an elementary school education.

In spite of these obstacles, the autonomous health care system evolved, over time, from a loose network of community-based health promoters into a well-developed health care infrastructure at the local and regional level. "Each community should have one or two general health promoters and also in each area of traditional medicine," said Magali, a midwife from La Realidad. "Each community should have its own *casa de salud* (community health center). Each community should also have a small pharmacy."[28] Often an unassuming structure, the *casa de salud* provides a physical space for the health promoters to see patients, hold meetings, and store medicine and herbs. Each of the five Zapatista regions also has a central clinic or hospital and a regional Health Commission, which oversees the work.

The overall impact of the autonomous health care system has been tremendous. According to Arnulfo: "We continue to suffer from malnutrition; our limited diet is a big problem. But before, there was much more illness. Now it's very rare that a child dies from a serious illness or because of lack of equipment or medicine. Almost all the children who are born

---

26 Regional women's gathering, handwritten transcription, Morelia, Chiapas, Mexico, June 9–10, 2001.

27 Testimony from the Third Gathering between the Zapatista People and the Peoples of the World "Comandanta Ramona and the Zapatistas," La Garrucha, Chiapas, Mexico, December 29–31, 2007.

28 Ibid.

survive. At least here in my community, young children, from the ages of one to three, do not die anymore like they did before."[29]

Education

There were no schools on the *fincas* where many indigenous peasants lived and worked. The villages that did have schools had a number of complaints—the poor quality of education, how common it was for teachers to mistreat their students, and the lack of respect for indigenous language and culture inherent in Mexican education policy which, for most of the twentieth century, focused on the assimilation of indigenous peoples.

Mauricio, a member of the Autonomous Education Commission in La Garrucha, explained:

> In the government's educational system they only teach one language [Spanish] and we want to be able to learn in our own language. The government wants us to take on their customs. They want to force us to have the same ideas as them. They told us things to make us lose our own culture, for example, that our ancestors did not know how to read and write, that they did not use mathematics. But now we know that's not true, that our ancestors did use math. They had a lot of knowledge.
>
> It was our parents' generation that started losing the culture of our ancestors. In the official educational system, our culture gets lost. Indigenous children are not familiar with their own culture and they feel ashamed of being indigenous.[30]

As with the autonomous health care system, Zapatista communities began by choosing education promoters who are then trained at the regional level. Each village is responsible for building a school and providing economic support to these community teachers—often in the form of working their cornfield for them. An Education Commission coordinates the work in each region.

The autonomous education system instituted some significant changes right away. The schools are open every weekday, for example, and teachers are not allowed to abuse the children. "The children feel comfortable telling us when they don't understand something," said Evita, a young education promoter from the autonomous municipality Francisco Gómez. Most of

29 From an interview with the author, originally published in Klein and Castro, "Health and Indigenous Autonomy."

30 From an interview with the author, originally published in Hilary Klein and Gustavo Castro, "Education and Indigenous Autonomy," CIEPAC (Centro de Investigaciones Económicas y Políticas de Acción Comunitaria) Bulletin *Chiapas al Día* 259, September 12, 2001.

the education promoters teach in the local indigenous language as well as Spanish so children will grow up speaking both languages. Core values of indigenous culture are upheld by the autonomous education system. "The thing we most want is to respect each other and be respected within our community. Our ancestors were very respectful," said Mauricio.[31]

The curriculum took longer to revise. At first, because the education promoters had no other model, the content of what was taught in the autonomous schools largely imitated the curriculum in government schools. With time, however, the Zapatistas structured the schools to more accurately reflect indigenous culture and daily reality. "We want the children growing up to know what freedom is and how to resolve their own problems," said Isabela, an education promoter from Santo Domingo in her late twenties. "That's why we teach them about the culture of their ancestors, and about their own history." Many of the materials developed and used in the autonomous schools focus on indigenous customs and traditions; they include information about land, nature, and agriculture; and they teach the history of Mayan civilization.

In the autonomous education system, girls' right to education is an accepted fact. "Now we know that women have the right to study too," said a group of Zapatista women from the Morelia region. "Things have changed because the rights of girls are respected and they can go to school. Community educators are chosen by each village, and women participate in the autonomous education system."[32]

In the late 1990s, the EZLN made the bold decision not to accept the presence of government teachers in its communities and to establish autonomous education as the primary education system in its territory. This move has been seen by some as a remarkable step forward for a liberatory education system and by others as foolhardy and premature. Internally consistent with its rejection of all government programs and services, the EZLN says that government schools do more harm than good. It has received criticism, however, that the Zapatista educational infrastructure was not sufficiently developed to adequately replace the government schools. In Zapatista communities without an autonomous school, children are growing up with no school at all. Criticism of this decision has come from within as well as outside the Zapatista movement. Some families living in villages with no autonomous school have chosen to prioritize their children's education and, in spite of a deep commitment to the Zapatista movement, have left the ranks of the EZLN.

---

31 Ibid.

32 From an interview with the author, originally published in *¡Viva Nuestra Historia! Libro de Historia de la Organización de Mujeres Zapatistas "Compañera Lucha"* (San Cristóbal de las Casas, 2003), 20–21.

In spite of the challenges, and while it is far from perfect, the Zapatistas have created an alternative education system, one that honors indigenous culture and respects women's right to study. In addition to an elementary school in most villages, there are now a number of regional high schools that function as boarding schools for the children from nearby villages. Before these regional high schools were built, it was rare for children to receive anything beyond an elementary school education.

Working Collectively in a Solidarity Economy

In addition to health care and education, the Zapatistas have also constructed an economic infrastructure designed to address the high level of poverty in their communities. Often called a "solidarity economy," the Zapatistas' autonomous economy offers a grassroots alternative to global capitalism. In a solidarity economy, the well-being of society is more important than the generation of profit, and solidarity is a strategy employed to improve the living conditions of the entire community.

Economic cooperatives generate resources that are invested back into the community. Because of the gendered division of labor, there are often men's and women's cooperatives. Men, for example, have coffee or cattle cooperatives, whereas women have artisan cooperatives, chicken-raising cooperatives, and collective vegetable gardens. Cooperative stores provide merchandise for community members at reasonable prices while also generating income. Money raised by the cooperatives is used to cover shared expenses, for example when the community's representatives travel to a regional meeting.

"Our ancestors lived and worked collectively," said Otelina. "Whenever they organized some community project, they included everybody. This way of working together, of living collectively, had been lost. People did their work individually, every person for themselves. For example, when somebody got sick, there was no structure to help each other out. So we began to think about whether there was another way to do things. We began to see that many solutions are possible if people work together. When indigenous communities began to work in collectives again it was because of the organization [the EZLN]."[33]

The economic cooperatives form the building blocks of the autonomous economy. These cooperatives have been a mechanism for economic self-sufficiency in Zapatista communities for more than a decade and have long provided material support to the Zapatista movement, but in more recent years they have been incorporated into a regional economy and have

33 From an interview with the author, originally published in Klein and Castro, "Women and Indigenous Autonomy."

played a concrete role in the project of indigenous autonomy. Although there is a limit to the resources that can be generated from communities that are so poor to begin with, funds generated by the economic cooperatives help pay for the autonomous government, health care, and education.

Conclusion

Zapatismo resembles anarchism in many ways: the Zapatista movement's critique of the state, its focus on social transformation rather than attempting to seize state power, its structures of direct democracy, and its philosophy of governance—to lead by obeying, its economic cooperatives, and its alternative institutions which challenge state power from below. Because of this, the Zapatista movement has attracted the attention of anarchist solidarity activists from all over the world, many of whom have traveled to Chiapas to better understand and support the movement. In spite of what it has in common with an anarchist tradition, however, the Zapatista movement is not an anarchist project. The political traditions that converged to form Zapatismo included Guevarism and Maoism, along with indigenous customs and traditions, a history of indigenous resistance, liberation theology, and the legacy of the Mexican Revolution. Each of these political traditions made significant contributions to Zapatismo and strands of each are still present in the Zapatista movement today. A manifestation of this is that, alongside a series of participatory decision-making structures, the EZLN has a guerrilla army with a hierarchical military structure. These two structures within the Zapatista movement—military and civilian, centralized and decentralized—are closely intertwined and each plays an important role in advancing the Zapatista movement.

Encountering this reality has represented a contradiction for some anarchists who have spent time in Chiapas participating in solidarity projects. I have known people who arrived to Chiapas as prominent anarchists and, after working in the Zapatista communities for a year and reexamining the relationship between revolutionary leadership and broad democratic participation, left Chiapas as communists. I have also known anarchists who grew disenchanted by the authoritarian element within the Zapatista movement. For me, this tension was one of the most fascinating things about living in Chiapas: witnessing the relationship between these two structures and how it has evolved over time as the Zapatistas themselves sought (and continue to seek) the right balance between the two. I also found that it is precisely the blend of political traditions that makes the Zapatista movement so vibrant, so unique, and so compelling, and harkens back to an earlier era of the Left when anarchists, communists, and socialists made common cause and were not always quite as narrow in how they defined themselves.

Selected Bibliography

Collier, George. *Basta! Land and the Zapatista Rebellion in Chiapas*. Oakland: Food First Books, 1994.

Gramsci, Antonio. *Selections from the Prison Notebooks*. Edited and translated by Quintin Hoare and Geoffrey Nowell Smith. New York: International Publishers, 1971.

Gunderson, Christopher. "The Making of Organic Indigenous-Campesino Intellectuals: Catechist Training in the Diocese of San Cristóbal and the Roots of the Zapatista Uprising," in Patrick G. Coy (ed.) *Research in Social Movements, Conflicts and Change, Vol. 31*, Emerald Group Publishing Limited, 2011: 259–95.

Gunderson, Christopher. "The Provocative Cocktail: Intellectual Origins of the Zapatista Uprising." PhD dissertation, New York: City University of New York, 2013.

Harvey, Neil. *The Chiapas Rebellion: The Struggle for Land and Democracy*. Durham, NC: Duke University Press, 1998.

LeBot, Yvon. *El sueño zapatista: Entrevistas con el subcomandante Marcos, el mayor Moisés y el comandante Tacho, del Ejército Zapatista de Liberación Nacional*. Barcelona: Plaza y Janés, 1997.

Marcos, Subcomandante Insurgente. *Relatos El Viejo Antonio*. San Cristóbal de las Casas: Centro de Información y Análisis de Chiapas (CIACH), 1998.

Muñoz Ramírez, Gloria. *The Fire and the Word: A History of the Zapatista Movement*. Translated by Laura Carlsen with Alejandro Reyes Arias. San Francisco: City Lights Books, 2008.

Physicians for Human Rights. *Excluded People, Eroded Communities: Realizing the Right to Health in Chiapas, Mexico*. Physicians for Human Rights and El Colegio de la Frontera Sur, Centro de Capacitación en Ecología y Salud para Campesinos-Defensoría del Derecho a la Salud, 2006.

Rovira, Guiomar. *Mujeres de Maíz*. Mexico City: Ediciones Era, 1997.

NO GODS, NO MASTERS, NO BRAHMINS: AN ANARCHIST INQUIRY ON CASTE, RACE, AND INDIGENEITY IN INDIA

Maia Ramnath

Somewhere that is nowhere, is Begumpura: the city without sorrow. There is no class or caste there, no taxation, no oppression. It is a place without masters or peripheries, built upon natural reason, equality, and joy. An anarchist's utopia? Perhaps. This one was described by the fifteenth-century bhakti poet Ravidas, considered a forerunner of contemporary anti-caste poetics and politics. How then might an anarchist understand the struggle against caste? This is a question imperative to ponder.

In previous work, I've suggested that a spectrum of anti-colonialist discourses in the global south shares a certain deep logic structure with the anarchist tradition in the global north, demonstrating a comparable range of responses to conditions produced by modernization.[1] I've suggested that a spectrum of anti-colonialist discourses in the global south shares a certain deep logic structure with the anarchist tradition in the global north, demonstrating a comparable range of responses to conditions produced by modernization. (In the colonial context, however, this process was experienced through a violent disruption by external forces and thus freighted with an extra burden of racialized alienation.)[2]

1 Maia Ramnath, *Decolonizing Anarchism: An Antiauthoritarian History of India's Liberation Struggle* (Oakland: AK Press, 2012); and Ramnath, "In Dialogue: Anarchism and Postcolonialism," in Carl Levy and Saul Newman, eds., *The Anarchist Imagination* (London: Routledge, 2015).

2 The fact that this was never a matter of a dynamic force acting upon an inert mass, but of complicities between particular external and internal actors, confronted by a spectrum of subalterns and dissidents, facilitated the continuities between "classical" and "neo" colonialisms, including "domestic" varieties proceeding from the independent Indian state's takeover of the British governmental apparatus, which it has since utilized in a precisely colonial fashion against those in economically, socially, or geographically marginalized but resource-rich areas of the territory it claims.

Correspondingly, I suggested that if decolonization could be defined as the most comprehensive possible degree of emancipation and autotransformation on all levels, from the largest socioeconomic structures to the most intimate dynamics of gender and psychology, this could also be compared to an anarchist ideal of collective liberation encompassing all axes of domination, oppression, and exploitation. In the South Asian context, caste lies at the intersection of all these axes; confronting it is by definition a battle against the purest social hierarchy. Decolonization in anarchist terms, then, is incomplete without dismantling caste.

Yet ironically, caste can all too easily slip from sharp focus via the same analytical lenses I had been using with precisely the intent to counteract the premises that South Asia by default refers to India, that Indian society is fundamentally Hindu, and that the culture known as Hinduism is essentially defined by a totalizing hierarchy. Meanwhile, anti-caste interventions historically have most often called upon, not opposed, modern state mechanisms. In stark contrast to Gandhi, who opposed the modern state while advocating a nation framed in a Hindu cultural language in which all were theoretically included but on an unequal footing, B.R. Ambedkar, the exemplary figure of caste abolitionism, held Hinduism to be fundamentally inegalitarian, and looked to the modern liberal state as universal guarantor of freedom, equality, and rights. Of course, such a solution to injustice is precisely the kind that anarchist thought avoids—indeed, cannot even see. Moreover, to the logic of an internationalist inquiry oriented toward to non- or anti-state movements, such interventions are less obviously legible. But, as with race in the United States, the denial of a principle's validity does not eliminate the material realities, entrenched practices, and pervasive structures of feeling based upon it.

So, then, to repeat the question: what is a useful anarchist approach to caste?

Although previously I flagged the (patriarchal, militaristic, xenophobic, homogenizing) dangers of the nation, even while acknowledging its historical uses by colonized populations, in indicting nationalism I was primarily blaming the *state* for tautologically legitimizing a community *as a nation* by equipping it with governmental, disciplinary, violence-monopolizing, and revenue-collecting mechanisms, which its minorities and discontents experience as irredeemably repressive. Now I needed to continue problematizing the nation, not in the abstract but specifically *as it was produced* in India: notably in the dominant Hindu version countered by radical anti-caste discourse, among other modes of subjugated knowledge.

But subjugated on what basis? Does caste function as an ideological shroud for class relations,[3] or as a mode of oppression that precedes and exceeds class? Was it a way of formalizing relations with an earlier colonized population? Does it name an internal or external relationship? Two modes of decolonial consciousness that weave through radical anti-caste discourse, sometimes in tandem and sometimes in tension, are indigeneity and race. Might we answer the question of how anarchism could relate to caste by examining how anarchism could relate to either indigenous or anti-racist struggles? If so, grappling with caste requires the anarchist anti-colonialist to sharpen her understanding of both race and indigeneity, as they intersect with unique historical and cultural formations, since other elements of radical anti-caste discourse reinterpret elements of liberalism, Marxism, and most innovatively, Buddhism,[4] as a rational ethical philosophy and indigenous challenger to Brahmanism.

Furthermore, an anti-caste intellectual history makes it clear that the story of colonization and decolonization in South Asia is not a simple binary clash of the British Raj versus the national liberation struggle, but rather a palimpsest.[5] Multiple waves of migration, settlement, synthesis, subjugation, dispossession, and incorporation have created interference patterns over thousands of years. To see oneself as anti-colonial in India then has not in all times and circumstances been to see oneself as anti-British: radical Dalit rhetoric locates the moment of foreign subjugation not by the East India Company in the eighteenth century CE, but by Vedic Aryans in the second millennium BCE.

Since the 1990s, however, several of these colonial timelines seem to be converging so that the once-distinct forces of Hindutva, neoliberal capitalism and the Indian state are now working synergistically with each other in relation to the prevailing structure of global empire. Accordingly, it may be that the dynamics of each wave form, including

---

3 On class analysis: see S.K. Thorat and R.S. Deshpande, "Caste System and Economic Inequality: Economic Theory and Evidence," in Ghanshyam Shah, ed., *Dalit Identity and Politics* (New Delhi: Sage Publications, 2001), 44–70; K. Balagopal, *Ear to the Ground: Writings on Caste and Class* (New Delhi: Navayana Publishing, 2011).

4 Gary Snyder, Robert Aitken, Hozan Alan Senauke, Joshua Stephens, and others have linked contemporary, social change-focused "Engaged" Buddhism to anarchism, while others, such as Peter Marshall in his omnibus history *Demanding the Impossible*, locate Buddhism as one of the philosophical traditions that preceded and prefigured anarchism, counter to the modern Western dominant paradigm of instrumental rationalism, hierarchical binarism, and domination. (Of course this pertains only to certain iterations of anarchism and Buddhism.) For a Buddhist anarchist attempt to grapple with caste and class, follow thread at http://www.dharmawheel.net/viewtopic.php?f=42&t=12046&hilit=anarchism. A fuller exploration of anarchism in dialogue with a specifically Ambedkarite Buddhism would be valuable, but well beyond the scope of this paper.

5 After writing this, I realized with chagrin that the "palimpsest" was Nehru's famous formulation of subcontinental history and culture in his *Discovery of India* (1946).

the counterforces they unleash, now have unprecedented possibilities to augment each other rather than cancel each other out. This may in turn create new opportunities for those borne upon any of those waves to learn from and act in concert with each other. These are the conjunctures to be explored here.

Opening Check-In

But first, in the spirit of "relentless self-interrogation"[6] required for accountable scholarship, it seems worthwhile to note a few things about methodological and locational biases. (Those impatient with such matters can skip ahead to the next section.)

As a logical extension of my initial questions about the practice of anti-systemic solidarities, I had originally explored historical connections between Western anarchists and Indian anti-colonialists from the transnational standpoint, from which what comes most into focus is imperialism as a world system, the continuity of classical colonialism and neocolonialism in the form of expanding global capitalism, and the insatiable incorporation of land, labor, and resources into that system. It is perhaps harder to see other aspects of struggle that are urgent for activist agendas and research questions embedded in the Indian local context. Of course, world systems and localized oppressions are connected; but according to positioning, angles and priorities may change. So, in privileging global systemic analysis over nationalist narrative, "South Asia" over Indocentrism, intersection with the Islamic world over Hindu cultural hegemony, history over ethnography, English, Hindi, and Urdu materials over those in languages such as Tamil or Marathi, what might a diasporic anarchist scholar pursuing interests springing from her location be inadvertently neglecting?

Moving from self-criticism to criticism: for anyone taking up the subject of caste—or neglecting to take it up—the likelihood of attack is approximately 99.99 percent. Some probable firing lines can be predicted: Indian Marxists may call me a right-wing reactionary for airing critiques of instrumental rationalism and industrial development. Hindu nationalists may accuse me of anti-Hindu hate speech, surely a symptom of either pathological guilt or cultural contamination. These I would refute, and the refutations are central to the alternatives I'm trying to highlight.

Radical Dalit activists and intellectuals may say that I should not presume to speak, due to lack of organic connection to Dalit movements and a middle-class/upper-caste background; or that I am taking up space

6 I am here recontextualizing a term for which I am indebted to several conversations with Skanda Kadirgamar.

better left to others. Native American activists and intellectuals may chide me for not sufficiently foregrounding and problematizing the location of my writing, on Lenni Lenape land. Lacking immediate solutions, I can only acknowledge these contradictions, while striving for what Taiaiake Alfred calls a clear head and a good heart to guide awareness during an endless process.[7] My overriding conviction is that if any headway is ever to be made toward the goals of dismantling oppression and exploitation while building freedom and equality, then avoiding talking about it is far worse than trying to talk about it, attempting to open dialogue (not to represent!), whoever and wherever we are, in however flawed a way.[8]

Finally, North American anarchists may feel (and have implied) that this topic is irrelevant, inaccessible, and less exciting than what they were expecting to hear: where are the itinerant revolutionists on whom to project their fantasies, meeting in clandestine, cosmopolitan locations? Where are the South Asian syndicalists and guerrillas they had anticipated adding to a rainbow coalition of familiar types? What such anarchists must realize is that the failure to think about caste in the past has doomed the revolutionary aspirations of those with whom they sensed affinity. So then let's think about it.

A Very Brief and Partial Account of Dalitbahujan Thought

"Dalit" is the preferred term for those previously marked as "untouchable," designating a transformation from a condition of subjugation and dehumanization to one of resistance and emancipatory struggle.[9] "Bahujan"

7 Taiaiake Alfred, *Peace, Power, Righteousness: An Indigenous Manifesto* (Oxford: Oxford University Press, 2009).

8 Wallace Shawn's 1985 essay "Morality," *Essays* (Chicago: Haymarket, 2010) inspires me here; more directly relevant are debates on Arundhati Roy's foreward to a new edition of Ambedkar's *Annihilation of Caste* (Navayana, 2014). For a sampling, see http://scroll.in/article/658279/Why-Dalit-radicals-don't-want-Arundhati-Roy-to-write-about-Ambedkar/; http://roundtableindia.co.in/index.php?option=com_content&view=article&id=7312:preface-politics-does-annihilation-of-caste-need-an-introduction&catid=119:feature&Itemid=132/; and http://roundtableindia.co.in/index.php?option=com_content&view=article&id=7283:an-open-letter-to-ms-arundhati-roy&catid=119:feature&Itemid=132.

9 In what follows I'm being slightly anachronistic in using the term "Dalit" throughout. It was introduced in common usage in 1931, and popularized more broadly in the 1970s. For a history of the terminology see Gopal Guru, "The Language of Dalit-Bahujan Political Discourse" in Shah, *Dalit Identity and Politics*, Vol. 2, 96–107. For a much more comprehensive introduction to the history and political theory of caste than space here allows, see, for example, Susan Bayly, *Caste, Society and Politics in India from the Eighteenth Century to the Modern Age* (Cambridge: Cambridge University Press, 2001); Gail Omvedt, *Understanding Caste: From Buddha to Ambedkar and Beyond* (New Delhi: Orient BlackSwan, 2011), *Dalits and the Democratic Revolution* (New Delhi: Sage Publications, 1994), and many others; Anupama Rao, *The Caste Question: Dalits and the Politics of Modern India* (Berkeley: University of California Press, 2009); Valerian

is the term for the literal numeric majority, the vast base supporting the social pyramid. The term "Dalit" sometimes refers to the bahujan samaj of Scheduled Castes, Scheduled Tribes and Other Backward Classes, all categories assigned by the 1935 Government of India act for the allotment of representation to socioeconomically marginalized communities, and later incorporated into the 1950 Indian Constitution. Other times it refers specifically to those designated avarna, outside caste society's four grades (as opposed to either savarna—within the four—or tribal).[10]

If dominant "Indic" civilization has been constructed as synonymous with Brahmanism—defined as Vedic/Aryan, northern, Hindi-speaking, patriarchal and hierarchical—then its submerged counter-discourses may correspond to non-Brahmin, Dravidian (southern), Tamilian, feminist, or Dalit locations. This multivalence opens up the possibility of principled alliances (or unstable situational coalitions) among critics of any facet of the dominant project. Dalitbahujan thought provides an alternate Indian intellectual tradition based on egalitarianism along the axes of both caste and gender.[11]

The accepted genealogy of modern anti-caste radicalism starts with Jotiba Phule (1826–1890), introducer of its central themes: the importance of dignity and self-respect; valorizing productive labor as ennobling, not defiling; the overdetermination of cultural/ideological and material/economic structures of domination; and a consistent linkage between

---

Rodrigues, "Dalit-Bahujan Discourse in Modern India," in V.R. Mehta and Thomas Pantham, eds., *Political Ideas in Modern India: Thematic Explorations*, Volume X, Part 7 (New Delhi: Sage Publications, 2006); Eleanor Zelliot, *From Untouchable to Dalit* (Manohar Press,1992); S.M. Michael, ed., *Untouchable: Dalits in Modern India* (Boulder, CO: Lynne Rienner, 1999).

10 See introduction to Dev Nathan, ed., *From Tribe to Caste* (Simla: Indian Institute of Advanced Study, 1997), 1–30.

11 I do not have space to accord Dalit feminism its due here, although anti-patriarchy is central to radical anti-Brahmanism. Phule's work was paralleled by that of his partner, Savitribai Phule, and contemporaries, Pandita Ramabai (1858–1922) and Tarabai Shinde (1850–1910). Unusual for the time, both women attained high levels of education while rejecting Hinduism on the grounds that its practices of caste hierarchy and patriarchy were not aberrational but intrinsic. Shinde, the daughter of a Satyashodhak Samaj member, was known for her fierce writings on women's rights. Ramabai dedicated herself to the service of (by definition disenfranchised) widows, and later founded an autonomous community made up of women of all castes living together. I am barely scratching the surface here but would rather cede the floor to those better equipped than myself to address it broadly and deeply, such as Uma Chakravarti, *Gendering Caste through a Feminist Lens* (Calcutta: Stree, 2003) and *Rewriting History: The Life and Times of Pandita Ramabai* (New Delhi: Zubaan Books, 2014); Sharmila Rege, *Writing Caste, Writing Gender* (New Delhi: Zubaan Books, 2013); B.R. Ambedkar, *Against the Madness of Manu* (New Delhi: Navayana Publications, 2013); Anupama Rao, ed., *Gender and Caste* (London: Zed Books, 2005). See also the current work of the All India Dalit Mahila Adhikar Manch, which may be accessed at http://www.ncdhr.org.in/aidmam/ and http://allindiadalitmahilaadhikarmanch.blogspot.com.

caste oppression and the oppression of women. These issues defined the confrontation with Brahmanism, understood as an all-pervading ideology fundamentally based on inequality.

Phule was born in Maharashtra in a relatively affluent family categorized as Shudra by the reigning social taxonomy.[12] His message was aimed not just at those condemned to untouchability but to all non-Brahmins: the bahujan samaj. Phule described caste as equivalent to slavery (gulamgiri), comparing the particular oppression of Dalits in India to that of blacks and Native Americans in the United States. His logical framework for this lay in the two races or Aryan invasion theory, according to which the (dark) Dravidian original inhabitants of the subcontinent were overrun by (light) Indo-European invaders. The newer Vedic culture was said to have destroyed the glories of the ancient Indus Valley civilization and enslaved its creators, leaving upper and lower castes as two distinct racial strata.

In 1873 Phule founded the Satyashodhak Samaj (Self-Respect Society). Political theorist Valerian Rodrigues writes, "If self-respect is the fundamental striving of this [Dalit] constituency, then Brahminism is its principal opponent . . . militating against self-respect by its tendency of ranking, which makes some inferior and others superior, irrespective of their merit and effort; for not relating desert[s] to effort; . . . [and] breed[ing] dependence and subservience."[13] Phule later launched the Sarvajanik Satya Dharma as a "religious alternative" to Brahminical Hinduism: a "nobleminded, equalitarian theism, which also projects a strong male-female equality."[14] His rejection of Hinduism was total, with no hope of reinterpretation or recuperation; other intellectual traditions native to the subcontinent might allow for more egalitarian, emancipatory social views. He favored knowledge, education, and science as tools of freedom, equality, and economic progress, while identifying patriarchy as a primary form of social oppression and promoting women's equality and education.

During his lifetime, Phule was little known beyond his own western region. There were other, more broadly influential movements in the south, where Iyothee Thass (1845–1914), drawing upon a vision of subcontinent-wide, pre-Aryan Dravidian civilization, pioneered a mode of Dalit Buddhism that was an important entry point for caste activists the early twentieth century. From this matrix, Periyar E.V. Ramaswamy (1879–1973) forged a new mass movement in the 1920s. Periyar cited three things that

12 Shudras were low in the hierarchy, but still within the system (savarna), not excluded from society as untouchables (avarna). Technically then they would fall within the category of bahujan, but not Dalit.

13 Rodriques, "Dalit-Bahujan Discourse in Modern India," 49.

14 Omvedt, *Understanding Caste*, 27.

needed to be destroyed in order to attain freedom: the Indian National Congress, Hinduism, and Brahmin domination. (Note that British rule is not on this list.) Through his Self-Respect League, founded in 1926, he called for both caste abolition and women's liberation; the following year he contested Gandhi's defense of varnashramadharma.[15] Unlike Phule, Periyar favored atheism over religion—making him a proponent of, in essence, a world with no gods, no masters, and no Brahmins.

Thass's Dravidan/Dalit reading of Buddhism also initiated the intellectual path of Chettiar Singaravelu (1860–1946). Part of India's first Marxist generation, Singaravelu contributed articles on socialism and historical materialism to Periyar's journal *Kudi Arasu*, and in 1932 Periyar and Singaravelu proposed a new program for the Self-Respect League: a form of socialism they called samadharma. But this sundered the more conservative non- or anti-Brahmins from the leftists, whose ranks otherwise tended to skew toward upper castes. In 1935 the anti-Brahmin faction formed the Justice Party while the leftists were absorbed into the Congress Socialist Party. This had the unfortunate effect of splitting a radical left movement that was now upper-caste by default and association, from a more conservative emergent regional/linguistic nationalism. As Periyar's anti-Brahmanism flowed into this channel, the Justice Party begat both the Dravidar Kazhagam, which still promoted his ideals of self-respect, anti-Brahmanism, and women's rights, and the less progressive regionalist Dravida Munnetra Kazhagam. Thus Ramaswamy's more expansive vision—not territorially bound, and capable of encompassing a plurality of identities—gave way to a more restrictive nationalistic logic.[16]

Nevertheless the 1920s and 1930s were a high point of Dalit mobilization linking caste radicalism to broader movements for national and class liberation through mass strikes, tax boycotts, worker and peasant formations, as well as more caste-specific agitations for access to public spaces such as temples and water tanks, from which they were excluded. The recurrent (and recurrently fractured) dream of linking caste and class politics has remained one of the most potent hopes of profound social transformation. Yet the failures of communist organizers to adequately acknowledge caste issues, or to accord them primary importance, inflicted lasting damage on the growth of intersectional movements.

---

15 This term refers to the fourfold division of society into the "traditional" functions of brahmin, kshatriya, vaisya, and shudra (priests, warriors, merchants, laborers/artisans).

16 This observation comes from the Pondicherry Group of Tamil Dalit intellectuals, described by M.S.S. Pandian in "Stepping Outside History? New Dalit Writings from Tamil Nadu," in Partha Chatterjee, ed., *Wages of Freedom: Fifty Years of the Indian Nation-State* (Delhi: Oxford, 1998), 294–98.

If Phule had introduced the main themes of Dalitbahujan thought, Bhimrao Ramji Ambedkar (1891–1956) brought them to fullest articulation.[17] Also Maharashtrian, Ambedkar came from a family of the Mahar caste. Defying the discrimination barring untouchables from education, he proved a brilliant scholar who went abroad to earn multiple doctorates in law and economics at Columbia University and the London School of Economics, taking the bar at Gray's Inn. After returning to India he rose to political prominence in the late 1920s. In 1932 he clashed with Gandhi on the place of Dalits in electoral politics. Gandhi wanted Dalits to be included within an undifferentiated Hindu constituency, whereas Ambedkar wanted a separate electorate in which Dalits would vote for their own slate of representatives. In the face of a Gandhian fast, he had little choice but reluctantly to accede to the mahatma's wishes, yielding the Pune Pact compromise in which Dalits, though remaining part of the Hindu electorate, would be allotted a certain number of reserved seats.

Ambedkar then founded the Independent Labour Party in 1936, as a Maharashtra-based leftist worker-peasant party linking anti-capitalist and anti-landlord agitations with resistance to caste oppression. At this period he identified a "dual-systems theory"[18] of capitalism and Brahmanism as the greatest enemies of the working class, criticizing the Left for recognizing only capitalism's but not Brahmanism's role as "negation" of his highest ideal, "the spirit of Liberty, Equality, and Fraternity."[19] During the 1920s and '30s Ambedkar was influenced by Marxism, and considered the "destruction of caste . . . a prerequisite to economic equality (socialism)," though his thinking evolved toward a more instrumental developmental state socialism, and later an emphasis on cultural issues and electoral politics.[20] The ILP morphed into the All-India Scheduled Castes Federation in 1942, and after his death into the Republican Party, named for the (American) party of Lincoln as emancipator of slaves.

17 Scholars such as Anupama Rao, Debjani Ganguly, and others make a strong case that Indian modernity cannot be understood without the category of the Dalit. In *Caste, Coloniality, and Counter-Modernity* (London: Routledge, 2009), Ganguly argues that in fact it is not only generated by but constitutive of Indian modernity, as opposed to a premodern remnant indicative of incomplete modernization, to disappear once that project is complete.

18 However, he didn't really articulate connections between the two, according to Omvedt, "Ambedkar and the Dalit Cultural Movement in Maharashtra," in Shah, *Dalit Identity and Politics*, Vol. 2, 146–47.

19 Gail Omvedt, *Ambedkar: Towards an Enlightened India* (New Delhi: Penguin, 2004), 82. For a more extensive elaboration of his definition of these three principles, see Ambedkar, *Annihilation of Caste* (1936), section 14, http://ccnmtl.columbia.edu/projects/mmt/ambedkar/web/index.html.

20 Economically he favored state socialism, though after independence he moved further right, toward pragmatic developmentalism including strategic nationalization of land and key industries.

Ambedkar played influential roles in government: labour minister under the British regime, law minister under Nehru. Above all he is remembered as the chief drafter of the Indian constitution. For Ambedkar at this stage, a crucial tool of social transformation was the modern state, as "the agency par excellence for safeguarding rights, when values deeply inimical to rights rule the roost in the domain of civil society."[21] Rule of law, and equality before the law, were paramount, even though existing inequities would first need to be adjusted through reservations in political, educational, and professional spheres.[22] Civic republicanism was the ideal, based in organized deliberative bodies undergirding a "self-governing political community in which citizens participate as equals to realize the good of both the individual [and] the collective."[23] Indeed, there could be "no meaning to self-rule without representation and participation,"[24] which is why issues of formal democracy, as at Pune, became so controversial. In *What Congress and Gandhi Have Done to the Untouchables* (1946), Ambedkar laid out his definition of Brahmanism: "graded inequality between the different classes" was its "official doctrine," entailing systematic disempowerment of Shudras and Untouchables—including the systematic denial of access to education, property rights, and officeholding—plus the "complete subjugation and suppression of women."[25] In a sense, the insistence on separate representation called liberalism's bluff on its claim to be blind to difference.

Unlike other Dalitbahujan thinkers, he put no stock in the two races theory.[26] Rejecting both class and race as the bases of social division, he turned to culture and ideology, sketching a historical narrative for caste

21 Rodrigues, "Dalit-Bahujan Discourse in Modern India," 65.

22 The term "reservations" in this context is roughly equivalent to affirmative action in the U.S. context. BRA also emphasizes throughout *Annihilation of Caste* that neither political nor economic adjustment is sufficient (if even possible) without a thorough transformation of social mentality and ideological commitments.

23 Rodrigues, "Dalit-Bahujan Discourse in Modern India," 62.

24 Ibid., 63.

25 Ibid., 49.

26 To quote from Ambedkar, *Annihilation of Caste*: "Some have dug a biological trench in defence of the Caste System. It is said that the object of Caste was to preserve purity of race and purity of blood. Now ethnologists are of the opinion that men of pure race exist nowhere and that there has been a mixture of all races in all parts of the world. Especially is this the case with the people of India. . . . The Caste system cannot be said to have grown as a means of preventing the admixture of races, or as a means of maintaining purity of blood. As a matter of fact [the] Caste system came into being long after the different races of India had commingled in blood and culture. To hold that distinctions of castes are really distinctions of race, and to treat different castes as though they were so many different races, is a gross perversion of facts. . . . [The] Caste system is a social division of people of the same race. Assuming it, however, to be a case of racial divisions, one may ask: What harm could there be if a mixture of races and of blood was permitted to take place in India by intermarriages between different

wherein he framed Brahmanism and Buddhism as the poles of primary contradiction within Indian civilization.[27] In Ambedkar's historiography, the Buddhist "revolutionary" period (circa 500 BCE–300 CE) was a golden age suppressed by a Brahmanist "counterrevolution" that imposed patriarchy, parasitic priesthoods, and social stratification, while appropriating from Buddhism whatever beneficent ideas and practices were later associated with Hinduism.

Though a thorough modernist, Ambedkar embraced those (non-Brahmanist) elements of tradition that could be deemed reasonable and salutary, thus effectively giving an ancient indigenous genealogy to principles generally considered modern and Western. Ambedkar presents "the Buddha's teachings and practices . . . as the very embodiment of reason, to which he found the Brahminical tradition of hierarchy, ritualism, superstitions, priest-craft, deceit and cunning to be in opposition." Significantly, though, this approach to reason is *not*, stresses Rodrigues, the utilitarian cost-benefit analysis of an atomized and context-free Descartean individual, but rather something "embodied in lived ways" that "locate . . . intersubjectively and in the communitarian context . . . the capacity to discern what is good and right, together with others."[28]

Ultimately Ambedkar's proposed redress for caste was twofold: politically, the legislative and juridical mechanisms of the liberal democratic-republican state, and culturally, a line of flight from Hinduism back to a South Asian-origin philosophy of rationalism, egalitarianism, atheism, and restorative morality: an autochthonous Enlightenment heritage in all senses of the term. This interpretation took the form of a liberation philosophy identifying *dukkha* with oppression and *dhamma* with social and economic justice.[29] Ambedkarite Buddhism thus made Dalits the agents of "opening the road to a society of equality and liberation" and the "carriers of . . . the liberatory message of Indian tradition."[30] Near the end of his life, he led a mass conversion of five hundred thousand to

---

castes?" See *The Annihilation of* Caste, section 5, http://ccnmtl.columbia.edu/projects/mmt/ambedkar/web/index.html.

27 This is discussed in several of his books including Ambedkar, *Untouchables: Who Were They and Why They Became Untouchables* (1948), accessible at http://www.ambedkar.org/ambcd/39A.Untouchables%20who%20were%20they_why%20they%20became%20PART%20I.htm.

28 Rodrigues, "Dalit-Bahujan Discourse in Modern India," 56.

29 See Ambedkar, *The Buddha and His Dhamma* (1957), accessible at http://www.ambedkar.org/buddhism/BAHD/45A.Buddha%20and%20His%20Dhamma%20PART%20I.htm. In Buddhist terminology dukkha represented the world's sorrow and suffering, from which liberation was sought; dhamma was the way of right thought and action for achieving it.

30 Omvedt, "Ambedkar and After: The Dalit Movement in India," in Shah, *Dalit Identity and Politics*, Vol. 2., 149.

this form of Buddhism.[31] This was a "quest for collective emancipation" above "individual salvation"; a call to "increase political participation so as to bring social transformation leading to an egalitarian social order."[32] In Omvedt's assessment, "[Ambedkar] had fought for a correlated but different freedom struggle," alongside Indian nationalism, "one for the liberation of the most oppressed sections of Indian society. This was a liberation movement wider and deeper than that of fighting colonialism, focusing on the kind of new nation that was to be built."[33]

While Ambedkar rejected racial categories, the Dalit Panthers, roaring onto the scene in 1972 from the slums of Bombay, explicitly linked caste to race and race to colonization as part of an international third world revolutionary movement. Representing an urban demographic with newly widening access to education, they fell within the ambit of a global wave of New Left militance. As their name indicates, they took inspiration from the Black Panthers in the United States, whose commitment to community self-defense, self-respect, and anti-capitalism they shared. Another stimulus was disillusionment with the bureaucratic cooptation of Ambedkar's Republican Party, and indeed with all political party and governmental solutions, amid a general atmosphere of corruption and a foundering economy. Like their Dalitbahujan predecessors, the Panthers were notable for their emphasis on the cultural dimensions of oppression, and harkening back to Ravidas and Tukaram, produced a literary flowering of radical poetry, memoir, and polemic.[34] They were also known for their political theater, offering "entertainment in the service of . . . mass education."[35]

In a compilation of Dalit literature put out by the Minority Human Rights Group on Untouchables, editor Barbara Joshi emphasizes the importance of culture and psychology as aspects of Dalit liberation: "underlying [a wide range of activist] tactics is the conviction that the most

---

31 Conversion to Christianity or Islam was seen as providing a comparable state of equality, but, it was claimed, at the cost of exile from one's own cultural heritage, unlike conversion to Buddhism, an indigenous philosophy. See Yoginder Sikand, *Islam, Caste, and Dalit-Muslim Relations in India* (New Delhi: Global Medial Publications, 2004); Abdul Malik Mujahid, *Conversion to Islam: Untouchables' Strategy for Protest in India* (Chambersburg, PA: Anima Books, 1989); Gauri Vishwanathan, *Outside the Fold* (Princeton, NJ: Princeton University Press, 1998).

32 Shah, *Dalit Identity and Politics*, Vol. 2., 34.

33 Omvedt, *Ambedkar: Towards an Enlightened India*, 157.

34 For an introduction, see Mulk Raj Anand and Eleanor Zelliot, eds., *An Anthology of Dalit Literature* (New Delhi: Gyan Pub. House, 1992); Arjun Dangle, *Poisoned Bread* (New Delhi: Orient BlackSwan, 2009).

35 Barbara Joshi, ed. *Untouchable! Voices of the Dalit Liberation Movement* (London: Zed Books, 1986), 91. See also Omvedt, "Ambedkar and After" in Shah, *Dalit Identity and Politics*, Vol. 2., 151–54; Thorat and Deshpande in Shah, 48–49.

important struggles are those within the minds of both the oppressed and their oppressors. . . . The result is direct and immediate Dalit confrontation with the world of the mind and the institutions that feed the mind." Therefore, "concurrent with efforts to mobilize against overt oppression and exploitation there have been efforts to repossess culture and self,"[36] equally important when one's humanity has been systematically denied.

In a famous essay of 1983, Marathi scholar and Dalit intellectual Gangadhar Pantawane spoke of redefining the word:

> What is Dalit? To me, Dalit is not a caste. Dalit is a symbol of change and revolution . . . Dalitness is essentially a means towards achieving a sense of cultural identity. . . . Now Dalitness is a source of confrontation. This change has its essence in the desire for justice for all mankind. In this sense, Dalitness is a matter of appreciating the potential of one's total being.[37]

The Panthers' founding Manifesto had used a similar definition to draw battle lines:

> **Who is a Dalit?** Members of scheduled castes and tribes, neo-Buddhists, the working people, the landless and poor peasants, women and all those who are being exploited politically, economically and in the name of religion.
>
> **Who are our friends?**[38] Revolutionary parties set to break down the caste system and class rule. Left parties that are left in a true sense. All other sections of society that are suffering due to economic and political oppression.
>
> **Who are our enemies?** Power, wealth, price. Landlords, capitalists, moneylenders and their lackeys. Those parties who indulge in religious or casteist politics and the government which depends on them.[39]

Panther franchises formed in other regions too, and the *Dalit Voice*, a biweekly published in English and Tamil, achieved a nationwide reach by the early 1980s. Sharad Patil, originally a CPI (Marxist) organizer, formulated a "Marx-Phule-Ambedkar" ideology, by which to fuse resistance against class-based exploitation to abolition of religiously sanctioned caste oppression. Founder of the Satyashodhak Communist Party in 1978,

---

36 Joshi, *Untouchable!*, 78.

37 Ibid., 80. Pantawane was founder of the main Dalit literary journal *Asmitadarsh* in 1967, serving as editor until the 1990s.

38 "Our" here presumably refers to anyone included in the preceding paragraph.

39 Joshi, *Untouchable!*, 145.

Patil wanted to "universalize Dalit identity as proletarian exploitation."[40] But tensions developed between the Buddhist and Marxist tendencies, represented respectively by Raja Dhale and activist poet Namdev Dhasal, both of whom were prominent among the organization's founders. By the 1980s the movement had fragmented, though mobilizations framed in terms of Dalit-Marxism, along with the radical practice of poetry, music, and theater activism, remain strong today.[41]

In the 1980s, Dalitbahujan mobilization ballooned in the form of electoral party politics,[42] but the 1990s produced some innovative articulations of Dalit political theory. Kancha Ilaiah (b. 1950) is a Dalit intellectual and activist, author of several books including the instant classic (and lightning rod for controversy) *Why I Am Not a Hindu* (1996). Like Pantawane, Ilaiah presents Dalitization as a qualitative, holistic transformation of Indian society, emphasizing that Dalitbahujan culture—beliefs, practices, kinship relations, economic relations, value systems, lifeways—is wholly distinct from Hinduism; and that in stark contrast to Hinduism, it is explicitly egalitarian and nonpatriarchal, and implicitly ecological. Based in valorization of labor and productivity, it organizes material and social life collectively, not individualistically.[43] It roots knowledge production in material practice, orality, intersubjectivity, nature, and experience, as opposed to textual abstraction. It is rich in technical ingenuity and practical expertise, and makes no split between mental and physical labor.[44] Nor is there a notional split between the public and private spheres.[45] Law comes from the community through participatory consultation, not from an authority outside and above. Thus the whole Brahminical value system is overturned: those once stigmatized for their work-function are from this perspective ennobled by it. That which had been proof of impurity is now the essence of productivity, hence value, while that which had been guarded as purity is now revealed as parasitism.[46]

---

40 Omvedt, *Understanding Caste*, 77.

41 For a spectacular recent document of this, see Anand Patwardhan's film *Jai Bhim Comrade* (2012). Anupama Rao's critical commentary of the documentary for *India Seminar* may be viewed at http://www.india-seminar.com/2012/633/633_anupama_rao.htm.

42 See, for example, the Bahujan Samaj Party founded by Kanshi Ram; his protegée Mayawati made history as a female Dalit chief minister of Uttar Pradesh four times between 1995 and 2012.

43 Kancha Ilaiah, *Why I Am Not a Hindu* (Kolkata: Samya, 1996), 99, 114–17, 124, 151–52, 155.

44 Ibid., 120, 127, 150; see also Kancha Ilaiah, "Dalitism vs. Brahmanism" in Shah, *Dalit Identity and Politics*, Vol. 2., 108–28; Ilaiah, "Towards the Dalitization of the Nation," in Chatterjee, *Wages of Freedom*, 266–91.

45 Ilaiah, *Why I Am Not a Hindu*, 39–40.

46 I would like to flag a critical concern, on both feminist and ableist grounds, about the implications of this theory of value, which skirts the risk of rating people in terms of the quantity of their productivity.

As portrayed by Ilaiah, then, the Dalitization of all society (in contrast to the historical trend of sanskritization) would usher in a more egalitarian order.[47] Actual (indigenous) alternatives to the Brahmanist dominant order were to be found in Buddhism, in tribal society, and in a possible future vision of "collective living and collective consciousness," in which the sharer would be "not only a collective being but also a secular social being . . . human relationships operate in a mode that has been sensitized to human needs. . . . Their social context is productive and distributive. Equality is its innate strength. . . . The material basis of the society is rooted not in wealth but in labor power."[48]

Dalitization, while reframing relations of production, went deeper than material class; it would require change in the whole culture, society, religion, philosophy, identity. Nevertheless, the caste-based producer/parasite relationship easily mapped onto capitalism, with upper castes proving all too amenable to its globalized form.[49] "In every industry the working masses are Dalitbahujans . . . whereas, the entrepreneurs and managers . . . are Brahmin, Baniya or Neo-Kshatriya," Ilaiah points out. "As a result, there is a total cultural divide between the managerial class and the working class."[50] Given this overlay, Ilaiah too postulates a truly caste-conscious Left as the great lost opportunity for true liberation.

But the nation constructed in the course of the liberation movement was botched. "While conducting the anti-colonial struggle, brahminical leaders and ideologues did not attempt to build an anti-caste egalitarian ideology,"[51] he says, lamenting not only that landowning aristocrats and urban bourgeoisie had been ensconced as the drivers of the national movement, but that Dalits had ceded even Marxism to the caste elites. "If only colonial rule in India had produced anti-Brahmin, organic, Dalitbahujan intellectuals who would have been the recipients of the revolutionary theory of Marxism, by now perhaps India would have undergone a Dalitbahujan socialist revolution."[52] But unfortunately, "the most revolutionary theory . . . fell into the hands of the most reactionary social forces."[53] This, in effect, destroyed Marxism's emancipatory potential. Ilaiah concludes, "It is only a conscious Dalitbahujan movement which

47 Ilaiah, *Why I Am Not a Hindu*, 114.
48 Ibid., 160–61; and in Chatterjee, 289.
49 Ilaiah *Why I Am Not a Hindu*, 52.
50 Ibid., 66.
51 Ibid., 113.
52 Ibid., 50.
53 Ibid.

can, step by step, decasteize society, socialize the means of production, and finally create humanitarian socialism in India."[54]

Perhaps one such alternative vision could be that expressed by the Pondicherry Group of Tamil Dalit intellectuals, exemplified by the writings of Raj Gowthaman.[55] He proposes an alternative to Dravidian nationalism which, rather than replacing a northern/Hindi with a southern/Tamil placeholder within the same logic structure, calls for a rejection of nationalist logic, statist historiography, and all forms of power. By refusing to organize on the basis of nationality, an "oppositional culture" of Dalit liberation could "travel beyond any bounded territoriality and mobilize . . . Blacks and . . . women in general . . . as well as tribals everywhere as the source of their new politics."[56]

As relayed by scholar M.S.S. Pandian, Gowthaman "identifies 'state, caste, religion, god, morals, justice, norms, regulated man-women relationship, ideology of family, literature'—all institutions that mark civilizational achievements—as institutions of discipline and power to be resisted."[57] Gowthaman knows, says Pandian, that caste elites will characterize "this cultural politics . . . as that of anarchists and barbarians,"[58] and that Dalits themselves might downplay this counterculture lest they be stigmatized as "uncivilized." For Gowthaman, though, refusing that civilizational teleology marks the necessary "beginning of Dalit politics."[59] Summing up this critical intervention, Pandian asks, "Can there be a nation without history and power (read state)? Indeed, it cannot be. Perhaps it is fifty years of freedom within the nation which has taught the Pondicherry Group that freedom lies outside the construct of the nation."[60]

Dalit Politics as Anti-colonial Thought: Indigeneity and Race

Let's return to the colonial palimpsest. Ambedkar names Hinduism "a form of imperialism."[61] Anand Teltumbde flags the "Dalit aboriginal iden-

54 Ibid., 52. Does this argument not contradict another frequent assertion, that the introduction of capitalism under the British was beneficial for Dalits? Perhaps this is what distinguishes Dalit liberalism from a Dalit Left.

55 Limited by language, I am reliant here upon the summarization of M.S.S. Pandian of what sound like remarkable Tamil texts by Gowthaman: *Dalit Paarvayil Tamil Panpadu* (Tamil Culture from a Dalit Perspective), 1994 and *Dalit Panpadu* (Dalit Culture), 1993. Pandian, "Stepping Outside of History? New Writings from Tamil Nadu," in Chatterjee, *The Wages of Freedom*, 302. See also Pandian, *Brahmin and Non-Brahmin: Genealogies of the Tamil Political* (Delhi: Permanent Black, 2007).

56 Pandian, "Stepping Outside of History?," 305; see also 306–8.

57 Ibid. quoting Gowthaman, *Dalit Panpadu*, 1993, 18.

58 Pandian, "Stepping Outside of History?," 306.

59 Ibid., 305.

60 Ibid., 309.

61 Bayly, *Caste, Society and Politics in India from the Eighteenth Century to the Modern Age*, 261–62.

tity" of "a highly civilized and peaceful people that was once dominant in the country but later subjugated and enslaved through Aryan conquest."[62] Movements based in the cluster of oppositional identities that define themselves through the prefix *adi*, designating original inhabitants (e.g., adivasi, adi-Dalit, ati-shudra, ad-dharm, adi-Dravida), claim allegiance to "a non- or even pre-Aryan Indian equalitarian tradition."[63] There is a double accusation here: the foundational violence of initial conquest, and the structural violence of a functioning system.[64]

There is also a double plaintiff in the categories of caste and tribe, frequently linked together by ethnography, law, and rhetoric. Yet it's necessary to distinguish between them as two historical locations and two modes of decolonizing thought. As J. Kehaulani Kauanui and Dean Saranillio remind us,[65] the two concepts of race and indigeneity, though related, do not function in the same way either structurally or analytically. In other words, each bears a different sort of relationship to, and names a different subjective experience of, colonialism/capitalism/imperialism; each tows behind it a different freight of symbolism.

A politics of indigeneity (Aryan invasion): The word "indigenous," in its neutral sense, denotes originally native to a place, as defined against newer arrivals. In many contexts "aboriginal" further implies not only native but "primitive," tribal, or nonmodern, as defined against urban/civic/modern populations. (Here is the line drawn between the anthropological and the sociological, or the colonizers and the colonized.)

According to one theory, the groups who were defeated and incorporated into Vedic society evolved into subordinate castes, whereas those who fled into hills and forests survived as autonomous tribes. Caste groups might then be assimilated along an incremental "civilizing" pathway of sanskritization, adopting the characteristics of Brahminical society. But several contributors to Dev Nathan's volume *From Tribe to Caste* challenge the notion that such a process was an improvement, asserting that it instead marked a devolution from an egalitarian, collective-property based condition to a more patriarchal, authoritarian, individual-property

62 Teltumbde, *The Persistence of Caste*, 23.

63 Ibid.

64 Conscious of the sharp ironies inherent in using a Hinduistic metaphor in this context, it strikes me that there are visible here violences of Brahma the creator, and Vishnu the preserver—in which case there remains only a violence of Shiva the destroyer. Would that mean genocide? Or could it suggest resistance, as in the case of the anti-caste dissident Virashaivite movement?

65 Both made complementary points as part of a panel presented at the American Studies Program Annual Conference, "Circuits of Influence: U.S., Israel, Palestine," at New York University, March 7, 2014.

based one.[66] (What doesn't seem fully articulated in accounts of such a shift is a distinction between hierarchy *among* distinct groups, and hierarchy *within* a particular group.)

Nevertheless, whether or not tribes and castes shared an ancient origin, they have since experienced different timelines of conflict.[67] Always on the front lines of encroachment, tribals launched frequent uprisings throughout the nineteenth and early twentieth centuries, chafing against incursions by both British and South Asian interlopers on forest lands.[68] In contrast, castes as such were not historically associated with militant rebellion, which might be interpreted as a difference between primary resistance and postsubjugation subversive behavior (though Teltumbde characterized Dalits as being more thoroughly beaten down). In other words, a tribal narrative is about being outside, on the frontier (vertical separation); a caste narrative is about being inside, down below (horizontal separation).

British colonial ethnographic practices worked to further fix and formalize these identity categories, ratifying them through decennial censuses from 1871 to 1931. The Criminal Tribes Act of 1871 linked the extraction of surplus, by means of establishing individualized, taxable land holdings, to a social engineering project by which tribal communities would be sedentarized as productive workers confined to heavily surveilled and disciplined villages, having been removed from traditional livelihoods centered upon more mobile shared land uses such as hunting, shifting cultivation, or harvesting of various forest plants and flowers. Criminality, tribal affiliation, landlessness, mobility, and "wild" places would now be conflated.[69] In this way the history of adivasi communities

66 See Nathan, "Introduction"; K.S. Singh, "Tribe into Caste: A Colonial Paradigm(?)"; B.B. Chaudhuri, "Tribe-Caste Continuum? Some Perspectives from the Tribal History of Colonial Eastern India"; Shalini Mehta, "The Legend of Evolution from Homo Equalius to Homo Hierarchicus"; Saguna Pathy, "From Tribe to Caste: Domination Reaffirmed"; and Baidyanath Saraswati, "Tribe as Caste"; all in Dev Nathan, ed., *From Tribe to Caste* (Simla: Indian Institute of Advanced Study, 1997). Gowthaman would share this view: Pandian notes that his reasoning is similar to Ramaswamy's, but that he lacks Ramaswamy's "meta-narrative of progress through reason and science" vis à vis a Tamil Dalit past of collectivistic, egalitarian "hill cultivators, hunters, fisherpeople, pastoralists and the like," 304.

67 Teltumbde, *The Persistence of Caste*, 162.

68 The literature on this is extensive within the Subaltern Studies volumes of 1982–87, and histories of criminality and insurgency in India. I would refer readers to the work of Ranajit Guha, Ramachandra Guha, David Arnold, David Hardiman, Crispin Bates, Anand Yang, John McLane, Swapan Dasgupta, K.S. Singh. These uprisings included the famous Santhal Hool of 1855; Birsa Munda's millennarian movement in 1898; and histories of tribal groups such as the Bhils, Konds, and Doms, as well as the northeastern Bodos, Nagas, Ahom, Chittagong hill tribes, et al.

69 On this process see Anand Yang, *Crime and Criminality in British India* (Association for Asian Studies, 1985); Sanjay Nigam, "Disciplining and Policing the 'Criminals by Birth,'"

more closely resembles notions (and histories) of indigeneity familiar in the context of the Americas.[70]

Dispossession and violent conquest, of course, are to be categorically condemned. Still, we should be wary of the implications of legitimating rights claims only through invoking prior habitation. For one thing, the language of nativity, spiritually linking a land and its people, its blood and its soil, is easily appropriated by racialist ethnonationalism, including the Hindutva which is the antithesis of Dalit politics. Similarly, are newness, alienness, and oppressiveness being presented as synonymous? This too can be risky, depending who is using it. Is it possible to find arguments and logics that are usable only for emancipatory projects?

Kauanui emphatically distinguishes indigenism from a nativism that might shade into exclusionary ethnonationalism or fascistic populism. Beyond denoting native or aboriginal, a contemporary critical politics of indigeneity also implies a particular way of being in relation to place and its (human and nonhuman) inhabitants, in which land and resources cannot possibly be commodified, and social relations are by definition nonstatist and noncapitalist.[71] An indigenist concept of sovereignty then would recognize a region of interdependent, nonanthropocentric cohabitation, as opposed to a nationalist sovereignty defined as ownership, control, and exclusive claim to development of the extractable wealth of a mapped territory.[72]

---

parts 1 and 2, *Economic and Political Weekly* 27, nos. 2 and 3 (1990); Henry Schwarz, *Constructing the Criminal Tribe in Colonial India* (Malden, MA: Wiley-Blackwell, 2010).

70 See Ramachandra Guha, *The Unquiet Woods: Expanded Edition* (Berkeley: University of California Press, 2000), *Varieties of Environmentalism* (London: Routledge, 1997), *Social Ecology* (New York: Oxford University Press, 1998); Ajay Skaria, *Hybrid Histories* (Delhi: Oxford University Press, 1999); Amita Baviskar, *In the Belly of the River* (Delhi: Oxford University Press, 1998), *Contested Grounds* (Delhi: Oxford University Press, 2008). This is also very much in the news. See cover story in *Frontline* 31, no. 3, February 21, 2014. (http://www.frontline.in/magazine/?date=2014-02-18&magid=5656026). A cluster of related features on tribal resistance to forest land acquisition in Chhattisgarh and mining operations in Orissa (among many other instances) detail how the Indian government takeover of land for use by multinational corporations leads to local communities' loss of livelihood and traditional access to resources.

71 Note that this does not necessarily require them to be nonhierarchical or nonpatriarchal, nor always and everywhere the same.

72 As Raymond Craib pointed out in a personal communication of January 5, 2014, "some might argue that the very notion of indigeneity as inherently pre-industrial and/or ecologically harmonious is a radically modernist notion." This can be seen as characteristic of particular indigenous societies (or the idealizations or aspirations thereof), rather than part of the universal definition of indigeneity itself. Again, this represents a discursive ideal type rather than a empirical sociology of contemporary individuals of indigenous heritage and their range of evolving relationships to urban, industrial conditions.

As this description suggests, in many ways a nuanced indigenist critique not only of capitalist modernity but of the dominant modes of institutionalized twentieth-century socialism is echoed by many anarchist critiques.[73] These include skepticism of an uncritical embrace of industrialization; resistance at the point of primary onset, as opposed to a struggle for seizure of the means of production once industrialization is complete (or, as some would put it, rejection of a whole mode of production as opposed to a more superficial change in relations of production and more equitable distribution within that mode); rejection of a unilinear teleological formula for progress and development, with capitalism and socialism representing the right and left expressions of post-Hegelian thought, sharing an assumption of limitless growth in productivity, as opposed to a more steady-state sustainable and renewable model prioritizing use-values and nonreified relationships.

But is a consciously indigenous perspective *by definition* an ecologically harmonious preindustrial worldview? Dalitbahujan thought has laid claim to an *anti-colonial indigeneity that is modern, rational and state-based.*[74] At the same time it legitimates this *alternate Indian modernity as the culmination of an alternate Indian tradition*, later subjugated by its upstart rival.[75] Does this mean that we need to rethink the meaning of

73 For such indigenist critiques, see, for example, Glenn Coulthard, *Red Skin, White Masks* (Minneapolis: University of Minnesota Press, 2014); Roxanne Dunbar-Ortiz, *Blood on the Border* (Boston: South End Press, 2005) and *An Indigenous People's History of the United States* (Boston: Beacon Press, 2014); Taiaiake Alfred, *Peace, Power, Righteousness: An Indigenous Manifesto* (Oxford: Oxford University Press, 2009), Vine Deloria Jr., *Custer Died for Your Sins* (Norman: University of Oklahoma Press, 1988). Jeff Corntassel, "Rethinking Self-Determination: Lessons from the Indigenous-Rights Discourse," in Jai Sen and Peter Waterman, eds., *World Social Forum: Challenging Empires* (Montreal: Black Rose Books, 2009). Given the irrefutable ecological crisis conditions of the twenty-first century, even Marxist theory has come to incorporate ecology as central its critique of capitalism: see, for example, the work of John Bellamy Foster, Brett Clarke, and the index of journals such as *Capitalism, Nature, Socialism.*

74 Ambedkar himself distinguished Dalits from adivasis in this way: one of his many critiques of Hindu society in *The Annihilation of Caste* is that due to its fixation on purity it excluded aboriginal tribal communities from the benefits of inclusion and the civilizing process. Section 8: "Apart from the question of whether their exclusion from the new Constitution is proper or improper, the fact still remains that these aborigines have remained in their primitive uncivilized state in a land which boasts of a civilization thousands of years old. Not only are they not civilized, but some of them follow pursuits which have led to their being classified as criminals. Thirteen millions of people living in the midst of civilization are still in a savage state, and are leading the life of hereditary criminals!!" (He seems to be taking for granted the taxonomy put in place by the Criminal Tribes Act.) Ambedkar, *The Annihilation of Caste*, section 8, http://ccnmtl.columbia.edu/projects/mmt/ambedkar/web/index.html.

75 In *Why I Am Not a Hindu*, Ilaiah traces this to pre-Buddhist counter-Vedanta traditions of the rational/skeptical Lokayatas and Charvakas, 113; points to tribal republicanism, 116; and associates the dhamma with a social contract, 118, 119. For more on suppressed

indigeneity for this context, or does it mean that we require a different logic-lens?

A politics of race (Aryan and Dravidian): A century-long history links black freedom struggle in the United States with both Indian anti-colonialism and caste emancipation.[76] Indians arriving in North America and African American observers of India alike recognized the social functioning of caste as comparable to race as a mode of internal subjugation. Anthropologist Kamala Visweswaran notes that B.R. Ambedkar and W.E.B. Du Bois were Ivy League contemporaries, and that even prior to communicating with each other, Ambedkar was using race to think caste while Du Bois was using caste to think race.[77] This "translation" of race and caste proved an effective way for people in either context to make sense of the other (and enhance their insights about their own) while also opening opportunities for solidarity.[78] In a sense, then, the linkage of caste abolition and racial justice posed a simultaneous challenge to the self-definition of both (American and Indian) national projects, exposing their blind spots and demanding not just inclusion in but expansion of their concepts of freedom and justice.

Still, Dalitness is differently constructed than blackness in the United States, although the differences soften if we open the field to include the whole history of New World slavery.[79] For example, the religiously explained purity/contamination (curse of Ham) model that preceded the pseudoscientific biological or eugenic model for race in Europe sounds not unlike the concept of ritual purity as basis for caste. And the caste system's graded hierarchy is more like the intricately stratified Latin American

counter-traditions and alternate readings of traditional texts, see note 83. On ancient materialisms and rationalisms, see Amartya Sen, *The Argumentative Indian* (New York: FSG, 2005). As Chakravarti notes (103), it's important to be able to access the precolonial critiques of brahminical patriarchy, such as those within the bhakti and Buddhist traditions, so that feminist and Dalit mobilizations cannot be discredited [by right-wing nationalists] as foreign imports, alien to the "true" indigenous Indian culture.

76 On the connections and cross-fertilizations between Pan-African and Indian anti-colonial and anti-racist movements, see, for example, Gerald Horne, *The End of Empires* (Philadelphia: Temple University Press, 2009); Nico Slate, *Colored Cosmopolitanism* (Cambridge, MA: Harvard University Press, 2012); Susan Pennybacker, *From Scottsboro to Munich* (Princeton, NJ: Princeton University Press, 2009); Minkah Makalani, *In the Cause of Freedom* (Chapel Hill: University of North Carolina Press, 2011).

77 Kamala Visweswaran, *Un/Common Cultures* (Durham, NC: Duke University Press, 2010), 12. Visweswaran identifies a "caste school of race relations" associated with the Chicago School of Sociology in the 1920s, interpreting race in the United States as, in effect, a caste structure. *Un/Common Cultures*, 114, 163.

78 Ibid., 152.

79 For a magisterial overview see Robin Blackburn, *The Making of New World Slavery: From the Baroque to the Modern, 1492–1800* (London: Verso, 2010); *The American Crucible: Slavery, Emancipation and Human Rights* (London: Verso, 2011); and *The Overthrow of Colonial Slavery, 1776–1848* (London: Verso, 2011).

spectrum than the North American black/white binary. In any case the *function* of caste in a Brahmin-supremacist society is very similar to that of race in a white-supremacist society.

At the UN-sponsored World Conference Against Racism in Durban in 2001, a Programme of Action was proposed in which caste was included as a form of racism. This proved controversial on both political and theoretical grounds. Politically, the Indian government was displeased, while other regimes too feared setting the precedent. Theoretically, sociologist of caste André Beteille argued that since race was a biological issue and caste a cultural one, there could be no equivalency.[80]

Yet segments of the Dalit movement had argued precisely that caste, too, was based in biological race.[81] And one can argue just as easily that race *is* a social/cultural construct, as that caste *is not* a biological fact. In other words the issue has more to do with whether race itself, as a social construct for organizing hierarchical difference, is to be defined as biological or cultural, than whether or not caste is analogous to race. In Visweswaran's reading—in the context of her framing question: what work does culture do, and when, where and how does it do the work of race?—the Durban debates implied "the reverse of asking whether caste is race. This question then asks when and how it has been productive to understand that race is caste—or more precisely, when the experience of casteism is seen to be the most compelling illustration of the experience of racism."[82]

Such a chain of logic, however, may leave intact the Aryan and Dravidian racial categories, long discredited by most historians as a slippage from the linguistic (cultural) to the biological register. Nevertheless that racial logic persists in underwriting both justifications for and indictments of the modern caste system; both racists and anti-racists can be racialist.[83]

---

80 See, for example, André Beteille, "Race and Caste," *The Hindu*, March 10, 2001, accessible at http://www.thehindu.com/2001/03/10/stories/05102523.htm/; Shiv Visvanathan, "Durban and Dalit Discourse," *Economic and Political Weekly* 36, no. 27 (July 2001) and no. 33 (August 2001).

81 Visweswaran, *Un/Common Cultures*, 150.

82 Ibid., 163.

83 In addition to the two-races theory, Hindu nationalism shares the premise with much radical anti-caste thought (not to mention the Indologist scholarship behind the once-conventional modes of history and anthropology) that brahminical Hinduism, as contained in authoritative readings of the Manusmriti, Dharmashastras, Ramayana and Mahabharata, is the essence of Indic civilization. This renders it irredeemable. Narrow dogma is accepted epistemologically, though it may be accepted or rejected morally. Other anti-caste and feminist scholars take a revisionist approach to Indic civilization, in which the spectrum of Hindu culture, philosophy, and practice may be reclaimed as a polyvalent tradition incorporating composite elements over millennia. This view holds that to define it solely in terms of patriarchal Brahmanism is an artificial and drastic

Regarding this persistence, Omvedt writes:

> The crude version of . . . Dalit anti-Aryanism, as scholars are quick to point out, is fallacious as well as a form of inverted racism. . . . Yet the imagery survives and for good reasons. The continual privileging of an Aryan identity and a Vedic-Upanishadic-Sanskritic core by almost all upper-caste definers of Indian tradition, the pride in being "white" in opposition to "black," the continual assumptions of northern superiority, the continual if always veiled forms of upper-caste arrogance: all of these make it almost inevitable that the angry Dalit-shudra masses will throw back the weapon of racial and ethnic identity and ask again, "Who was the first invader? Who was the first outsider?"[84]

Putting it together: Historian Gyan Pandey, in his recent work comparing the structures of oppression facing African Americans and Dalits,[85] characterizes both as "internally colonized" groups. But he also notes that neither, dispersed throughout the social body and integral to its functioning, could be easily identified as a foreign entity to be allotted a separate sovereign territory, as sought by Native Americans or South Asian Muslims (or Tamilians, Sikhs, Manipuris, Assamese, Mizo, Naga, etc.). But it seems to me that in groping to define some sort of special subcategory of the racialized as colonized, Pandey too may not be fully acknowledging the distinction between two historically specific types of subordination.

Kauanui and Saranillio remind us that just as neither race nor nation is synonymous with indigeneity, imperialism is not synonymous with settler colonialism. Settlement is a precise phenomenon, which imperialism *may*

---

restriction of its meaning that impoverishes its heritage, diminishes its referents, and erases its many valid variants. See Wendy Doniger, *The Hindus: An Alternate History* (New York: Penguin Books, 2010) and *On Hinduism* (Oxford: Oxford University Press, 2014); Paula Richman, ed., *Many Ramayanas* (Berkeley: University of California Press, 1991) and *Questioning Ramayanas* (Berkeley: University of California Press, 2001); A.K. Ramanujan, "Three Hundred Ramayanas in *The Collected Essays of A.K. Ramanujan*, ed. Vinay Dharwadker, (Delhi: Oxford University Press, 1999); Romila Thapar, *The Past Before Us* (Cambridge, MA: Harvard University Press, 2013), *Somanatha: The Many Voices of a History* (London: Verso, 2005). The operative point, though, is that regardless of one's deep logic, or one's definition of "true" Indic civilization, the structures, institutions, practice, prejudices, sanctioned social relations (and resultant exploitations, exclusions, dehumanizations) of the narrowly brahminical version do exist now and must be opposed.

84 Omvedt, *Understanding Caste*, 99.

85 Gyanendra Pandey, *A History of Prejudice: Race, Caste, and Difference in India and the United States* (Cambridge: Cambridge University Press, 2013), 62. Equating Dalit liberation with conversion (to Buddhism, or to an alternative social ethic and political position), he links this choice in turn to the core of a decolonization process.

include among its goals or instruments.[86] It may be helpful here to utilize George Fredrickson's typology of administrative, plantation, mixed settlement, or pure settlement colonies. In the Indian case, the Vedic-Aryan arrival could be characterized as mixed settlement (in which indigenous populations are not exterminated but are incorporated into the complex racial and class stratifications of dominant settler culture, often including modes of exploitation through land or labor); and the British arrival as administrative (in which the goal is military and economic control of a region for politically strategic benefit, with foreign in-migration on a limited scale). By contrast, the mode most formative of the United States was a combination of plantation (with settlers relatively few in number but laying claim to massive land acreage, and importing enslaved or indentured laboring populations to produce monoculture crops) and pure settlement (in which the native population faces extermination, or removal and concentration).[87]

Andrea Smith's "Three Pillars of Heteropatriarchy" are also relevant here. Smith articulates three distinct modes of white supremacist racial logic applicable in the U.S. case, operative respectively toward Native Americans (the conquered, the savage), African Americans (the enslaved), and Asians/Arabs/Muslims (the eternal other, the enemy).[88] In the Indian case, from the perspective of Brahmanist Aryan supremacy we could place adivasis, Dalits, and Muslims in these three positions.

Despite the occasional blurring of Scheduled Castes and Scheduled Tribes, then, we might still distinguish adivasi and Dalit political projects, each facing distinct modes of internal colonization, although both may overlap and coexist. In the adivasi paradigm—if I may be schematically simplistic—oppression is visited upon those subhumanized as primitive, and exploitation is leveraged at the point of land and resources; key issues intersect around land rights, sovereignty, ecology, development, and militarized security. In the Dalit paradigm, oppression is visited upon those subhumanized as polluted, and exploitation is leveraged at the point of labor; key issues intersect around civil rights, poverty, discrimination, and sexual and social violence.

If indeed the most serviceable analogy for caste as a structure of oppression is a mode of race, then it still remains to identify the relationship

86 Talks given at American Studies Program Annual Conference, New York University, March 7, 2014. On the native-settler-slave triad see also Eve Tuck and K. Wayne Yang, "Decolonization Is Not a Metaphor," *Decolonization: Indigeneity, Education & Society* 1, no. 1 (2012): 1–40.

87 George M. Fredrickson, *The Arrogance of Race: Historical Perspectives on Slavery, Race and Social Inequity* (Middletown, CT: Wesleyan University Press, 1988), 218–20.

88 INCITE! Women of Color Against Violence, *The Color of Violence: The INCITE! Anthology* (Boston: South End Press, 2006).

between racism and colonialism—and an appropriate anarchist attitude to both. Perhaps we can formulate a three-sided comparison. Anarchist scholar Andrew Cornell has traced the intellectual genealogies of both the pacifist and militant traditions within contemporary American anarchism to pacifist and militant strands within American anti-racist movements, identifying anarchist heirs to both the King-Gandhian tradition, and the Malcolm X–Panther tradition.[89] Anti-caste movements also link to both these traditions. We have noted the circuit of inspiration from Black to Dalit Panthers in the 1970s, in the context of postwar decolonization, while the influence of Ambedkar's great antagonist, Gandhi, on King and the Congress on Racial Equality is well-documented. What this suggests is that at any point within these three historical spectrums of activist discourse, there are points of correspondence with the other two. So only one leg of a double triangle is left to be imagined: a link between anarchism and anti-casteism, as there is for anarchism/anti-racism, and anti-racism/anti-casteism.

Interference Patterns: Decolonizing Today?

Earlier I suggested that colonization in South Asia is an incompletely erased palimpsest, a field in which subsequent wave-forms have set up interference patterns with each other. I also hinted that some of these factors may now be converging, whereas in earlier periods they were arrayed at conflicting angles to imperial formations and to each other. For example, whereas Dalits perceived British and Mughal rule as mitigating the effects of Brahmanism, it now appears that postcolonial capitalism has reinforced the control of upper castes over Indian society and production,[90] in contrast to the earlier portrayal of British-introduced social and economic changes as providing opportunities for modern mobility. Indeed, the destruction of "Dalitbahujan productive structures, culture, economy and . . . positive political institutions," in Ilaiah's words, has proliferated in post-independence India.[91]

Yet was the earlier period really so good—for Dalits, if not for adivasis? The British Raj utterly reconfigured the *conditions in which* all narratives of conquest and conflict were deployed, even if *textually external* to accounts of Dravidian versus Aryan, or Hindu versus Muslim. Economically, British intervention drove South Asian incorporation into the circuits of global capitalism (liberalization since the 1990s has driven a second

89 Andrew Cornell, "'White Skin, Black Masks': Marxist and Anti-racist Roots of Contemporary US Anarchism," in Dave Berry, Ruth Kinna, Saku Pinta, and Alex Prichard, eds., *Libertarian Socialism: Politics in Black and Red* (New York: Palgrave Macmillan, 2012).

90 Ilaiah, *Why I Am Not a Hindu*, 113–14.

91 Ibid., 113.

round). Politically, British control introduced the notion of paramountcy, a unified governmental jurisdiction replacing more decentralized forms of segmented power relations. This consolidation removed many matters from adjudication by the "village-level caste bodies" (panchayats) which had previously "functioned as local governments."[92] In this way, contemporary anti-caste thinkers argue that the modern state and capitalism mitigated the traditional oppression of Dalits.[93] According to Teltumbde, British colonialism, "in addition to creating an enabling environment through its institutional regime . . . made two direct contributions to the emerging anticaste ethos": by opening up opportunities to untouchables for education and economic betterment, including employment with the military or infrastructure projects, all of which, along with the concomitant growth of urban areas, resulted in greater social mobility.[94]

Yet Dalitbahujan writings also concede that British colonialism reinforced Brahminical hegemony.[95] Rodrigues weighs the duality: "On the one hand [British rule] introduce[d] newer and more intense forms of exploitation; on the other it create[d] the conditions and resources to undermine not merely colonial exploitation but also other forms of oppression."[96] According to the familiar subalternist reading, the subordinated were caught between two mirrored elite narratives: the colonial and the nationalist, both equally guilty of erasing their agency and colluding in the task of Orientalist knowledge production. What became the dominant national paradigm was largely a co-creation of eighteenth-century European Indologist scholars and (Brahmin) clerical elites who were able to position themselves self-servingly as "expert" native informants, establishing the textually authoritative version of a misleadingly monolithic Indian tradition.[97] Precolonial Brahminical patriarchy was therefore reinforced, though not invented, by the colonial regime.[98]

---

92 Teltumbde, *The Persistence of Caste*, 20–21. How selective is Teltumbde being in noting laws which undermined caste? Were there other laws which reinforced it? One thinks for example of the Criminal Castes and Tribes Act, and of course the decennial censuses. Perhaps it's fair to say that the categories were produced and strengthened, but the material condition of the people in some of those categories may have improved, or at least been afforded pathways toward improvement?

93 See Shah, *Dalit Identity and Politics*, Vol. 2, 19, 39.

94 Teltumbde, *The Persistence of Caste*, 21–22

95 Ilaiah, *Why I Am Not a Hindu*, 9; Rodrigues, "Dalit-Bahujan Discourse in Modern India," 57.

96 Rodrigues, "Dalit-Bahujan Discourse in Modern India," 58.

97 On this process see Nicholas Dirks, *Castes of Mind* (Princeton, NJ: Princeton University Press, 2001); Thomas Metcalf, *Ideologies of the Raj* (Cambridge: Cambridge University Press, 1997); Bernard Cohn, *An Anthropologist Among the Historians* (New York: Oxford University Press, 1998).

98 Another aspect of this reinforcement via the colonial juridical system can be hypothesized through the designation of certain areas as "personal" as opposed to civil law,

Recalling this historiography modifies the sense in which opposition to the Aryan invasion is an anti-colonial stance: instead of taking sides *within* the narrative (of conquerors vs. indigenes, whichever side one chooses to designate as savage or civil), it's possible to object to the creation *of* the narrative itself. That is to say, opposing not just the Aryan invasion but "the Aryan invasion theory" shifts the anti-colonial emphasis from an anti-Hindu to an anti-British resistance, and from a mythic to a historical episteme, without acquitting Hindutva ideologues of their violent and discriminatory uses of the Aryan/Dravidian binary. In this way opposition to British colonialism and to Brahmanism could be connected. Here is the interference pattern at work.

The development of mainstream nationalism empowered an elite who identified it with themselves and their own interests. This was also a nationalism more acceptable to the colonial regime, which saw therein "a possibility of manipulation of institutions, parties and organizations" in order to shape the character of post-independence India in accordance with its own mentality and class interests, foreclosing its revolutionary possibilities. "Therefore they helped these [elite] forces to play the double role of articulating the national interest, and opposing colonialism in a limited form" conducive to preservation of the social status quo. This meant, in effect, favoring upper castes, landowners, industrialists, and the right over lower castes, peasants, workers, and the Left. "If the colonial authority had wanted to create a strong, anti-brahminical social base," Ilaiah declares, "it could have done so very easily," yielding quite a different sort of postcolonial society.[99] Nevertheless radical caste activists sometimes appealed to the British at the height of the anti-colonial struggle, when new political arrangements and proportional representation mechanisms were being hammered out, as being more likely to safeguard their interests than the dominant Hindus.

From 1950, when Ambedkar's constitution was instituted, to the 1980s, Dalits placed emancipatory hopes in the ideal of the post-colonial democratic republic. Even now, after much disenchantment with the emancipatory potential of the Indian state, given its failure to deliver on the promise of egalitarian redistribution, challenges are most often aimed not at the law's core principles, but at abuses or inconsistencies of implementation. Nevertheless the 1990s reversal of principles, as commitment

as a zone of colonial non-interference relegated to the control of Hindu and Muslim authorities, in order to avoid social destabilization potentially leading to insurgency. Instantiated as they were through strict endogamy and interdining practices, caste and gender structures could be cemented under the umbrella of culture and religion rather than coming into the domain of politics, public space, or civil rights.

99 Ilaiah, *Why I Am Not a Hindu*, 49.

to the market superseded commitment to welfare as the state's guiding ethos, meant that it could be challenged on the basis of its successes and not just on its failings.[100]

What now is the condition of "caste in a globalizing India"?[101] Neoliberalism, Teltumbde notes, is merciless to the poor and disadvantaged, caste aside. It brings indebtedness to rural areas, job loss to small scale industries, and the withdrawal of state subsidies and protections. Thus neocolonialism in the form of globalization has had the effect of strengthening caste inequities.[102] It also appears that the rise of capitalism has reinforced the class-like aspect of caste. According to Teltumbde, as Dalits engaged collectively in class struggle only to face brutal collective punishment, anti-communist reprisals have manifested as caste-based atrocities and vice versa.[103]

Another new twist within conditions of late capitalism is that due to economic competition, the rising OBCs, with rising anxieties matching rising ambitions, are perhaps even more hostile to Dalit aspirations in many localities than higher caste groups.[104] This has led to a shocking increase in incidents of caste-based violence, often with the tacit or open complicity of police and legal systems.[105] "It is commonplace Dalit experience that state/police intervention does not help them combat the perpetrators of caste violence; on the contrary, the state emboldens nonDalits" by both its omissions and commissions. Beyond the biased application of justice (with leniency fostering the general perception of tolerance of atrocities, thus encouraging more boldness in their perpetration), the police have even been known to join in the mayhem. Thus the "state machinery" has played an active role in caste atrocities.[106]

Under the 1989 Prevention of Atrocities Act, the state is supposed to guarantee the protection of Scheduled Castes and Tribes, and punish perpetrators of hate crimes, but it seldom works that way in practice. Here too it is suggested that implementation is the real problem, not the law itself, because the interface of the population with the law—that

100 Teltumbde, *The Persistence of Caste*, 62.
101 Ibid., 31.
102 Ibid., 154–56.
103 Ibid., 60–61.
104 Even so, the Mandal agitations of 1990 too could be seen in part as reaction to fear by upper caste people of limited economic means at losing their own precarious access to educational opportunity to reservations.
105 Teltumbde offers an exhaustive account of this in relation to the Khairlanji killings of 2006, in which government involvement ranged from tolerance of the violence (90–112) to actual complicity in caste atrocities (116–35). A similar dynamic applied to the Gujarat massacres of Muslims in 2002.
106 Atrocities are defined as "the violent manifestation of social prejudice against dalits." Teltumbde, *The Persistence of Caste*, 154–55.

is, of society with the state—primarily occurs at the local level, where caste prejudices prevail.[107] But is this really such a new phenomenon? Those prejudices are very old. Teltumbde links the rise of atrocities since the 1980s to a combination of factors: the weakening of the anti-caste movement, the new impacts of capitalism, and the resultant shifts in the economic fortunes of different groups. The combination of old prejudice and late capitalist precarity makes a toxic mix.

All these threads—state repression, global capitalism, accelerated encroachment on resource-rich forest and agricultural lands—converge upon a reinvigorated militant left movement that has primarily mobilized adivasi communities, but in some regions (according to Teltumbde) can also be significantly characterized as a Dalit phenomenon: Naxalism.[108] The movement originated in 1967 with a *tribal* youth, and *tribal* peasants killed in an "encounter" over the cultivation of contested land near Naxalbari in West Bengal. But its branch in Bihar centered on a Dalit teacher named "Master" Jagdish Mahto, who was first the Ambedkarite publisher of the *Harijanistan* newspaper, and then a Marxist after 1968. He and others established Bhojpur as a Naxalite hub by 1975. The upshot was that Naxalism in Bihar was, in effect, "caste politics in a different guise."[109]

This may be even truer in the twenty-first-century form, wherein the interference patterns are visible yet again, if indeed neoliberal interests and global ambitions stand behind the Indian state's policies toward those it identifies as security threats. In other words, if the U.S.-led imperialist "war on terror" is a rhetorical cover justifying the annihilation of obstacles to the expansion of a neoliberal regime, post–Cold War India is its aspiring partner in that project. Thus, Teltumbde accuses, as the "war on teror" has "justified demonizing every other Muslim as a potential terrorist, India's Hinduistic state has taken the US model even further, invoking the label 'naxalite' for Dalits and adivasis to violently suppress any kind of dissent on their part. The naxalite rhetoric of 'armed struggle,' 'people's war,' 'guerilla zone,' 'liberated area' and so on fits the profile of an 'enemy' that the state wishes to have" in order to justify its militarization.[110]

On the other hand, given the negative impact of neoliberalism on the disadvantaged, *both* "Dalits and adivasis have been attracted in

107 Ibid., 87. On the good intentions of the law, see 78–79. Note again this blurring or conflation of Scheduled Castes and Scheduled Tribes, including in the UPA government's Common Minimum Program of 2004.

108 Ibid., 158.

109 Ibid., 161, drawing on Mendelsohn and Vicziany, *The Untouchables: Subordination, Poverty and the State in Modern India* (Cambridge University Press, 1998), 59. Teltumbde, *The Persistence of Caste*, 204. He identifies Dalits as central also to the Telangana uprising of 1947, marked as precursor to Naxalbari, 159.

110 Teltumbde, *The Persistence of Caste*, 156.

large numbers to the naxalite movement, and, by and large, constitute its combat force."[111] Because of this demographic, the state's crackdown on Naxalism through special laws and paramilitary forces "directly precipitates antidalit and antiadivasi atrocities."[112] SCs and OBCs, Dalits, and adivasis are the most frequent "encounter deaths."[113] But just because such instances of state violence fall under the rubric of anti-Naxalism doesn't mean they shouldn't also be viewed as caste atrocity, Teltumbde argues. The use of anti-Naxalism as cover for cracking down on the protests that followed the multiple murders of a Dalit family in Khairlanji in 2006 is central to his story.[114]

So it seems the rubric of Naxalism can mask caste relations in both directions: just as those killed as Naxalites are disproportionally Dalit or adivasi, people attacked for their caste (or people defending those people) are liable to be tagged as Naxalites—a blanket excuse to criminalize activists, rights workers, or gadflies, just as select tribes were interpellated as criminals in the late nineteenth century.[115] In this way the state, capital, and caste elites have achieved a new collusion of interests. Can anti-state, anti-capitalist, and anti-caste radicals do the same?

In Lieu of Conclusion: Questions and Observations

Indigenist discourse makes "nation" a possibly recuperable idea, conceivable within nonstate forms of sovereignty. By contrast, Dalitbahujan thought asserts the possibility of a recuperable state deployed against a dangerous nation. Previously, when I suggested (somewhat provocatively, I admit) the possibility of liberating the nation from the state, I was trying to hold onto a capacious reference point that could encompass many examples of anti-colonial struggle; to come to terms with primary resistance to conquest, and assertions of survival, from the Americas to Africa to Asia to Australia.

But every context is particular, layering critiques upon a hypothesis in the process of testing it for relevance. This is fine; the point of such a hypothesis is not to defend it against challenge and gain ideological points, but to dialogically carry forward usable, actionable understandings of real conditions. Anyone listening tends to apply these propositions to their own specific location, though in reality there is no ideal type against which to specify qualifications and exceptions. What becomes clear is that it is inaccurate to draw conclusions in the abstract, outside of a context. The

111 Ibid.
112 Ibid.
113 Ibid., 163.
114 Ibid., 156.
115 Ibid., 164–66.

terms we plug into "let x equal . . ." change the graph of the function in historically and politically significant ways.

Attempting to test such terms, I conclude, inconclusively, with questions.

Closing Check-in

It is easy to see the struggles of forest-dwelling tribal communities against land appropriation and enclosure of the commons as direct continuations of anti-colonial resistance, unbroken across British and Indian regimes.[116] The ways in which a radical anti-caste political/philosophical framework crosshatches an anarchist/anti-colonialist one are slightly more complicated.

1) Annihilating caste is, in India, the ultimate struggle of equality against hierarchy. How can anarchism, classical or contemporary, enter into meaningful dialogue with anti-caste thought and praxis? Here is Malatesta on the articulation of freedom and equality: "No man can achieve his own emancipation without at the same time working for the emancipation of all men around him."[117] This is true if individuals are not atomized monads of the kind imagined by classical liberal theory, but interdependent components of society. Emancipation thus must be achieved systemically and symphonically, through—and here is Bakunin—a "restructuring of society from below, according to the principle of free association and federation."[118] This restructuring occurs both positively, in the development of social potentialities through education and material well-being for all, and negatively, in the revolt against "all forms of transcendental authority" whether human or divine, including both nation and state (Bakunin having denounced nationalism, long before Benedict Anderson, as a "new form of political theology").[119] Crucially though, such revolt opposes not only the transcendent but the immanent, not only sovereign but governmental power: namely the "tyranny of the society" that is

---

116 Much of the content of colonial Indian Forest Acts (1865, 1878, 1927) was incorporated into postcolonial land rights and tribal land use legislation. For comparative global perspectives, see Alexander Reid Ross, ed.. *Grabbing Back: Essays Against the Global Land Grab* (Oakland: AK Press, 2014).

117 Errico Malatesta, "Notes on Anarchist Social Organization," referenced on February 19, 2014 at International Institute for Organization Research, http://www.anarchy.no/malat1.html. Also quoted in the context of Chiara Bottici, "Black and Red: The Freedom of Equals," in Bottici, Jacob Blumenfeld, and Simon Critchley, eds., *The Anarchist Turn* (London: Pluto Press, 2013), 16.

118 Bakunin, "Stateless Socialism." http://dwardmac.pitzer.edu/Anarchist_Archives/bakunin/stateless.html.

119 Bakunin, "God and the State." http://dwardmac.pitzer.edu/Anarchist_Archives/bakunin/godandstate/godandstate_ch1.html.

"exercise[d] through customs, traditions, sentiments, prejudices, images and habits, on both our material and intellectual life."[120]

While Ambedkar repeatedly invoked the revolutionary republican principles of liberty, equality, and fraternity, he left no ambiguity about equality's preeminence. In fact, from the anti-caste perspective, liberation itself could be defined as the attainment of equality. Similarly, for anarchists, liberty and equality are reciprocally generated. But whereas for anarchists that condition requires the elimination of the state, Ambedkar sought to use the state as tool of emancipation against social tyranny. For Bakunin or Malatesta such a strategy was inconceivable.

Anti-statist political thought in India is mainly associated with (some would say tainted by) the Gandhian tradition and the sarvodaya movement, leading toward various branches of environmentalism that in turn influenced key adivasi-based mobilizations, including the Chipko movement.[121] These lineages are for the most part viewed askance by the established left parties, which extend their suspicion to the notion of decentralized organization and village-scaled economies. But after the experience of the Emergency in the 1970s (in which Indira Gandhi suspended civil liberties and constitutional government for two years, brutally crushing dissent with military rule), and the transition from quasi-socialism to economic liberalization in the 1990s, many social movements are more likely now than during the first decades after independence to view the state as a force of repression inimical to human rights and civil liberties. It has repeatedly claimed internal (usually Naxalite), external (usually Islamist), and separatist threats (in which case the internality or externality is the crux of the conflict, as in the Northeast or Kashmir) as a pretext to intensify its special military and policing powers.[122]

In Debjani Ganguly's meta-account of caste logic, drawing upon the formulation introduced by Hegel and embraced by Mill, the state is the

---

120 Quoted in Bottici, 17.

121 Chipko was a movement initiated by Himalayan tribal groups in the 1970s, whose activists were famous for using their bodies to protect trees from being logged after the Forest Department awarded lumber contracts to a sporting goods company; the tactic was part of a larger mobilization in defense of local sovereignty, ecological sustainability, and traditional rights of access to and use of forest resources. See sources cited in note 70.

122 Here I am not talking about the post-liberalization trope that the state must retreat before the markets—this is not reality. The state is equally big, or even bigger, just reoriented to serve markets and the interests of global capital and the emergent layer of Indians who identify with it, rather than the interests of redistribution and social welfare. Kanchan Chandra, "The New Indian State," lecture, February 16, 2013, Fifth Annual Global South Asia Conference, New York University; Rupal Oza, *The Making of Neoliberal India: Nationalism, Gender, and the Paradoxes of Globalization* (London: Routledge, 2006).

historical embodiment of rationality and freedom in its most advanced/advancing form. Mill's liberalism (and therefore canonical social science) defined Indian society as the opposite of this: India was defined by the absence of the state, and thus by its negations, hierarchy and despotism. Much Indian social and political thought internalized that notion, which outlived the colonial politics that had produced it. But the anarchist's definition of the state is the opposite: if the state is by its very structure and function a producer of hierarchy and despotism, the negation of the state would promote freedom.

Since both pre- and post-colonial states have been used to institutionalize and enforce caste through uppercaste domination of symbolic and material economies, control of resources, and monopoly of coercion, was the colonial state then an exception, from the perspective of Dalit emancipation?[123] If, in the current configuration, state-based mechanisms are insufficient (or inimical) to combat caste, does anarchism have anything to offer to this struggle?

2) Regardless of one's own biases, is it possible for people in a given situation—in this case, Dalits in post-independence India—to conceive of reform within an existing system as revolutionary, or is reform always counterrevolutionary? What if the establishment of that system itself was considered revolutionary, or at least the result of revolutionary intentions? In other words, when, if ever, do incremental changes that make use of official channels, even highly problematic ones, move things in a direction that creates conditions of possibility for revolutionary change, and when do they shore up the status quo? For example, one might argue that ensuring the conditions basic for survival and humane living when these have previously been denied is, in addition to being an ethical imperative, a prerequisite for anyone to have the capacity, time, and energy to organize toward revolutionary futures. These questions have also been discussed within Western anarchist discourse: Colin Ward, Murray Bookchin, and others have proposed pragmatic coexistence with or even strategic utilization of existing institutions.[124]

---

123 Precolonial examples include the Maharashtrian peshwai state described by Chakravarti, 105–13; and the classical Gupta state in which the Dharmashastras were made normative. The early postcolonial Ambedkarite/Nehruvian years could also be included within the period of a pro-Dalit state that I'm suggesting was anomalous.

124 While this has sparked accusations of halfhearted reformism, it also obliges us at least to consider the obscured routes by which we might navigate from the society in which we actually live to that in which we would like to live I'm not taking a stance here, merely puzzling it out. For a taste of these discussions, see, for example, Colin Ward, *Anarchy in Action* (London: Freedom Press, 1973) and *Anarchism: A Very Short Introduction* (London: Oxford University Press, 2004); Howard Ehrlich, ed., *Reinventing Anarchy, Again* (San Francisco: AK Press, 1996); and Murray Bookchin, *Social Anarchism or Lifestyle Anarchism: An Unbridgeable Chasm* (Oakland: AK Press, 2001).

On the other hand, caste radicals seeking constitutional redress may need to consider whether or not top-down changes in state policy are sufficient—even assuming they are consistently enforced—when in truth what's needed is a profound and pervasive change in social attitudes and cultural norms, which cannot be legislated.[125] As the saying goes, when the mores are sufficient, the law is unnecessary; when the mores are insufficient, the law is ineffective. But the same applies from the bottom up. Decentralized organization, if it is informed by patriarchal Brahmanism in village councils, for example, is by no means guaranteed to be egalitarian or emancipatory. A litany of ugly newspaper stories illustrates how khap panchayats have been primarily a vehicle for punitive caste and gender violence. Form without content, structural devolution without a shift in values, is not enough.

3) Omvedt has characterized the new social movements since the 1980s as linking cultural and socio-economic critique—a trait she associates with the spread of a "Dalit consciousness"[126]—along with their increasing opposition to centralization.[127] Could these strands (including those focused on the environment, gender and sexuality, as well as peasant, worker and student concerns) as be unified into a "total liberatory theory," as Omvedt hopes?[128] Pandey too, echoing Ilaiah and Pantawane, suggests that the Dalit liberation paradigm of egalitarian emancipation offers a future to all people, not just Dalits. In other words, might a political vision based in radical Dalitbahujan thought, if enhanced by a stringent critique of political forms, be the foundation of a movement based on intersectional (anti-oppression, anti-capitalist) grassroots (anti-statist, anti-authoritarian) logic? And might it magnify decolonizing solidarities with anti-authoritarian, intersectionally minded activists with anarchist affinities elsewhere in the world?

4) If colonial encounters in India are a palimpsest, not a simple polarity, what opportunities for solidarity appear where multiple colonialities converge?

5) Is it only relative power calculus—a quantitative measure—that determines whether a newly introduced element is a threat, a vulnerable guest, or an assimilable additive, as in the Parsi story of sugar sprinkled into milk? How can we also evaluate the qualitative? After all, one could

---

125 Even in the 1970s and '80s, prior to the emergent symbiosis of Hindutva and neoliberalism, and aside from the state's active collusion in caste oppression, a turn to electoral politics itself was seen as a neutralizer of social movements, sapping energy from more radical transformations and diluting constituencies for the sake of mass appeal. See Adi Dalit pamphlet.

126 Omvedt, *Understanding Caste*, , 81.

127 Ibid., xii.

128 Ibid., 87–88.

just as easily sprinkle the milk with salt, or cyanide. What political work is done by distinguishing the need to restore what was lost as a benefit to all because of its intrinsic (e.g., egalitarian or ecologically sustainable) character, from the condemnation of conquest on principle, regardless of the character of the conquered society?

6) Finally, some object to mobilizing caste (or race) as a political identity on the grounds that doing so reinforces and perpetuates the logic on which it is based. Can you reject the epistemology of caste (or race), *and* the material conditions, privations, and power imbalances of caste or race? The former may be a construct, but the latter are very real. Does denying the former before the latter is dismantled simply leave the latter intact? Perhaps the key is to deny its legitimacy, but not its existence. That way, it's possible to hold both in one's head at the same time (koan-like, though that's a different branch of Buddhism than Ambedkar's). This is not quite the same thing as strategic essentialism—more like a distinction between what does exist and what should, could, and must exist, while trying to move actively from one to the other.

7) Can an anarchist navigate a route to Begumpura?

Selected Bibliography

Ambedkar, B.R. *The Buddha and His Dhamma.* Bombay: Siddharth College Publications, 1957.

———. *The Essential Writings of B.R. Ambedkar.* Edited by Valerian Rodrigues. Oxford: Oxford University Press, 2002.

———. *The Annihilation of Caste with a Reply to Mahatma Gandhi.* New York: Columbia University Press, 2004. (orig. R.R. Kadrekar, 1937.)

Anand, Mulk Raj, and Eleanor Zelliott, eds. *An Anthology of Dalit Literature.* Gyan Publishing House, 1992.

Chakravarti, Uma. *Gendering Caste Through a Feminist Lens.* Calcutta: Stree, 2003.

Dangle, Arjun. *Poisoned Bread.* Hyderabad: Orient BlackSwan, 2009.

Dirks, Nicholas. *Castes of Mind.* Princeton, NJ: Princeton University Press, 2001.

Ganguly, Debjany. *Caste, Coloniality, and Counter-Modernity.* New York: Routledge, 2009.

Guru, Gopal. The Language of Dlit-Bahujan Political Discourse." In Ghanshyam Shah, ed., *Dalit Identity and Politics.* Vol. 2. New Delhi: Sage Publications, 2001.

Ilaiah, Kancha. *Why I Am Not a Hindu.* Calcutta: Arunima Printing Works, 1996 (2012 edition).

———. "Towards the Dalitization of the Nation." in Partha Chatterjee, ed., *The Wages of Freedom: Fifty Years of the Indian Nation-State.* Delhi: Oxford University Press, 1998.

———. "Dalitism vs. Brahmanism: The Epistemological Conflict in History." In Ghanshyam Shah, ed., *Dalit Identity and Politics.* Vol. 2. New Delhi: Sage Publications, 2001.

Joshi, Barbara, ed. *Untouchable! Voices of the Dalit Liberation Movement.* London: Zed Books, 1986.

Kannabiran, Kalpana, and Vasanth Kannabiran. "Looking at Ourselves: The Women's Movement in Hyderabad." In M. Jacqui Alexander and Chandra Talpade Mohanty, eds., *Feminist Genealogies, Colonial Legacies, Democratic Futures*. New York: Routledge, 1997.

Mamdani, Mahmood. *Define and Rule: Native as Political Identity*. Cambridge, MA: Harvard University Press, 2012.

Natarajan, Balmurli. *The Culturalization of Caste in India: Identity and Inequality in Multicultural Age*. London: Routledge, 2012.

Nathan, Dev, ed. *From Tribe to Caste*. Shimla: Indian Institute of Advanced Study, 1997.

Omvedt, Gail. *Dalits and the Democratic Revolution: Dr. Ambedkar and the Dalit Movement in Colonial India*. New Delhi: Sage Publications, 1994.

———. "Ambedkar and After." In Ghanshyam Shah, ed. *Dalit Identity and Politics*. Vol. 2. New Delhi: Sage Publications, 2001.

———. *Ambedkar: Towards an Enlightened India*. New Delhi: Penguin, 2004.

———. *Seeking Begumpura*. Navayana Publishers, 2008.

———. *Understanding Caste: From Buddha to Ambedkar and Beyond*. New Delhi: Orient BlackSwan, 2011.

Pandey, Gyanendra. A History of Prejudice: Race, Caste, and Difference in India and the United States. Cambridge: Cambridge University Press, 2013.

Pandian, M.S.S. "Stepping Outside of History? New Writings from Tamil Nadu." In Partha Chatterjee, ed., *The Wages of Freedom: Fifty Years of the Indian Nation-State*. Delhi: Oxford University Press, 1998.

Rajshekar, V.T. *Dalit: The Black Untouchables of India*. Atlanta: Clarity Press, 1987 [orig. *Apartheid in India* (Bangalore: Dalit Action Committee, 1979)].

Rao. *The Caste Question: Dalits and the Politics of Modern India*. Berkeley: University of California Press, 2009.

Rao, ed. *Gender and Caste*. London: Zed Books, 2005.

Rege, Sharmila. *Writing Caste, Writing Gender*. Zubaan Books, 2013.

Rodrigues, Valerian. "Dalit-Bahujan Discourse in Modern India." In V.R. Mehta and Thomas Pantham, eds., *Political Ideas in Modern India: Thematic Explorations*. Vol. X Part 7. New Delhi: Sage Publications, 2006.

Schwarz, Henry. *Constructing the Criminal Tribe in Colonial India*. Malden, MA: Wiley-Blackwell, 2010.

Shah, Ghanshyam, ed. *Dalit Identity and Politics*. Vol. 2. New Delhi: Sage Publications, 2001.

Sikand, Yoginder. *Islam, Caste, and Dalit-Muslim Relations in India*. New Delhi: Global Media Publications, 2004.

Teltumbde, Anand. *The Persistence of Caste*. London: Zed Books, 2010.

Thorat, S.K., and K. Newman. "Caste and Economic Discrimination: Causes, Consequences and Remedies," *Economic and Political Weekly* 42, no. 41 (October 13, 2007): 4121–24.

Vajpeyi, Ananya. *Righteous Republic: The Political Foundations of Modern India*. Cambridge, MA: Harvard University Press, 2012.

Visweswaran, Kamala. *Un/Common Cultures*. Durham: Duke University Press, 2010.

Zelliott, Eleanor. *From Untouchable to Dalit*. Delhi: Manohar Press, 1992.

———. "The Meaning of Ambedkar." In Ghanshyam Shah, ed. *Dalit Identity and Politics*. Vol. 2. New Delhi: Sage Publications, 2001.

YPSILANTI VAMPIRE MAY DAY

Peter Linebaugh

OCCUPY YPSILANTI 2012

Dedicated to the students, young and old, of southeastern Michigan and northwestern Ohio

Dracula

On May Day sometime in the 1890s, an ordinary Englishman boarded a train in Munich.* His destination was a castle in Transylvania, a country wedged between the Danubian provinces of Moldavia and Wallachia. It was a dark and stormy night when he arrived, and the wind was howling hard.

"Do you not know that tonight, when the clock strikes midnight, all the evil things of the world will have full sway?" asked the landlady of a nearby hotel, and she implored him to reverse his course. Other commoners then warned him it was a witch's Sabbath. Heedless, he persisted to the castle where pure terror awaited him in the personage of a bloodsucking monster. Count Dracula was at once as smooth, polite, and persuasive as President Obama, and as terrifying, shape-shifting, and diabolical as George W. Bush. He was undead—a zombie, or a werewolf—and lived only as long as he was able to suck human blood.

As for the crisis of our own lives, in 2009 Matt Taibbi assigned blame to the banks, calling Goldman Sachs "a great vampire squid wrapped around the face of humanity, relentlessly jamming its blood funnel into anything that smells like money."[1] Reverend Edward Pinkney of Benton Harbor, Michigan, referring to the emergency manager which was wrapped around the face of his city, said "he's for the corporations that suck the life out of people." Banks, insurance companies, and corporations belong to the total circuit of capitalism whence the sucking originates. When Alan Haber, the first president of Students for a Democratic Society (SDS), spoke last winter at the Crazy Wisdom Book Shop and Tea Room in Ann Arbor about his experiences at Occupy Boston and Occupy Wall Street, he concluded his remarks by reminding everybody that "Capital is dead labor, which vampire-like, lives only by sucking living labor, and lives the more, the more labor it sucks."

As May Day 2012 approaches Ypsilanti, by all means let us tell stories of flowers and fertility rituals and of the ancient festivals on the commons; and let us, for sure, commemorate the great struggle for the eight-hour workday that reached a climax in Chicago at the Haymarket in May 1886, and gave birth to the holiday of workers around the planet, east and west, north and south. As the prospect of the appointment of an emergency manager (EM) looms over Ypsilanti—with powers to abrogate union

---

* Thanks to Kate Hutchens of the University of Michigan Library's Labadie Collection; to the Ypsilanti Historical Society; to Constantine George Caffentzis; to Kate Khatib of AK Press; to Professor Ronald Grigor Suny; to Anna of Thessaloniki; to Lia Yoka of Thessaloniki; to Jeffery Pollock and Eric Albjerg of the University of Toledo; and to Michaela Brennan and Riley Linebaugh.

1 Matt Taibbi, "The Great American Bubble," *Rolling Stone*, July 9, 2009, http://www.rollingstone.com/politics/news/the-great-american-bubble-machine-20100405.

contracts, close schools, sell public assets, expropriate municipal lands, and whose very word is law—we must also greet the day with the realistic gloom that comes from an uncertainty about health, roof, studies, and livelihood. The tooth is at our throat!

Our green parks are turned into toxic brownfields and our common lands have been laid waste as collateral for unspecified "development."

Our eight-hour workday is lengthened by multiple part-time jobs, or by the time-consuming caretaking of elders without pensions or children without day care. Our lives now are in the grip of mysterious forces called securitization or financialization, to which we submit in dumbfounded helplessness, though the blush on our faces reminds us that these forces are but the bloodsuckers of old. Voltaire wrote that "stock jobbers, brokers, and men of business sucked the blood of the people in broad daylight . . . these true suckers live not in cemeteries but in very agreeable palaces."[2]

We face a crisis of production, yes, but also a crisis of reproduction. Production pertains to factories, sweatshops, mines, and fields; it is the realm of commerce, technology, and commodities. Reproduction pertains to kitchens, families, schools, neighborhoods; it is the realm of society, service, and a very special "commodity"—actually no commodity at all, rather: human beings. Reproduction takes place over various cycles of duration. It may mean the daily preparation for the next day or week—the shopping, the cooking, the cleaning, etc. Or it may mean the preparation of the next generation, beginning with its creation and extending from diaper changing to graduate school. Michaela Brennan, a public health nurse at the Packard Community Clinic outside Ypsilanti, sighed in near despair: "So many people need looking after!"

Reverend Pinkney and Greece circa 2012

Benton Harbor is on the other side of the state, but its tale is Ypsilanti's too. Reverend Pinckney opposed the expropriation of the parklands which had been deeded to the city a hundred years ago, to belong to it "forever." Such places are common lands. Whirlpool Corporation wanted the land and so did the developers who had in mind a golf course for executives and the Chicago summer people. The people's park had to go, and so did the people. When they squawked, an emergency manager was forced on the town. Its commons were then privatized by the 1 percent.

One aim of this book is to oppose EMs—in the name of democracy!—and, in the name of the commons, to oppose the capitalist system behind them. We are being hoodwinked.

In 2007 Reverend Pinckney quoted scriptures to a judge:

> Cursed shalt thou be in the city, and cursed shalt thou be in the field. Cursed shall be thy basket and thy store. Cursed shall be the fruit of thy body, and the fruit of thy land, the increase of thy kine, and the flocks of thy sheep. . . . The Lord shall smite thee with a consumption, and with a fever, and with an inflammation, and with an

2 *Philosophical Dictionary* (1764).

> extreme burning, and with the sword, and with blasting, and with mildew; and they shall pursue thee until thou perish.[3]

The judge found these lines threatening and ordered Edward Pinkney to prison for three to ten years. Pinkney kept up the fight inside jail, where despite the mutual resentment of blacks, whites, and browns, he coordinated with each group and collectively they won better food for themselves.

An emergency manager is a dictator. In ancient Rome, Sulla was one of the patricians who opposed the *populares*, who were still in mourning for the death of the fraternal people's tribunes of Caius and Tiberius Gracchus, whose Agrarian Law redistributed the land of the patricians and preserved the common lands of the people, or the *ager publicus*. Sulla ravaged Athens until its streets ran with blood; in Rome he slaughtered five thousand prisoners. Under an emergency, he had himself declared "dictator" and murdered his friends. His word was law, and law was death. The Roman people were offered bread and circuses; we are offered McDonald's and golf. In Benton Harbor the *ager publicus* has been privatized; it now has no people and eighteen holes.

This phenomenon is worldwide. Take Greece, for instance. From Thessaloniki a woman named Anna writes me, "I don't know if you are aware that since last fall, instead of having an elected government, the IMF [International Monetary Fund] and the European Bank have appointed an emergency government to manage the crisis." The manager used to work for Goldman Sachs. He puts the funnel in to draw some blood.

In December of 2008, in an autonomous neighborhood in downtown Athens, a fifteen-year-old high school student named Alexis Grigoropoulos was deliberately shot to death by a policeman. Lia Yoka, another colleague in Greece, writes me that the people of Nafplion—Ypsilanti's sister-city in that country—protested by occupying the Town Council and the Theatre Department of the University of Peloponnese. A generation of young Greek people roused themselves from a decade's torpor and sprung into outrage: high school and university students, immigrants, the unemployed, precarious workers, and others occupied the streets in riotous protest, and turned them into an urban commons. This occurred amid the economic "shock therapy" that has accompanied the response to the Greek debt. A state of exception was declared.

The minimum wage in Greece has been sliced by 25 percent, making it the lowest in Europe. Allowances, benefits, pensions have been destroyed. Youth unemployment is at 51 percent. What was once a welfare state providing relief "from the cradle to the grave" has become a penal state that

---

3 Deuteronomy 28:14–22.

incarcerates some immigrants in special detention units and criminalizes others, including those who wear hoodies! Six out of ten Greek households are in arrears with their mortgage payments; seven out of ten are in arrears with consumer loans; one out of two are in arrears with credit card payments. This is a crisis of reproduction, and women are the hardest hit.

Fiscal terrorism operates emotionally as well as economically. Crisis is experienced as a multitude of personal failures; collective guilt and self-blame become commonplace, and neither trade unionism nor politicians have been able to respond successfully. One-day general strikes, sectional strikes by subway workers, bus drivers, secondary school teachers, hospital doctors, bank employees, and truck drivers have also been unable to halt the bulldozing of the Greek working class. Suicides have increased. The most effective antidepressant is collective action, yet this is criminalized.

The situation does indeed resemble Count Dracula's castle: the barred windows of banks; the impregnable battlements of securitization; the bolted doors of financialization; the endless corridors of credit default swaps; the twisting stairways of lost mortgages; the heavy portcullis of fiscalism. Every view is hemmed in by enclosure, and each citizen is watched over by the omniscient Evil Eye of surveillance cameras. Even the Greek minister of labor has declared "there will be blood."[4] We yearn to escape.

Here, then, as if from a nineteenth-century poet, is an Ypsilanti vampire story; only, this is not just a story. It is real, instructive, and documented history, and may also be a shadow from the future cast back onto the past. It may—it should—curdle your blood, quicken your heart, and rouse you to fury. We have been bamboozled.

De-Bamboozling

Howard Zinn's *A People's History of the United States* was first published in 1980. Even if you possess only a single shelf for books and spices, this should be on it, right next to the salt! What is radical history? Zinn quotes sociologist E. Franklin Frazier, as he speaks to black college students in Atlanta: "All your life, white folks have bamboozled you, preachers have bamboozled you, teachers have bamboozled you; I am here to debamboozle you."[5]

The B-24 was built at Willow Run in the township of Ypsilanti. As a young bombardier, Howard Zinn did not fly "The Liberator," as the B-24

4 I am especially grateful to two articles by "Children of the Gallery," a Greek collective: "The Rebellious Passage of a Proletarian Minority through a Brief Period of Time" and "Burdened with Debt: 'Debt Crisis' and Class Struggles in Greece," in Vradis and Dalakoglou, *Revolt and Crisis in Greece* (Oakland and London: AK Press and Occupied London, 2011), 115–31, 245–78. I am also grateful for a message from Anna in Thessaloniki.

5 Howard Zinn, *The Politics of History* (Boston: Beacon Press, 1970), 45.

was called, but instead in a B-17, a "Flying Fortress." Zinn remembers that "the crews who flew those planes [B-24s] died in great numbers. We who flew the more graceful-looking B-17s sardonically called those other planes B dash 2 crash 4." The B-24 had a longer range and could carry a heavier payload, but it tended to catch fire.[6] It was "the worst piece of metal aircraft construction I have ever seen," according to Charles Lindbergh.

Of World War II Zinn wrote, "I thought it was a just cause. Therefore you drop bombs." He was the first to drop napalm, which he regretted for the rest of his life, and lived to remember a pilot who perished and who had told him, "You know, this is not a war against fascism. It's a war for empire. England, the United States, the Soviet Union—they are all corrupt states, not morally concerned about Hitlerism, just wanting to run the world themselves. It's an imperialist war." This unnamed casualty de-bamboozled Howard Zinn, who became one of the most influential peaceniks of the second half of the twentieth century. Like Zinn, Albert Parsons changed his mind. In the Civil War, he had ridden cavalry on behalf of Confederate slave masters. Parsons and Zinn excelled at what they did, but after bitter experience each came to reject as false the virtues of valor and bravery when in service of war or slavery, but as true when in the service of peace and the working class. That is why, comrades, we must *never give up* on those who disagree with us.

At the base of the Ypsilanti water tower there is a marble bust of a Greek who looks grand despite having weathered eighty-four years since its creation. Demetrios Ypsilantis stares into the Michigan skies, with a splendid high collar to hold up his chin, dashing military braids to enlarge his chest, a gallant sash, and brush-like epaulettes that broaden his shoulders.

Demetrios and his brother Alexander, an *aide-de-camp* to Alexander I, Czar of Russia, had been officers in the military of the Russian Empire until the spring of 1821 when Alexander Ypsilantis, along with a small contingent, invaded Moldavia from the east; Demetrios entered Wallachia from the west. They thus fought the first battles of the decade-long war of Greek independence from the Ottoman Empire. It is an accident of history that the Greek War of Independence commenced in the Danubian provinces of Moldavia and Wallachia, the very region and setting of *Dracula*. And there is still more to it: in these same provinces we discover a key genesis of the transition from expropriation to exploitation which

6 Howard Zinn, "The Greatest Generation?" *The Progressive* 65 (October 2001): 12–13. See also his *Failure to Quit: Reflections of an Optimistic Historian* (Monroe, ME: Common Courage Press, 1993), and *You Can't Be Neutral on a Moving Train: A Personal History of Our Times* (Boston: Beacon Press, 1993).

characterizes capitalist modernity and the crisis we currently suffer. We confront three losses: the loss of blood, the loss of names, and the loss of commons. Only as a result of such a confrontation may we regard May Day and the beauty it promises. A green beauty and a red promise.

1. The Loss of Blood

The Battle of Waterloo put an end to Napoleon. Across Europe the jaws of a devouring darkness clamped upon the light of freedom. The wars against the French Revolution were finally over. Crippled soldiers and emaciated sailors returned home to haunt and to starve in city slums. The enclosed peasantry of England cried "bread or blood." The gallows executed followers of Ned Ludd. The mechanization of production had begun. Anyone who dared even peep in demurral was imprisoned. Ireland was smashed; starvation prevailed. In America, slave-holders and Indian-killers ruled supreme.

Giant landlords owned England, the country that Percy Shelley, Mary Shelley, and Lord Byron fled. In an immense carriage that carried his library, dining service, and *lit de repos*, Byron roamed across Europe to Switzerland. One famous evening of idleness and boredom, on the shores of Lake Geneva, these friends amused themselves by telling ghost stories. Mary Shelley told her *Frankenstein* tale, and Byron told a story which his physician, Dr. John Polidori, wrote down and published in 1819. It was a story titled *The Vampyre*.

The stories were cathartic allegories of the historical forces engulfing Lord Byron and the Shelleys: slavery, or proletarianization, and mechanization, or technological innovation. These were the means by which the ruling class squeezed every drop of surplus-labor from the people. Slavery forces more people to work harder. Migrations, the Middle Passage, child labor, natalism for women, expropriation from land and subsistence: people are forced to enter factories or plantations. And what is it, this "factory," if not a former West African slave-trading post and subsequently a housing for coal-fired steam engines? Machines merely made things more cheaply, using less labor per unit, and made more units in gross profusion. Human endeavor amounts no longer in cornucopia but in waste dumps.

How did this exploitation work? Alienation turned human beings into zombies, the undead. Monstrous forces sucked the life from women and men: either they produced absolute surplus-value, or else they produced relative surplus-value. The former lengthened the entire working day, while the latter shortened only that part of it which produced necessary value. But what is this value, and how is it extracted? *Frankenstein* was the prototypical tale of the hidden forces of technology and of the

Faustian pride of creation. The technocrat combines the new, scarcely understood energy of electricity and applies it to body parts that have been collected by body snatchers, and in so doing he creates a new kind of creature. The tale's subtitle compares him to Prometheus, the Greek demigod who stole fire from the gods and used it to create humankind.

Frankenstein was published in 1818. A year later John Polidori published his prose version of Byron's ghost story, *The Vampyre*. Polidori drew on ancient peasant folklore and started a craze that reached its apogee with *Dracula*. The protagonist of *The Vampyre* is a philhellene—a lover of Greece and Greek culture—amusing himself in Greece by traipsing over ancient ruins and temples, but who is soon distracted by a beautiful and innocent country girl. He is smitten. In her childhood, her nurse had entertained her with a vampire story whose veracity is confirmed by the old men of the village. The vampire attacks in the woods. "Upon her neck and breast was blood, and upon her throat were the marks of teeth having opened the vein: to this the men pointed, crying, simultaneously struck with horror, 'a Vampyre, a Vampyre!'"

The socioeconomic context of the story is provided by the expropriations of the era. Such superstition "constitutes a sort of religion applicable to the common household necessities of daily life," writes a scholar of that time.[7] Inasmuch as it had functioned to protect the household, the story belongs to the realm of reproduction. And nearly everyone is familiar with this story: what had once been the folklore of an exploited peasantry is now a universal truth for the 99 percent, and as such has become the fable of the world's proletariat. Yet in its first, literary iteration, the bloodsucker became an aristocrat who bides his time with gambling, rape, and the biting of the neck that transforms life into living death. The story's setting is a forest in Greece, and a year later the real forests of the Balkans and Greece will erupt in revolution. Demetrios and Alexander Ypsilantis are at the center of these conflicts.

We must keep these two stories in mind because one is a fable of technology and the intensification of labor, and the other is a fable of slavery and the extension of exploitation.

Philhellenes

By the beginning of the nineteenth century philhellenism had become a distinct ideology, one with powerful and lasting effects in Europe and America. It arose at the peak of the Atlantic slave trade and one of its principle effects was the disparagement of Africa. The Nile River valley,

7 William Wilkinson, *An Account of the Principalities of Wallachia and Moldavia* (London: Longman, 1820).

the great pyramids, and Egypt itself were no longer considered the birthplace of civilization. Christian bigotry, the growth of the doctrine of white supremacy, the teleological doctrine of progress, and romantic Hellenism each contributed to philhellenism, which in turn would help justify the expansion of the cotton regime and its death camps, called plantations.[8]

The German concept of *Altertumswissenschaft*, or the science of antiquity, came to dominate research and school curricula. The "Classics"—the Greek and Latin languages—became the foundation of the curriculum at the same time that Greek-letter fraternities originated as chauvinist and anti-intellectual organizations. Sports also originated in the philhellene craze: the 26 miles, 285 yards of the marathon is a distance that commemorates the run of Phidippides, who carried to Athens the news of a Greek victory over the Persians at Marathon, in 490 B.C.E.

> The mountains look on Marathon—
> And Marathon looks on the sea;
> And musing there an hour alone,
> I dream'd that Greece might still be free.

So Lord Byron mused (*Don Juan,* Canto III, st. 86). After 1821 the love of freedom revived, and the Greek War of Independence commenced, in the wake of a protracted reaction against the French Revolution.[9] Shelley's *Hellas* was composed in 1821 and published the following year: "We are all Greeks. Our laws, our literature, our religion, our arts all have their roots in Greece . . ." Philhellenism begins to turn into hellenomania. "This is the age of the war of the oppressed against oppressors, and every one of those ringleaders of the privileged gangs of murderers and swindlers, called Sovereigns, look to each other for aid against the common enemy, and suspend their mutual jealousies in the presence of a mightier fear." True enough.

The philhellenic movement grew in Germany, Russia, and England.[10] All told, a thousand volunteers went to fight in Greece. They were mostly German, French, and Italian, but included in their ranks ninety-nine British and sixteen Americans. Byron (*Don Juan*, Canto VII, st. 18) took a jaundiced view of some.

> Then there were foreigners of much renown,
> Of various nations, and all volunteers;

8 Martin Bernal, *Black Athena: The Afroasiatic Roots of Classical Civilization*, Vol. 1, *The Fabrication of Ancient Greece, 1785–1985* (New Brunswick, NJ: Rutgers University Press, 1987).

9 William St. Clair, *That Greece Might Still Be Free: The Philhellenes in the War of Independence* (London: Oxford University Press, 1972).

10 L.S. Stavrianos, *The Balkans, 1815–1914* (New York: Holt, Rinehart and Winston, 1963).

Not fighting for their country or its crown,
But wishing to be one day brigadiers;
Also to have the sacking of a town;
A pleasant thing to young men at their years.

Byron himself died in 1824 in Missolonghi, fighting for Greece. In 1824, Samuel Gridley Howe, a Harvard medical student, established a free hospital. Relief committees formed across the United States. In 1826, the Independence movement's greatest enemy was neither the Turks nor the Arabs, but starvation. In 1827, eight shiploads of supplies sailed to Nafplion, Ypsilanti's present-day sister city. Villages had been ruined and tens of thousands massacred. Starving families fled to the mountains and lived on herbs, grass, and worms. The governor of Massachusetts took a Greek orphan into his household.

2. The Loss of Names

The town of Ypsilanti has had other, earlier names. Rev. Mr. Harvey C. Colburn's *The Story of Ypsilanti* (1923) is a history *of* white property-owners *for* white property-owners and therefore relies on an ample paper trail. Frenchman Gabriel Godfroy and his partners claimed large tracts of land by 1811. "The various treaties with the Indians made by Governor St. Clair and the extinguishment of their land claims resulted in their retirement westward." Extinguishment! Land claims! Retirement! This is pure bamboozlement. Robbery, rather.

In 1790 the Potawatomis lived four days upstream from Detroit, in a place known as Sanscrainte's Village among the *coureurs de bois*, the trappers and traders who scorned regulation and married Indian women.[11] Although the land was common, "the women did all the work" of growing peas, corn, beans, and wheat. Jean Baptiste Romain dit Sanscrainte was a *métis*; that is, part Indian and part not. He was a trader and an interpreter in the network of Sauk Trail pelt trappers and traders, and sold, for instance, 73 kegs of whiskey and 170 kegs of tobacco to Anthony Wayne, a commander of the United States Army. In 1795 Sanscrainte signed the Treaty of Greenville, in which Ohio and Michigan lands were ceded by Native Americans.

In September of 1819, Lewis Cass "signed a treaty at Saginaw by which the future Washtenaw County passed forever out of Indian possession." The Potawatomis along the Huron River neglected to harvest their corn

---

11 Jim Woodruff, *Across Lower Michigan by Canoe 1790* (typescript, Bentley Historical Library, 2004). This is an account of a modern canoe trip following the route taken in 1790 by Hugh Heward as described in his journal. See also Karl Williams, "Gabriel Godfoy Wasn't the First," *Ypsilanti Gleanings* (April 9, 2009).

and left it standing in their rush to go to Greenville to hear the Shawnee Prophet, who preached sobriety, restraint from wife-beating, and disassociation from the Long Knives (white men). In 1813 the Shawnee Prophet's followers made new villages on the lower Huron River, and a force of Potawatomis established themselves twenty miles further upstream. Tecumseh's confederacy of Kickapoos, Winnebagos, Sacs, Shawnees, Wyandots, Miamis, Munsee Delawares, Potawatomis, Ojibwas, Ottawas, Senecas, and Creeks retreated to Canada with twelve hundred warriors and their families in canoes. Several hundred Potawatomis refused to budge and remained in their villages on the Huron, under the leadership of Main Poc, a ferocious warrior, bullying drunk, and former foe of the Long Knives.

If this constituted the remnant that was to survive wars and settle in what eventually became Ypsilanti, its recent experience was one of defeat, retreat, and division.[12] The skin must be cut before blood flows. The Founding Fathers made the incision, and the Robber Barons drew the blood.

In 1823 the Woodruff brothers arrived. Sleep was fitful, as they were unfamiliar with the howling of wolves. Indians had prepared the fields for corn, and the European settlers took them over. The indigenous commons was thus expropriated. Some "families bought no farms but squatted on bits of unoccupied land, threw up shacks and proceeded to gain a livelihood in haphazard and dubious manners."[13] This was Woodruff's Grove.

In the spring of 1825: "Land was cleared and fenced, dooryards inclosed and crops planted . . . and the wild life of the forest began to disappear." Augustus Brevoort Woodward—a disciple of President Jefferson, a defender of slave masters, and an expropriator of the Detroit commons—bought the land (612 acres!) and platted the village, naming it Ypsilanti. He had studied Greek at Columbia University, and he published using the pseudonym Epaminondus, a mighty commander in ancient Greece. Woodward was involved in a lucrative Detroit currency and banking swindle. He was also a founder of the University of Michigan, which, possessed as he was by a very strong case of hellenomania, he termed a *catholepistemiad* with thirteen *didaxia*, or professors.[14] He contemplated naming the upper peninsula "Transylvania."

With ax, cart, and plough, "every stroke of his hand made him a capitalist, every uplifting of himself in the new community made of his

---

12 John Sugden, *Tecumseh* (New York: Henry Holt, 1993), 148, 362.

13 Harvey C. Colburn, *The Story of Ypsilanti* (Ypsilanti Committee on History, 1923), 35, 37, 40.

14 Frank B. Woodford, *Mr. Jefferson's Disciple: A Life of Justice Woodward* (East Lansing: Michigan State College, 1953).

children ladies and gentlemen." What did this mean? The land is turned into the foundational means of social reproduction; it becomes constant capital, or merely "dead labor" (the Potawatomi land clearings are forgotten) to be revived by "living labor" in the vampiric manner. Within a decade, after the fright of the 1832 Black Hawk War had passed, the first churches, tax assessments, railroad, and banks were established in Ypsi. In that same decade, Wallachia and Moldavia became connected to the Black Sea grain trade. The Danubian provinces thus become the principle supplier of Constantinople, whose bakers now depend on those *boyards* who had expropriated not just the woodlands but the peasant's rights to such commonages.

Michigan toponymy is stratified, with names derived from its past inhabitants. Sanscrainte (*métis*), Godfroy (French), Woodruff (English), Ypsilanti (American). This is the loss of names. Doubtless the name will change again, but exactly when it will change or what its new name will be will depend upon the nature of those who occupy it.

Shall we hasten that day?

Phanariots

The Ypsilantis family were Phanariots, or Greeks who ruled Moldavia and Wallachia on behalf of the Ottoman Empire as princes or hospodars, invested by the Grand Vizer of Constantinople as "God's Annointed."[15] Phanariots were named after a lighthouse in the Phanar district of Constantinople. (Is the Ypsilanti city water tower inspired by this lighthouse?) Although they also belonged to the Filiki Eteria, a "society of friends" (modeled on the Italian Carbonari and on Freemasonry) that conspired to lead the Greek War of Independence, the Phanariots were not liked at home. Indeed, an English historian of the region writes, "It is impossible to conceive a more disheartening task than that of recording in detail the history of these hundred years in Wallachia and Moldavia . . ."[16] So many names, so many kings, so much oppression.

Alexander Ypsilantis, Demetrios Ypsilantis's grandfather, had "reformed" the tax code of the Danubian provinces, making it so rigorous "that a peasant would sometimes kill his cattle to escape the . . . cow tax, or even destroy his house to avoid the . . . chimney tax." Young Alexander, brother of Demetrios, encouraged his troops to acts of terror, and it is therefore not surprising that to the peasants he was identified with rapacity and extortion, while to the boyards, or landlords, as an intruder. The common people had a proverb against Phanariot families: "the winter

15 Wilkinson, *An Account*, 155–66.

16 R.W. Seton-Watson, *A History of the Roumanians from Roman Times to the Completion of Unity* (Cambridge: Cambridge University Press, 1934).

of Hângerli, the earthquake of Ypsilanti, the famine of Moruzi, the pestilence of Caragea." Although Alexander Ypsilantis ignited the war, his ill-disciplined, excessive force did not last long, and others, including the philhellenes, picked up the torch. Alexander himself was confined to a fortress in Munkács, Transylvania!

3. The Loss of Commons

The Greek War of Independence (1820–1832) bore certain similarities to the American War of Independence (1775–1783): a brilliant outpouring of rhetoric in opposition to empire, and financing from abroad. These wars also resembled each other in an oblique way: they were both land grabs. This is one of the reasons we call them "bourgeois revolutions."

Demetrios Ypsilantis was appointed commander by the Society of Friends. He and his brother were given to making grandiloquent, ceremonious proclamations, and one such proclamation inaugurated the Greek War of Independence. In 1832, following two civil wars, multiple invasions, countless massacres, widespread famine, epidemic pestilence, international diplomacy, and huge bank loans, the war drew to a close.

The common patrimony of a Greek village before the War of Independence was called the *hotar*. "The bulk of the hotar consisted of meadows, grazing, and woodland, and these were used jointly by the whole village." This was the commons. Economically speaking, the commons was a subsistence regime anterior to capitalism. Its disappearance could be sudden or it could occur bit by bit, as was the case in Wallachia and Moldavia. A boyard petition of February 28, 1803 shows that before they could take any surplus from the "boundary," they first had to ask permission from the villagers. The essential customs of the people were traditional and unwritten. "Of these customs evidently none concerned the people so much as their right to the land, a right which remained unaffected by the historical events that were taking place."[17] But a vampire haunted the village borders, which were the location of communal lands.

In the middle of the eighteenth century some ancient rights (e.g., timber for building and fuel) were granted in exchange for eight to twelve days of labor servitude. But what was a day? It was not measured in the peasant's actual labor time, but fixed "the quantity of labour which, according to its nature, each peasant must perform in one day. This *nart* was twice or thrice as heavy as that which a normal man could do in a normal day."

17 David Mitrany, *The Land & the Peasant in Rumania* (London: Oxford University Press, 1930), 7, 9, 17, 19.

"The peasants also lost the valuable right to wood for fuel and building which they had enjoyed throughout the worst Turkish times." The first attempt to restrict the peasants' access to timber was in 1792. A British consular report of 1812 recommends a sweeping commercial program—the export of forest timber, and the reduction of fast and feast days to 240![18] In 1820 the British consul observed: "There does not perhaps exist a people laboring under a greater degree of oppression from the effect of despotic power and more heavily burdened with impositions and taxes than the peasants of Wallachia and Moldavia."

The Treaty of Adrianople of 1829 put Russia in charge of Wallachia and Moldavia. Kiselev, a *philosophe* in the school of Voltaire and Diderot, became governor. He was a reformer and passed something like a constitution, the Règlement Organique. Boyards sought to restrict peasant cultivation of all lands, with concessions dependent on an extension of days of labor and servitude. The free use of wood from the commons was abolished, and forced service increased to fifty-six days a year. Rents tripled and wheat prices skyrocketed. Karl Marx was upset.

It was Marx, in fact, who said "Capital is dead labor, which vampire-like, lives only by sucking living labor, and lives the more, the more labor it sucks." You'll find these words in "The Working Day," which is the tenth chapter in volume one of *Das Capital*, and is certainly the most powerful description of nineteenth-century capitalism.[19] Part of its power derives from the authenticity of its vampire reference. In part four of this chapter, Marx refers to capitalism's "vampire thirst of the living blood of labor," and in part five he refers to its "blind unrestrainable passion, its werewolf hunger for surplus-labor . . ." In the following part he mentions stock-exchange wolves, and concludes the chapter by referring once more to the vampire.[20] Marx drew for this chapter not only upon his massive reading and upon the tireless research of his daughter, but he was also drawing upon the "superstitions of the household" which, as a male Victorian scholar, he would not usually credit.

If not a black man, Karl Marx was certainly dark in complexion, his ancestors having come from Portugal and, before that, from North Africa. His children affectionately called him "the Moor." The Moor defended the people's access to the forest and its resources. What happened in the

18 Seton-Watson, *A History of the Roumanians*, 7, 9, 19, 141.

19 I once encountered evidence that German railway workers in St. Louis, Missouri, were the first to translate this tremendous chapter into English, but I've since been unable to track it down.

20 Mark Neocleous, "The Political Economy of the Dead: Marx's Vampires," *History of Political Thought* 24, no. 4 (Winter 2003). I also recommend Amedeo Policante, "Vampires of Capigal: Gothic Reflections between Horror and Hope," Cultural Logic, 2010, http://clogic.eserver.org/2010/Policante.pdf.

Balkans would soon happen to the people's estovers in the Mosel River valley where the Moor grew up. (Estovers is the English name describing wood that a commoner may take; it derives from the French *estover*, or "that which is necessary.") "The community of several thousand souls to which I belong," wrote Marx, "is the owner of most beautiful wooded areas . . ." Statutes and executive orders dating to 1816 distinguish naturally distributed firewood and material for making household articles from building timber, if it is not used for communal building or to assist individual members of the community in cases of damage by fire, etc. It was the criminalization of such customs which led Marx to develop his materialist methodology. Nameless timber companies dealing to international markets bought up the forests of the Mosel where Marx's parents had a share in a vine or two. The forests of central and eastern Europe were rapidly being consumed by buyers in western Europe. Marx was as powerless to stop the loss of humble subsistence customs as Warren Kidder was to stop the expropriation of his family farm at Willow Run years later. Because of the distress caused by the lack of firewood in the Mosel and its environs, Marx made plans to write a new article: "The Vampires of the Mosel Region."[21] Look closely and you will find puncture wounds on Marx's neck, too.

The temporal coincidence between the Greek War of Independence and the expropriation of the customary rights of peasant commoners, both of which occurred in the 1820s and reached their climaxes in 1832, can be understood in several ways. From the viewpoint of traditional political economy, each was an example of a straightforward transition from "primitive communism" to "capitalist agriculture." From the standpoint of the bourgeoisie, Greece's independence meant liberation from the Ottoman Empire and rebirth as an independent nation-state. From the standpoint of neoliberalism, it illustrated the conformity between political independence and market relations. For those on the ground, however, it was an emergency: forest, pasturage, and field commons were lost to a regime of increased work, more working days, and more surplus labor. Though it could genuinely appear either as a Greek national liberation struggle or a transition to capitalism—economic development and modernization—to commoners it was bloodsucking. The destruction of the arboreal canopy in Michigan and in central and eastern Europe occurred at the same time. With the disappearance of Michigan woods "all [was] changed," wrote George Perkins Marsh a few years later. "The face of the earth is no longer a sponge but a dust heap."

21 *Rheinische Zeitung*, January 15, 1843.

Walker's *Appeal* (1829) and the Monstrosity of Race

David Walker, a black Bostonian used-clothes dealer, wrote an *Appeal to the Coloured Citizens of the World* in 1829. In it he challenged the hypocrisy of American support for the Greek independence struggle:

> But oh Americans! Americans! I warn you in the name of the Lord (whether you will hear it or forbear) to repent and reform, or you are ruined ! ! ! Do you think that our blood is hidden from the Lord because you can hide it from the rest of the world, by sending out missionaries and by your charitable deeds to the Greeks, Irish, &c.? Will he not publish your secret crimes on the house top?

On May Day we celebrate the workers of the world: blue collar, white collar, pink collar, in hoodies or prison green, this day belongs to the *entire* working class. It's not the color of her skin but the clothes that maketh the woman. It is a day of *human* agency. Yet the fact remains that in America, built as it is on African slavery, the human beings who led the original workers' struggle were African American. Walker demolished Thomas Jefferson's lame notions of white supremacy, and he did so with stand-up language.

David Walker was born to a slave father and a free mother in North Carolina in 1785. He belonged to the African Methodist Episcopal Church in Charleston, South Carolina, and was to take part in the Denmark Vesey conspiracy, a slave revolt planned for 1822. Slave masters put thousands of dollars on his head. He studied Sparta and the equality of conditions under Lycurgus. The arts and sciences originated in Egypt and then migrated to Greece, according to Walker. People of color "are the most wretched, degraded and abject set of beings that ever lived since the world began."[22] "But I tell you Americans! That unless you speedily alter your course, *you* and your *Country are gone ! ! ! ! ! !*" He also compares whites to vampires: "The whites have always been an unjust, jealous, unmerciful, avaricious and bloodthirsty set of beings, always seeking after power and authority." He helps us understand that the system of racism is a monstrosity.

In 1825 William Lloyd Garrison completed his typesetting apprenticeship in Boston. With his shirt collar unbuttoned in the manner of Lord Byron, he dreamed of sailing off to fight with the Greeks for their freedom. But because he suffered from seasickness, he spared himself the long voyage and stuck around, only to be moved by Walker's *Appeal*, and he became one of the greatest anti-racists of his (or any) time, proving that not all white men are monsters!

---

22 Peter P. Hinks, *To Awaken My Afflicted Brethren: David Walker and the Problem of Antebellum Slave-Resistance* (University Park: Pennsylvania State University Press, 1997).

The American working class of the time was organized around color: red, white, and black. An Egyptian army of six thousand soldiers invaded Greece in 1824 on behalf of the Ottoman Empire, and this army included many people described as "Negroes," who roundly defeated the ill-organized Greeks and enslaved those whom they did not kill. Lord Byron led a small band of fighters—two hundred, according to some estimates—as well as many black women who'd been tasked with caretaking them as laundresses and cooks. Byron himself was chauffeured by a black West Indian named Benjamin Lewis, who was the poet's groom and responsible for the care of his team of horses. Lewis befriended two black women who had been slaves of the Turks, but who had been liberated and were now starving. He begged for Byron's help. "My determination," said Byron, "is that the children born of these black women, of which you may be the father, shall be my property, and I will maintain them."[23] Although a martyr to Greek freedom, how can we claim that this Romantic hero was an abolitionist of slavery?

Elijah McCoy (1843–1929) helped to grease the wheels of industry and then to sprinkle the lawns of suburbia. A conductor on the Underground Railroad, he used the space beneath the false bottom of his wagon to transport fugitive slaves to Wyandot, from whence they were ferried over the river to Canada. His parents had fled the slave state of Kentucky by crossing the Ohio River. On their way to Canada they passed through and then later returned to Ypsilanti. McCoy spent five years as an engineer's apprentice in Edinburgh, Scotland; he too returned to Ypsi, and in 1872 took out a patent for an Automatic Steam Chest Locomotive Lubrication Device. Discerning engineers called this device "The Real McCoy," while the rest referred to it as a lubrication cup. Thus Elijah McCoy oiled trains that hauled the coal and iron that together formed the foundations of industrial civilization. What was his role in the railway strikes of the 1880s? Eugene V. Debs, a locomotive man, union organizer, and socialist, united the engine drivers and the brakemen. When the powers-that-be tried to shift labor's holiday from May 1 into September, Eugene Debs came to its defense. "This is the first and only International Labor Day. It belongs to the working class and is dedicated to the revolution."[24]

As for reproduction, we remember Elijah McCoy for his lawn sprinkler patent. Following the destruction of the prairie, the sprinkler became a necessary item for the prettification of the suburban front lawns of the 1950s, when ticky-tacky houses for nuclear families were all the rage.

---

23 Fiona McCarthy, *Byron: Life and Legend* (New York: Farrar, Straus and Giroux, 2002), 507. European racial slavery begins with the Romany people, or Gypsies.

24 Philip S. Foner, *May Day: A Short History of the International Workers' Holiday* (New York: International Publishers, 1986), 77.

McCoy died irritable and irascible. We might more easily remember his wife, Mary, who wrote an appeal against lynching: "Justice, where art thou? Thou Church of the Living God, why slumberest thou? Awake! Awake! And hear Ethiopia's cry for her people!"[25] Like David Walker or Percy Shelley, Mary McCoy prophesied by hurling anathemas at bloodsuckers in a voice intended to awaken the dead.

Let us follow her forward. She resisted the terrorism of the monstrous regime of labor created a hundred years earlier, at the beginning of the industrial-mechanical transformation. Death by lynching or execution reduces the value of life to point zero. Its exploitation depends, as we see in both *Frankenstein* and *The Vampyre*, upon dead labor. Now that we have addressed the losses of blood, names, and the commons, we may turn to the beautiful promise of May.

The Green . . .

Approaching Ypsilanti from the west, one passes the notoriously phallic water tower and is reminded of the traditional rhyme,

> Hooray! Hooray! The First of May!
> Outdoor f***ing begins today!

Across the globe people celebrate the arrival of spring, with its "fructifying spirit of vegetation." We do this in May, which takes its name from Maia, who in Greek mythology is a mother of gods. The Greeks had sacred groves, the Druids worshipped oaks, and the Romans played games in honor of Floralia. In Scotland, herdsfolk formed circles and danced around fires. Celts lit bonfires on hilltops to honor Beltane, their own god. In the Tyrol, people encouraged their dogs to bark and made music with pots and pans. In Scandinavia fires were built and out came witches.

The world over, people went a-Maying. They went into the woods and returned with leaf, bough, and blossom, with which to garland their bodies, homes, and loved ones. Acts of theater featuring characters like "Jack-in-the-Green" and the "Queen of the May" were performed out of doors. Trees were planted and maypoles erected. There was dancing, music, drinking, and lovemaking. Winter was over. Spring had sprung.

In Wallachia and Moldavia, home to Dracula as well as to those rulers from whom the city of Ypsilanti takes its name, there was a May spirit. Emily Gerard, an English folklorist who tramped through the region in the 1870s, describes it: "The *Gana* is the name of a beautiful but malicious witch who presides over the evil spirits holding their meetings on the eve of the 1st of May. *Gana* is said to have been the mistress of Transylvania

25 Albert P. Marshall, *The "Real McCoy" of Ypsilanti* (Ypsilanti: Marlan, 1998).

before the Christian era. Her beauty bewitched many, but whoever succumbed to her charms, and let himself be lured into quaffing mead from her ure-ox drinking horn, was doomed."

Despite its complexities, whether May Day has been observed by sacred or profane ritual, by pagans or by Christian, Muslim, or Jewish monotheists, by magic or not, by straights or gays, by gentle or calloused hands, it has always been a celebration of all that is free, green, and life-giving in the world. Whatever it was, it was not a workday, and therefore was attacked by those in power.

. . . and the Red

Don't be bamboozled about the red May Day: it began here in America. There are two essential stories about this; one is Merry Mount and the other, Haymarket.

Let's begin with Merry Mount. Gloomy Puritans wanted to isolate themselves ("the city on the hill") and, having accepted the hospitality of native peoples, proceeded to wage war against them and to make them sick. Thomas Morton, on the other hand, arrived in 1624 and desired to work, trade, and enjoy life with the natives. He envisioned a life based on abundance rather than scarcity, and three years later he celebrated May Day with a giant Maypole: "a goodly pine tree of eighty feet long was reared up, with a pair of buckhorns nailed on somewhat near unto the top of it." William Bradford, who landed the Mayflower in Massachusetts, thought Indians were agents of the Antichrist. Of Thomas Morton and his crew, Bradford wrote in total disgust that "they also set up a maypole and dancing about it many days together, inviting the Indian women for their consorts, dancing and frisking together like so many fairies, or furies, rather, and worse practices. [It was] as if they had anew revived the celebrated feasts of the Roman goddess Flora, or the beastly practices of the mad Bacchanalians." Myles Standish destroyed Merry Mount, as Morton's commune was called, and in so doing brought America's first red May Day to a bloody end. Despite this, we remember Flora, the frisky fairies, and the beastly practitioners.

And we remember Haymarket. The movement for an eight-hour work day began at the conclusion of the civil war that abolished slavery. Ira Steward of the International Workingmen's Association, along with the National Labor Union, called for it. The American Federation of Labor (A.F. of L.) resolved in 1884 "that eight hours shall constitute a legal day's labor from May First, 1886 . . ."

We want to feel the sunshine;
We want to smell the flowers.

> We're sure God has willed it.
> And we mean to have eight hours.
>
> We're summoning our forces from
> Shipyard, shop and mill;
> Eight hours for work, eight hours for rest,
> Eight hours for what we will.

Work—Rest—Play: it's a persuasive program, is it not?

Accordingly, a huge march was held in Chicago on May Day in 1886. Iron workers of the Molder's Union struck at the McCormick Reaper Works in Chicago. Police killed some of the workers, and to protest their murders a meeting was called for May 4 at Haymarket Square. Militant workers and armed police faced off, a stick of dynamite was thrown (nobody knows by whom), and all hell broke loose. Sam Fielden, August Spies, Albert Parsons, Oscar Neebe, Michael Schwab, Adolph Fischer, George Engel, and Louis Lingg were found guilty in a spectacularly unfair trial. Four of them were hanged on November 11, 1887, despite an international campaign against the trial's injustice. The way was thus prepared for the Gilded Age of American capitalism, and May Day became a day of worker's solidarity everywhere in the world *except* the United States. We have been bamboozled.

Now that we know, we shall not forget.

Whereas Green celebrations were carnivalesque and temporarily turned the world's economic classes and power relations upside down, Red demonstrations sought to turn May Day into a revolution that had the abolition of the class system as its aim. While the Red and the Green stand together in opposition to avarice and privatization, there are ways in which they differ. Green May Day is related to the realm of the commons (the location of subsistence on the ground), while Red May Day is related to the public sphere (formed in relation to institutions of the state). The commons tend to be invisible until taken away, while the public realm is all too visible as a spectacle of not much more than purchase and sale. An Ypsi man named Oakley Johnson was both: a Green commoner and a Red revolutionary.

Oakley Johnson Learns "Take It Easy"

Oakley Johnson was born in 1890 in a log cabin in Arenac County, Michigan. He split wood, speared fish, and fell asleep at night to the sound of bullfrogs and whip-poor-wills. At school he read Aesop, ancient history, and Darwin. He attended Baptist, Methodist, and Congregational churches, but after reading Tom Paine and Colonel Ingersoll ("the great agnostic") he began to doubt that "Jesus was the *only* son of God," and was asked not to return to Bible class.

Johnson had learned "The Deserted Village," Oliver Goldsmith's long poem about the ruling-class theft of English and Irish common lands. Goldsmith (1730–1774) was Irish and had investigated the matter.

> Ill fares the land, to hastening ills a prey,
> Where wealth accumulates and men decay.

Debilitation, drunkenness, and depression awaited the 99 percent. As for the 1 percent,

> The man of wealth and pride,
> Takes up a space that many poor supplied;
> Space for his lake, his park's extended bounds,
> Space for his horses, equipage, and hounds;
> The robe that wraps his limbs in silken cloth,
> Has robbed the neighboring fields of half their growth.

Not only did the wealthy landowner wrest away communal lands and sculpt them into picturesque views, he also monopolized the game (rabbits, pheasants, deer) and raised rents in order to be able to purchase his luxuries.

> Those fenceless fields the sons of wealth divide,
> And even the bare-worn commons is denied.

And if the commoners objected, as frequently they did by rioting, poaching, and even playing football, the terrorism of capital punishment might await them.

> While the proud their long-drawn pomps display,
> There the black gibbet glooms beside the way.

Surely Oakley compared his remarkable achievement of memory (it is a *long* poem!) to his own life-experience, which included time spent in an Ojibwa village near Harbor Springs. There he would have thought about the commons, which at that moment was the subject of worldwide conversation. In 1912 he attended what is now Ferris State University, where he became a revolutionary socialist.

In Davenport, Iowa, he attended Industrial Workers of the World ("Wobbly") street meetings, and got to know Frank Little, whom he asked about sabotage. "We don't advocate destruction of the products of our labor, that would be folly," said Little, whose mother was Native American. "But if conditions don't permit us to quit work, we can work more slowly, can't we? That would be striking on the job. The workers of Europe call this 'Ca Canny,' or 'Take it easy.' If the bosses refuse to pay us a full day's wage, why should we give them a full day's work?" In 1995 Ypsilanti became the headquarters of the IWW, with an office at 103 West Michigan Avenue.

Frank Little was lynched in Butte, Montana, in 1917 by agents of the copper bosses. Johnson signed up for his red card and attended the Michigan State Normal School, which still stands opposite the water tower and the white marble bust of Demetrios Ypsilantis. Johnson then took a position as a principal at Grant High School in Ypsilanti. Midway through the school year, Johnson was yanked out of his classroom by representatives of the U.S. Department of Justice, who removed him to Grand Rapids in order to interrogate him about his nationality and to learn why he had contributed money to a legal defense fund established for Wobblies who were undergoing prosecution. Johnson refused to be bullied, and the following day he called a school assembly at which he recounted the entire story.

"From that day, the atmosphere changed," Johnson later recalled.

> The students and the farmers round about were on my side. In June, on the day before graduation, an out-of-town mob gathered at the school house to get me, but my students spirited me and my young wife out the back way, where farmers in automobiles rescued us and gave us hospitality for the night. The next day Professor Hoyt of Ypsilanti gave the graduating address, and expressed regret, I was told, that the mob on the preceding night had to go home empty handed. My graduating class refused to sit on the platform because I was not there. They picked up their diplomas later, after the "exercises" were over.

In October of 1920 Johnson starting teaching at the University of Michigan, where he remained until 1928.

May Day 1934 and the Curriculum

On May Day in 1934, on the front cover of its journal the *New Masses*, the Communist Party in America issued a poetic call by "Joe Hill" author Alfred Hayes:

> Into the streets May First!
> Into the roaring Square!

Hayes casts his gaze back to Haymarket Square. For us the "roaring square" is an analog of Cairo's Tahrir Square, where people set in motion the momentous events of 2011, which in turn flowered into such phenomena as Occupy Ypsilanti. Hayes was calling people to march to Union Square in Manhattan.

> Shake the midtown towers!
> Shatter the downtown air!

We remember and mourn the loss of three thousand fellow workers in the World Trade Center catastrophe of 2001.

> Come with a storm of banners,
> Come with an earthquake tread,
> Bells, hurl out of your belfries,
> Red flag, leap out your red!
> Out of the shops and factories,
> Up with the sickle and hammer,
> Comrades, these are our tools,
> A song and a banner!

The hammer and sickle represented the alliance of industry and agriculture, or wage workers and peasants.

> Roll song, from the sea of our hearts,
> Banner, leap and be free;
> Song and banner together,
> Down with the bourgeoisie!
> We hurl the bright bomb of the sun,
> The moon like a hand grenade.

This poem was composed well before Hiroshima, Nagasaki, Three Mile Island, Chernobyl, and Fukushima.

> Pour forth like a second flood!
> Thunder the alps of the air!
> Subways are roaring our millions—
> Comrades, into the Square!

Despite its limitations, this attempt to compare the energy of the 99 percent to sublime terrestrial and cosmic forces should be a challenge to our own movement and its creativity. In Egypt, Madrid, and Oakland, how can we translate the energy of the square into the beauty of the circle?

In the same issue of the *New Masses*, Oakley Johnson published two articles concerning "Education Under the Crisis." He described how thousands of PhD's were looking for work, thousands of college teachers were laid off, and thousands of students who "normally" work their way through college could not do so; many who formerly paid tuition had nothing to pay with. He wrote, "*there are no jobs . . .*" Tuition was raised by 25 percent at Columbia. White-collar workers—chemists, engineers, accountants, physicians—were also without work.

The people yearned to comprehend their economic situation; they were thirsty for knowledge in general. Book circulation jumped from thirty-three million to forty-three million in one year alone, while education budgets were reduced from $11.5 million to $8 million dollars. Langston Hughes castigated the leaders of Negro colleges for reactionary policies, and half of the teachers at those institutions believed in the notion of the inherent inferiority of African Americans. Furthermore, graduate student assistants were expected to work "*for nothing*."

Administrators believed that "education" could be a palliative to the injuries caused by economic disaster, that it could treat the depressed as if it were no more than Valium, Prozac, or Wellbutrin. Even the "starving poor" were expected to go to night school and passively ingest self-help classes. College deans and presidents advised unemployed PhD's to lead discussion groups and nature hikes for Boy Scouts. Medical schools weeded out any applicant who lacked a "gracious personality." They were fearful of the "new leisure"; idle people should have hobbies. In Lansing, a "People's University" was organized by the YMCA; its instructors were businessmen, and its meetings took place at a bank. Students empowering themselves on picket lines? Satisfying their hunger at integrated lunch counters? Cutting class in order to march on May Day? Blacks and whites dancing together? No, no, no, and no!

"The gigantic attack on the colleges," Johnson wrote, "made under cover of the 'depression,' is in fact an attack upon intellectuals as a class,—an attack upon middle class professional and white collar workers. It is an attempt not only to reduce the standard of living of teacher-intellectuals, but to reduce the over-production of intellectuals by striking at higher education.... Students and teachers and professional workers must resist the attack. Particularly must college teachers, last to wake up and last to act, organize for struggle."

In an earlier article, "A Five-Inch Shelf of Booklets," Johnson had tried to fashion a revolutionary answer to Harvard University President Charles William Eliot's philhellenist bamboozlement in *The Harvard Classics*. Theoretical writing requires study, and Johnson warned that "the inquiring and newly radicalized intellectual must watch his step." His study of political economy is essential to this inquiry and should not be postponed. Johnson recommended *Socialism: Utopian and Scientific* by Friedrich Engels, a work which featured an essay on the commons ("The Mark"). He also suggested the study of Alexander Trachtenberg's *History of May Day*, and Lenin's *Imperialism*, itself sorely in need of a revival.

Bob Marley also de-bamboozled the issue:

De Babylon system is the vampire, falling empire,
Suckin' the blood of the sufferers,
Building church and university,
Deceiving the people continually.

Between 1923 and 1928 the Negro-Caucasian Club met in Ann Arbor, at the University of Michigan. Oakley Johnson, then a teacher of English literature and of rhetoric at the university, was the club's faculty sponsor as well as the chaperone at its dances. With his wife he hosted the group in their home. The club was started by Lenoir Smith, a student from Mississippi; another early leader was a young West Indian man by the name of Fairclough. One day, following an all-nighter and a morning hectic with lectures, exams, and papers, Smith went out for a quick lunch, and in the midst of her fatigue was stunned to be refused service at the lunch counter. The club came to her aid and held a sit-in at the restaurant. Was it the first of its kind? Shall Ann Arbor, led by Ypsilantian Oakley Johnson, claim priority in the lunch counter sit-in movement?

The group also attempted to integrate college dances, as well as the university swimming pool and gymnasium, but without success. The dean—who was "more than hostile" and boasted that his grandfather had owned slaves in Virginia—insisted that "the name of the University not be used in connection with the activities of the Negro-Caucasian Club."[26] The guest speakers the club brought to town included Alain Locke, W.E.B. Du Bois, Jean Toomer, and Clarence Darrow.

Willow Run and the Birth of Ypsitucky

Ypsilanti is sometimes called Ypsitucky. Here's why.

Willow Run was built in 1940 and became the biggest factory in the world; it was a mile in length, and produced a bomber an hour. A quarter of a million people moved into southeast Michigan, "some tens of thousands of hillbillies, CIO unionists, and transients from the ends of the continent." Ford recruited from Tennessee and Kentucky, establishing in "Ypsitucky" a cultural divide within its working class. At its peak in 1943 it employed more than forty thousand workers. Although there were fifty-six showers available at the factory, no provision was made for worker housing. Here was a crisis of both production *and* reproduction.

Warren Kidder was expropriated at Willow Run.

"Government conscription of our land . . . forced us off the farm . . ." With the roar of bulldozers echoing in his ears, the barn was burned, the woods were cleared, and the tree stumps left in place. "The horrors of what was happening to me and to my family left scars and hidden forces below the surface of the land and in my mind that even time would never cease."

---

26 *Negro History Bulletin* 33, no. 2 (February 1970) or the *Michigan Quarterly Review* (Spring 1969). See also, "Trying to Live '*Really Human*,'" an autobiographical typescript written by Oakley Johnson for his grandchildren, located in a folder marked "Other Papers" in Box 2 of the Johnson Papers, Labadie Collection, University of Michigan.

Harry Bennett was Ford's pistol-packing director of personnel. He ruled "with his collection of Purple Gang mobsters and political fixers" and instilled terror throughout the hierarchy of Ford management.[27] His "theory of supervision" consisted of the belief "the worker is never right." Armed guards oversaw production in factories that suffered high turnover (at a rate, in some years, of as much as 100 percent). Among the top complaints of the factory workers was that there was "No Place to Stay," even, in some cases, after having worked at the factory for years; another complaint was "Ran Out of Money."[28] Theft of tools was another problem (how to build a shack?), as was absenteeism (and when to build it?).

This insufficiency of worker housing resulted in "the worst mess in the whole United States." The housing that did exist was lousy: tents, tarpaper shacks, or trailers with outdoor toilets. "Unless the husband had built a vestibule,—prohibited in government camps—muddy shoes and rubbers tracked good old Michigan mud into the living room after every rain—spring, summer, fall, or winter. It was always wash day for trailer wives and mothers."[29] A woman's work was never done.

The government solution to this housing shortage was to construct the first "free way" (toll-less government road) in the United States. An automobile commute enabled the workers to live as far away from their jobs as Detroit, for instance.

Rosie the Riveter, a phantom composite who proliferated in song and print, was in fact a representation of millions of women.[30] In 1942 Betty Oelke, an eighteen-year-old, newly married farmgirl, traded a dress for slacks, punched a clock and went to work. She stood on her feet nine hours a day, six days a week, building bombers at the Willow Run plant. "I'd drill all day, and another girl would put the rivets in," she said. The work was repetitive and her bosses were male and mean. "They would stand right there and time you." In hindsight she acknowledged "it was the beginning of women's liberation."

Women's liberation would take some time—two or three decades. Meanwhile, right after the war, women were expelled from the factories, and a process of racial segregation was developed in the housing policies of Willow Village. A 1967 report by Alan Haber to the federal government stated that the black community suffered from "hate and self-hate, apathy, hostility and hopelessness, dead-end jobs, and a family and community life barren of the enrichments and varied opportunities for pleasure and

---

27 Warren Benjamin Kidder, *Willow Run: Colossus of American Industry* (1995), 39–41. The Purple Gang muscled in on labor as it had during the Cleaners and Dyers War of 1927.
28 Lowell Carr and James Stermer, *Willow Run* (New York: Harper, 1952), 9, 36, 104, 208.
29 Kidder, *Willow Run*, 184.
30 Ypsilanti Historical Society archives. Willow Run Collection, "Rosie the Riveter" file.

growth that are taken for granted in the affluent, white community. The whites, too, are often deformed by racism, identifying the Negroes as an enemy group, which threatened their status, security, and physical welfare."

A golf course divided the white community from the black. In 1965 a community action project had been designed to mobilize poor people on their own behalf, "with maximum feasible participation," as was the phrase of the day. It failed. The report reached two remarkable conclusions to account for this failure. First, "there was almost no 'utopian thinking,'" and second, "the project lacked a sense of history."[31] These words were written almost fifty years ago, and anticipate both Howard Zinn's people's history project as well as our Occupy Wall Street–inspired dreams.

X^2: Or, a Theoretical Excursus

We began by invoking two horror stories that were conceived at a moment of world crisis. One of them led us to the name of Ypsilanti and helped us to develop an international perspective. Both stories contribute to our understanding of two malignant structures of social life: first, the utter destructiveness of capitalism to body and soul, and, second, the monstrosity of racism. The former drains the body of life and the latter perverts the soul. If we could return to the structures of thinking of the peasant cultures whence the vampire story originates, the solution to its evil appears magically: garlic, or a stake in the heart. We might even dream up symbolic meanings to these ancient remedies. The spirit of May Day, however, requires that we take practical steps.

What is the relation between the bulldozers destroying homes at Willow Run and the construction of the world's largest factory? What is the relationship between Goldsmith's deserted village in Ireland, the Indian village of Sanscrainte, and the Communist proletarians of 1934? What's the relationship between the golf course in Benton Harbor and economic austerity in Ypsilanti? And what of loss of fuel rights in Transylvania and the expansion of slavery in the United States? Here we find a morass of bamboozlement!

What is the relation between the loss of our commons—their *expropriation*, so often achieved, according to the Moor, via letters of blood and fire, which for us means drones, Structural Adjustment Programs, invasions, civil wars, "sectarian" violence, "ethnic" violence, and school-closings, factory-closings, foreclosures, and enclosures—and the subsequent cuts to our social wages and institutions? Our schools, libraries, health

31 Alan Haber, *The Community Organization Approach to Anti-poverty Action: An Evaluation of the Willow Village Project*, Report to the Office of Economic Opportunity (typescript, University of Michigan, 1967), 53, 313, 315.

clinics, city parks, medical insurance, and jobs have been knifed. With the expansion of mandatory overtime and the contraction of our vacations, our workdays and workloads—our working lives!—are lengthened.

I call this phenomenon "X squared," to show that *expropriation* compounds *exploitation*. For economist David Harvey, X^2 means "exploitation by dispossession." If you refuse to abide by this criminal racket (cunningly referred to as "entrepreneurship") what awaits you is wage-stagnation, poverty, or prison.

How might we relate X^2 to the crises of production and reproduction? Expropriation, as we have seen, refers to the theft of our commons and common goods. Our reproduction depends upon common land as well as the *action* of commoning. Even government-as-commoning has been possible, as Nobel laureate Elinor Ostrom has shown. When all is said and done, however, the solution to our crisis of reproduction is to discover and then reclaim our commons.

You don't need to be an avid follower of the Occupy movement to know that in Washtenaw County the crises in housing and education are on everyone's mind. Foreclosure is expropriation, while higher education fees and the massive student debt they incur constitute exploitation. In Ypsilanti, school district budget overruns coupled with diminishing state funding for education mean the imminent appointment of an emergency financial manager. The housing crisis results in such things as Camp Take Notice, a homeless tent community outside Ann Arbor, a city whose own Occupy group has devoted its energies to the establishment of a twenty-four-hour, seven-days-a-week "warming center" for the shivering homeless. This initiative failed, as did plans to establish a commons on top of the multistory underground parking structure next to the downtown branch of the Ann Arbor Public Library.

The creature produced by the technocrat Dr. Frankenstein wandered all over the face of the earth, without any regard for national borders. Likewise, the vampire ignores national, sexual, and racial differences so long as the blood is red! Capitalist hunger for surplus value is international and achieves its exsanguinary goals by relocating plants, equipment, genes, data, and people as it pleases. When the International Monetary Fund met in October of 2011 in Nafplion, the trade unions organized a huge demonstration against it under the following banner:

YOUR WEALTH, OUR BLOOD!

Bloodsuckers are international, but then so are we, if we only . . .

AWAKEN! AROUSE! ARISE! OCCUPY FOR MAY DAY

Bloodsucking is not only symbolic. Around the corner from the University of Toledo, where I work, are three shops that share a parking lot: a plasma shop, a check-cashing store, and a liquor store. They've stayed put, and have apparently prospered, while many University presidents have come and gone, and they conveniently enable that patently American lifecycle whereby a man sells his blood, cashes his check, and then gets plastered.

The land of zombies! Home of the undead. Oh, shame!

The dictator Sulla was wholly bent on slaughter and no sanctuary of the gods, hearth of hospitality, or ancestral home could defend against his wrath. But Sulla came to a bloody end, too. According to Plutarch's *Lives*, it went something like this: his bowels were ulcerated ("his very meat was polluted") and even his skin attracted lice, which no amount of picking or bathing could destroy. Having been told that a magistrate had allowed someone to defer the payment of a public debt, Sulla berated the man and then had him strangled. But his screaming and exertion were too great a strain on him, and with "the imposthume [abscess or cyst] breaking, he lost a great quantity of blood" and died. Even though, as David Graeber reminds us, credit and debt have always been backed by violence, it is rare for a dictator's days to conclude so poetically, expiring by his own medicine.[32] Remember Sulla!

"And forgive us our debts, as we forgive our debtors," advised a carpenter's son. Let us also remember David Walker, Karl Marx, Mary McCoy, and Albert Parsons.

And let us not forget Howard Zinn, Oakley Johnson, Mary Shelley, and Reverend Pinkney.

There will be a test!

Let us not forget the English romantics, the Chicago anarchists, or the New York Communists. We brought an end to one kind of slavery: plantation racial slavery. We brought an end to one kind of capital punishment: lynching by mobs. Can we bring to an end the vampirine dictatorships of corporations and their emergency managers? Or do we simply mourn the eight-hour workday and our commons as dead and gone?

There will be a test!

Though we are the 99 percent, few Americans identify as "working class": in our country this term has been seriously compromised, despite the fact that the world is yearning for a solidarity that might overthrow the princes, modern-day hospodars, CEOs, Caesars and Sullas, emergency managers, and the rest of the 1 percent. More of us are proletarian—lacking the means of subsistence—than ever before.

---

32 David Graeber, *Debt: The First 5,000 Years* (Brooklyn: Melville House, 2011).

May Day is the day we perceive anew who we are and what we want. We dissolve the "I" into the "we" on this glorious and revolutionary day of unity, and by our words and actions we decide what kind of union we desire to build. Trade union, craft union, industrial union, marriage union, family union, national and tribal union, one big union, or even class union: these are our unions of production and reproduction. May 1 is a practical day; we discover who are our brothers and sisters and in so doing we forge solidarity. This is how we create the future: with collectivity and cooperation.

What are our responsibilities this May Day? We must preserve the General Assemblies of the 99 percent. Together we must occupy common space, and what better spaces to inhabit than the squares, parks, halls, streets, libraries, factories, schools, and plazas which have been privatized or simply abandoned? And what about the stolen-land-turned-golf-course in Benton Harbor? We should fill the streets and make our presences known to one another by sight, sound, and touch. We are Many, they are Few.

We must have a Maypole. We must preserve Ypsilanti's public assets. We must fill the streets so that we may actually see we are the 99 percent. We must welcome fellow creatures who are undocumented. We must drive a stake through the heart of the monstrosity of white supremacy. We must avoid dictatorship even as it masquerades under pseudonym. We must envision for our children a future without prison. We must de-bamboozle what is offered to them in school. We must turn brownfields green. We must reclaim our commons and create new ones. None can accomplish this alone. Let us vouchsafe to ourselves that together in common we can, if we only

AWAKEN!
AROUSE!
ARISE!
OCCUPY FOR
MAY DAY!

THE
BEGINNING
is
Near

Selected Bibliography

Boal, Iain, Janferie Stone, Michael Watts, and Cal Winslow, eds. *West of Eden: Communes and Utopia in Northern California.* Oakland: PM Press, 2012.

Brecher, Jeremy. *Strike!* Oakland: PM Press, 2014.

Caffentzis, George. "On the Notion of a Crisis of Social Reproduction: A Theoretical Review." In *Women, Development and Labor of Reproduction: Struggles and Movements*, edited by Mariarosa Dalla Costa and Giovanna F. Dalla Costa. Trenton, NJ: Africa World Press, 1999, 153–87.

Federici, Silvia. *Revolution at Point Zero: Housework, Reproduction, and Feminist Struggle.* Oakland: PM Press, 2012.

Graeber, David. *Debt: The First 5,000 Years.* Brooklyn: Melville House, 2011.

Green, James. *Death in the Haymarket: A Story of Chicago, the First Labor Movement, and the Bombing that Divided Gilded Age America.* New York: Pantheon Books, 2006.

Harvey, David. *The New Imperialism.* Oxford: Oxford University Press, 2003.

Hawthorne, Nathaniel. "The Maypole of Merry Mount." In *Twice-Told Tales.* Boston: American Stationers Co., 1837.

Linebaugh, Peter. *The Magna Carta Manifesto: Liberties and Commons for All.* Berkeley: University of California Press, 2008.

Marsh, George Perkins. *Man and Nature; or, Physical Geography as Modified by Human Action.* New York: Charles Scribner, 1864.

Marx, Karl. *Capital: A Critique of Political Economy.* Vol. 1. Translated by Ben Fowkes. London: Penguin Books, 1976.

McNally, David. *Monsters of the Market: Zombies, Vampires and Global Capitalism.* Historical Materialism Book Series, Vol. 30. Leiden, Netherlands: Brill, 2011.

Morton, Thomas. *The New English Canaan.* London, 1637.

Rosemont, Franklin, and David Roediger, eds. *The Haymarket Scrapbook.* Chicago and Oakland: Charles Kerr and AK Press, 2012.

Stoker, Bram. *Dracula* (1897). Edited by Nina Auerbach and David J. Skal. New York: W.W. Norton & Co., 1997.

Trachtenberg, Alexander. *History of May Day.* New York: International Publishers, 1947.

Vradis, Antonis, and Dimitris Dalakoglou, eds. *Revolt and Crisis in Greece: Between a Present Yet to Pass and a Future Still to Come.* Oakland and London: AK Press and Occupied London, 2011.

Walker, David. *Appeal to the Coloured Citizens of the World.* 1829.

Zinn, Howard. *A People's History of the United States.* New York: Harper & Row, 1980.

Comrades' vigil over the corpse of Takiji Kobayashi, tortured and murdered by the police, February 20, 1933

A THOUSAND LINKS: TRANSNATIONAL LINES IN AN ANARCHIST AGE

We never live only by our own efforts, we never live only for ourselves; our most intimate, our most personal thinking is connected by a thousand links with that of the world.

Victor Serge

LET'S DITCH SCHOOL AND BE UNMANAGEABLE

Adrienne Hurley

Preamble

I hope this chapter is adequately responsive (affirmatively so) to the argument of the authors of the pamphlet *Who Is Oakland*, who write, "Anti-oppression, civil rights, and decolonization struggles clearly reveal that if resistance is even slightly effective, *the people who struggle are in danger.* The choice is not between danger and safety, but between the uncertain dangers of revolt and the certainty of continued violence, deprivation, and death."[1] I have no conclusion to offer here beyond the expression of my desire that those of us currently making a living as authority figures and salaried agents of repression devise our exit strategies and defection plans so that we can use more of our energy to support the abolition of institutions that inflict so much harm instead of having so much of our vitality funneled back into the maintenance of those institutions. Maybe this is a wild desire, to imagine a mass exodus of professors, police, and other professional authorities from our posts given our years of education, professionalization, and socialization, but sometimes circumstances can make ditching school, abandoning one's post, disobeying an order, resigning, or shutting down one's place of work irresistible despite all our training never to do such things. My examples are drawn from contexts I know in Japan and Québec, but none are representative of anything especially Japanese or Québécois/e.

---

1 CROATOAN, *Who Is Oakland: Anti-oppression Activism, the Politics of Safety, and State Co-optation*, by ludmilap, is accessible at http://escalatingidentity.wordpress.com/2012/04/30/who-is-oakland-anti-oppression-politics-decolonization-and-the-state/.

Part One: There Have Always Been Cops on Campus. They Call Us Professors.

The Liberal government of Jean Charest was voted out in Québec in September of 2012 after a massive student strike. The Liberals had championed the tuition hikes that invited the nearly seven-month-long strike and fueled it with highly repressive legislation and policies. Over three hundred thousand students across the province were on strike at the highest points, and we had monthly mass demonstrations and daily confrontations with police, as well as a proliferation of militant and creative street tactics.[2] What made Charest's government possible in the first place has not disappeared with his ouster, as ongoing actions, such as those against the Plan Nord, continue to make clear.[3] The tuition resistance is far from over as well. Although the corporate media predictably suggested the Liberals' loss meant at least some kind of victory for Pauline Marois and the Parti Québécois (PQ), the streets continue to make clear that, at least for some of us, conflict with the Liberals and the PQ is the same—and not over. In other words, the PQ, while sporting a different brand or packaging, presents continuations and variations of the same problems we find throughout settler colonial society in the Americas, problems such as repression, neoliberalism, austerity, authoritarianism, white supremacy, policing, and the like. Many of these problems are not unique to the settler colonial context where I live, in Montréal. I work at McGill University, which has occupied Mohawk territory for almost two hundred years. It is no wonder the authoritarianism on campus can be hard to bear. McGill was built in the context of settler colonial state-building and made possible by profiteering, expropriation, and slave labor. This is not only a historical issue but deeply implicated in what McGill is today and how it works.[4] The same can be said of Québec and of many schools and places.

2 The following videos and articles provide some anarchist perspectives on the student strike in Québec. The Submedia short documentary *Street Politics 101* provides an accessible overview of this recent history with participant interviews: http://www.submedia.tv/stimulator/2013/05/26/street-politics-101/. "The Quebec Student Strike: Red Squares, Black Flags and Casseroles," by Maria Forti and Becca Yu appears *in Fifth Estate* 47 (Winter 2013). "While the Iron Is Hot: Anarchist Analysis of the Revolt in Québec, Spring 2012" is accessible via CrimethInc at http://www.crimethinc.com/texts/recentfeatures/montreal1.php. "Vivre de Combat: A Critique of CL(ASSE)" by Akher is accessible via Montréal Counter-Information at http://mtlcounter-info.org/english-vivre-de-combat-a-critique-of-classe/?lang=en.

3 The Plan Nord opens up more of Québec's northern territories, more indigenous territory, to mining and gas exploitation. For images and commentary on the April 20, 2012, demonstration against the Plan Nord, see http://www.sabotagemedia.anarkhia.org/2012/04/riots-and-street-battles-in-the-financial-district-of-montreal-during-the-plan-nord-job-fair-w-pics-vidz/.

4 The group Demilitarize McGill is currently active in documenting and challenging "the university's history of complicity in war and colonialist violence, by ending military

In the thick of student strike actions in the spring of 2012 and before Charest's defeat in the polls, Maria Forti and Becca Yu explain, "the Liberal Party provincial government passed what became known as Special Law 78, which, among other things, made gatherings of more than 50 people illegal unless the participants gave their route and time line to the police in advance. It also imposed heavy fines on student associations who advocated striking and banned demonstrations within a certain distance of university campuses."[5] The following spring, new provisions were added to a municipal bylaw, P-6, which further criminalized protests in Montréal by outlawing the wearing of masks at demonstrations and requiring that itineraries of any demonstration be given to police in advance.[6] P-6 tickets have been compared by many to parking tickets (albeit with heftier fines), yet police have used the law as justification to kettle, cuff, film, detain, and deny bathroom access to hundreds of protesters at a time for up to nine hours in some cases (treatment rarely suffered by those who receive parking citations).[7] The repression continues, as do efforts to fight back and resist. With thousands of arrests (which continue) and related injuries and trauma, the courts will be busy for quite some time. In his essay "Outlaw Universities," Thomas Lamarre argues that the Québec government played by the university governance handbook when it adopted Special Law 78, and much the same could be said of P-6. Lamarre writes: "What passes for business as usual on university campuses is in fact a mode of governance that works through extralegal procedures to criminalize

research at McGill"; see: http://demilitarizemcgill.com/en/. For an account of how James McGill, the founder of McGill, amassed wealth, see Gustavus Myers, *A History of Canadian Wealth* (Chicago: Charles H. Kerr and Company, 1914), especially chapter 5. In a recent (March 31, 2014) op-ed for the *McGill Daily*, rosalind hampton notes, "McGill was founded on the wealth of a European colonizer and has refused to recognize and compensate the Iroquois Six Nations for an outstanding debt incurred in 1860, when according to the Six Nations, McGill borrowed $8,000 from the Six Nations Trust Fund held by the colonial government in trust for Six Nations land." See http://www.mcgilldaily.com/2014/03/indigenous-control-of-indigenous-education/.

5 Maria Forti and Becca Yu, "The Quebec Student Strike: Red Squares, Black Flags and Casseroles," *Fifth Estate* 47, no. 3 (Winter 2013): 32.

6 Readers unfamiliar with the need to mask up may find it helpful to know that police routinely use chemical weapons/irritants (such as tear gas and pepper spray) on demonstrators in Québec (as is the case in many other places). A mask can lessen the effects of such irritants. Vinegar-soaked rags (another method of dealing with chemical irritants) have been alleged by police to be "weaponized" material in some cases. Police also engage in profiling and targeting of oppressed people and identifiable activists, so masks are also a basic form of self-defense, especially for those who may be vulnerable to other types of repression and oppression (such as those who might be targeted for deportation or with more extreme violence). Masks do not, of course, address all risk factors and usually cannot, for example, minimize the impact of projectiles and bullets, rubber or otherwise.

7 For more on P-6, see: Fred Burrill, "Why Montrealers Must Resist By-Law P-6," *Maisonneuve*, May 10, 2013, accessible at http://maisonneuve.org/post/2013/05/10/why-montrealers-must-resist-bylaw-p-6/.

political action and expression in advance. In its attempt to redefine forms of political assembly, association, and expression as forms of misbehavior or obstruction that justify government response outside or beyond existing legal channels, the Charest government has, unknowingly or not, adopted extralegal procedures that are already customary practice on university campuses."[8] Lamarre's exposé of the university governance model provokes critical questions about the role and function of schools, universities in particular, and, by extension, the policing role of the professoriate.[9]

The student disciplinary regime at McGill University, where both Lamarre and I teach, exemplifies this mode of governance, but I suspect it is not so different at other universities. The active participation and consent of professors is necessary for McGill's student disciplinary regime to function. Professors serve as disciplinary officers and prosecutors in proceedings and kangaroo courts convened to punish students for behavior the university (or a particular professor) deems to be in violation of its code of student conduct, such as participation in on-campus protest actions that are considered disruptive.

I began to learn more about the extent of on-campus policing performed by colleagues in the aftermath of November 10, 2011. On that day, as afternoon was giving way to evening and a large protest of students from across the province was ending in front of McGill University in downtown Montréal, police on bicycles and riot police attacked those of us who were gathering in front of the James Administration Building. Many of us were there to support fourteen people who were inside on the fifth floor in what was called an "occupation," though some who were also pepper-sprayed, tear-gassed, and beaten just happened to be passing by.[10]

---

8 Thomas Lamarre, "Outlaw Universities," *Theory and Event* 15, no. 3, 2012 Supplement, available at http://muse.jhu.edu/journals/theory_and_event/toc/tae.15.3S.html.

9 This could be extended to include all teachers. In her book *Wild Children—Domesticated Dreams: Civilization and the Birth of Education* (Winnipeg: Fernwood Press, 2013), Layla AbdelRahim avoids the hackneyed question as to how schools are "failing" students and presents a more complex and challenging claim that so-called "failing" schools are actually successfully accomplishing precisely what they were designed to do. Her study forces a reconsideration of what teaching work in schools means. By reading together narratives of social control and narratives of those who actively and directly resist it (such as so-called "eco-terrorists"), AbdelRahim charts out some of the storytelling regimes that structure education regimes.

10 An open letter from the fourteen students on the fifth floor that evening was published by the *McGill Daily* and is accessible here: http://www.mcgilldaily.com/2011/11/letter-from-the-5th-floor-occupiers/. An open letter to those students by supporters was posted online and is accessible at http://10novembre.wordpress.com/. One student journalist's account of his experiences appeared as a feature article of the November 28, 2011, issue of the *McGill Daily* and is accessible at http://www.mcgilldaily.com/2011/11/pepper-spray-and-milk/.

The next day, we had new T-shirts with a photo from the previous night and the caption "No Cops on Campus." Initially, I was troubled only by the exceptionalism suggested by the words "on Campus," but I wore the shirt in solidarity because at least it said "No Cops." Over the next few months, I became increasingly troubled as the work of professors seemed more and more like the work of police. I started to think "No Cops on Campus" needed to include us too.

As the militancy and creativity of student activism buoyed in the lead-up to a massive student strike that would begin in February of 2012, more and more of my students were subjected to disciplinary proceedings for on-campus protest actions, and I saw professors devoting countless hours to campus law enforcement work, as well as professors eager to serve as informants and accusers. Some even cast themselves as victims of disruptive strike activities in grievances that were used as evidence in disciplinary proceedings. The people who summarily banned students from campus, who identified and harassed known student radicals (KSRs), who convened lengthy disciplinary "interviews" and hearings, and who argued students should be admonished or even expelled were professors. They were performing administrative job duties (sometimes in conversation and cooperation with campus security and surely often with their higher-ups). McGill University employees who served on the Committee on Student Discipline (CSD), which is akin to a judicial board in disciplinary hearings, were also compensated in some way. For example, professors are compensated for their CSD service with professional credit for salary increases, promotion, and tenure. The same was not true of professors who supported the targeted students as volunteer defense advisers. Though they spent hundreds of hours in their efforts to support targeted KSRs, their service was not institutionally organized, recognized, or particularly welcome.

Significantly, while many universities have in place similar codes, procedures, and policies to police and punish student activists, there seem to be fewer disciplinary mechanisms in place to police and punish professors who participate in on-campus protest actions if McGill's example is representative. I assume this is because it has not been necessary to create such mechanisms for an already highly disciplined workforce that is used to policing itself. At McGill, some professors and staff openly supported and a few openly participated in the same on-campus protest actions for which students were subjected to disciplinary proceedings, yet, to date, none of those professors or staff have been subjected to any disciplinary measures, reprimands, or the like.

The admonition to be collegial and relentless job pressures in a hierarchical work environment are typically enough to dissuade most professors who might be so inclined (already a minority of the professoriate) from what might seem to be risky activism (especially on campus), but sometimes it happens nonetheless. In the spring of 2012, McGill University had procedures in place to discipline KSRs, but apparently not professors or staff for conduct unbecoming in on-campus protests. For example, there is no disciplinary officer, to the best of my knowledge, for faculty. Might administrators have considered calling the police and pressing charges against protesters—faculty, staff, and students alike—to end the unwanted protests? Perhaps, but after the publicity surrounding the actions of riot police on campus on November 10, 2011, had been so negative and many blamed the administration, there may have been some reluctance to call in the police and file criminal charges against those who, for example, spent the night (or multiple nights) in the James Administration Building again in February of 2012.[11] The desire to avoid negative publicity that we might imagine as underwriting the decision not to call the police and press charges in February would surely have been a very conditional desire, shaped by that particular context. The opening that February for professors and staff to be able to disobey with impunity at McGill was not predictable and might not have emerged under different circumstances. After all, there are also cases when university administrations cooperate with and defer to police to assist in the arrest of a professor for protest activity. The experiences of two Japanese academics are noteworthy in this respect.

Professor Masaki Shimoji, who teaches economics at Hannan University in Japan, was arrested by Osaka prefectural police on December 9, 2012, held for twenty days, and released without charge. One can be arrested and held without charge for up to twenty-three days in Japan.[12] The Hannan University administration was informed that police intended

11 For those interested in the specifics of the February events at McGill, my understanding is that a forthcoming book about the Québec student strike of 2012 that will be published by Between the Lines will include a chapter on the events known as #6party. In the meantime, rich archives of #6party and related material are accessible via the #6party Tumblr site (http://6partylive.tumblr.com/), the archive of documents released via McGill (http://mcgillileaked.wordpress.com/category/6party/), and the many *McGill Daily* reports from February of 2012 (searching their online archive via: http://www.mcgilldaily.com/). For a satirical publication that was active at the time, see the Milton Avenue Revolutionary Press, Canada's Most Alternative Maoist Hate Blog (the MARP) at http://miltonrevolutionarypress.wordpress.com/. Of broader interest is the publication "Blockade, Occupy, Strike Back," accessible at: http://zinelibrary.info/files/strikeback-web.pdf (English) and http://zinelibrary.info/files/grevesauvage-web.pdf (French).

12 This has many implications. One can lose a job during this time, and known or suspected activists can be arrested and detained prior to a protest to prevent them from organizing. One can be interrogated during this time as well, and it is not uncommon for police to question family members, coworkers, and friends of those detained without charge.

to arrest Shimoji in advance, and they provided police with access to his office and actively cooperated with the investigation into his participation in a small demonstration that took place in a train station in Osaka several months earlier, on October 17. At that time, Shimoji and others were protesting the distribution and incineration of radioactive rubble from Fukushima. Shimoji was arrested two months after the fact for walking through a train station with some other people en route to a city office to protest the city's plan to burn radioactive debris from Fukushima. He was arrested, held almost the maximum amount of time allowable by law, and released without charge, and his employer actively participated in his arrest and detention.

Professor Koji Shima, who taught in the Faculty of Business at Hannan University, was one of the very few if not the only member of the Hannan community to show open solidarity with his targeted colleague. One year before he was scheduled to retire, Professor Shima resigned at the end of the 2013 spring semester in protest and exasperation over the administration's treatment of Shimoji and his colleagues' (and students') silence. Our socialization as professors can beat the will to resist out of us as we are admonished to be collegial always as we hustle for a tenure-track position, and if we get it then we hustle for tenure, promotion, the promises of a pension, and the like, always chasing after the next carrot. This is certainly the case at Hannan and McGill, as well as many other (if not all) universities. When faced with the reality that his employers actively worked with police to make the arrest of a colleague possible and his colleagues (and students') silence, Koji Shima had had enough. The psycho-emotional toll of pushing for institutional reform in this context was simply too great and held such little promise. He concluded, admirably I believe, that it was not worth it.[13] We are in a moment when many agree that fundamental, big change is needed, yet many, particularly we oversocialized professors, are trained to pull our own leashes when they are not being pulled for us. In this context, the decision of an academic so close to the end of his career and pension to walk away is very inspirational.

Part Two: Practicing Fearlessness and Dealing with Being Scary

It is not necessarily easy to recognize the ways in which our capacity is misrepresented to us, as I have learned from the work of Chizuko Naitō, a feminist theorist and literary/media studies scholar who has researched

13 Koji Shima's statement regarding the dissolution of the solidarity group formed to support Masaji Shimoji and announce his retirement plans is accessible online thanks to the Atomic Age blog: http://lucian.uchicago.edu/blogs/atomicage/2013/02/01/to-the-members-of-the-group-in-support-of-professor-shimoji-masaki-from-shima-koji/.

recurring stories of anarchists, Ainu, Koreans, and women in late nineteenth-century and early twentieth-century Japanese media that still show up today.[14] I will sketch out some of what I have learned from Naitō by way of the old story that anarchists are scary, a story Naitō investigates in great detail. There is now well over a century of formulaic storytelling that casts anarchists as a problem, as troublesome, ineffective, unruly, dangerous, and scary. Naitō characterizes this storytelling pattern as resulting in a conflation of the words "anarchism" and "violence" (or the words "anarchism" and "assassination"), and through extensive archival research she demonstrates how the media at the time depicted anarchism as a disease that had spread to Japan. My students often notice the newspaper articles and commentaries about anarchists in Japan in the late nineteenth and early twentieth centuries that Naitō cites and analyzes seem very contemporary when compared to characterizations of Black Bloc tactics and anarchism that appear in North American mainstream media today. For example, many have been quick to compare the writings of Christopher Hedges, who decried Black Bloc as "the Cancer of Occupy," with journalistic accounts of anarchism as a disease that appear in Naitō's book.[15] These predictable stories tend to be distorted and pathologizing, designed to elicit fear, revulsion, and perhaps some fascination too. That is not to say that anarchists do not find value in being scary or threatening to power. We do. But it is not always a choice we make to be scary, and, obviously, it is not always or simply exhilarating or empowering to be scary either.

On December 25, 2011, in Tokyo, I joined a "reality tour" to the home of Tsunehisa Katsumata, the chairman of TEPCO, the power company responsible for the Fukushima reactors. Over a hundred tour participants were attempting to deliver letters of outrage and demands for accountability for the nuclear disaster. Delivering the letters was the expressed purpose of the tour, but it also made clear the extent to which police would be mobilized to prevent us from doing such a seemingly simple thing as walking on the sidewalks to leave letters at someone's residence. I had learned about this tour from anarchist friends and saw some anarchists there when I arrived, but not all the "tourists" were anarchists. There were some who had come from the ongoing sit-in of angry mothers in front of the Ministry of Economy, Trade, and Industry in Tokyo, as well as journalists, and various kinds of anti-nuke activists. The only visibly

14 While not yet available in English translation, some of Naitō's writings will be available in *A Documentary History of Anarchism in Japan*, which will be published by PM Press. Those who can read Japanese might refer to: Chizuko Naitō, *Teikoku to ansatsu: Jendaa kara miru kindai nihon no media hensei* [Empires and Assassinations: a Gender Analysis of the Organization of Modern Japanese Media] (Tokyo: Shinyosha, 2005).

15 Hedges's screed is accessible at http://www.truthdig.com/report/item/the_cancer_of_occupy_20120206/.

foreign participants in the tour were my partner and I, but one French reporter was also there covering the event/action. We met in a very busy urban shopping district, surrounded by high-rises filled with stores and restaurants and massive electronic advertising screens and billboards.

Although there were over a hundred of us, there were of course many more people walking by, shopping, and looking at us as if we were scary. This was surely reinforced by the presence of police who were watching and following us. Nevertheless, a few passersby joined us too. Two women ended up walking next to me once the tour departed, and we chatted most of the way to Katsumata's street. We made fun of the fairly obvious undercover cops and ranted about police in general. One of them talked about how she had stopped using electricity in her home and how much is possible without electricity even in an urban space. She had begun doing this because she could not afford to pay bills on her measly pension. We cursed the patriarchal state, which allocates significantly less pension funding to women, and talked about how demoralizing it is to appeal to bureaucrats. They shared food with me, and one of them lent me a poncho when it started to get chilly. At the post-tour rally, we cheered together after the short speech of a young person, someone I knew to be an anarchist who had recently been released from jail. As things were winding up, they asked if I wanted to hang out with them for dinner. I was touched, but had to tell them I already had plans to meet up with some anarchist friends, and as soon as I said the word anarchist, they both said almost in unison, "Ew, scary" (*iya kowai*).

The "ew, scary" reaction was not new to me, which is probably why I was not very surprised, even though we had just enjoyed what I had experienced to be an anarchist and feminist bonding session. They spoke and described living in what I understood to be anarchist ways or with anarchist sensibilities. If there were a checklist of what makes an anarchist, I would have been able to tick off a lot of categories based on our conversation. Furthermore, we had just participated in something that anarchists had played a big part in organizing. Yet the storytelling around what anarchists are that underwrites the "ew, scary" reaction is something I also understood, and not just from research. I used to have the same reaction to anarchism before anarchist youth of color taught me I was an anarchist. What has been happening in Japan over the past few years also has made me aware of how I have responded similarly to certain kinds of anarchism, anarchisms that had inspired an "ew, scary" response in me even after I started calling myself an anarchist—specifically anarcho-primitivism, anti-civ, or green anarchism.

I used to think of anarcho-primitivism, green anarchism, anti-civ thought and the like as peripheral, wingnut, and usually racist strains of anarchism that distracted from the urgent work at hand, which for me meant abolishing prisons, cops, capitalism, colonialism, white supremacy, and heteropatriarchy. I felt repelled by what little I knew, and I made no attempts to try and learn more until after the Fukushima disaster began when many of my comrades and friends in Japan and elsewhere were talking about what sounded like anti-civ or primitivist ideas even though I was not encountering familiar references to Zerzan, Jensen, or even Kaczynski. Suddenly it no longer seemed farfetched or so crazy to cast the net of my abolitionist desire much further. I had to go back and revisit a lot of what I had ignored or missed. There was certainly no shortage of thought and art produced in Japan that I knew well, like the fiction of Tomoyuki Hoshino, that had already been challenging civilization, but perhaps because I was carrying my own anti-anti-civ baggage with me and had not paid attention to what I had already encountered when reading Hoshino's works, I think I had missed a lot. It has been a big and ongoing learning for me, so it is not as if I can lay claim to any deep understanding or answers here. However, I can write about what I am learning.

What seem to me like critiques of civilization in the post-Fukushima context are not at odds with organizing and anti-oppression work, or liberation struggle, some of the typical critiques I learned about anti-civ anarchism in North America (leaving aside the question as to what extent those critiques are actually warranted). Anarchists who had been doing things like organizing sound demos, DIY skillshares, anti-capitalist and anti-oppression organizing, G8 and G20 protests, homeless solidarity work, and the like in Japan for years have been critical to the tremendous anti-nuclear organizing that has been happening. Some have been subjected to multiple targeted arrests. There are many engaged in anti-U.S. base, anti-capitalist, anti-racist, and other draining work who continue all that other organizing even as they deal with the ongoing anti-nuke/de-nuke struggle, including through actions and arguments against civilization. Understandable feelings of desperation, fatigue, and urgency have not stopped people from continuing these other day-to-day struggles that had been underway before March 11, 2011, along with the ongoing anti-nuke work.

As an example, Takurō Higuchi appears in Franklin López's *Amateur Riot*, a short film that focuses on some examples of DIY radiation monitoring, anarchist organizing, and anti-nuke/de-nuke protests in Japan in recent years.[16] This film was made when López was touring his feature film *END:CIV* to packed houses in many cities in Japan.[17] In *Amateur Riot*,

16 *Amateur Riot* is viewable at http://www.submedia.tv/stimulator/2011/12/27/amateur-riot/.

17 *END:CIV* is viewable at http://www.submedia.tv/endciv-2011/. The extensive blog for the *END:CIV* Japan tour is accessible at http://endcivjp.wordpress.com/.

Higuchi says, the "main goal" of the anti-nuke movement in Japan is, "of course to stop all nuclear power plants," but he adds, "the problem is not only nuclear power plants. We have to note that our civilization produced nuclear power plants. It also produces plutonium. So when the disaster happened, I felt like this is a kind of answer . . . that the civilization that human beings created ended up like such a disaster. This is a very deep problem. We have to change how to live." This sensibility, shared by the women at the Reality Tour who said, "ew, scary," is touched by grim reality. Despite the admonitions and coaching to act as if everything is okay, the evidence of the scope and severity of the problems are not hard to find, whether in the mutations observed in butterflies near Fukushima or the 35 percent increase in the rate of infant mortality documented after March 11 on the West Coast of North America.[18] Some anarchists in Japan continue to inspire by making sure the weight of this awareness does not stall or immobilize their organizing, and they are doing a lot despite the massive challenges they face. It is especially hard to keep pushing, to maintain momentum, and to believe we really can be "in it to win it" when people are also very tired and worn out by the toll of the repression, repeated arrests, detentions, and trials, not to mention everything that comes with radiation. As a friend said of our situation in Québec, everyone who fights back gets hurt in some way.

Sabu Kohso, an independent scholar based in New York, and Go Hirasawa, a cinema researcher based in Tokyo, visited Montréal in 2011 for the Anarchist Bookfair, just a few months after the Fukushima disaster started. They had been to Montréal before to show solidarity with local struggles in Québec and share information about G8 protest plans in Japan, so there were already some relationships of solidarity in place. Kohso, Hirasawa, and I composed a short statement for the workshop time we shared at the Bookfair:

> What is happening in Japan cannot be deemed merely a situation particular to one nation-state, but a new phase of human history, an opening toward a future unknown equally for the global powers and the people. It is a universal experience in the sense not only of its economic and environmental impact but also in terms of the self-destruction of the apparatus that the modern world has been

18 See, for example, Janette D. Sherman and Joseph Mangano, "A 35% Spike in Infant Mortality in Northwest Cities Since Meltdown," *Counterpunch*, Weekend Edition, June 10–12, 2011. Accessible at: http://www.counterpunch.org/2011/06/10/is-the-increase-in-baby-deaths-in-the-us-a-result-of-fukushima-fallout/. Also: Azeen Ghorayshi, "Has Fukushima Radiation Created Mutant Butterflies?," *The Guardian*, August 16, 2012, accessible at: http://www.guardian.co.uk/environment/2012/aug/16/fukushima-radiation-butterflies.

> building up on a planetary scale. While the Japanese government is desperately attempting to sustain its sovereignty, it is revealing its incapacity to solve the amassing problems. Its national territory is being divided up into enclaves of inaccessible regions, the national economy is sinking into the abyss, and all this could result in a fundamental disequilibrium, the possibilities of which we'd like to discuss.

Although the words we use as individuals are often different, Kohso, Hirasawa, and I share what I would call an abolitionist desire, a desire to abolish that which harms us, and they especially are engaged in the struggle of trying to understand something that touches us everywhere, all the time in harmful ways. They call it the apparatus.

It can be daunting to think about disobeying and rebelling against something as massive as an apparatus that touches every aspect of our lives. Our stories about how we have tried, where we have been effective when trying, and the openings that we have found are worth sharing (when we are able to share them) because we can help one another expand the limits of what we imagine as possible for ourselves. The fact that anarchists in many places are in touch creates skill-sharing and tactic-sharing opportunities today, just as it did over a hundred years ago, except that now perhaps more of us are in touch and able to share more of what we learn and do.

Anarchists in Japan advertised actions that became huge, massive monthly demonstrations like Japan had not seen for decades by using tumblrs, blogs, and other websites that were not necessarily or clearly tied to any individual or group.[19] New sites would appear for new actions. Sometimes there would be spaces where visitors could post solidarity messages, opening up space for a variety of voices and also autonomous organizing of various local groups and communities. There were sometimes translations of call-outs for demonstrations in multiple languages, as well as solidarity messages in multiple languages and archives of solidarity actions held around the world. Had the call-outs been published on existing anarchist or anti-capitalist sites, the results might have been different given the "ew, scary" factor, and the translations of the call-outs allowed for a broader readership. A similar blog was created to announce, in multiple languages, a convergence in Montréal in August of 2012 to block the

19 For one example of such a site, see 5.7 Stop Nukes Demo, http://57nonukes.tumblr.com/. For an example of a video made to critique targeted arrests at such demonstrations, see *Police Academy TV,* which is accessible at http://www.youtube.com/watch?v=Dpg9-qi2Swg.

return to classes after the strike.[20] This invitation was not likely to bring tens of thousands to town since it was clearly a call for people willing to confront heavily armed police, and, in fact, it did not. But the site did show that some people would respond to such a call and that it would be noticed.

This kind of knowledge sharing does not happen with the blessing of universities, even if it sometimes emerges on campus. Ditching school and ditching the institutional roles schools require of us is ultimately a necessity, I think, which is why I felt touched when I read the description that Ray Craib and Barry Maxwell wrote for the conference that led to this book. Specifically, I was moved by these opening lines of their conference description:

> The diffusionist line—anarchism was in areas outside of Europe an import and a script to be mimicked—has faced the challenge in recent years of research that reveals anarchism in its plural origins and sheer multiplicity of local variants. In this sense one might go so far as to argue that early twentieth century anarchists were—in their emphasis on the world as their home, in their peripatetic radicalism, in the fact that anarchist perspectives could be born from (rather than prior to) migration, in their critique of the constant efforts to divide and hierarchize people—the first postcolonial theorists. To reflect on the histories and cultures of the anti-statist mutual aid movements of the last century, then, will be one aim of this conference.

The limits of what they call the "diffusionist line" when it comes to explaining the presence of anarchisms in different places were familiar to me in the white supremacist context of North American schools, particularly in a discipline like area studies, and all the more so at a colonial Anglocentric and elitist institution like McGill. Just as it cannot account for all the anarchisms and anarchists over a hundred years ago, the diffusionist line cannot suffice to explain what happens (and what we do) now either. It also cannot explain anarchisms, or what sure seem like anarchisms, that happen without (or even despite) the presence of anarchists. Rather, the diffusionist line can lend itself to the replication of hierarchies and formations that gave rise to something like area studies in the first place.

When anarchists are in touch and attentive to our respective local and shared struggles, it can strengthen our resistance and practice of fearlessness in the face of increasing repression. This is surely the case when it comes to Black Bloc and similar tactics, which have been used to great effect in Montréal and elsewhere. Because it is true, as the authors of the

20 This website is still accessible at http://bloquonslarentree.com/en.

pamphlet *Who Is Oakland* argue, that those who resist are in danger, we also learn from one another how to think about and deal with the dangers of struggle, with grief, frustration, burnout, and resilience.[21] And the conversations made possible by these anarchist touchings can also disrupt and open up familiar debates and understandings, even of what kinds of anarchists we are and what we can do. I think that is worth ditching school for today, any day, and every day for as long as it takes.

To that end, I will conclude with a discussion of situation that is begging for the kind of disobedience and anarchist exchanges I have described above. As is the case in Québec and elsewhere, some students in Japan have been protesting tuition hikes and other harmful university and government policies over the past several years. When such protests take place on campus, university administrations tend to respond by increasing the general level of repression and expanding disciplinary policies and procedures. At Hosei University's Ichigaya campus in Tokyo this approach has taken the form of routine surveillance, harassment (including of students' parents and family members), disciplinary proceedings, and a variety of legal and extralegal punishments. Hosei's administration has also called upon professors to block students from protesting on campus.

As I have argued above, repression on campus is typically carried out at least in part by professors. This is particularly true of professors on the Ichigaya campus who are being tasked with performing what most would associate with typical police work. For example, they physically restrain and forcibly remove protesting students from campus.[22] Some justify this as an institutionally understandable response to decades of student radicalism, sectarianism, and "outside agitation" on the Ichigaya campus. More commonly, professors and administrators alike explain it as a matter-of-fact response to "disruptive" activities on campus. My understanding is that, at least as of August 2013, no professor has refused these policing duties.

When I first began discussing the similarities between the work of professors and police casually with friends, I often hedged my comparisons by saying our work was like police work without the physical violence. Although it is chilling to view footage of professors tackling and carrying off their students and see that line crossed, I also can imagine professors at other universities doing what Hosei faculty are doing. Some colleagues

21 As an example of one recent contribution to such discussions, see "Neither Oblivion nor Ceremony: Against the Cult of the Carrion," accessible at http://www.non-fides.fr/?Neither-Oblivion-Nor-Ceremony.

22 Footage taken at a demonstration on October 19, 2012, shows professors in suits and business attire working together with contract security personnel (and perhaps undercover police agents) to restrain and remove protesting students. This video is accessible on YouTube: http://youtu.be/ELar6vSU1lo.

at universities in North America have expressed similar concerns when learning about the situation at Hosei. One wrote, "How would we do in the U.S." if our employers told us to do the same? Her initial reaction was not to see Hosei professors as especially deserving of rebuke, but rather to see the situation on the Ichigaya campus as a signal or warning to us all of potentialities in our own workplaces.

Nevertheless, I have heard from faculty on the Ichigaya campus who describe their university as "unique" or "peculiar" when discussing this situation. The "unique culture" on the Ichigaya campus is, they suggest, beyond the comprehension of those who do not live and work in it, and they deride or dismiss students who have traveled from other campuses to support protesting students at Hosei as "naïve" and "completely uninformed." The invocation of Hosei's uniqueness serves as a way to deflect criticism of professors who are quite literally policing their students. In other words, we are cautioned not to judge what we, all of us who do not teach on the Ichigaya campus, do not know and cannot understand. One can surely find faculty at any university who will say their institution is unique, particularly when on-campus repression is evident, and there are, of course, aspects of any university that are, in fact, unique. Indeed, I have not heard of this happening at any other university. At the same time, I understand what Hosei professors are doing to be something like an extension or expansion of the kind of work already done by professors who teach in universities everywhere. This is why it is not hard for many of us at other universities in other places to imagine that the majority of our colleagues would do exactly what Hosei professors are doing if instructed. Some would surely do so eagerly.

The story is not over, and we may still see Hosei professors resist calls to policing duty and perhaps make common cause with the students who mobilize against repression on-campus and off-campus. Among the Ichigaya campus faculty are professors who have written supportively of earlier student movements and who have their own histories of student radicalism. There are also some who identify as "leftists" and who criticize state repression in their work. Their compliance with the administration's directives to police student demonstrations has predictably inspired the heightened outrage of students and others who have referred to them as "betrayers" and "hypocrites." My hope is that, as one friend so aptly phrased it, at least some professors on the Ichigaya campus will learn "how to make a 180 degree turn" and that more and more of us who are still teaching in universities will be ready and willing to do the same on our campuses too.

KABYLIA'S 2001 HORIZONTALIST INSURRECTION

David Porter

> The only democracy worthy of interest is direct democracy, and it is in Algeria, in the wilayas of Béjaïa, Bouira, and Tizi-Ouzou that one can see the best contemporary prospects. The struggle of the Kabyle citizens' movement is a movement to study and follow, not only for all of Algeria, but also for the rest of the planet.
>
> —French anarchist, 2001[1]

Beginning in April 2001 and more or less lasting into 2004, the mountainous Algerian Berber region of Kabylia experienced a massive insurrection, at the core of which was the movement referred to above. This area east of Algiers, about the size of Massachusetts, had a dense population of roughly five million at the time, the vast majority of whom participated in one way or another in the insurgency. With its size, duration, and anarchic features in form and program, the Kabyle revolt against the Algerian state inevitably drew enthusiastic responses from French anarchists and anti-authoritarians at the time, but it was little known elsewhere.[2] To add this important historical experience to our understanding of "spaces of anarchy," as Mohammed Bamyeh describes, is to help us transcend the sometimes confining limits of ideological definition.[3] This essay introduces the specific origin and dynamics of the Kabyle insurgency, highlights its accomplishments and problems, and draws from it broader

1 Manuel Sanschaise, "Algérie: l'élection du président," *Le Monde Libertaire* 1356 (April 22–28, 2004).

2 Various praising statements across the anarchist and anti-authoritarian spectrum are translated and presented in my book: David Porter, *Eyes to the South: French Anarchists and Algeria* (Oakland: AK Press, 2011) and are quoted further below.

3 Mohammed A. Bamyeh, *Anarchy as Order: The History and Future of Civic Humanity* (Lanham, MD: Rowman and Littlefield, 2009), 216–18.

observations of potential generic significance for a wider analysis of anarchism and anarchy.

Sparks igniting the Kabyle insurrection, also known as the "Black Spring," were similar to those in various Arab Spring contexts a decade later. On April 18, 2001, eighteen-year-old Massinissa Guermah was taken to gendarme (national police) headquarters in his community of Beni Douala, twelve miles south of Kabylia's second largest city, Tizi-Ouzou. While in custody for three days, he was accused of theft and shot dead by a gendarme within the station. Algeria's interior minister described him falsely as a twenty-six-year-old delinquent. On April 22, gendarmes in Amizour, forty-five miles to the east (ten miles southwest of Béjaïa, Kabylia's largest city) claimed that three lycée students had insulted them in an earlier demonstration and arrested them in the presence of their teacher.

Both events enraged local youth who immediately launched street protests. News of the events spread rapidly and lycée students were joined by local young workers, university students and the jobless, and youth from nearby villages. Gendarmes were especially hated for their persistent harassment of youth. Throughout the region, street marches culminated in angry attacks against gendarme stations with stones and Molotov cocktails, apparently the only way to be heard politically. Besieged, but not in imminent danger, gendarmes in many locales retaliated by intentionally shooting to kill demonstrators with live ammunition.[4]

During the last week of April, of the dozens of youths murdered, a large number were targeted in the head. Many hundreds were wounded, some paralyzed for life. After some lulls in these confrontations, gendarmes again launched new waves of murderous repression in the weeks that followed. The death toll by mid-June was 55. A similar deadly wave of gendarme attacks occurred in early 2002, resulting in further Kabyle outrage. Within about 20 months, at least 126 had been killed in the region, the vast majority of whom were young men.[5] (To appreciate this impact, consider that this was comparable, proportionally, to killing 7,560 in a U.S.

4 This included the use of sniper rifles and explosive bullets.

5 Details of the violent dimension of the insurgency and state repression are found in International Crisis Group, "Algeria: Unrest and Impasse in Kabylia," *Middle East/North Africa Report* no. 15 (June 10, 2003), accessible at http://crisisgroup.org, (henceforth ICG Report), accessed August 15, 2012, http://www.crisisgroup.org/en/regions/middle-east-north-africa/north-africa/algeria/015-algeria-unrest-and-impasse-in-kabylia.aspx; Ligue Algérienne de Défense des Droits de l'Homme (LADDH), "Rapport Algérie: La Répression du Printemps Noir, Avril 2001–Avril 2002"; Mohand Issad, *Rapport préliminaire de la Commission nationale d'enquête sur les événements de Kabylie*, July 2001; and Farid Alilat and Shéhérazade Hadid, *Vous ne pouvez pas nous tuer, nous sommes déjà mort: l'Algérie embrasée* (Paris: Editions 1, 2002).

population of 300 million, but all in a tightly circumscribed area.) The ugly, blunt face of the state was more strongly revealed than ever.

These immediate sparks easily ignited a longtime simmering and potentially explosive social context. As in later Arab Spring locations, throughout Algeria and in Kabylia specifically, large numbers of young people felt entirely marginalized. Though a majority of the population, they had a huge unemployment rate,[6] faced a badly inadequate housing supply, were frequently hassled by police and tortured if jailed, and constantly experienced the *hogra* (a term connoting contempt, arrogance, and corruption) of local officials. Young men were justified in feeling abandoned by the state, at all levels, and many tried to flee to European shores in dangerous, often deadly, voyages across the Mediterranean in small boats. One of the common slogans they expressed in wall graffiti and when facing off in the streets against police was "You Can't Kill Us, We're Already Dead." More broadly, most Algerians felt oppressed and neglected by the authoritarian military-dominated regime that ruled since national independence in 1962. A previous decade of large-scale murderous conflict (two hundred thousand dead) between the military and armed Islamists, with civilians caught in between, further extended centralized power and exhausted hopes for a more democratic future fostered in Algeria's own "Arab Spring" opening in 1988–91.

Street clashes of this sort had occurred in the past, most dramatically in Algiers in October 1988 and more recently a decade later after the shocking and apparently political murder of highly popular, defiantly anti-authoritarian Kabyle singer Lounès Matoub. Especially unique about the 2001 insurrection, however, was the prolonged, extensive revolt throughout all of Kabylia (and some areas elsewhere[7]), and the crucial creative intervention and long-range involvement of older generations.

In Beni Douala itself, the district of the first Kabyle martyr spontaneously formed a coordination body with delegates from area villages to provide unified support for grievances of local youth, to demand the arrest and prosecution of Guermah's murderer, and to insist on withdrawal

6 Much of the region's economy depended on retirement income and small business or agricultural investments from Kabyle immigrants in France (Hamid Chabani, *Le printemps noir de 2001 en Kabylie: le cas de la coordination communale d'Aïn-Zaouia* (Paris: L'Harmattan, 2011), 14–15.

7 Some areas adjacent to Kabylia developed a comparable movement and sent delegates to regional meetings. Street demonstrations and riots elsewhere in Algeria were similar to those in Kabylia initially, led by youth and the jobless and concerned with the same socio-economic issues and the *hogra* of gendarmes and other state officials. Roughly two-thirds of Algerians were aged twenty to twenty-five and younger. But aside from several local communities, nothing comparable to the organized Kabyle movement emerged with which the latter could federate. Local quick-lived upheavals in fact continued throughout the country for the whole next decade.

of the gendarmes. Very quickly, by the first week of May, responding to similar shock and bloodshed throughout the region, similar local communitarian structures emerged elsewhere to express similar demands and to "channel the violence of the young" into a more organized structural and programmatic approach.[8]

This grassroots coordination movement took the unique form of horizontalist, federalist direct democracy based on a political model already available in Kabylia's political culture. It was variously referred to as the "citizen's movement," the "assemblies movement," or the "*arch* or *arouchs* movement." The term *arch* traditionally referred to a tribal identity mobilized in the face of severe external threat and thus was reappropriated by some for motivational and legitimacy purposes. But the media's common use of this label, in turn, became itself a matter of political manipulation and controversy because of its archaic connotation.[9] Because of the latter issue and the misleading liberal democratic connotation of the "citizens" term, I will refer only to the "Assemblies Movement" since that label best conveys the notion of horizontalism and accountability to the grassroots.

Organizational forms and procedural policies emerged spontaneously and by emulation in the first weeks of the uprising. They were formally adopted for the region as a whole a few months later and lasted for several years. These principles of form and process, along with the frequent street revolt and certain programmatic aspects, established the anarchic nature of the insurrection. Rapidly emerging was a multilayered confederation with power emanating from below—beginning with the village or neighborhood general assembly (though almost exclusively males), then extending with delegates through commune (municipality)[10] and *daira* (district) levels to that of *wilaya* (province) coordination bodies and finally, on June 4, 2001, to an inter-*wilaya* coordination body, the CIADC. (Kabylia consisted of mainly three *wilayas* and parts of three others.) This highest level coordination met about thirteen times during the first year.

The Tizi-Ouzou *wilaya* coordination body (CADC[11]) was officially created on May 17 and came to include some forty delegations. The Béjaïa

8 Chabani, *Le printemps noir de 2001 en Kabylie*, 17, 35.

9 A small minority of locales chose to label their coordination bodies as *archs*, not in a tribal sense, but as local federations in the face of severe threat. Others in the Assemblies Movement found the term offensive because of its "premodern" connotation. This definitional issue, including the resulting bias-producing press misrepresentation, is discussed in detail in Chabani, *Le printemps noir de 2001 en Kabylie*, 61–64 and Mohammed Brahim Salhi, *Algérie: citoyenneté et identité* (Tizi-Ouzou, Editions Achab, 2010), 152–60.

10 Details about the functioning of one such communal coordination body, that of Aïn-Zaouia, south of Tizi-Ouzou, are presented in Chabani, *Le printemps noir de 2001 en Kabylie*, 68–71.

11 Coordination des archs, dairas et communes.

wilaya coordination (CICB) was established two months later, largely replacing a separate popular committee (CPWB) created by students, trade unionists, and Trotskyists.[12] The other most important *wilaya* coordination was that for Bouira (CCCWB). One writer in 2004 estimated that about two thousand delegates were involved, apparently often with professional backgrounds.[13]

In the Tizi-Ouzou *wilaya*, each next lower coordination body sent two delegates to the CADC body. Periodic meetings of the latter shared information, wrote minutes of all discussions, and provided these to all delegates. Plans were made for future meetings as well as activities in between. All decisions were to be made by consensus. Separate permanent commissions dealt with solidarity and internal disputes and temporary commissions with "actions and reflections" and with the imprisoned or disappeared.[14]

The intent was to create, as authentically and quickly as possible, a united statement of grievances and demands as well as to coordinate actions across the region. The most obvious contradiction was the nearly universal exclusion of women, except as observers, apparently based on the traditional *tajmat*[15] (village assembly) model and the exclusion of women from public political roles generally in rural communities.[16] If even consciously considered in May 2001, presumably the exclusionary logic was to avoid divisive social issues, as much as possible, that might weaken the unified resolve of Kabyle men.

By implication, the same logic extended as well to the ultimate decision of the inter-*wilaya* coordination body not to take a programmatic stand against the retrograde Algerian Family Code that relegated women

12 Salhi, *Algérie*, 151–52; and "L'Algérie en mouvement," *Lutte de classe* 63 (January 2002), accessed June 21, 2013, http://www.lutte-ouvriere.org/documents/archives/la-revue-lutte-de-classe/serie-actuelle-1993/tribune-l-algerie-en-mouvement.

13 Karima Direche-Slimani, "Le mouvement des âarchs en Algérie: pour une alternative démocratique autonome?" *Revue des mondes musulmans et de la Méditerranée* 111–12 (March 2006): 183–96, accessed September 5, 2012, http:remmm.revues.org/2873.

14 Chabani, *Le printemps noir de 2001 en Kabylie*, 71–73.

15 Traditionally, attendance at the *tajmat* was mandatory for all adult village males and all could speak, though until the 1980s strong deference was given to village elders. Decisions were made by all village family representatives. The *tajmat* established a local moral code, mediated internal village disputes, organized local public works and other projects of mutual aid (*la touisa*) and guaranteed village honor. Against the distant, repressive and unresponsive centralized Algerian state, the *tajmat* was an experience of direct democracy for males of the village.

16 Though not given access to the *tajmat*, says Hamid Chabani, "females were often consulted within the family circle" (*Le printemps noir de 2001 en Kabylie*, 17). Deep cultural codes traditionally regulated women's roles in village public space and prevented formal political participation (Alain Mahé, *Histoire de la Grande Kabylie, xixième–xxième siècles: anthropologie du lien sociale dans les communautés villageoises* [Paris: Editions Bouchène, 2001], 546).

to legally subservient and male-dependent status.[17] The decision was rationalized by the resolve to avoid issues specifically identified with one or the other rival Kabylia-based political parties, despite strong support for such a stand by the CPWB.[18] Nevertheless, at least several instances of female participation in village-level assemblies were reported and, after several months, the inter-*wilaya* coordination council reversed itself, approving women's involvement.[19] In its programmatic explication of October 2001, it insisted on women's equality with men "in every realm."[20] In the meantime, some women, especially of younger ages, participated alongside men in movement demonstrations.

Following the procedural model of the traditional village assembly and consistent with the goal of a unified voice, decisions were to be made after open discussion and consensus, a process that often resulted in long meetings, sometimes over two days, and that was later modified to permit three-fourths majority decisions.[21] Attempting to avoid a potentially divisive leadership elite at the highest level, inter-*wilaya* coordination meetings were arranged and presided over on a revolving basis, with a three-person presidential body of the immediate past, present, and next presidents working together. To assure accountability to the base, delegates were pledged to express only the position of the body they came from, not to make independent judgments about the issues. Violators of this mandate could be recalled from below.[22] Meanwhile, "the whole population" could attend and observe, but not speak, at coordination assemblies."[23] After delegates reported back on consensual decisions made

---

17 Meant to appease the rising tide of Algerian Islamism, the 1984 Family Code gave men the rights to polygamy, unilateral divorce, supervision of women, and inheritance privileges, leaving women in a status as legal minors.

18 "L'Algérie en mouvement."

19 Emma Tilleli, "Le mouvement citoyen de Kabylie," *Pouvoirs*, 106 (3e trimestre 2003), 157, accessed September 5, 2012, http://www.revue-pouvoirs.fr/Chronique-Le-mouvement-citoyen-de.html; Nicole Logeais mentions one specific example: economist Kamira Naïd Sid, an organizer of the May 6, 2001, Tizi-Ouzou women's march, selected by her neighborhood committee to be a delegate to the *wilaya* CADC (Nicole Logeais, "Paroles d'une femme kabyle," September 19, 2003, accessed March 15, 2013, http://yessis-n-teryel.forumculture.net/t11-paroles-de-femmes-de kabylie-par-nicole-logeais).

20 The Platform Explication document appeared on several websites, including http://www.tamazgha.fr?Plate-forme-d-El-Kseur-explicite,208.html, accessed April 15, 2013.

21 Daniel Cefaï, "Entretien d'Alain Mahé: itinéraire d'une recherche. L'engagement civique d'un anthropologue en Kabylie," *Cultures et conflits* 47 (Autumn 2002): 11, accessed September 5, 2013, http://conflits.revues.org/844. Emma Tilleli claims that the new vote majority accepted was 2/3 ("Le mouvement citoyen,"154).

22 During the important June 2001 inter-*wilaya* coordination meeting at El Kseur to develop an official Assemblies Movement program, the Tizi-Ouzou *wilaya* coordination (CADC) recalled its delegates for lack of confidence and required new discussions (ibid., 155).

23 Chabani, *Le printemps noir de 2001 en Kabylie*, 69.

at the coordination level, it was up to local assemblies to decide how to act and at these meetings everyone could speak.[24] In general, according to one observer, delegate ages averaged under forty, while the vast majority were not traditional village notables.[25] As well, some youths in their twenties were selected as local assembly leaders.[26]

Also adopted at an early stage,[27] a Delegates' Code of Honor, agreed to as a condition of selection, was designed to further ensure process consistent with horizontalist principles and full independence of the movement from the state and statist political parties. Four requirements were set forth in this effort to maintain *de facto* Kabyle political autonomy. Most basic of all, delegates were pledged never to carry out any action aimed at creating direct or indirect ties with the regime or its collaborators. To assure that statist political parties and its members would not use the movement for partisan ends or tarnish its unified voice, delegates could not manipulate people in order to gain votes in elections or for any other possibility of gaining power. Likewise, to protect the movement from contamination and manipulation by the state, delegates could "never accept a political position (elected or appointed) in an institution of power." To further assure accountability to the base, delegates were not allowed to make statements to the media in the name of the movement without authorization. Any violators of these horizontalist and political autonomy provisions were subject to "ostracism and isolation."

Hamid Chabani described the code of honor at the communal coordination level for Aïn Zaouia. In effect, the coordination served as a mediation or arbitration body to resolve any citizen disputes based on the "law" established by community collective opinion. As with the traditional village *tajmat*, the coordination body could impose a sanction for those who violated the community code of honor. The most severe sanction was banishment or ostracism (the person should not be served, transported, or spoken to). Anyone who assisted such a person, defined as a "traitor," was also in turn subject to the same sanction. These more local codes of honor were then eventually synthesized at the *wilaya* coordination level.[28] The rapid choice and acceptance of this horizontalist form of resistance

24 Ibid., 69. Surely he means "all males" by this statement.

25 Robert Vasseur, "Dossier: l'Algérie libertaire, entretien sur la situation en Algérie," *Combat Syndicaliste* (CNT-AIT), 183 (September–October 2002), accessed June 21, 2013, http://www.theyliewedie.org/ressources/biblio/fr/Vasseur_Robert_-_L%27 Algerie_libertaire.html.

26 Kahina Aït Tafouneste and Jugurta Aït Amchiche, "Le second printemps berbère: nous casserons plutôt que de plier," *Le Combat Syndicaliste International* (CNT-F), July–August 2001.

27 September 27–28, 2001.

28 Chabani, *Le printemps noir de 2001 en Kabylie*, 70–71.

throughout Kabylia was based primarily on several factors, none of which apparently included any explicit Western-type anarchist ideological consciousness. At a pragmatic level, it was the easiest and fastest way to mobilize, coordinate, and unify local populations throughout the region for immediate action and to stop the horrendous bloodshed. Recognizing the virtue of full grassroots discussion in formulating community response assured greater creativity and legitimacy both, important in facing off against powerful repressive state forces in the immediate and longer-range contexts of crisis.

The egalitarian village assembly *tajmat* model was a readily available resource in Kabyle political culture.[29] While actually functioning well at the time in apparently only a small minority of locales, and certainly not at all in urban settings, it was a familiar historical practice integral to the sacred cohesion and identity of the "traditional" village. According to French anthropologist Alain Mahé, the *tajmat* was one of the four most essential dimensions of historical village identity (along with honor, Islam, and magical rites).[30] Its deep roots in Kabylia's past were acknowledged by a number of nineteenth-century French colonial observers and French colonial practice indeed did not attempt to suppress it.

As both Mahé and Algerian political scientist Salhi underline, just because the *tajmat* was an essential component of traditional culture did not mean that its form and principles could not be effectively adapted to current social conditions. In 1951, Algerian anarchist Mohamed Saïl stressed in an article the central importance of anti-authoritarianism, village self-governance, federalism, and mutual aid in Algerian (especially Kabyle) political culture and foresaw that their deep roots would bode well for an anarchist future for Algeria once French colonialism was overthrown.[31]

Both the 1963–64 guerrilla movement in Kabylia against the new Algerian government[32] and Kabyle Berber activists' defiant three-week resistance (occupations, street resistance, and general strikes) to the

29 The *djemma* counterpart in Algerian areas beyond Kabylia was also a historical tradition in Arab culture but survived much less because of conscious French colonial policy.

30 Mahé, *Histoire de la Grande Kabylie*, 144.

31 See Saïl's 1951 essay "The Kabyle Mind-Set," in Robert Graham, ed., *Anarchism: A Documentary History of Libertarian Ideas, Vol. II: The Emergence of the New Anarchism (1939–1977)* (Montreal: Black Rose Books, 2009), 157–60.

32 The maquis base was apparently strongest in villages where village institutions were also strongest, as was the case during the war for independence from France. These were also the villages with the highest level of worker migration to France, the deepest schooling in French and the most modern political and trade union culture. At the same time, the FFS 1963 party program, complementing the guerrilla struggle, emphasized the importance of the *tajmat* tradition (Mahé, *Histoire de la Grande Kabylie*, 436, 441, 443–44).

central regime in the Berber Spring of April 1980 were strong indicators of a more egalitarian political culture, still strongly committed to solidarity and jealous defense of individual and collective honor.[33] Other factors were surely important as well, such as the disproportionally high worker immigration of Kabyle men to France and their subsequent exposure to Western socialist ideals in trade unions, as well as strong identity with the Berber language and culture and the need to protect and enhance them politically against the dominant trends and power base of authoritarian Arabo-Islamism within the nationalist movement and post-independence regime.

Following the inspiration and violent repression of the Berber Spring in 1980, centered initially among Kabyle university students and faculty, many young people returned to their villages and sought to revive the *tajmat*, opening it to younger male participants instead of solely village elders. While only partially successful in the next few years, their efforts revalorized the *tajmat* in modern terms.[34] From 1984 to 1987, the average age of village committees went from 60–70 years to about 40–50 years.[35] Such activism also stimulated use of this local egalitarian model for widespread organizing and functioning of village cultural associations, following Algeria's brief relaxation of political restrictions in 1988–91 that opened the door to legal voluntary associations for the first time in independent Algeria. Using the same horizontalist principles of egalitarian participation, including substantial young female involvement,[36] these Kabyle cultural associations, even more than surviving and functioning *tajmats*, became the most vital political experience nourishing the younger generation's egalitarian hopes and expectations for full participation while simultaneously contributing to a revival of Berber culture throughout the region. Thus, one longer-range effect of the earlier Berber Spring was "to open breaches in the political arena, until then closed and fossilized, to

33 Detailed discussions of the roots and nature of the Berber Spring and the subsequent Berber Cultural Movement are found in Salhi, *Algérie*, chapters 3–4 and Mahé, *Histoire de la Grande Kabylie*, 465–95. Also of interest is an autonomist account of the Berber Spring: Un groupe d'autonomistes algériens, *L'Algérie brûle* (Paris: Champ Libre, 1981).

34 Another motivation for this return to villages and local activism at that time was the new official blockage of immigration to France and the experience of relative freedom immigration had provided (Mahé, *Histoire de la Grande Kabylie*, 480). The "modernist" nature of the Assemblies Movement's demands and functioning was explicitly emphasized by participants and supporters.

35 Ibid., 480.

36 Camille Lacoste-Dujardin, "Géographie culturelle et géopolitique en Kabylie: le révolte de la jeunesse Kabyle pour une Algérie démocratique," *Hérodote*, 4e trimestre 2001, 67, accessed September 6, 2013, http://www.cairn.info/revue-herodote-2001-4-p-57.htm; and Mahé, *Histoire de la Grande Kabylie*, 546.

a movement of return to the local in the villages and more precisely in the *tajmat.*"[37]

The 2001 Assemblies Movement extended this model into a federated structure at levels of the *commune* or *daira*, the full *wilaya*, and between the several *wilayas* involved. This larger territorial scope and federation also had deep historical roots, as for coordinated military resistance in times of imminent French military threat to Kabylia in the mid-nineteenth century.

The immediate choice of the inclusive horizontalist model in 2001, based on face-to-face familiarity in villages or urban neighborhoods, also prevented easy infiltration and manipulation by the regime's powerful and ubiquitous political police (the DRS). After decades of active political interference and repression, the latter was viewed as potentially controlling much of Algeria's political life through its secret files and pressures on elites at every level, including the media.

Finally, the horizontalist structure and Delegates' Code of Honor directly excluded opportunistic partisan efforts by either of the two rival regionally based political parties, the FFS and the RCD.[38] Despite initial enthusiasm in Kabylia for each party, as well as roots of each in the Berber Cultural Movement, both had failed to deliver significant social and economic gains to the region in their twelve years of competition and both showed similar tendencies to corruption in local political offices. Each had strongly denounced the other in bitter electoral competition and had brought their divisiveness into local *tajmats*, directly contradicting the emphasis on consensual decision-making.[39] The alienating and manipulative competition between two bitter rivals was antithetical to forging a strong and coherent resistance solidarity in the face of immediate murderous repression by the military regime. Both parties were surprised and somewhat paralyzed by the events of April–May 2001. Neither party could credibly represent grassroots demands of the region or act as a mediator with the state. At the same time, neither party dared to oppose the nonpartisan principles of the new movement, though party activists were free to participate alongside others in their communities if they did not obviously promote their party agendas.

As Hamid Chabani states summarily in his study of the Assemblies Movement, "this horizontalist system shows how totally discredited are

37 Chabani, *Le printemps noir de 2001 en Kabylie*, 42. By 1995, more than a thousand cultural associations had emerged in Kabylia's mountain villages. Jane Goodman, "Berber Associations and Cultural Change in Algeria: Dancing Toward 'La Mixité,'" *Middle East Report* 200 (Fall 1996), accessed September 3, 2012, http://www.merip.org/mer/mer200/berber-associations-cultural-change-algeria.

38 The Front des Forces Socialistes and the Rassemblement pour la Culture et la Démocratie.

39 Chabani, *Le printemps noir de 2001 en Kabylie*, 49, 60.

the state institutions and the vertical mode of State functioning." The horizontalist mode of functioning "places the individual, the citizen, at the center of this organization and of the movement of contestation."[40]

The Assemblies Movement structures and the insurrectionary communities of Kabylia carried out a wide variety of resistance and solidarity activities. In the first several weeks, the movement planned and successfully produced large street marches in several locales. In Tizi-Ouzou, the capital of the *wilaya* of the same name, at least five hundred thousand demonstrators, the largest in the city's history (over twice its population), filled the streets on May 21. Prefiguring part of the movement's formal overall June program, chants and placards denounced the "Assassin Regime," proclaimed "No Forgiveness," and demanded closure of the gendarme stations, trials for those who shot protesters, and restitution for the families of the dead and wounded.

Three weeks later, approximately a million people engaged in a similar march on the nation's capital, Algiers. While thus demonstrating massive support for the insurrection and intending to present a platform of demands to President Bouteflika, the march was meant implicitly, as Jaime Semprun observed, to carry the anti-regime insurrection itself to the heart of the state, "proclaiming to the Algerian people that the time had come to settle accounts with the oppression experienced since 1962."[41] While huge numbers descended in cars, buses, and trucks from the mountains of Kabylia sixty miles away, they were joined by hundreds of thousands of Kabyles and others in that city.

Fearing indeed that this could be the beginning of mass revolts throughout the country aimed at toppling the regime, the latter mobilized its repressive machinery to stop the momentum. Police and the army harassed and blocked demonstrators at the outskirts of the city and prevented access to the center. Along with police repression, numerous DRS recruits as well as released jail inmates were directed to infiltrate, provoke, and attack the marchers, resulting in hundreds of wounded and eight deaths. Government-controlled TV and radio coverage was entirely one-sided and racist, portraying the demonstration as a regionalist effort to subvert the rest of Algeria and a direct threat to the lives and property of Algiers residents.[42] Nevertheless, the unprecedented size of the march, the largest in Algerian history, succeeded in gaining international atten-

40 Ibid., 77–78.

41 Jaime Semprun, *Apologie pour l'insurrection algérien* (Paris: Editions del'Encyclopédie des Nuisances, 2001), 26. The entire document appears on line at: http://infokiosques.net/lire.php?id_article=376.

42 Details on this march and its repression are in Alilat and Hadid, *Vous ne pouvez pas nous tuer*, chapters 16 and 20. Various videos of the march and repression are still posted on YouTube as of 2013.

tion and was generally regarded by Kabyles as a dramatic assertion of their passionate determination and grassroots power.[43] At the same time, the failure to cause change and the regime's use of large-scale repression helped to further radicalize the movement.

Locally, within Kabylia, a wide variety of direct action methods were employed, spontaneously and otherwise, to maintain pressure against state institutions, to defend control of the streets and to attack symbols of state authority.[44] Efforts to surround gendarmes' barracks and to resist their intrusions into the streets continued on a more or less permanent basis. Street and roadway barricades frequently were erected to prevent circulation of security forces. Self-defense was organized to protect meetings and the wounded in hospitals. Public buildings and offices of local government and government agencies were often sacked and burned, under siege, or at least the objects of sit-ins.[45] Such actions carried over as well to attacks on and burning of many offices of the two regional political parties, the FFS and the RCD, since each seemed dedicated to recuperating the insurrectionary movement to its own partisan advantage. Kabyles were discouraged from paying taxes and public utility bills, military draft notices were ignored, and local general strikes of one or several days were frequently called.[46] Anyone dealing in any way with gendarmes was isolated and treated as a traitor. Hotels, restaurants, villas, cafés, and shops of "liars and wheeler-dealers of various sorts" were burned to the ground.[47]

---

43 Unfortunately, international attention to events in Kabylia drastically diminished after Al-Qaida's attacks on September 11, 2001.

44 Said University of Algiers historian Daho Djerbal, "This important mass movement has found no other expression than the immediate. . . . It doesn't represent a political alternative. A revolt that is basically anarchist in character, refusing centralized leadership, administration and representation" ("Une entrevue de Daho Djerbal," *La Tribune*, December 13, 2001, accessed September 6, 2012, http://www.algerieinfos-saoudi.com/article-daho-djerbal-la-visibilite-n-existe-pas-88490625.html). Several months later, Djerbal added: "It is the expression of a total revolt. . . . Their protest is a protest against society as a whole. They target not only the state but also the new bourgeoisie that has taken over the distribution of national revenue to further its interests. So sweeping is the protest that it shuns the traditional symbols of power and the hierarchical nature of governance. . . . Their mode of protest is immediate, direct action, that rejects authority. . . . The only representatives of these disaffected youths are themselves, acting in the here and now" (Djerbal, "Sidelined Youth Has No Choice But to Riot," *Algeria Interface*, June 21, 2002, accessed August 30, 2012, http://www.algeria-watch.org/en/articles/2002/riots.htm).

45 For insurgents, said two observers, the notion of "public property" didn't exist since the whole of the country had been privatized by the regime for its own benefit (Alilat and Hadid, *Vous ne pouvez pas nous tuer*, 169).

46 Association Aït Ghobri Solidarité, *Algérie: le mouvement citoyen en Kabylie* (Paris: L'Harmattan, 2007), 31; Florence Beaugé, "La Kabylie s'installe progressivement dans l'anarchie," *Le Monde*, October 17, 2001, accessed August 30, 2012, http://www.algeria-watch.org/farticle/revolte/anarchie.htm.

47 Semprun, *Apologie pour l'insurrection algérien*, 12.

Walls were covered with political graffiti[48] and some municipal spaces were renamed with plaques after martyrs of the revolt.[49]

More strikingly, the movement carried out a massive boycott of national legislative elections in May 2002, an event one supportive writer called "insurrectionary."[50] Warning against voter participation, it declared a general strike regionally before the voting day and some polling stations themselves or trucks delivering ballots were attacked and burned. Nevertheless, there were significant disagreements with this policy within the various coordination bodies and the population.[51] The two regional parties refused to pose candidates so that only names from the ruling government coalition parties appeared. Despite government efforts to truck in "voters" from outside the region,[52] the announced official voting rate was no more than 2 percent.[53] A few months later, for October municipal elections, virtually the same scenario unfolded, although the FFS resisted pressure by running candidates anyway, thus objectively collaborating with the regime against the movement. But some FFS candidates finally withdrew under threats, and those elected were pressured to leave their towns. Nevertheless, voter participation still was no higher than 2 percent. Meanwhile, the rival RCD apparently fully supported the Assemblies Movement position of continued resistance.[54]

Beyond these militant forms of resistance, more positive assertions were occasional urban squats and the effort to organize immediate assistance to families of the wounded and martyrs. Such support involved not only local residents but also organized efforts in France by emigrants from the areas concerned.[55]

Despite the Assemblies Movement ban on political party or other organizational representatives (such as from trade unions) participating as such within local assemblies, other groups could and did organize

48 One young Azazga martyr even wrote "Liberté" ("Freedom") on a wall with his own blood before dying. Moh Si Belkacem, *Chronique de la Kabylie martyrisée* (Paris: L'Harmattan, 2004), 27.

49 This commemorative reappropriation of public space included naming a central square in Tizi-Ouzou after singer Matoub. Nassim Amrouche, "Histoire, mémoire et tribus ou les *aarch* de 2001 en Kabylie," *Conserveries memorielles: revue transdisciplinaire de jeunes chercheurs* 9 (2011), accessed September 4, 2012, http://cm.revues.org/816.

50 Belkacem, *Chronique de la Kabylie martyrisée*, 53.

51 Chabani, *Le printemps noir de 2001 en Kabylie*, 99.

52 Belkacem, *Chronique de la Kabylie martyrisée*, 53

53 Essentially, it was local members of the state repressive apparatus who voted—gendarmes, police, the army, and their families. Ramdane Redjala, "Le FFS et la question électorale: bilan d'une stratégie calamiteuse (II)," *Le Matin DZ*, April 5, 2013, accessed April 5, 2013, http://www.lematindz.net/news/11507-le-ffs-et-la-question-electorale-bilan-dune-strategie-calamiteuse-ii.html.

54 ICG report, 29.

55 Association Aït Ghobri Solidarité, *Algérie: le mouvement citoyen*, 70, 73, 76.

autonomous activities as part of the overall insurrection. Schoolteachers, hospital workers, and students (including many women), for example, organized separate strikes on many occasions. At least one female attorney was part of the free lawyers' collective for defending Black Spring victims and arrested Assemblies Movement delegates.[56] Most impressive, however, was a women's collective's organizing of a massive women's march in Tizi-Ouzou on May 24, 2001, where an estimated fifty thousand took part.[57] Despite the initial exclusion of women from local assemblies and traditional pressures against independent public roles generally,[58] Kabyle women nevertheless actively and enthusiastically participated in the insurrection in the conventionally domestic realms of affective daily support, as well as through providing resources, care for the wounded, and safe houses for those involved in direct action.

Articulating a program for the overall Assemblies Movement was a multiphased process as discussions and resolutions gradually proceeded upward from mid-May until June 2001. At an inter-*wilaya* meeting in the town of El Kseur (near Béjaïa), just three days before the march on Algiers, delegates from the *wilayas* of Tizi-Ouzou, Béjaïa, Bouira, Boumardes, Sétif, Bordj Bouareridj, and Algiers and the Collective Committee of Algiers Universities approved a fifteen-point platform of demands. But this programmatic statement and its later detailed "explication"[59] also demonstrated that within the movement itself were potentially competing orientations.

Of the fifteen points in this El Kseur Program, some were clearly reformist and some, in essence, revolutionary—given the tight authoritarian nature of the ruling regime. On the reformist side were issues concerning immediate consequences of the violent clashes, recognition of Berber culture, and demands for specific anti-poverty programs regionally and for all of Algeria. In effect, the Algerian state was clearly recognized and charged with fulfilling certain direct objectives. Concerning repercussions of the violence, the Platform demanded that the state compensate all the wounded and families of the martyred, that it give official martyr status to all victims during the events and protection of witnesses, that it drop all judicial charges against demonstrators and acquit those already judged, that it immediately stop all "punitive expeditions, intimidations and provocations against the population," and that it dissolve commissions

56 Logeais, "Paroles d'une femme kabyle."

57 Ibid.

58 Given the traditional taboo, it is understandable that many young village women would be reluctant to participate in movement assemblies even after some experience in mixed public activities in universities or village cultural associations.

59 At a meeting in Larbaa-Nath-Irathen, about seven miles southeast of Tizi-Ouzou, on October 31, 2001.

of inquiry initiated by the regime (because of obvious bias and expected whitewashing). None of these measures, if instituted, would threaten the survival of the regime.

Aside from the rather vague demand for an emergency socio-economic plan for all of Kabylia, the other major regionally based concern was the demand for "unconditional Amazigh [Berber] recognition in every dimension (identity, civilization, linguistic, and cultural) without referendum and consecration of Tamazight as a national and official language." While these Berber cultural demands were not an initial focus of the insurrection, as the revolt spread and discussions ensued, the immediate grievances of concern to youths in the street were viewed, especially by older Kabyles, as one more layer of overall Berber oppression, especially including the key cultural elements so emphasized in the still commemorated Berber Spring.[60] Obviously, such a demand also was understood to reinforce the notion of common unified struggle in the region and the specific legitimacy of the Assemblies Movement.

At the same time, the El Kseur Program articulated in several of its more radical demands that the Assemblies Movement was concerned with the oppression and liberation of Algeria as a whole. Despite claims by the regime and other opponents, the Assemblies Movement was never oriented toward Kabyle autonomy or independence. But subverting its efforts to gain national support,[61] a minority separatist political organization did emerge at the same time, headed by popular singer and former Berber Cultural Movement activist Ferhat Mehenni. This Movement for Kabyle Autonomy (MAK), announced opportunistically in June 2001, advocated a status for Kabylia within Algeria comparable to that of Catalonia within Spain.

At least six demands of the El Kseur Platform were implicitly revolutionary in nature, especially when the Assemblies Movement decided at the end of August that the Platform was nonnegotiable. While on the surface, the wording of these demands suggests a continuing Algerian state, their complete fulfillment would imply the toppling of the regime and a much more liberated political system. If combined with the guiding procedural principles of the movement itself, they could reasonably suggest potential evolution toward a substantially anarchic political system for Algeria generally, even if no one in the movement openly proclaimed that ultimate goal or expectation.

---

60 Chabani, *Le printemps noir de 2001 en Kabylie*, 83–84; Salhi, *Algérie*, 172; ICG report, 11.

61 Djamel Benramdane, "Hugh Roberts: Kabylie, un déficit de représentation politique," *Algérie Interface* website, June 12, 2003, accessed August 29, 2012, http://www.kabyle.com/forum/threads/12692-Kabylie-Un-D%C3%A9ficit-De-Repr%C3%A9sentation-Politique%C2%BB.

To have opened the door to that anarchic political possibility through the revolutionary nature of these six demands articulated by a mass horizontalist movement added a radically new vista to the ongoing evolution of Algerian politics. As Chawki Amari, a prominent op-ed writer for the influential Algiers daily, *El Watan*, expressed in the paper nine years later, Algerians by nature are far more fit for the anarchy of Bakunin than for the anarchy/chaos of the Bouteflika regime.[62]

The six *de facto* nonnegotiable revolutionary demands were as follows: (1) All authors, organizers, and secret sponsors of crimes [of repression] must be expelled from the security services and public office. (2) All gendarme brigades and Republican Security units must be withdrawn from local communities. (3) The state must guarantee all socio-economic rights and democratic freedoms. (4) All executive functions of the state and the security corps must be placed under the authority of democratically elected bodies. (5) *Hogra* and all forms of injustice and exclusion must end. (6) The politics of underdevelopment, of pauperization, and of homelessness of the Algerian people must be reversed.

Given the regime's visceral commitment to repression and *hogra* for keeping itself in power and to massive corruption to fill its pockets, genuine fulfillment of the first, fifth, and sixth demands would decimate the vast majority of state functions and officials, from top to bottom. The second demand would eliminate, at least in Kabylia, the immediate potential for state repression.[63] Fulfilling the third and fourth demands would transform the very nature and purpose of the polity and could potentially lead to a horizontalist direct democracy for the whole country.[64] Real control of the "state and the security corps" by political bodies democratically selected by horizontalist principles and where "socioeconomic rights and democratic freedoms" were assured would in any case surely make Algeria one of the most liberated political systems in the world.

Faced with these dimensions of radical challenge, the regime sought to repress and undermine the insurrection. Its immediate and most

62 Chawki Amari, "Cette terre ingouvernable," *El Watan*, March 29, 2010, accessed June 21, 2013, http://www.djazairess.com/fr/elwatan/155079.

63 Gérard Lamari, an original leading figure in the Berber Spring and Berber Cultural Movement and author of several detailed articles about Kabylia in the French anarchist press, regarded this demand in particular as anarchistic (Gérard Lamari, "Carnet de voyage—cinquième partie," *Tamazgha: le site Berber* website, April 9, 2007, accessed August 29, 2012, http://www.yasni.fr/ext.php?url=http%3A%2F%2Fwww.tamazgha. fr%2FKabylie-Trouver-la-voie-entre-l-accroche-au-passe-recent-et-son-devenir%2C1969.html&name=G%C3%A9rard+Lamari&cat=other&showads=1).

64 In the ICG report he authored, Hugh Roberts agreed that these two demands implied that the Assemblies Movement was "revolutionary," "seeking the fundamental transformation of the regime" (ICG Report, 20). Algerian political scientist Salhi concurred that the fourth demand especially would imply the self-removal of the regime (Salhi, *Algérie*, 186).

vicious response was its organized violent attacks, as with the murders, wounding, and arrests of thousands of demonstrators, as well as prisoner torture, an institutionalized habit in Algerian jails. Though attacks on demonstrators never ceased, this approach was used most dramatically in the spring of 2001 and early 2002. The danger of further violence through sudden house and street raids was a continuous forceful threat affecting every aspect of evolving Kabyle response and the sense of constant threat was no doubt intensified by memories of the 1990s decade of military massacres of civilians in its war against Islamist guerrillas.

In March 2002, the regime arrested and imprisoned several hundred Assemblies Movement delegates, especially those of a more radical orientation.[65] Immediate street battles, followed by demonstrations on the outside and hunger strikes inside, preoccupied the movement until the release of most in August, but ongoing threats and actual new arrests had a chilling effect on the movement and on the willingness of some to continue resisting dialogue.

For most of the first two years of the insurgency, the regime chose simply to avoid serious political engagement with the region itself, evading official response to the El Kseur Program, no doubt to drain the vitality of the movement as an active political force. At the same time, it alternated denunciations of "hooliganism," subversion of Algerian nationhood, and alleged foreign plots with sudden conciliatory speeches and meetings with selected nonradical delegates. Indeed, in July 2003, President Bouteflika abruptly invited dialogue for implementation of the El Kseur Platform.[66] Such tactics no doubt intentionally aimed to accentuate divisions and an eventual split between reformists and radicals in the Assemblies Movement, thereby draining its claim to legitimacy as the unified voice of the region.

As well, from April 2001 onward, the regime's constant propaganda domestically and abroad not only asserted that the insurrection and Assemblies Movement were supported by unnamed foreign interests but that they were purely a Kabyle regionalist and ethnic phenomenon,[67] despite continuing movement statements that their program was for national transformation. This second claim by the regime was made easier by inclusion of the Berber language demand in the El Kseur Program and demonstrations, as well as the publicized creation of the MAK in

65 Not surprisingly, prisoners were subjected to great pressure to change their resistance to "dialogue" before their release (Vasseur, "Dossier").

66 R.N., "Bouteflika invite des arouch au dialogue," *Le Quotidien d'Oran*, July 21, 2003, accessed June 19, 2013, http://www.algeria-watch.org/fr/article/pol/revolte/ boutef_arouch.htm.

67 Chabani, *Le printemps noir de 2001 en Kabylie*, 97–98.

2001. One result, as French leftist Jaime Semprun commented in late 2001, was overall French disinterest in the insurrection. "For the moment, the insurgents of Algeria are alone, more alone than revolutionaries have ever been in the past."[68]

Based apparently on the reformist/radical split (including the dispute about electoral participation) but also on personality issues, by late 2002 and throughout 2003, coordination meetings of the movement at *wilaya* and inter-*wilaya* levels were increasingly wracked by strong verbal attacks and counterattacks, with claims by each side of violations of the Delegates Code and subsequent sharply contested de-credentialing. Already, in June 2002, an inter-*wilaya* coordination meeting had to be dedicated to discussing and resolving various sorts of violation of horizontalist principles.[69] Increasingly, in this atmosphere, suspicions also grew concerning some degree of DRS or other government infiltration, adding to this volatility.[70]

Dialoguists and anti-dialoguists each formed their own bonds of informal and increasingly formalized alliance, now with competing *wilaya* coordinations claiming the allegiance of specific villages in the region. Additionally, it became clear that certain delegates were more influential in decision-making, through their charisma and self-promotion,[71] that the consensus principle was not being respected, and that most coordination delegates were no longer returning to the village base for discussions.[72] The coherent insurrectionary message was thus diffused and the movement gradually and irreparably divided, much to the regime's satisfaction. As one reporter observed, "Kabyles no longer knew who was who and who wanted what in the *arch* structure."[73]

Eventually, by January 2004, the movement had quite visibly split and an official delegation of earlier anti-dialoguists, led by previously imprisoned Belaïd Abrika, negotiated with the regime for implementation of six reforms, though mainly not from the original El Kseur Program.[74] A

68 Semprun, *Apologie pour l'insurrection algérien*, 59.

69 "Rapport de synthèse: Treizième conclave de l'interwilaya," accessed April 15, 2013, http://www.tamazgha.fr/Treizieme-conclave-de-l-Interwilaya,234.html.

70 Chabani, *Le printemps noir de 2001 en Kabylie*, 100. The DRS itself was adept at circulating such rumors, thus to increase the level of distrust within the movement generally.

71 Ibid., 100. Most notable, in part because of media attention, were university lecturer Belaïd Abrika of the CADC and Ali Gherbi of the CICB.

72 Alain Mahé, "Mobilisation citoyenne en Kabylie: la révolte des anciens et des modernes," *Alternatives internationales* 7 (March–April 2003), accessed March 5, 2013, http://www.mondeberbere.com/presse/200303_mahe_altint.htm.

73 Malik Boumati, "Les arouch divisés en plusieurs tendances," *La Tribune*, March 21, 2004, accessed September 7, 2012, http://www.algeria-watch.org/fr/article/pol/presidentielles/ arouch_tendances.htm.

74 Specifically, ending the arrests of Assemblies Movement delegates and other demonstrators, the return of fired workers, dismissing charges against previous arrestees, a fiscal amnesty for regional businesses affected by the events, finding solutions to the

subsequent protocol agreement was signed on January 15, 2005. Earlier, in March 2002, President Bouteflika had agreed to bring to justice everyone responsible for the severe repression and especially those responsible for deaths. In fact, however, even by several years later, only the constitutional recognition of Berber as a "national language" had been carried out, but it was still not granted status as an "official language." One writer called this latter move "a moral and psychological attack on a whole people."[75] As M.A. Haddadou points out, while the status of "national language" "confers a certain prestige, it is official language status that gives it real rights: the right to be used in the administration, in schools and in the media."[76]

Additionally, some gendarme units were withdrawn from the region and some jailed demonstrators were released. As well, the regime agreed to some financial restitution for some victim families and some judicial proceedings against guilty gendarmes.[77] But while a few involved in the repression were relieved of duty, and twenty-four were arrested, none were judged in court. Meanwhile, none of those responsible higher up in encouraging and permitting the massacres were ever prosecuted.[78]

The splits, mutual accusations of betrayal, and grassroots discouragement led to the virtual disintegration of the organized movement. Nevertheless, Abrika continued to lead a sort of rump Assemblies Movement, with a website and occasional local demonstrations and meetings all the way to the present. In effect, it became no more than one more voluntary association among others, stripped of its influence and power and largely ignored.

Though the FFS and RCD resumed partisan rivalries and the MAK claimed greater followings than before, the defiant insurrectionary spirit was kept alive to the present only by local insurgent youths in one locale after another (throughout the rest of Algeria as well), launching demonstrations, road blockades, and confrontations with the police in desperate attempts to gain some recognition and relief, especially with jobs and

---

nonpayment of electric bills since May 2001, and revocation of local and village legislature presiding officers based on the boycotted elections of October 2002.

75 Belkacem, *Chronique de la Kabylie martyrisée*, 48.

76 M.A. Haddadou, "L'Etat algérien face à la revendication berbère: de la répression aux concessions," *Glottopol: revue de sociolinguistique en ligne* 1 (January 2003), 137, accessed September 5, 2012, http://www.univ-rouen.fr/dyalang/glottopol/telecharger/numero_1/gpl1_05grand.pdf.

77 Chabani, *Le printemps noir de 2001 en Kabylie*, 107. However, at least some families rejected the concept itself of state payments for killing their sons (Vasseur, "Dossier").

78 Farid Alilat and Slimane Khalfa, "Onze ans après la marche du 14 juin, 2001, l'état s'est renie: 126 morts, 1 gendarme jugé," *DNA Algérie.com*, June 15, 2012, accessed September 11, 2012, http://www.dna-algerie.com. Only the gendarme responsible for the original murder of Massinissa Guermah was jailed.

housing, from local authorities.[79] But these local insurgencies, usually of only one or several days duration, remained too uncoordinated and to the present too vulnerable to quick repression for substantial broader-level effect. As well, Kabyle voters continued to resist electoral politics through very low participation at the polls—consistently lower than substantial abstention rates elsewhere in Algeria.

Outside commentaries on the insurrection and Assemblies Movement demonstrate competing conceptions of what it was about. The government-controlled press and unsympathetic observers abroad referred to it as essentially a retrograde phenomenon rooted in archaic, localist, and rural or tribal identities, an orientation and organizational form unfit for political representation and negotiation in a context of modern politics.[80]

From his very different democratic pluralist perspective, FFS leader Hocine Aït-Ahmed called it publically a "fascist populist movement," a "Loch Ness monster," exerting "authoritarian hegemony" in totalitarian fashion, promoted and subsidized by the political police in order to isolate the Kabyle insurgency from those in the rest of Algeria, thus to prevent emergence of a nationwide democratic opposition and possibly to prepare the way for the regime to commit a Rwandan-type massacre.[81]

A third, typically liberal, position was articulated in the 2003 report of the outside observer International Crisis Group. While validating legitimate Kabyle grievances concerning government repression and economic and social neglect as well as general violations of democratic practice and human rights, the report also viewed the street violence and the Assemblies Movement's more revolutionary demands and refusal to dialogue, as a dysfunctional response that only led to an unproductive impasse and failure of reform.[82]

A fourth view of the insurrection and Assemblies Movement was enthusiastic endorsement of its basic principles by anarchists and post-situationists writing in France. While critical of various aspects, such writers abundantly praised its general direction as a worthwhile model to emulate. In the publications of almost every major French anarchist organization

79 During 2010, for example, there were over 112,000 riots, demonstrations, or other acts of public defiance resulting in police intervention reported throughout Algeria. See Adiène Meddi, "Edito: rien ne vas plus," *El Watan*, January 7, 2011, accessed June 21, 2013, http://www.elwatan.com/archives/article.php?id_sans_version=106144.

80 Semprun, *Apologie pour l'insurrection algérien*, 44–45.

81 Hocine Aït-Ahmed, "Arch, la tribu, les Arouchs, les tribus; note politique du 26 mars 2002," posted on *Algeria-Watch* website, accessed August 30, 2012, http://www.algeria-watch.org/farticle/ffs/arch_arouch.htm.

82 ICG Report, iii, 22, 32, 34. Hugh Roberts, the report's British author and academic specialist on North Africa, was well-respected as a knowledgeable and astute writer on Algerian affairs. Yet the limits of his perception were the frames of his liberal democratic perspective.

and in several leading independent French anarchist periodicals, positive columns were devoted to the Kabyle insurrection.

Georges and Hassina Rivière wrote in *Alternative Libertaire*, "The quasi-insurrectional movement in Kabylia includes elements that deserve our deep support. It's not only solidarity on our part; we identify with its process, its mode of struggle, and its modernity in reinventing democracy." They explained that it belongs to the tradition of direct democracy and autonomous self-management.[83]

The French anarchist website, *Le Jura Libertaire*, published an April 2003 article on the movement by "Some French Friends of the *Aarchs*." They said that the present Kabyle insurrection, with its commitment to the concept that "no movement can pretend to struggle for democracy without itself genuinely functioning democratically" is in the same line as Kronstadt and other such upheavals. But "few historical movements of this sort have so quickly formalized their anti-hierarchical position as the *aarch* movement did with its code of honor and published guiding principles and with their refusal to collaborate with the regime or state institutions."[84]

Meanwhile, the French CNT-AIT posted on its own website most of the extensive pamphlet text by post-situationist Jaime Semprun, "Apology for the Kabyle Insurrection of 2001," as well as an extensive supportive article by Robert Vasseur from a similar perspective.

Along with praise and enthusiasm from French anarchists and anti-authoritarians for the 2001 Kabyle insurrection, especially in its first phase, came critiques of certain faults and weaknesses. Heading the list was the failure of the Assemblies Movement to include and encourage full participation by women. If such an invitation had been genuine, it is obvious from the enthusiastic successful organizing of the women's march in Tizi-Ouzou and the growing participation of young women in village cultural associations in the 1990s that many would have seized the opportunity. At the very least, in this circumstance, it seems far more likely that the Assemblies Movement would have added, as some men wanted, a rejection of the notorious Family Code to the movement's Platform.

The failure to devote enough effort to outreach to other regions, beyond Kabylia, was another negative factor in the movement's vulnerability. This would have removed the "regionalist" or "ethnic" label used by the regime and others and obviously created far more momentum for overthrowing the regime itself. A spread of worker and student strikes in

83 Hassina Rivière and Georges Rivière, "Solidarité totale avec la révolte de Kabylie: démocratie en Algérie," *Alternative Libertaire* 99 (September 2001).

84 Quelques Amis Français des Aarchs, "Lettre à Mohand Chelli," Paris, April 18, 2003, *Le Jura Libertaire* website, juralib.noblogs.org/.

the context of an immense wave of local street battles across the country could have been crucial. But without organized horizontalist linkages throughout the country, the nature of the political outcome would have been difficult to forecast. No doubt the fear of resumed terrible violence, as experienced in the 1990s, inhibited many from serious radical political organizing.

A third common critique was the Assemblies Movement's failure to expand its activities beyond resistance and demands on the state to efforts at positive construction of local and regional non-state-dependent social and economic alternatives.[85] Beyond encouraging greater resistance sustainability, such engagement could have further enhanced confidence and enthusiasm for longer-range commitment to the alternative politics of horizontalist structures and processes.

One other critique concerned the failure of the El Kseur Program to denounce the radical Islamism that was partly (with the military) responsible for the devastating internal war of the 1990s—with two hundred thousand deaths, and thousands more wounded and disappeared.[86] Despite the apparent retreat of most Islamist guerrillas from open warfare by 2001, there were still active units of the GIA (later Al-Qaida in the Islamic Maghreb) in the countryside and a strong conservative Islamist presence and influence in Algeria's political life,[87] clearly contrary to the ideals of the Assemblies Movement. Most likely, this failure came from the desire to not add potential distance from those of other regions they wished to influence as well as bring about a possible *de facto* truce with remaining Islamist guerrillas still in Kabylia who could have severely disrupted the movement's anti-state focus and who themselves rather approved of the movement's denunciations and actions against the repressive nature of the regime.[88] Nevertheless, some movement supporters attacked "the hidden theocratically inspired forces largely manipulated by the regime" among the traits of the existing system[89] and the regime's failure to satisfy any social demands as encouraging the proliferation of fundamentalist

85 Ibid.; Robert Vasseur, "La Kabylie, six ans après," Paris, October 22, 2007, posted on the *Le Jura Libertaire* website, accessed January 7, 2008, juralib.noblogs.org/.

86 Semprun, *Apologie pour l'insurrection algérien*, 53.

87 Islamism never had a strong base in Kabylia where laicism is the rule. Kabyle activist Gérard Lamari stated in 2001 that Kabyle youth were deeply secular or even atheist ("Où va la Kabylie?" *Courant Alternatif,* 110 [June 2001]). In the 1991 last legislative elections before the 1990s war, the Islamist FIS party received only 5.5 percent of the vote in Kabylia despite gaining a majority in the rest of Algeria. Relatively few guerrilla attacks subsequently followed in the region during the 1990s war and apparently, for this reason, was a favored assignment in this period for police and gendarmes (Alilat and Hadid, *Vous ne pouvez pas nous tuer*, 41).

88 "Entretien avec Nadir," *L'Oiseau-Tempête* 9 (Summer 2002).

89 Association Aït Ghobri Solidarité, *Algérie: le mouvement citoyen*, 56.

Islam.[90] As well, the El Kseur Program Explication of October 2001 at least demanded that religious indoctrination in the schools be entirely banned.

The Kabyle Assemblies Movement brought to the fore a number of important generic issues relevant to the study and effectiveness of anarchist, anarchic, and anti-authoritarian contexts everywhere. The failure to be fully inclusive to one half of the community (women) in every aspect seriously deprived the movement of its fullest potential. There is a single continuum of the same general phenomenon that includes both the traditional inhibitions and restrictions on women in Kabylia and the subtler but still strong sexist factors influencing women's less frequent and less egalitarian participation in anarchist movements in the West,[91] which needs to be fully and continuously addressed.

Internal contradictions in consciousness and vision are far more obvious in movements of negative resistance only, as is eventually clear in any crisis community practicing spontaneous mutual aid in contexts of disaster. The shared commitments to community defense and more egalitarian relations and responsibilities during the immediate period of crisis do not automatically translate into a longer-range common anarchic social imaginary for ongoing political relations. Shared experiences of such times surely have the potential to generate long-range horizontalist commitment (as with many veterans of '60s activism), but the relative impact and motivating strength of that temporary liminal community differ from one individual to another because other preexisting or later political values and experiences. Such differences make this type of movement vulnerable sooner or later to other sorts of counter-appeals, targeting other elements in the political consciousness of many, thus making the movement susceptible to eventual internal rifts and outside manipulation. Contradictions and vulnerabilities are obviously more evident the larger the movement concerned and the longer it persists. But rather than fatalistically accepting that dynamic, this raises the issue of how militants might more effectively encourage deeper and more durable anarchic "social visions" in the midst of crisis contexts, among those not previously exposed.

Related to this is the important issue of dissidence in the midst of crisis. The role of shunning, "quarantine," or exclusion for those who apparently betrayed the Delegates' Code of Honor in Kabylia was a

90 Ibid., 65.

91 Addressing this reality among French anarchists are Mimmo Pucciarelli, "Qui sont les anarchistes?" *Alternative Libertaire* (Belgium) 219 (Summer 1999), accessed March 14, 2009, http://www.anarchie.be/AL/pdf/219.pdf; and Simon Luck and Irène Pereira, "Les pratiques dans les organisations anarchistes," *Réfractions* 24 (Spring 2010), accessed June 21, 2013, http://refractions.plusloin.org/spip.php?article529.

nonviolent form of community discipline to strengthen the commitment to consensus-based program and actions. But beyond the threat to individuality involved by this form of "social death," the rule became increasingly dysfunctional to the degree that those excluded or their allies interpreted their mandates or the movement program differently and felt ill-treated by the domination by "consensus," or two-thirds majority votes, or the excessive influence of Assemblies Movement spokespeople or leaders.

The Assembly Movement's *de facto* temporary "dual power" coexistence with the Algerian state was only a large-scale demonstration of the limits of freedom in "anarchy-in-the-cracks" or temporary autonomous zones constantly under the threat of repression and contradictions from within. Nevertheless, however liberating temporarily or disappointing in ultimate defeat, these ruptures in the dominant social reality provide potential momentum in consciousness and experiential knowledge for ongoing revolutionary struggle and potentially larger gains.

A final generic lesson from the Kabyle experience is the importance for anarchists everywhere to be attentive to horizontalist or anarchic (as broadly defined) potentials and dispositions within indigenous political cultures, outside of Eurocentric anarchist movement definition. From the Siberians observed by Kropotkin or the Aché by Pierre Clastres in Paraguay a century later to the current movements of Zapatistas and Oaxaca communes in Mexico, potentials and realities exist for freer and more egalitarian political societies, reliant upon anarchic traits separate from but similar to Western anarchist visions. Such societies and movements should be learned from and supported by anarchists of the West, in addition to explicitly self-labeled anarchist experiences and movements throughout the world.

Finally, and this is too early to assess, how did the experience of the insurrection and, specifically, the Assemblies Movement encourage or discourage the development of stronger anti-authoritarian consciousness and motivation in Kabylia and Algeria more generally? Apparently, the number of local *tajmats* has sharply declined.[92] Certainly, the general economic, social, and political situation of Kabylia and Algeria overall has not improved since the 2001 insurrection. Localized, short-lived insurgencies continue throughout the country and the *hogra* of the regime is as bad as ever. Despite continuing pride in the uprising,[93] and its forced removal of many gendarme units and continued resistance to their reimplantation in the region, the general failure to change the broader political, economic,

92 Chabani, *Le printemps noir de 2001 en Kabylie*, 107.

93 There were various commemorations of the insurrection in Kabylia on its tenth anniversary (D.M., e-mail message to author, March 31, 2013).

and social conditions through the insurrection and Assemblies Movement was an immense and bitter disappointment.

Is the reported current depoliticized and individualized perspective and activity of much of Kabyle youth[94] due in part to its perception that even the Assemblies Movement ultimately merely channeled street rage into dead-end politics? In the end, is the legacy of this experience, as some suggest, at best simply an education in participatory citizenship within a hierarchical state system?[95] Or, in fact, are the deep cultural egalitarianism, solidarity and anti-authoritarianism so prominent in Kabyle society, like similar traits in Spain before the arrival of Bakunin's emissaries,[96] the strongest forces of the future—with the 2001 insurrection and Assemblies Movement of millions added as one more political rupture contributing to ongoing changes in Kabyle and Algerian political cultures and the possibilities of more liberated existence?

94 Chabani remarks in 2011 that "youth seem no longer to believe in the future of their country." Prostitution, alcoholism, suicides, emigration (including young females) and religious extremism are increasingly visible (*Le printemps noir de 2001 en Kabylie*, 106). Another Algerian observer remarked about today's escapist consumerism and the prevalence of apolitical music. As he said, "the trend is now for forgetfulness" (Aziz B., e-mail message to author, September 14, 2012).

95 Chabani notes the "second wind" given to participatory values through creation of new sociocultural associations (*Le printemps noir de 2001 en Kabylie*, 107).

96 Bakunin's Italian emissaries came to Spain in 1868 to propagate his new explicit anarchist ideological formulation, a message greeted in Spain by those already familiar with such tendencies from their own political culture. In neither the Spanish nor the Kabyle cases, of course, should such tendencies be construed essentialistically or as elements of a deterministic narrative of progressive liberation.

EL PROCESO CONTRA LOS ANARQUISTAS

Casimiro Ramos Fernández.

El ex-sacerdote don Juan José Julio Elizalde, más conocido por el "Pope Julio.

Luis Blejer Hepel.

El Ministro señor Artorquiza, sigue con actividad digna de enconio el proceso que se na instaurado contra los elementos anárquicos que por desgracia estaban comenzado a infestar el país. Publicamos en esta página varios de los indeseables que ya han sido expulsados del país. Al centro, figura el célebre Pope Julio, que ha sido reducido a prisión por atribuírsele propaganda antipatriótica.

Luis Cuadry Matabelli.

Vicente Amoró Pozo.

Octavio Palmiro Martínez.

Nicolás Gretana Ramos.

Marcos Dukelsky Dukelsky

Anarchists expelled from Chile, July 1920, including Casimiro Barrios (upper left).
Courtesy of the International Institute for Social History, Amsterdam.

THE HORIZON AT THE CENTRE: NO PERIPHERIES

Social space . . . is the horizon at the centre of which they place themselves and in which they live.

Henri Lefebvre

ANARCHISM AND ALTERITY: THE EXPULSION OF CASIMIRO BARRIOS FROM CHILE IN 1920

Raymond Craib

How far does something need to travel to be an import?* The question, by the sheer manner in which it is asked, not only presumes the predominance of the nation-state but mimics the language of capital. In 1973 Augusto Pinochet, along with three military co-conspirators, led a successful and violent *coup d'etat*, overthrowing the democratically elected government of Salvador Allende. Once installed, Pinochet promised to purge Chile of "alien ideas," by which he meant the varied and rich veins of Marxist, Trotskyist, and anarchist thought and practice, all of which had long been robust parts of the country's political culture. Soon after, Pinochet, his advisors, and the so-called Chicago Boys of economist Milton Friedman, forcefully imposed—as only a brutal military dictatorship could—a neoliberal program of unprecedented intensity upon which he would build his personalist regime and personal fortunes.

This was, of course, hardly the first time that ideas, that thought itself, had been ascribed a place, a genealogy, and an origin. A half century earlier

* Acknowledgments: Previous versions of this essay were presented at the Cornell Department of History Americas colloquium, the Trans-Americas colloquium at the University of Buffalo, and the No Gods, No Masters, No Peripheries conference sponsored by the Institute for Comparative Modernities at Cornell University. I thank participants in those venues as well as Barry Carr, Susana Romero, Dalia Muller, Camilo Trumper, Hal Langfur, Victor Muñoz, Mario Araya, Sergio Grez, and Alberto Harambour. Special thanks to Barry Maxwell, Steven Hirsch, Geoffroy de Laforcade, Andrej Grubačić, and all the participants at the ICM gathering for comments and suggestions. Special thanks to Jorge Barrios Pulgar and his family. Research for this article was funded by a Franklin Grant from the American Philosophical Society and by the Deans' Research Fund, College of Arts & Sciences at Cornell University. A slightly different version of this essay appears in Geoffroy de Laforcade and Kirwin Shaffer, eds., *In Defiance of Boundaries: Anarchism in Latin America* (Gainesville: University of Florida Press, 2015) and is reproduced here with their permission.

Chile's oligarchs ascribed a similar "alienness" to anarchism and to those who espoused it. Through their eyes anarchists appeared as the epitome of barbarism: a political philosophy espoused by itinerant, stateless radicals bent on the violent destruction of the state itself. One such individual, caricatured and persecuted, was Casimiro Barrios Fernández. Accused of being a subversive and an anarchist, Chilean security personnel escorted Barrios out of the country on July 19, 1920.

In ordering his expulsion, the administration relied on multiple notions of alterity: not only was Barrios purportedly foreign, so too were the ideas he supposedly espoused. This chapter takes up the question of anarchism as alterity by following the activities, and eventual expulsion, of Barrios. It is, in many ways, and despite Barrios's Spanish origins, a very local story rooted in Santiago, Chile. I stress this for a simple reason: the politicians and critics of labor and its allies at the time were all too keen to emphasize the foreign origins of political opposition and, in particular, anarchism and anarcho-syndicalism. They leapt at every opportunity to suggest such "agitation from without." My aim is to emphasize that organizers and militants were often quite rooted: they were long-term residents of a place, with families and communities and political projects to whom and to which they were intensely committed.[1] The myth of the place-less radical was oftentimes precisely that: a myth. Moreover, as will become evident in this chapter, Chilean militants and organizers bristled at the repeated and patronizing suggestions that the ideals they held dear were somehow foreign or imported, just one more finished product from the metropole shipped off for consumption in the periphery.[2] This is, in some ways, then, an exploratory exercise in (forgive the anachronism) import subsitution radicalization.

Errant Swallows

Casimiro Barrios Fernández arrived in Chile in 1904 at the age of fourteen. He was one of a wave of young immigrants from the sierra of Cameros in La Rioja, Spain, to set their sights on South America. His hometown of Nieva de Cameros was characteristic of many of the small villages that clung to the mountainsides of the sierra, where the population had traditionally devoted itself to sheep herding. Transhumant paths coursed across old Castile to the edges of Extremadura while the wool cloth from

1 I discuss this issue in more detail, and in relation to the recent "transnational turn," in Raymond Craib, "Sedentary Anarchists," in Constance Bantman and Bert Altena, eds., *Reassessing the Transnational Turn: Scales of Analysis in Anarchist and Syndicalist Studies* (London: Routledge, 2014).

2 James Morris long ago pointed out trenchantly the degree to which intellectuals continued to reproduce this kind of importation narrative, a discourse of docility. See Morris, *Elites, Intellectuals and Consensus*, 112–14.

the sierra made its way to many of the commercial centers of the plateau and as far south as Andalucia in the eighteenth century.[3] The sierra had increasingly seen an outmigration of its young population in the late nineteenth century, prior to a larger outflux from the Ebro Valley regions of La Rioja, due to the herding and wool industry decline in the nineteenth century, combined with the phylloxera plague which devastated La Rioja and a more general crisis in agricultural production.[4] Initially many of these adolescents migrated south, either to Extremadura or to Andalucía, many perhaps following centuries-old pathways.[5] But gradually, and especially by the late nineteenth century, the migration shifted toward South America with young migrants leaving directly from their villages and towns in the sierra.[6] Most were in their teens, opting to leave upon finishing their basic schooling at thirteen or certainly prior to being subject to mandatory military service upon turning twenty-one.[7]

Transportation changes facilitated this shift toward trans-Atlantic migration as did the increased existence of agents actively recruiting migrants. Indeed, throughout La Rioja agents of colonization companies sought to tempt potential immigrants to make the move with offers of free travel to Chile. After Argentina, Chile was the destination of choice and the Chilean Colonization Agency had a representative in Arnedo and branches in Logroño, Calahorra, Cervera, and Haro.[8] Although migrants had to be wary—stories circulated of phony agents and fake companies, such as the Spanish American Iron Company, whose agents promised passage to Cuba on a ship that in reality sailed for the Transvaal—many found their way to Buenos Aires, Santiago, and Valparaíso after departing from Barcelona, Santander and Galicia.[9]

The Barrios family was no exception. Four of the five Barrios brothers left the slowly contracting village of Nieva de Cameros around the turn of the twentieth century, a decade before an even larger boom in

3 David Ringrose, *Spain, Europe and the "Spanish Miracle," 1700–1900* (Cambridge: Cambridge University Press, 1996), 273.

4 Pedro A. Gurría García and Mercedes Lázaro Ruiz, *Tener un Tío en América: La emigración riojana a ultramar (1880–1936)* (Logroño: Instituto de Estudios Rio-janos, 2002), 26–29.

5 Juan Antonio García-Cuerdas, "Los almacenes Giménez," *Boletín Informativo de la Asociación Benéfico Cultural Nieva de Cameros y Montemediano* 2008, no. 24 (2009): 65–68.

6 Gurría García and Lázaro Ruiz, *Tener un Tío en América*, 27, 31.

7 Gurría García and Lázaro Ruiz note that the highest outmigration was among young men, between the ages of thirteen and twenty-one. By the age of thirteen they had completed enough schooling to read and write, and twenty-one was the age for mandatory military service—by 1908, with the war in Morocco, many young men emigrated in part to avoid the war (*Tener un Tío en América*, 39–40).

8 Ibid., 86.

9 On the Spanish American Iron Company, see ibid., 86n113.

outmigration from La Rioja.[10] While Eleuterio Barrios, like most of his fellow *neveros*, headed for Buenos Aires, the eldest brother, Ciriaco, traveled to Taltal, in northern Chile, followed shortly thereafter by his brothers Rogelio and, in 1904, Casimiro.[11] Taltal was a dusty port-town of fifteen thousand souls but growing quickly as the demand for saltpeter, copper, and nitrates, all mined from the surrounding Atacama desert, expanded rapidly for export to North America and Europe. The Barrios brothers were drawn there for other reasons: their uncle, Julián Barrios, needed help in his two small shops, "El Sol" and "Las Novedades."[12]

Barrios would not remain long in Taltal. With the deaths of his brother Rogelio (1905) and Ciriaco (1908) he may have had little reason to remain.[13] By 1911, he had apparently relocated to the capital city of Santiago. One of the first tasks he set himself on arriving was to have Ciriaco's poetry published. It took some time but he eventually succeeded, the volume appearing with a small eulogy from Casimiro in the prologue.[14] Ciriaco was six years Casimiro's senior. In Taltal, as well as working in his uncle's shop, he had established a reputation for himself, under the pen-name Gil Güero, as a poet and a correspondent with Santiago's *El Heraldo de España*.[15] His poems revealed an attention to social inequalities and seemed to evoke the plight of La Rioja's peasants while others, such as "Nostalgia," reflected the difficulties of migration: "Pobre golondrina errante!/ no bien ensayado el vuelo/ con rumbo a remoto suelo/ mi tibio nido dejé," (Poor errant swallow!/ not well tested in flight/ for a land remote/ I left my warm nest).[16] Just how much he had established himself as an ally of working people is suggested by the editorial that appeared in *La Voz del Obrero* upon notification of his death: "The cause of social

10 On the statistics for migration from La Rioja, see ibid. chap. 2.

11 According to an interview with Barrios, in late 1918 or early 1919, he had been in Santiago for fourteen years and he was twenty-eight years old. See "Un extremo de la ley de residencia: Dura lex, sed lex," clipping from the weekly *Zig-Zag*, International Institute for Social History, M. Segall Rosenmann Collection f. 14 (1919) [hereafter MSR]. On immigration to Chile see Fernández Pesquero, "España en Chile: Preliminar," in Fernández Pesquero, *Monografía Estadística de la Colonia Española* 5. For data on the destinations of inhabitants of Nieva de Cameros, see Ramón Arrellano, "Aquellos emigrantes," *Boletín 2008 Asociación Benefíco-Cultural Nieva de Cameros*, 58–59, http://issuu.com/asociacionnievadecameros/docs/2008.

12 García-Cuerdas, "Los almacenes Giménez," 66; Arrellano, "Aquellos emigrantes," 58–59.

13 García-Cuerdas, "Las desventuras de dos anarquistas cameranos en el norte de Chile," *Revista de Cultura Popular y Tradiciones de La Rioja* 9 (2009): 52–57.

14 Casimiro Barrios, "A mis padres," in Barrios, *Recuerdos.*

15 Jose Angel Barrutieta. "Ciriaco Barrios: Un poeta nevero en ultramar," *Boletín 2008 Asociación Benéfico-Cultural Nieva de Cameros*, Año 2007, no. 23 (2008), 66–75. http://issuu.com/asociacionnievadecameros/docs/2008 [accessed June 28, 2010].

16 Ibid., 80–81.

justice has suffered an irreplaceable loss: with the death of señor Barrios it has lost one of its next apostles."[17]

How much of an ideological influence Ciriaco had on his younger brother is unclear but Casimiro clearly shared his brother's sympathies for the plight of workers in Chile's burgeoning industries. This perhaps is not surprising: as well as the influence of his brother, Barrios must also have been impacted by the massacre of workers, and their wives and children, at the nearby Escuela Santa María de Iquique in 1907.

At some point after arriving in Santiago Barrios married a *chilena*, with whom he raised a number of children. He had saved enough money to establish his wife with a *cigarerría*, with sales of nearly 200 pesos a day, while he worked as a clerk in a garment shop on San Diego Street just south of the city center.[18] But the Great War (or, as Barrios put it, "the goddamn war") quickly put an end to his wife's business although he later was able to set her up with a small milk stand.

By the second half of the decade, Barrios had become, with his energy and eloquence, a fairly prominent figure in the political Left of Santiago.[19] From his counter, Barrios would watch the happenings on the busy street outside. When a demonstration arose in the streets nearby, Barrios would leave his post for an hour—with his employer's permission, no less—unleash "a torrent of fiery (inciting) words and then return to selling cloth."[20] He acquired a reputation for being particularly outspoken regarding the lack of enforcement of existing labor laws, such as the 1914 "ley de la silla," requiring employers to provide a chair for each of their clerical workers, and the 1907 "ley dominical," which provided for a day of rest each week.[21] Although on the books, these laws were rarely enforced. In other instances he spoke openly and frequently about the need for new legislation: for a minimum wage, a limit to the number of hours one could work, and a reduction in the interest lending houses could charge.[22] Eloquent and well-informed, living and working in the

---

17 This excerpt from *La Voz del Obrero* appears in the prologue to Barrios's posthumously published drama *La Patria del Pobre*, 6–8, and reproduced in Barrutieta, "Ciriaco Barrios," 69–70.

18 "Un extremo de la ley de residencia: Dura lex, sed lex," clipping from the weekly *Zig-Zag*, MSR f. 14 (1919).

19 His "elocuencia indiscutible" comes from Vicuña Fuentes, *La Tiranía en Chile: Libro escrito en el destierro en 1928* (Santiago: LOM Ediciones, 2002 [1938]), 111.

20 José Santos González Vera, *Cuando era muchacho* (Santiago: Editorial Universitaria, 1996 [1951]), 136. See also González Vera, "Los anarquistas," reprinted in Carmen Soria, *Letras Anarquistas. Artículos periodísticas y otros escritos inéditos* (Santiago: Planeta, 2005).

21 On these and other labor laws, see Peter DeShazo, *Urban Workers and Labor Unions in Chile, 1902–1927* (Madison: University of Wisconsin Press, 1983), 40.

22 Fuentes, *La Tirania en Chile*, 111; Unsigned report titled "Asamblea Obrera de Alimentación Nacional" and dated November 11, 1919, Intendencia de Santiago

heart of one of Santiago's busiest commercial districts, Casimiro Barrios would eventually feel the wrath of the business owners who feared the enforcement of such measures.

The Residency Law

On November 22, 1918, upward of a hundred thousand people took to the streets of Santiago. The demonstration was organized by the Asamblea Obrera de Alimentación Nacional (Workers' Assembly on National Nutrition, AOAN), created in 1917 by the labor movement, in conjunction with university students from the Chilean Student Federation (FECh), to address the scarcity and rapidly escalating costs of basic foodstuffs and staples at a time when the major growers were increasing their exports. A remarkably inclusive organization, the AOAN was composed of workers from various industries, *empleados* of both sexes, university students, and middle-class professionals.[23] The key issues were a demand that the government reduce or stop exports of cereals and that farmers be permitted to sell directly to consumers. These were the demands that brought a remarkable number of people together on the central streets of Santiago that November day.[24] Among those in the leadership of the AOAN was Casimiro Barrios, who by this point had also joined the Santiago branch of the Partido Obrera Socialista (Socialist Workers Party, POS), speaking at meetings and demonstrations protesting the cost of food and basic necessities.[25]

The November protest clearly captured the government's attentions. In the wake of the demonstrations, Sanfuentes's administration issued an order suspending the exportation of foodstuffs for the remainder of 1918 and for all of 1919 in order to ensure the provisioning of the country.[26] But the regime responded in other ways also: it organized patriotic rallies in Santiago, ratcheted up repression against labor and its allies, and

[hereafter IS], v. 496, Archivo Nacional de Chile [hereafter AN]. On the passage, and non-enforcement, of the ley de la silla and the ley domenical, see DeShazo, *Urban Workers and Labor Unions*, 39–40. There is more than a little irony in the fact that the article on Barrios was titled "Dura lex sed lex," (which roughly translates as "the law is harsh but it is the law") given that Barrios was fighting to in fact have labor laws enforced.

23 On the AOAN, see Ignacio Rodríguez Terrazas, "Protesta y soberanía popular: las marchas del hambre en Santiago de Chile 1918–1919," thesis (Santiago: Pontificia Universidad Católica de Chile, 2001); DeShazo, *Urban Workers and Labor Unions*, 159–60; Sergio Grez Toso, *Historia del comunismo en Chile: La era de Recabarren, 1912–1924* (Santiago: LOM Ediciones, 2007), chap. 6.

24 DeShazo, *Urban Workers and Labor Unions*, 160.

25 "De Hace Medio Siglo," *El Mercurio* (September 30, 1968), MSR f. 13. For his leadership role in the Santiago branch of the POS, see Rodríguez Terrazas, "Protesta y soberanía popular," 47.

26 29th session, November 26, 1918, in *Cámara de Diputados*, 684.

circulated alarmist claims of Peruvian plots to take back the northern districts of Tacna and Arica, captured by Chile in the War of the Pacific (1879–1883). Such claims were largely hyperbolic responses to Peruvian attacks on a number of Chilean consulates in Peru earlier in the month but combined with the powerful appearance of the AOAN, they provided a strategic opportunity for the regime to push again for the enactment of a residency law.[27]

Calls for the enactment of such a law were not entirely new and had increased in recent years as officials battled strikers who threatened to cripple the ports of Valparaíso and Iquique.[28] They also battled Australian officials who had seemingly adopted Chile as their first choice of destination for agitators subject to deportation in their own country: three times over the course of 1918 Australian authorities marched their unwanted Wobblies—English, Irish, Danish, American, and Spanish—onto ships bound for Valparaíso.[29] Such deportations led to moments of diplomatic strife and eventually, according to British ambassador Francis Stronge, a "hope that the incident would serve as a lever for bringing about prohibitive or restrictive legislation" within Chile.[30]

And it did. While the imagined plots brewing in Peru were the stuff of fantasy, the Residency Law soon became reality. Enacted in December 1918, the law prohibited entrance into, or residency in, Chile by "undesireable elements."[31] Like other exclusionary laws, this one also noted that entrance would be prohibited for foreigners condemned or currently under prosecution for common crimes, those without employment, individuals engaged in illicit activities, and those with certain illnesses.[32] The law also gave power to Intendents to force foreigners to register with local officials and to obtain personal identity *cédulas*. But the impetus for the law was to prohibit immigration to Chile by people with political ideals that challenged the status quo and, just as crucially, to allow for the

27 DeShazo, *Urban Workers and Labor Unions*, 160–61. On the attacks on the consulates, see William E. Skuban, *Lines in the Sand: Nationalism and Identity on the Peruvian-Chilean Frontier* (Albuquerque: University of New Mexico Press, 2007), 172.

28 On previous calls for the creation of a residency law, see Julio Pinto V. and Verónica Valdívio O., *Revolución proletaria o querida chusma?* (Santiago: LOM Ediciones, 2001), 54; and Ignotus, *Los Anarquistas: Vidas que se autoconstruyen* (Santiago: Ediciones Spartacus, 2011), 151n9.

29 Cain, "The Industrial Workers of the World: Aspects of Its Suppression in Australia, 1916–1919," *Labour History* 42 (May 1982): 54–62.

30 Cited from ibid., 60.

31 Ley no. 3446: Impide la entrada al país o la residencia en él de elementos indeseables. Published in the Diario Oficial no. 12,243, December 12, 1918 (reproduced in Brian Loveman and Elizabeth Lira, *Arquitectura política y seguridad interior del estado: Chile, 1811–1990* [Santiago: DIBAM, 2002], 82–83).

32 In Chile it also included pimps and "ruffians": thus anarchists are lumped together with the idle, the ill, and the illicit.

expulsion of non-Chileans who were perceived to be creating problems for the administration and its allies. The first to feel its wrath was Barrios, who was ordered, on December 18, 1920, expelled from the country for "preaching the violent overthrow of the social and political order and provoking protests against the existing order."[33] Fourteen years after immigrating to Chile, enticed perhaps by Chilean colonization agents scattered in and around La Rioja, Barrios now found himself the first person to be ordered expelled under the new law.

A Constant Sentinel

Barrios was not expelled. At least, not immediately. In early January 1919, the authorities stayed his expulsion order.[34] The reasons why are worth considering in some detail. In part, it resulted from an intense campaign on the part of some POS members in Santiago and of organizers in the AOAN.[35] Barrios had established himself as a powerful and admired presence among Santiago's working sectors and various organs of the POS—*La Aurora* and *La Bandera Roja*—published editorials condemning the Residency Law and the order for Barrios's expulsion.[36] But Barrios had defenders in other quarters also. Only two days after the issuance of the initial expulsion decree, deputies and senators from the Alianza Liberal in Chile's Parliament voiced concerns on the floor of their respective chambers.[37] Over the course of two weeks, from December 18 to January 4, they returned repeatedly to the case of Barrios, debating at great length and with great intensity. While complicated, the issues raised by defenders of Barrios can be distilled down to four: first, why was the law applied to Barrios (in other words, a question of applicability)? Second, was the retroactive application of the law legal (essentially a question of law)? Third, on what basis were decrees of expulsion founded (questions of evidence)? And fourth, could ideas, rather than actions, serve as the basis for expulsion or other forms of persecution (questions of scope)?

All of these deserve due consideration. For example, when a deputy in the Parliament publicly questions the reliability of police reports, remarking at one point that "[I] wouldn't trust the Security Section's methods

33 The circumstances of Barrios's arrest and order of expulsion are reviewed in Intendencia de Santiago to Sr. Ministro del Interior, June 19, 1920, AN/IS v. 497; the initial expulsion decree is Decreto 760 de Intendencia de Santiago, dated December 18, 1918. For the administration's explanation for the suspension of the expulsion decree, see the remarks of Quezada in 71st session, January 7, 1919, *Cámara de Diputados*, 1840.

34 Decreto 2, Intendente de Santiago, January 4, 1919, referenced in Intendencia de Santiago a Sr. Ministro del Interior, June 19, 1920, AN/IS v. 497.

35 Rodríguez Terrazas, "Protesta y soberanía popular," 82.

36 *La Aurora: Organo del Partido Obrero Socialista* 132 (January 10, 1919), 2; on *La Bandera Roja* see Rodríguez Terrazas, "Protesta y soberanía popular," 82.

37 61st session, December 20, 1918, in *Cámara de Diputados*, 1413.

[*procedimientos*] as far as I could spit," there are clearly issues worth pursuing.[38] So too does the wrangling over whether or not the law could be applied retroactively, particularly given that Barrios himself submitted a writ of habeaus corpus to the courts in his defense precisely on this point, while others claimed that of course the law was meant to be "preventive" (perhaps preemptive?) against men such as Barrios who led others in to the "thicket of social disorganization, of disorder, and in the end, the utopia of men without country and without possessions."[39]

The strongest arguments made repeatedly in defense of Barrios were that he was not an individual to whom such a law ought to be applied. The reasons offered were numerous: he worked hard; he had lived in Chile for much of his adult life (an implicit questioning of what constituted a "foreigner"); he had married a Chilean woman and had children with Chilean nationality; and that he was not a subversive but in fact simply worked to ensure existing laws were upheld.[40] Take, for example, the long disquisition of Senator Torrealba, someone who had worked with Barrios while president of a Santiago artisan society and who spoke at great length in his defense of Barrios, even while emphasizing that Barrios was a member of a party "that calls itself the Socialist Worker" and not Torrealba's own Democratic Party.[41] Barrios, he noted, had joined the Sociedad de Empleados de Comercio (Business Employees' Society) and had begun to campaign hard for the enforcement of the Sunday Rest Law. To ensure compliance with, and enforcement of, this law and others that had been passed for the benefit of working people, Barrios had organized demonstrations and meetings. He had also begun to preach among workers of the need for abstention from alcohol.

> For these reasons, I imagine that this man has attracted persecution from the business owners [*comerciantes*] and distributors

38 See his comments in 69th session, January 3, 1919, in *Cámara de Diputados*, 1717–19. The translation here attempts to capture the slang and derision of Pinto Duran's original phrasing: "y yo no meto un brazo al fuego por los procedimientos de la Sección de Seguridad." It could be also translated as "I would not vouch for the procedures of the Security Section" although I have opted for something a bit more derisive.

39 On Barrios's writ, the quote is from Minister of the Interior Quezada explaining Barrios's petition in 71st session, January 7, 1919, *Cámara de Diputados*, 1845. On "preventive" applications of the law and "thickets," see Sánchez Gárcia de la Huerta, 71st session, January 7, 1919, *Cámara de Diputados*, 1839.

40 69th session, January 3, 1919, in *Cámara de Diputados*, 1718. Even the minister of the interior, who was asked to visit the Parliament to explain the suspension of Barrios's expulsion order, made note of Barrios's long-term residency in Chile and of his domestic situation. 71st session, January 7, 1919, *Cámara de Diputados*, 1844; see also the summation in Intendencia de Santiago a Sr. Ministro del Interior, June 19, 1920, AN/IS v. 497.

41 Session of December 24, 1918, in *Cámara de Senadores*, 907

> [*espendedores*] of alcoholic beverages, above all those who have their businesses in the barrio of San Diego, who do not want to see him continue his campaign. He has been, in effect, a constant sentinel who has forced them to close their shops on the days required by law. I imagine that these businessmen, tired of putting up with the continuous vigiliance of this citizen, would have denounced him to the Santiago Intendent, accusing him of being an anarchist and a dangerous man. I believe this to be the real motive behind the accusation that, without a doubt, they have made against him.[42]

Had perhaps the Intendent been swayed by such commercial interests, Torrealba suggested, particularly given that the government had nothing more than a report from a Security Section agent upon which to base their decree of expulsion? Regardless of how outspoken (*mui hablador*) Barrios might be, that did not make him a threat to the internal security of the nation, he argued.[43]

On the floor of the Deputies' Chamber similar defenses unfolded. Deputy Pinto Durán referred to Barrios as an "hombre de bien," and a "modest worker," one concerned with those who were less well-off (to which a conservative deputy responded: "Then let him go preach in his own land! There is a lot more misery there than in Chile.")[44] The well-off, Pinto Durán noted, see the principles that structure society as naturally indisputable, but if one were to see through the eyes of those who work ten or twelve hours per day and still cannot earn enough to feed themselves and their children, the world would look quite different. The comment provoked a heated and revealing response from a conservative deputy: there was plenty of work in the *campos* at good pay, he claimed, but workers in the city did not want it and instead chose to pass their time in the taverns.[45] He and other *agricultores* offered four or five pesos a day for work in the fields plus room and board but still could not find workers. The root cause of the high prices of foodstuffs, he argued in a revealing shift, was the fact that the labor force was poorly distributed.[46]

All of these comments—whether from defenders or accusers of Barrios—point to the heart of why a significant group of Parliamentarians spoke in favor of a residency law and the expulsion of Barrios: large landowners and growers had just watched, in Sanfuentes's response to the

42 Ibid., 906–7. Note the interesting fact that Torrealba refers to Barrios as a "citizen."

43 Ibid., 907.

44 69th session, January 3, 1919, in *Cámara de Diputados*, 1717–18.

45 I say "heated" because Pinto Durán calls him out for "arranques un poco violentos" (69th session, January 3, 1919, in *Cámara de Diputados*, 1718).

46 Ibid., 1719.

AOAN demonstrations, their export possibilities and profit margins radically curtailed, while businessmen in the central commercial district of Santiago had to suffer Barrios's constant efforts to get labor laws enforced.

They clearly would have preferred not to admit that such was the case. Instead, they unsurprisingly embraced the canard of the foreign agitator. Yet in Barrios the authorities had someone who hardly fit such an image. As he himself noted in an interview with *Zig-Zag*, having arrived in Chile at the age of fourteen he had lived there for half of his life.[47] He clearly was not *that* foreign. Moreover, he had over the course of the previous decade, become a prominent and important figure in Santiago's labor movement and had developed close relationships with members of Chile's political class. He was a fixture in Santiago's political, social, and commercial life. Just as important, members of the Parliament defended him, and it seemed unlikely he could so easily be conflated with bomb-throwing fictions of the kind circulating at the time. In other words, the assertions of alterity hardly fooled many, even in the centers of government.

Misplaced Ideas?

Nor did they fool working people.

Shortly after Barrios's expulsion order was stayed, tram operators in Santiago went on strike. Meanwhile, the AOAN pushed to capitalize on the momentum by calling for nationwide demonstrations in early February 1919. Having been caught off guard by the size of the demonstrations the previous November, and reeling from both the tram strike and congressional criticism of cancelling Barrios's expulsion order, Sanfuentes's ministers and party stalwarts saw such mobilizations as an opportunity to regain ground and to move against the labor movement under the pretense of a subversive threat.[48] Despite the peaceful nature of the demonstrations, authorities increasingly responded with repression and threats of extensive violence. Presses were shut down; union leaders were arbitrarily detained; workers were beaten; a multitude of others were arrested under false pretenses; and claims of maximalist conspiracies were circulated.[49] One paper reported that the military presence sent to the northern pampas to suppress the AOAN organizers was of a magnitude not seen since the civil war of 1891.[50] In the midst of this crackdown, Deputy Urrutia Ibáñez took to the floor of the Parliament:

47 "Un extremo de la ley de residencia: Dura lex, sed lex," MSR f. 14 (1919).

48 That such was the case was all too clear to Recabarren who noted that the repression had little to do with fear and everything to do with weakening the labor movement. See Rodríguez Terrazas, "Protesta y soberanía popular," 92.

49 Rodríguez Terrazas, "Protesta y soberanía popular," 89–92.

50 *La Opinión*, cited from ibid., 91.

> This past week has been one of apprehension and anxious concern; one could not forsee the characteristics the strike would take; it was known that there were reckless agitators preaching sedition among the workers, and it was feared that foreign anarchists could be hatching sinister plans against the social order; and it was even feared that the 'red flu,' as maximalism is called, might have spread among our popular classes. . . . These events . . . should serve to teach us and serve as an example. They show us that international anarchism takes on a very dangerous form in countries of incipient organization: it does not now throw bombs [*prepara ya atentados*] at the heads of government; it provokes the rebellious mass to rise up against work, discipline, and the social morality that exists, has existed, and always will exist in all States.[51]

Urrutia again returned to the argument that the strikes and conflicts erupting in Santiago and elsewhere were the work of foreign agitators, and particularly anarchists. He could hardly have been unaware of the existence of domestic anarchists: after all they had been organizing and agitating for some two decades in Chile.[52] But the possibility of both negating the possibility that such strikes and conflicts stemmed from legal and domestic organizations with legitimate grievances and of equating anarchism with foreignness was too much to pass up. Indeed, such perspectives had become commonplace in the press. Editorialists and politicians repeatedly blamed the foreign—persons and ideas—for the supposed agitation of the otherwise content Chilean worker. In his interview with Barrios, the reporter from *Zig-Zag* concluded with a predictable insult: "he is a victim of the criminal propaganda that circulates among workers in old Europe who, through the university or through books, are imbued with utopian theories which, if they don't fit there, are even less appropriate here in Chile where currently our greatest evil is an excess of liberties."[53]

These efforts to assert the presence of "misplaced ideas" and placeless agitators were obvious to many at the time. Juan Gandulfo, a medical student and prominent member of the FECh, seemed to have Barrios in mind when he scathingly remarked that "Chilean journalists, among whom there are two or three who really understand the social question,

51 The speech was given on January 16, 1919. Cited from ibid., 87.

52 For excellent studies, see Sergio Grez Toso, *Los anarquistas y el movimiento obrero: La alborada de 'la idea' en Chile, 1893–1915* (Santiago, Chile: LOM Ediciones, 2007); Víctor Muñóz Cortés, *Armando Triviño* (Santiago: Editorial Quimantú, 2009) and Muñóz Cortés, *Cuando la Patria Mata* (Santiago: Editorial Usach, 2011); and Mario Araya Saavedra, "Los Wobblies Criollos," thesis (Santiago: Universidad ARCIS, 2008).

53 "Un extremo de la ley de residencia: Dura lex, sed lex," MSR f. 14 (1919).

have chileanized the 'professional agitator,' in order to satisfy their bosses and the commercial businesses which advertise in this country's newspapers."[54] Barrios's own colleagues understood as much. In a revealing exchange during a meeting of the central committee of the AOAN immediately following the expulsion decree, Enrique Huerta noted the following: "It is not possible that they can claim that Barrios came to Chile as a foreigner to preach subversive ideas: I have known this man for nine years and his principles *were taught to him by Chileans*. First he was an anarchist and then a socialist." Evaristo Rios agreed, remarking that Barrios had learned his ideas in Chile and that his only "crime" was to be a foreigner.[55] In other words, neither anarchism nor socialism were somehow "alien" or "mis-placed" ideas, and immigrants could discover them in the societies in which they landed rather than necessarily importing them from whence they came: no idea that resonates in a given context can be said to be out-of-place.[56]

A Capacious Left

Even so, the stigma of being accused an anarchist could be hard to shake and a worrisome accusation for some. An incident at a POS meeting in March of that year (1919) is revealing. Victor Roa Medina, long-time POS militant and the party secretary, hosted a gathering at his home at which he suggested that the name of a weekly publication, *La Bandera Roja*, most likely modeled after the publication of the same name in Buenos Aires, be changed. Barrios in particular seemed to take offense at the

---

54 Cited fron Ignotus, *Los anarquistas*, 4–6. The "importation" paradigm persisted: James Morris would lament in the 1960s that Chile's Marxist historians continued to understand historical radicalization as merely ideational and a result of the increased circulation of texts, from Europe to the "periphery." That said, the diffusionist paradigm—whether in the history of science, of ideas, or of politics—has been subject to repeated and withering critique over the years. See, for example, the varying critiques in Kapil Raj, *Relocating Modern Science* (New York: Palgrave Macmillan, 2007); Mary Louise Pratt, *Imperial Eyes* (London: Routledge, 1992), in particular the elaboration on Fernando Ortiz's concept of transculturation; Fernando Coronil, "Beyond Occidentalism," *Cultural Anthropology* 11, no.1 (February 1996): 51–87; and more broadly Bruno Latour, *We Have Never Been Modern* (Cambridge, MA: Harvard University Press, 1993). Particularly useful in understanding the context within which such ideas are generated is Roberto Schwarz, *Misplaced Ideas* (London: Verso: 1992), and the recent engagement with that work by Elías José Palti, "The Problem of 'Misplaced Ideas' Revisited," *Journal of the History of Ideas* 67, no. 1 (January 2006): 149–79.

55 Unsigned report by Sección de Seguridad on the AOAN, dated December 21, 1918, of a meeting held on December 20, in AN/IS, v. 470. My emphasis.

56 There may indeed have been a nationalistic sentiment at work here, certainly for those militants in the POS who identified clearly with socialism, but it is worth at least proferring a complementary possibility: that such arguments were, in effect, kinds of early post-colonial critiques of Eurocentricism, and ones that anarchists in particularly were well-positioned to offer.

suggestion, observing that changing the name of the paper would be a problem, because it was by that title that the paper was known both in Chile and Argentina, but perhaps also in part because *La Bandera Roja* had been organized in response to the expulsion order directed at him. Regardless, he responded to Medina's suggestion with sharp words, calling Roa Medina a coward and ridiculing his knowledge of socialist doctrine.[57] But what is especially striking is the response by Roa Medina and his allies who argued that Barrios was in fact not a socialist but an anarchist and that his subversive ideas were going to get him expelled from the country and that his continued participation in the party would ruin it.[58] A vote was taken on whether or not to expel Barrios: he survived the vote and Roa Medina did in fact step down while Barrios took over the publication of *La Bandera Roja*.

This dispute between Roa Medina and Barrios occurred at a particular juncture: in the wake of the tramworkers' strike, Sanfuentes was granted powers of martial law and, under the threat of violence, the leadership of the AOAN cancelled a set of demonstrations, an act that angered many, particularly workers' organizations that were largely anarchist in orientation, including shoemakers, tailors, and typesetters.[59] New confederations appeared, including a Gran Confederación de Trabajo that began to meet regularly on Wednesdays at the offices of the Chilean Student Federation.[60] It was in this context—of heightened repression combined with internal divisions over strategy—that the dispute between Roa Medina and Barrios unfolded.

The dispute is revealing of something worth emphasizing: while on the one hand it seems to suggest a kind of sectarianism it also points toward the various ideological threads that made up the POS. Clearly ideas are important and I have no desire to dismiss the ascriptions people appropriated for themselves, or to disparage the communities they formed and the ideological glue that held those communities together. But I also do not wish to mimic the language of the police or reinforce the inclinations

57 Unsigned report dated March 16, 1919, Sección de Seguridad, AN/IS v. 476 (Comunicaciones 1919); unsigned report dated March 17, 1919, Sección de Seguridad, AN/IS v. 476 (Comunicaciones, 1919).

58 Unsigned report dated March 17, 1919, Sección de Seguridad, AN/IS v. 476 (Comunicaciones, 1919).

59 For an excellent discussion, see Rodríguez Terrazas, "Protesta y soberanía popular," 84–92; see also "El comité de Alimentación Nacional," *Verba Roja* 1, no. 6 (February 1919): 2.

60 Rodríguez Terrazas, "Protesta y soberanía popular," 101. The importance of the FECh to anarchist and labor politics at the time is worth emphasizing. For more on the linkages between students, workers, and worker-intellectuals, see Raymond Craib, "Students, Anarchists and Categories of Persecution in Chile, 1920," *A Contracorriente* 8, no. 1 (Fall 2010): 22–60; and DeShazo, *Urban Workers and Labor Unions*.

to sectarianism that occasionally hold sway and that insist on dogmatic coherence rather than lived experience. Barrios was someone hard to pin down and in this I do not believe he was exceptional for the time. As one colleague noted, Barrios began as an anarchist and became a socialist; yet we have a POS militant accusing Barrios of being an anarchist; yet other POS militants defending Barrios and noting that he served as the secretary of the Santiago branch of the POS. (A similar ambivalence appears in the historiography in which Barrios appears.) The fact is that such efforts to rigidly situate Barrios are revealing on two fronts: first, that there were unsurprisingly differences of opinion regarding strategy, tactics, and so forth; and second, that there was a capaciousness to the Left after the Great War and anarchists and socialists, if not indistinguishable from each other, certainly overlapped strongly. Was Barrios an anarchist? A socialist? Both or something else entirely? Barrios himself avoided too rigid a label: at various points in an interview with *Zig-Zag* he referred to himself as a socialist, a radical, a free-thinker, and a "militant in the most advanced parties," while also noting that he had mellowed over the years![61]

In fact, as was the case in many parts of the globe prior to 1920 or so, in Chile the line between anarchists and socialists could be relatively fluid.[62] University students espoused anarchist ideas as they sold copies of Trotsky's writings recently translated in to Spanish; others sustained a relationship with the Radical Party yet similarly embraced anarchist ideas and writings; meanwhile, contributors to *Verba Roja*, who self-identified strongly as anarchists, warmly embraced Lenin and the Bolshevik Revolution as a welcome "prologue" to a communo-anarchist future.[63] These should not be taken as evidence of incoherence or, conversely, of sectarianism, but perhaps instead of the capaciousness of the Left in a specific place at a specific time: a city experiencing dramatic labor unrest

61 "Un extremo de la ley de residencia," MSR f. 14 (1919).

62 See, for example, Anderson, *The Age of Globalization*, and Khuri-Makdisi, *The Eastern Mediterranean*.

63 For the selling of Trotsky's writings, see the July 1920 interrogation of university student Rigoberto Soto Rengifo in "Proceso contra Pedro Gandulfo Guerra, et al.," Segundo Juzgado del Crimen de Santiago, AN, Judicial de Santiago/Criminales, legajo 1658 (f. 50). For the comments on the Russian Revolution, see "El maximalismo" in *Verba Roja* 1, no. 17 (August 29, 1919): 3; "Lenin," *Verba Roja* 1: 14 (July 1919): 2; and "La dictadura del proletariado: El el Prologo del comunismo anárquico. Lenin, Trotsky y los maximalistas rusos van hacia él," *Verba Roja* 1, no. 14 (July 1919): 1. As much as this reveals that divisions were not necessarily strong, it also reveals the degree to which, as it unfolded, the Russian Revolution had a number of possible paths, some of which appeared agreeable to those with more anarchistic persuasions. It was with the massacre of the Ukranian anarchists that the split began to widen. Even then the divide between communists and anarchists was not all-encompassing. As late as the early 1940s Manuel Rojas, a lifelong anarchist, would pen a beautiful obituary of Trotsky in the intellectual journal *Babel*.

and social change, in the wake of the Great War, and in the midst of an unfolding and inspiring revolution in Russia.

Expulsion

Despite the Intendent's warning to steer clear of politics, over the course of 1919 Barrios continued to organize and agitate with the POS and the AOAN, something well known to the Intendent through his spies in Santiago's Security Section who kept close watch on Barrios and his immediate circles. Through the winter of 1919 Barrios worked closely with what remained of the AOAN, organizing to get lending houses to reduce their interest rates.[64] But it was a report that identified Barrios as one of the main instigators of a September 1919 general strike. In response to a police assault on the local office of the Federación Obrera de Chile in Limache, beer workers struck in Santiago, followed immediately by tram workers, chauffeurs, and shoeworkers. This soon led authorities to order Barrios to appear yet again in the Intendent's office.[65] "With his characteristic mode of innocence," reported the Intendent, Barrios denied the accusations and assured the Intendent that, "as a foreigner, he would not intervene in workers' movements nor preach his ideas in public."[66] Barrios clearly had cheek. A short time after this appearance, he evidently returned of his own accord and suggested to the Intendent that the police be more proactive in enforcing the law requiring Sunday as a day of rest, concluding his piece of unsolicited advice by "threatening" the Intendent that if this did not happen he would "raise the issue with workers' societies."[67] Shortly thereafter, Barrios was accused of issuing public threats against officials who had drawn up the Residency Law.

The authorities were losing patience with Barrios. But just as crucially, as the year ended and the June elections approached, they were losing patience with the labor movement and its allies as a whole. As the

64 Unsigned report titled "Asamblea Obrera de Alimentación Nacional," November 11, 1919, AN/IS v. 496. He also worked to wage a campaign against the "apuesta mutuas en los Hipódromos."

65 On the general strike see Rodríguez Terrazas, "Protesta y soberanía popular," 134–35. The strike in September had again raised the specter of expulsions as an editorial in the leading daily *El Mercurio* pointed to the United States as an exemplar of how to handle undesireables: "El noble gesto con que la Federación Obrera de los Estados Unidos señaló la puerta de la expulsión a los elementos maximalistas, es la mejor demonstración de que la educación política del pueblo norteamericano le permite distinguir con claridad la verdadera democracia de la demogagia anarquista." From "De hace medio siglo (el Mercurio del 17 de septiembre de 1919)" MSR f. 14.

66 Intendente de Santiago al Sr. Fiscal en Comisión don Fidel Araneda Luco, July 7, 1920, AN/IS v. 505 (Gobernadores, Prefectos y Varias Autoridades, 1920). These are the Intendent's words, not Barrios's.

67 Ibid.

presidential election scheduled for June 1920 approached, and the candidacy of opposition candidate Arturo Alessandri garnered momentum among labor, those in power sought to find ways to control the circumstances surrounding the election and the political demography of the country. They did so through a number of mechanisms. For example, the Chilean state successfully forged agreements on immigration with some of its neighbors—Brazil, Argentina, and Uruguay—in order to "defend workers" from "undesireable elements," including persons who sought the "violent or revolutionary transformation of society."[68] The government also attempted to enforce more strictly the order that all foreigners resident in Chile register with the Intendent in their zone of residence. Barrios received such an order in March.[69] The requirement that foreigners register and acquire identity cards had been a part of the 1918 Residency Law but clearly it had been only minimally enforced. Partially this resulted from a bureaucratic infrastructure not yet prepared to handle the demands that such a requirement entailed, despite the existence of an Office on Identification.

Identification itself could be a tricky business but also a profitable one. For example, seeing the possibilities, Roberto Matus and Humberto Ducci approached the Intendent's chief of the Office on Identification at the end of 1919 to offer their services: a recently patented procedure for preparing personal identity cards, one which "absolutely impedes any substitution of the original picture."[70] Their letter hinted at the concerns with which any registration program would have to contend: "We have seen that with a simple change in the picture of an identity card, which has been stolen from its rightful owner, thieves can pass for capitalists or businessmen [or] public employees; for diplomats; and even for Agents in the Security Section." They concluded ominously that this "could happen any day, if it hasn't already."[71] In a suggestive analogy, they noted that during the war in Europe officials would falsify identity cards of prisoners simply by changing pictures and thus giving easy access to enemy territory. Thus Matus and Ducci developed a process that used a paper with a particular

68 See the convenio outlined in Enrique Cuevas [head of the Chilean Legation in Uruguay] al Ministro de Relaciones Exteriores, March 16, 1920, vol. 801b, Archivo General Histórico, Ministerio de Relaciones Exteriores de Chile.

69 Decreto of March 5, 1920 (f. 60), AN/IS, v. 504, Decretos, 1920.

70 Matus and Ducci al Señor Jefe del Gabinete de Identificación, December 30, 1919, included in Coronel-Prefecto al Intendente de la Provincia, January 24, 1920, AN/IS v. 504 (Decretos), 1920. On the creation of the Office of Identification, see Decreto 715 of the Ministry of the Interior.

71 Ibid. Such passing, of course, had already happened, just not as Matus and Ducci imagined it: agents in Santiago's Security Section were passing themselves off as organizers and agitators.

sheen that would disappear if tampered with.[72] Their work dovetailed with long-standing efforts by the police to improve identification techniques, in particular through training in dactyloscopy (fingerprinting and fingerprint identification and classification), anthropometry (the physical measurement of bodies—especially the head and face—to create a detailed description), and photography. These techniques were adopted and used as a means not only to identify individuals, but to track them, which explains why labor and anarchist leaders, such as Onofre Chamorro of the Industrial Workers of the World, intensely resisted efforts to make photographs mandatory for work permits and sought to avoid having their faces photographed.[73]

The registration and identification systems advanced in lock-step with the increased surveillance apparatus deployed by the Chilean state in 1920. In early July 1920, the Santiago Intendent was asking that it be better financed and restructured.[74] His request came in part as a result of increased efforts to register, identify, and track foreign nationals living in Chile. He issued an order, simultaneous with his request for increased funding, that all foreigners resident in Santiago register in a special registry overseen by Santiago's police prefect and to also obtain a government-issued identity card.[75] In subsequent days he designed a system to facilitate the process of registration at the Identification Office, organized according to country of origin. Included near the top of the list were Russian nationals, beginning with men ages fourteen to twenty-five, to be followed by Spanish nationals. Given the fears of revolutionary and anarchist activity that seemed to drive the registration process in the first place, this is not surprising. But neither of these categories topped the list. That sad privilege went to Peruvian nationals.[76]

---

72 Ibid.

73 For a detailed discussion of the possibilities, limits, and applications of identification techniques at the time, see Prieto Lemm, *Identificación de las personas*; on Chonofre and photography see Pinto and Valdívio, *Revolución proletaria o querida chusma?*

74 Intendente de la Provincia al Sr. Ministro de Interior, July 5, 1920, AN/IS, v. 506. The space within which the Santiago staff worked was so narrow that it not only made working conditions difficult but simply could not accommodate the much-needed increase in staff, a situation that the Prefect suggested was responsible for the limited success at filling the registration rolls, rather than administrative laziness or resistance by foreigners: by the end of November 1920, six months after the new decree, the Santiago office had managed to register only some seventeen thousand of an estimated sixty thousand foreigners. Coronel-Prefecto al Intendente de la Provincia, December 21, 1920, AN/IS, v. 500 (December 1920).

75 Decreto of July 7, 1920 (f. 290), AN/IS, v. 504 (Decretos 1920).

76 *El Mercurio* (Saturday, July 17, 1920), 1. Space limitations prevent me from discussing this issue further. I discuss the manner in which the government would conflate anarchists and Peruvians, as diseases of the social body, in Craib, *The Cry of the Renegade: Subversive Santiago, 1920* (New York: Oxford University Press, forthcoming).

The government also increasingly turned to the Residency Law and applied it with full force. It had not been uncommon for the occasional ruffian or pimp to be expelled under the law but by March of 1920 the law began to be applied to individuals perceived to be propagating doctrines incompatible with the established order.[77] Such was the case, in March, for Ecuadorian-born Lisandro Paladines and Peruvian-born Nicolás Gutarra Ramos.[78]

And such was the case for Casimiro Barrios: in early July 1920, after months of being superintended, surveilled, spied on, and registered, Barrios was summoned to the offices of Santiago's police commissioner of investigations and *fiscal*, Fidel Araneda Luco, accused of distributing subversive propaganda.[79] It did not help that Barrios purportedly had been "insolent" toward the Santiago Intendent who then reported that he "had to force him to leave the room."[80] Such things made it evident, the Intendent reported, that Barrios was "a dangerous foreigner . . . who did not respect the authorities, and a danger to public tranquility."[81] Briefed on the case, Araneda rescinded Barrios's stay of expulsion and had Barrios sent to Valparaíso for deportation.

Escorted by a senior police official from Santiago, he arrived in Valparaíso where the government's efforts soon ran into problems. The steamship company refused to take Barrios because he had no passport; Chilean authorities could not grant him one as he maintained his Spanish

77 For examples of foreigners expelled "por ser rufianos conocidos i dedicarse a esplotar la prostitución" see the cases discussed in Coronel-Prefecto al Intendente de Santiago, January 20, 1919 and Sub-Prefecto al Coronel-Prefecto, January 18, 1919, both in AN/IS v. 496.

78 For Paladines, see Decreto of March 11, 1920 (f. 72), AN/IS, v. 504, (Decretos 1920); Nicolas Gutarra of Peru was ordered expelled on 18 May, and placed on a steamship for Arica and expelled from the country on June 5, 1920. Gutarra had initially been expelled from his native Peru for the same reason, "por propagar ideas contrarias al orden establecido." For Gutarra, the original order is in Decreto of May 18, 1920 (f. 178), AN/IS, v. 504, (Decretos 1920); the actual date of expulsion is given in Coronel-Prefecto al Intendente de la Provincia, June 14, 1920, AN/IS, v. 496.

79 Fidel Araneda Luco, Comisario de Investigaciones, al Señor Intendente de la Provincia, July 7, 1920, AN/IS, v.497.

80 Intendencia de Santiago a Sr. Ministro del Interior, June 19, 1920, AN/IS, v. 497. Such "insolence" should not be underestimated: the writer and anarchist José Santos González Vera would remark that it was the perception of insolence and breach of social protocols that led to the brutal detention and death of the poet José Domingo Gómez Rojas. See González Vera, *Cuando era muchacho*. On the death of Gómez Rojas, see Fabio Moraga Valle and Carlos Vega Delgado, *José Domingo Gómez Rojas* (Punta Arenas: Editorial Ateli, 1997); Craib, "Students, Anarchists and Categories of Persecution"; and Craib, "The Firecracker Poet: Three Poems of José Domingo Gómez Rojas," *New Letters* 78, no. 1 (Fall 2011): 71.

81 Intendencia de Santiago a Sr. Ministro del Interior, June 19, 1920, AN/IS, v. 497. The minister of the interior confirmed the expulsion on 28 June. See Ministerio del Interior al Intendente de Santiago, June 28, 1920, AN/IS, v. 496.

citizenship. This should not have been unexpected: the Intendent of Valparaíso noted in a letter to his counterpart in Santiago that "the difficulties that arise in each case regarding the application of the Residency Law have not been few. It would be convenient if the authorities throughout the country were to explain these circumstances to the Government so that they can resolve them."[82] The paradox of documentary regimes is precisely that they cannot be controlled solely for repressive means: it is fitting that an individual accused of being an anarchist reveals the paradoxes to be found in systems of nationalist identification.

The Valparaíso Intendent had a solution: he suggested having Barrios taken as far as Arica, where he would then disembark and be transported overland to either the Peruvian frontier or Bolivian border.[83] By July 9, Barrios was on board the steamship *Palena*, bound for Arica, where he disembarked, accompanied by a Santiago Security Section agent.[84] After being granted permission to withdraw funds from Caja Nacional de Ahorros for his family, Barrios was transferred to the custody of the police in Tacna.[85] Some in the government wanted to put Barrios on a train to Bolivia but instead, on July 19, he was taken to the border with Peru, across from Sama, and expelled.[86]

His expulsion carried multiple meanings. For one, and perhaps most obviously, it represented the state's efforts to assert control over the social order: to expel individuals perceived as threatening to the political and social stability of the state. It carried a second meaning: a reassertion of spatial order. The choice of the Sama, rather than say the border with Bolivia, was a strategic choice in that Chilean officials had long held the Sama to constitute the northern boundary of the provinces of Tacna and Arica, against the protestations of Peru.[87] Escorting subversives to the banks of the Sama for expulsion constituted a symbolic affirmation of that claim. What better way to reaffirm the social and spatial order of the

82 Intendente de Valparaiso al Señor Intendente, don Francisco Subercaseaux, July 7, 1920, AN/IS, v. 497.

83 Ibid.; Telegram de García de la Huerta al Gobernador de Arica, July 9, 1920, Archivo del Siglo XX de Chile [hereafter ARNAD], Fondo Ministerio del Interior [hereafter MI], v. 5427.

84 Telegram de García de la Huerta al Gobernador de Arica, July 9 1920, ARNAD/MI, v. 5427; Telegram de García de la Huerta al Gobernador de Arica, July 10, 1920, ARNAD/MI, v. 5426.

85 Telegram de García de la Huerta al Gobernador de Arica, July 9 1920, ARNAD/MI, v. 5427; Certificate, Policia Fiscal, Tacna, July 16, 1920, AN/IS v. 498.

86 Telegram de Fernando Edwards al Prefecto de Policia, Santiago, July 28, 1920, AN/IS v. 498; on the idea of expelling him to Bolivia see telegram from Fernando Edwards, Intendente de Tacna, al Intendente de Santiago, August 1, 1920, AN/IS v. 498. See also Sub-Prefecto Jefe al Coronel-Prefecto, July 30, 1920 and Casimiro Barrios, "Desde Lima," *Claridad* 1, no. 9 (December 11, 1920): 9.

87 Skuban, *Lines in the Sand*, 185.

state than by expelling "foreign agitators" across a contested boundary, a simultaneous policing of national and ideological borders?

The expulsion of Barrios was followed shortly thereafter by a series of other deportations. People who hailed originally from countries as diverse as Russia, Spain, Italy, Argentina, and Cuba were given, over the course of some four days in late July, expulsion orders and more expulsions followed in August, all for "propagating doctrines incompatible with the unity and individuality of the nation and with public order," or, as the press was eager to note, for being "anarchists."[88] Interestingly enough, these expulsion orders came in part at the behest of a specially appointed minister, José Astorquiza, to oversee the prosecution of subversives who himself had been born aboard a ship at sea, sailing under the Peruvian flag.

Coda

Upon being expelled, Barrios made his way to Lima where he continued his efforts to organize workers.[89] By January of 1921, the Intendent was apprised of the fact that Barrios was back in Santiago.[90] Like many immigrants to Chile—whether from Spain, Russia, Italy, or Peru—Barrios had made a life for himself there. He had labored and loved in Santiago for his entire adult life. Santiago was home.

He would remain in Santiago another six years. In 1927, under the government of Carlos Ibáñez, he would be expelled again, this time not for being an anarchist but a communist (a label presumably Barrios would not have contested: he named his son, born in 1925, Santiago Lenin Barrios).[91] He was not alone. A number of members of Parliament, as well as a number of well-known intellectuals, would also be expelled. Some would end up on Chilean islands in the Pacific—the outposts of Más Atierra and Más Afuera made famous by the story of Robinson Crusoe, or Isla Pascua (Easter Island).[92] Others would voyage to Europe. Barrios would

88 See Decreto 2900, July 24, 1920, ARNAD/MI, v. 5393; Decreto of July 26, 1920 (f. 314); Decreto of July 26, 1920 (f. 317); Decreto of July 28, 1920 (f. 324); Decreto of July 28, 1920 (f. 325), Decreto of August 18, 1920 (f. 388), Decreto of August 19, 1920 (f. 390), all in AN/IS, v. 504 (Decretos 1920); Coronel-Prefecto al Intendente de la Provincia, September 9, 1920, AN/IS, v. 502.

89 Telegram from Fernando Edwards to Prefecto de Policía, Santiago, 28 de julio de 1920, AN/IS v. 498; Sub-Prefecto Jefe al Coronel Prefecto, July 30, 1920; Casimiro Barrios, "Desde Lima," 9.

90 Coronel Prefecto to Intendente de la Provincia, 6 de enero de 1921, AN/IS, v. 506.

91 I am indebted to Casimiro Barrios's grandson, Jorge Barrios Pulgar, for the numerous conversations he had with me about his grandfather and his family.

92 For a remarkable account of his exile on the Juan Fernández island of Más Afuera, see Roberto Meza Fuentes, *Los trágicos días de Más Afuera* (Santiago: LOM Ediciones, 2006), originally published as a series of articles in the daily *Las Ultimas Noticias*, from August 1 to September 23, 1931.

end up in La Paz, Bolivia, where he would organize with the Bolivian labor movement under the leadership of the radical tailor and attorney Luis Salvatierra.[93]

At some point in 1930 he attempted to reenter Chile, as he had done at least once before.[94] Barrios's picture had been circulated among the carabineros and police agents for fear that he might try to reenter, particularly given that Barrios had purportedly publicly "declared war without quarter against Ibáñez and all those who keep him in power."[95] He was soon recognized, stopped by two or three carabineros out patrolling the remote border. This time, they wasted no time on passports or transit papers: in the Valley of Azapa they executed Casimiro Barrios.[96]

93 Guillermo Lora, *Historia del movimiento obrero boliviano* (La Paz: Editorial "Los Amigos del Libro," 1967), 63.

94 Marcos Burich Parra, Carabrineros de Chile, Prefectura de Tarapacá, a la Sub-Prefectura de Carabineros 'Arica' Guarnación, September 24, 1930 in Brian Loveman and Elizabeth Lira, *Los Actos de la Dictadura* (Santiago: LOM Ediciones, 2006), 290–91.

95 Ibid., 290.

96 González Vera, *Cuando era muchacho*, 136. His family, including his widow, Rosario Riveros Martínez, were paid reparations by the government in 1931, as part of the political investigations and reparations regarding the Ibañez dictatorship (Lira and Loveman, *Políticas de reparación* [Santiago: LOM Ediciones, 2005], 25). At the time of Barrios's execution, in his hometown of Nieva de Cameros, his father was finishing a term as mayor and his brother Juan was assuming a role on the municipal board. Both would be murdered by Franco's forces in 1936. Aguirre González, "Nieva: El largo verano del '36," *Boletín Informativo de la Asociación Benéfico-Cultural Nieva de Cameros* 2006, no. 22 (2007): 38–42.

THE GHOSTS OF INSURGENCIES PAST: WATERFRONT LABOR, WORKING-CLASS MEMORY, AND THE CONTENTIOUS EMERGENCE OF THE NATIONAL-POPULAR STATE IN ARGENTINA

Geoffroy de Laforcade

Syndicalism typically receives attention in Argentine labor historiography between 1916 and 1921, generally as evidence of Radical Civic Union elected President Hipólito Yrigoyen's unprecedented profession of "neutrality" in conflicts between capital and labor. Anarchism—at least the tradition represented by the historic FORA (Federación Obrera Regional Argentina), at its height the second largest anarchist labor confederation in the world, is assumed to have withered following the repression unleashed in 1910, and to have vanished altogether after the 1930 military coup. As often occurs in narratives of working-class history that analyze organized labor and its platforms—which is not itself an unworthy task—these tentative "snapshots of relevance" tell us little about either syndicalism or anarchism. Their scorekeeping decontextualizes the actual practice of militancy and disembodies, by seldom viewing them as anything but instruments of abstract ideals, the real people who were involved. Like the memories of those individuals and communities, organizations tell stories about the times and places, possibilities and limitations, intentions and contingencies, cathartic transformations and dull routines of their protagonists, as well as adversaries and onlookers. This can be illustrated through the story of longshoremen and mariners—all men, but woven into a community tapestry that included less gender-segregated spaces—and their consistent engagement with anarchism and syndicalism over the course of a half century, leading up to the direct intervention of their unions by the first Peronist administration after World War II. This chapter will frame the story of organized labor movements among port workers in Buenos Aires through the prism of local history in La Boca del Riachuelo, spanning the four decades that followed the disarticulation of the "first" great "anarcho-syndicalist" insurgent wave in Buenos Aires by the Argentine State in 1906–1907.

The setting is the densely populated "*porteño*" neighborhood of La Boca, which had been the cornerstone of Buenos Aires's riverine and transatlantic shipping trade in the age of sail and was the epicenter, in the urban and industrial transition phase of the city's late-nineteenth and early-twentieth-century *Belle Époque* of anarchist (as well as socialist) activism.[1] The story begins, fittingly, with a celebrated community protest movement, the tenement dweller's strike (*huelga de inquilinos*) of August–December 1907, spearheaded by a "Committee of La Boca" headquartered in the building of the revolutionary syndicalist Argentine Naval Workers' League (Liga Obrera Naval Argentina or LONA) where the FORA itself was stationed. Numerous *conventillo* (tenement) dwellers throughout the Riachuelo district joined forty thousand-odd tenants in Buenos Aires in demanding a 30 to 50 percent reduction in monthly rents.[2] The Feminine Anarchist Center (Centro Anarquista Feminino) led by Juana Rouco Buela and Virginia Bolten, both veteran anarchist orators whose harangues were familiar to quayside workers in La Boca, spearheaded the movement in which women played a key role, confronting the police, organizing neighbors, and harboring fugitive strikers. Several of the subsequently deported leaders of this uprising were also activists of anarchist resistance societies. Violently repressed,[3] the movement was followed by a resurgence of the anarchist and syndicalist unions during a victorious mariners' strike over hiring prerogatives and working conditions, emboldening the clandestine and decimated FORA to attempt, unsuccessfully, a nation-wide general strike against the 1902 Residency Law and deportation of immigrant activists.[4] As the decade drew to a close, anarchist activists regrouped during the "red week" of 1909, an uprising against police chief Ramón Falcón that provoked a series of violent incidents in La Boca. Anarchist port workers' unions reemerged as key players in the movement, orchestrating massive public gatherings in the streets and marketplaces of the quayside district. The strike rapidly extended to the suburbs of the capital, to major cities

1 See Graciela Silvestri, *El color del río: Historia cultural del paisaje del Riachuelo* (Quilmes: Editorial de La Universidad Nacional de Quilmes, 2003), 27–82.

2 *La Protesta*, September 28, 1907, and October 2, 4, and 5, 1907.

3 See Juan Suriano, "La huelga de inquilinos de 1907 en Buenos Aires" in Diego Armus, ed., *Sectores populares y vida urbana* Buenos Aires: Consejo Latinoamericano de Ciencias Sociales (CLACSO), 1984.

4 *La Vanguardia*, November 20 and December 11, 1907; *La Razón*, January 14, 1908; *Boletín del DNT* 4 (March 31, 1908): 84–87.

such as Rosario and Bahía Blanca, and to several ports of the littoral, mobilizing some 150,000 workers. It failed to achieve either the liberation of eight hundred prisoners or Falcón's renunciation. The police chief was later executed by Ukrainian anarchist Simon Radowitzky, sending shockwaves through the ruling establishment and provoking another state of siege as well as the militarization of the port, from which hundreds of activists and foreigners were once again deported.[5]

As was often the case during a nationwide mobilization of workers involving local federations in the ports of the littoral, the sailors' unions played a crucial role in the spread of information. In the summer of 1909, when a new general strike on the ships resulted in the unprecedented acceptance by a renegade union leader, Juan Colmeiro, of police mediation and a negotiated settlement, the decade-old assembly-based culture of deliberation promoted by anarchists resulted in a rank-and-file vote of defiance and continued direct action. Traditional practices of community mobilization gave the workers' movement momentum. In the end, the strikers succeeded in renewing their leadership, expelling informants from their ranks, blocking the recruitment of blacklegs, and imposing their terms on the ship owners while circumventing police or State mediation.[6] It was in this context that the LONA was dissolved and a new Maritime Workers' Federation (Federación Obrera Marítima, or FOM) created, with the goal of federating all categories of river and seafaring labor into a single bastion of maritime unionism. It lost the quasi-totality of its leadership to arrest or deportation under a state of siege in 1910. In an effort to preempt the use of anti-immigrant legislation (the "Law of Social Defense") to suppress the FOM, its remaining activists then elected Francisco García, a former railway worker from Santa Fe province with strong libertarian credentials, to coordinate the reorganization drive. Capitalizing on a decade of anarchist insurgencies, local community activism, and sympathy among workers on the ships and their landed allies, the FOM under his leadership would grow into one of the two largest and most powerful Argentine unions (alongside railwaymen) by 1915. This was the context of the birth of large-scale syndicalism, which advocated the coordination of workers' organizations in a single trade in lieu of the

5 Diego Abad de Santillán, "Evocación del Primero de Mayo de 1909" in Agustin Souchy, ed., *Una vida por un ideal: Simon Radowitzky* Mexico: Grupo de Amigos de Simón Radowitzky, 1956; Prefectura General de Puertos, *Copiador interno* no. 11 (1909–1910): May 6, 8, 10, 13, 1909 and November 24, 1909; *La Razón*, November 16, 1909.

6 *La Protesta*, March 4, 9, 15–17, 20–22, 1910; *La Razón*, March 12, 15–17, 19, 21, 1910; Prefectura General de Puertos, *Copiador interno* no. 11 (1909–1910): March 19 and 22, 1910.

solidarity across crafts, localities, and affinity groups that had characterized the loosely federated anarcho-communist FORA since 1905.[7]

Seemingly vindicating the advocates of stronger "class-based" unions was the militarization of the labor process in the port, where contractors and abusive foremen ruled with impunity under the protection of an employer-backed "free labor" militia of armed inspectors while the daily wages of longshoremen, cartmen, and casual day laborers in the warehouses and shipyards dropped to turn-of-the-century levels. The longshoremen's resistance society (Sociedad de Resistencia Obreros del Puerto de la Capital, or SROPC)—until 1907 the most powerful force in anarchist labor activism—itself lowered its guard in the defense of unyielding direct action: it belatedly agreed to government arbitration in 1912, in the midst of a new wave of strikes on the docks and ships. For the first time ever, on the eve of the promulgation of a law of universal male suffrage, National Labor Department (DNT) officials acknowledged that the workers' wage demands were justified given soaring rents and food prices. All but one of the powerful owners' organizations—contracting agencies, export firms, and shipping companies—denounced collusion between the State and anarchist strike leaders and loudly decried DNT mediation. An assembly of several thousand port workers voted in favor of accepting arbitration as a means of forcing the owners to bend under pressure from the government.[8] Thus State intervention in favor of workers' interests against powerful capitalist lobbies was not entirely inconceivable in this era of political conservatism, as most historians of prewar Argentina have assumed. That a heavy-handed State crackdown befell striking railway workers that same year underscores how critical it was for the State to guarantee smooth export operations, and how influential anarchists and their allies remained on the docks. Heeding the advice of an interior minister, Serafín Romero—the same ultrarevolutionary anarcho-communist who had advocated a head-on confrontation with contractors and the State in 1907—now publicly accepted the usefulness of government arbitration, a heretical departure from the precepts of classical anarchist trade unionism. These are too often hailed or refuted by historians (and activists) inclined to hypostasize doctrine to the detriment of contextualizing working-class experience. What really occurred here is that a feared tool of militarized labor control, the "free labor" militia, was

---

7 See Geoffroy de Laforcade, "Federative Futures: Waterways, Resistance Societies, and the Subversion of Nationalism in the Early 20th Century Anarchism of the Rio de la Plata Region" *E.I.A.L. Estudios Interdisciplinarios de América Latina y el Caribe* 22, no. 2 (July–December 2011): 71–96.

8 *La Nación*, December 28–29, 1911 and January 13, 1912; *Boletín del DNT* 19 (December 31, 1912): 872–73 and documents; *Review of the River Plate*, December 22, 1911 and January 26, 1912.

handily defeated. A breach in capitalist solidarity opened by government partiality in favor of the workers had defused the utility of a drawn-out confrontation which, some dissenters still believed, might have resurrected the redemptory appeal of anarchist intransigence.[9]

As open-air anarchist proselytizing resumed in the crowded streets and marketplaces of La Boca, social Catholics resumed their early-century mantle of defense against the "disorder" of working-class radicalism, resurrecting their moribund longshoremen's union with the backing of a major employer's association and vying for the hearts of the poor. They and others succeeded, in a context of economic depression and high unemployment, in preventing the full restoration of anarchist authority on the docks.[10] The anarchist presence would remain significant, however, for decades to come, even as the role of the State was durably altered by public awareness of the endemic misery and social distress which stranded tens of thousands of workers on the shores of the Rio de la Plata. Their resistance societies remained influential both within and without the FOM, whose leader Francisco García was elected secretary of the predominantly syndicalist national labor federation (FORA-IX) by the Ninth Congress in 1915. Dissident resistance societies regrouped to preserve the historic anarchist federation, renamed the "FORA-V" (after the Fifth Congress in 1905, which had adopted anarcho-communism). In October of the following year, Radical Civic Union reformer Hipólito Yrigoyen became the first Argentine president ever to be elected by universal male suffrage. Nationalism, which local labor movements had equated in the past with atavistic nativism and anti-immigrant repression, emerged as new factor in the political equation.

It was not just that naturalizations increased with the onset of voting rights for men; Radical Civic Union reformers also vowed to assert sovereignty over the nation's ports and rivers. The nation's largest shipping company, owned by Dalmatian-born magnate Nicolás Mihánovich, and the German-owned Hamburg-South America line had been blacklisted by Great Britain. A wartime coal embargo befell an Argentine merchant marine already diminished by fleet requisitions, sell-offs, and disloyal competition from foreign-owned railways, and in 1917 Mihánovich surrendered a majority of its shares to British capital.[11] The shared resentment of foreign domination in a critical area of the export industry would

9 Prefectura General de Puertos, *Copiador interno* no. 14 (1911–1912): March 2, 1912.

10 Prefectura General de Puertos, *Copiador interno* no. 14 (1911–1912): February 23 and 29, 2012, and March 4, 1912; *Review of the River Plate*, February 2, 1912; *La Vanguardia*, January 28, 1912.

11 Prefectura General de Puertos, *Memoria annual* (1915–1916), 1–2; Gerencia Asesoria Juridica, *Libro de Actas de la Cia. Argentina de Navegación Nicolás Mihánovich* (1914–1918), no. 1, 46.

soon give syndicalist trade unions leverage, and a modicum of common ground, with the newly elected authorities, pitting them both against much of the shipowning establishment. Predictably, the issue would sharply divide veteran labor organizers in La Boca, causing anarchists in particular to sharpen their differences with surging syndicalist rivals, even when their federalist aims, participatory ideals, work grievances, proclivities for direct action, and places of everyday sociability converged in practice. Social revolution remained the objective of both, and social discipline was still the goal of the new government. While anarchism might have been expected to fold in the years between 1907 and 1912—indeed, mainstream Argentine history assumes that for the most part, it did—in La Boca the movement was braced for renewal. News of social revolutions in Mexico and Russia and a postwar wave of labor insurgencies worldwide would conspire against social peace when exports recovered. The key actors of postwar Argentine labor politics, and of a new era in relations between unions, capital and the State, were in place.

It is well-known that in the years immediately following the war organized syndicalist unions would present an unprecedented challenge to the established order. Less often noticed is that the FOM was rooted in legendary anarchist and revolutionary syndicalist-led upheavals since the turn of the century, and that its headquarters functioned in the heart of La Boca where traditions of solidarity and social activism ran deep. The nearby anarchist longshoremen's resistance society would play a momentous role in postwar labor insurgency as well. High unemployment and diminished influence notwithstanding, its diehard nucleus of veterans had assembled regularly to debate anarchist doctrine, world events, and local grievances, and even organized peace marches of port workers into the center of the city during the war.[12] As always the strong identification of the SROPC with the immigrant heritage of La Boca provided fodder for nationalist enmities. Members of the resistance society itself sometimes framed their weariness of workplace competition and low wages in terms that were unflattering to uprooted migrants from the interior provinces, whose illiteracy or ignorance of European events and revolutionary canons they were not above pointing out.[13] Rivals generally claiming representation of "true" Argentine workers emerged in the modern port facilities of Puerto Madero and across the Riachuelo River in Dock Sud. Still, casual port workers recruited through the anarchist resistance society translated their image as outcasts into a fierce defense of individual sovereignty, direct democracy, and loose institutional ties

12 SROPC, *Actas de reuniones*, 1913–1915, 30–76; *La Vanguardia*, June 28, 1915.
13 SROPC, *Actas de reuniones*, 1913–1915, 18, 38, 50–52, 61.

between craft unions and affinity groups outside of the labor movement. Maritime workers' unions, on the other hand, who were equally committed to their independence from the State, became increasingly receptive to a collectivist ideal of industrial unionism federating all branches and hierarchies of the industry, which they articulated through the doctrine of syndicalism, workers' control, and a language of class. Their rivalry grew in intensity as the respective local and nationwide influences of the two FORAs expanded.

The ideologues of syndicalism developed a theory of direct action and organizational autonomy as the assertion of a revolutionary counterculture within capitalism but outside of its institutions (parliaments, political parties, schools), rooted in the experience of class struggle and workplace solidarity, and in which the emancipatory future was conceived as an ongoing creation of everyday life, collectively embodied in the internal democracy of trade unions. Political neutrality was theorized as a defensive mechanism against the encroachments of bourgeois political culture and tentacular State control, circumscribing the field of direct action and meaningful worker participation to the conflictual arena of workplace relations, where class boundaries drew their ritual and symbolic meaning from the palpable experience of confrontations between labor and capital. The doctrine, which allowed for partial strikes and solidarity pacts as necessary expressions of immediate working-class interests, became structured around the Sorelian myth of proletarian moral regeneration, through the collective assertion of force epitomized in the general strike: a triumphal celebration of higher ethical values and of the salvation of humankind through the ultimate expropriation of the means of production by the producers themselves.[14] Few resistance societies or trade unions before 1915 had fully espoused syndicalism, but it became the dominant force in the Argentine labor movement thereafter and would remain so for the next two decades.

Large shipping concerns typically responded to maritime workers' invocations of craft pride with disdain, sometimes phrasing their denials of the skilled nature of seafaring in terms biased against Italians who had dominated the rivers since the colonial era and were the most influential ethnic community in La Boca. Argentine élites and foreign investors stereotyped their unions as a source of social disorder, and their communities as a refuge of the laboring poor. In response, manifestoes and press statements issued by early anarchist resistance societies among them,

14 See Wayne Thorpe, *"The Workers Themselves": Revolutionary Syndicalism and International Labour* Amsterdam: International Instituut voor Sociale Geschiedenis, 1989; Edgardo Bilsky, "La diffusion de la pensée de Sorel et le syndicalisme révolutionnaire en Argentine," *Estudos* 5 (November 1986): 25–32.

which were almost always bilingual, glorified—as had their mutualist predecessors—the folk traditions and popular rituals of Italo-Argentine seafarers, countering the stigma of "floating peons" with lyrical projections of masculine valor, class unity, and craft respectability.[15] As a growing "traveling population" of provincial Argentine or *criollo* sojourners worked and associated with immigrant mariners on the coastwise fleet, the syndicalist FOM recruited workers from remote outposts of the littoral, socializing them into industrial unionism and developing far-flung networks of patronage and influence that enhanced its national power. It comes as no surprise, then, that when the 1916 electoral campaign kicked in, Radical Civic Union and Socialist Party political forces—both influential in La Boca—sought inroads among the voting men represented by the federation. Radical sympathies ran high among ship captains, machinists, and officers of the smaller lighter fleets who advocated national sovereignty over their industry, whereas maritime cooks and stewards were organized in La Boca by the local Socialist Party section. Pressing for strict political neutrality and assertive direct action against employers were the anarchist remnants still active in the FOM's sailors' section, which was always the most numerous. The challenge, then, for the syndicalist leadership of the union was to federate all of these disparate sensibilities among its rank-and-file, which it did by allowing their representation at the same time that it strictly separated labor advocacy from the political sphere. For example, two leaders of the maritime cooks and stewards, Ramón Suarez and Marcelino Lage, would rise to prominence in the leadership of the FOM first as socialists and later as communists;[16] as would Antonio Morán, an anarchist sailor who became an influential revolutionary syndicalist in the 1920s. Francisco García himself would develop ties to the Radical Civic Union. The syndicalist emphasis on strict autonomy from political parties and the State allowed them to coalesce, more or less consistently, behind a shared adherence to the union's independence, its principles of federalism, assembly-based deliberative decision-making, and class unity. What historians often overlook is that they socialized and organized together, even at times with their anarcho-communist rivals among the cargo handling trades and in the community when major strikes erupted that required coordination and solidarity. The ideological "purity" often invoked in propaganda and intellectual accounts does not easily account for divided loyalties, separate arenas of action (workplace

15 *La Aurora del Marino*, August 1905–December 1906.

16 *Boletín Oficial del Sindicato Union Cocineros, Mozos y Anexos de a Bordo*, January 1, 1922; *Informe del Comité de Propaganda Gremial, Mayo 12, 1914–Agosto 31, 1917* (Buenos Aires: n. ed., 1917).

vs. electoral), tactical compromises, and the shades of grey inherent in class struggle as in everyday life.

Much is often made of the insurgent labor movement's diatribes against the State, yet it was the owners' association that refused to accept State mediation in the conflict with the FOM in 1916. This was because the newly elected Yrigoyen government acknowledged the need for a resolution of the explosive "social question," and framed its offer to mediate in a language attentive to the unions' security, wage, poverty relief, and work-related concerns. Interior Minister Ramón Gómez responded to the capitalists' refusal by appealing to their patriotism, and admonishing them to consider "the common good of society."[17] Thus it was not pro-government connivance, but the State's unprecedented neutrality—motivated by a conjuncture of mild political reformism—that gave union leaders grounds for launching class warfare against the shipping establishment. A spectacular rebirth of direct action and solidarity ensued, this time without mercenary or military intervention to crush the workers, and with a newfound public sympathy, in mainstream media, for their cause.[18]

The theater of labor insurgency in the Riachuelo district, with its riotous transgression of law and order on the ships and in public spaces, mirrored the annual strike movements of the early-twentieth-century anarchist heyday. Traditions of rank-and-file deliberation and community outreach were revived. Canvassing for donations was carried out by a citizens' committee in La Boca; daily assemblies were held in the popular Verdi Theatre; makeshift dining halls sprang up, staffed by maritime cooks and stewards and supplied with foodstuffs from the Garibaldi and Solís markets; wandering strike commissions informed incoming crews and discouraged longshoremen from replacing sailors in stevedoring tasks; local anarchist resistance societies provided assistance in the form of printing materials and fundraising picnics; and grievances voiced by the families of striking men were addressed by the union through a special relief committee.[19] Shipping firms one after another conceded bread-and-butter victories to the union, dividing the business coalition and strengthening the FOM, until the president himself endorsed negotiations to end the economically debilitating movement. On December 23 a massive and tumultuous workers' assembly voted 967 to 461 to do so after winning 90 percent of the union's demands, and the streets of La Boca erupted in celebration

17 José Elias Niklison, "La Federación Obrera Marítima," *Boletín del DNT* 40 (February 1919): 39; *La Prensa*, November 29, 1916.

18 *La Vanguardia*, December 7, 1916; *La Época*, December 8, 13, and 14, 1916; *La Prensa*, December 13 and 14, 1916.

19 *La Prensa*, December 13, 1916; *La Época*, December 15–16 and 17, 1916.

of the most significant labor victory in a decade.[20] The momentum was not just on the side of reformists; legends of anarchist prepotency on the docks were, according to police reports which warned of a major subversive danger, revived in tavern conversation by the outcome of the 1916 strike, and refugees from the war in Europe were alleged to spread talk of revolution in sailors' binges. The perception among local authorities was clearly that insidious foreign manipulation of working-class discontent posed an immediate threat to the national interest.[21]

The ship owners soon coalesced around Mihánovich's decision to retaliate by creating a new "free labor" instrument, the Sociedad Obrera Marítima Protectora del Trabajo Libre (Maritime Workers' Society to Protect Free Labor, or "Protectora"), based minutes away from FOM headquarters in La Boca.[22] Its dissolution instantly became a rallying cry for the FOM and its allies in the larger labor movement. Within weeks a massive FOM boycott of the Mihánovich fleet was triggered, and this time, police and military forces were dispatched to restore order as violent clashes broke out in the streets. When President Yrigoyen ordered the withdrawal of troops from the port and again professed his government's neutrality, the owners denounced a capitulation and issued a lockout order. Several Mihánovich competitors dissented, however, and sought out the union to resume navigation along the Paraná River, which effectively consolidated FOM control over the hiring and work inspection process throughout the ports of the interior.[23] The boycott and lockout also drove a wedge between employers and supervisory officers—ship captains, pilots, machinists, deck-masters, and radio telegraph operators—on board the vessels. Their recently organized unions walked out in March 1917, and for the first time ever the FOM backed their leaders, sealing a powerful federalist cross-class alliance that would soon propel maritime unionism to the fore of the national labor movement. Ship captains would thereafter view the FOM as a trustworthy ally in their battle with administrative tutelage, against the costly mismanagement by outsiders of a labor process in which informal relations and familiarity prevailed.

By April, in another resounding victory for the workers, Mihánovich had capitulated and the Protectora was dissolved. By revealing the government's inability to enforce the agreement signed in January with Yrigoyen's backing, the FOM had demonstrated the ineptitude of legal action by itself

20 Niklison, "La Federación Obrera Marítima," 41; Prefectura General de Puertos, *Copiador de Notas* no. 22, December 28, 1916; *La Vanguardia*, January 4, 1917.

21 Policía de la Capital, *Copiador de Notas* no. 15, sección 24, January 9, 1917.

22 *La Vanguardia*, March 24, 1917; Companía Argentina de Navegación Nicolás Mihánovich Ltda., "Directiva a los oficiales de buques," in Prefectura General de Puertos, *Copiador de Notas* no. 8, April 20, 1917.

23 *La Vanguardia*, April 3 and 6, 1917.

and fulfilled its promise to resort to direct action. It also showed that a strong boycott could shatter the resistance of the State and capitalist interests as effectively as an industry-wide general strike, while facilitating the implementation of work standards and union hiring prerogatives on ships still in activity. Moreover, all of this could be achieved in conjunction with the sworn enemies of a not-so-distant past, ship captains and officers, who had grown increasingly weary of open-shop drives. This, much more than doctrinal wavering and political opportunism, helps explain why the meteoric ascendancy of the revolutionary syndicalist FOM was accompanied by a more tactical approach to strikes, and well as a seemingly paradoxical "institutionalization" of workplace cooperation between mariners and the highest authorities on board. The informal and decentralized structure of work in the expanding merchant marine, combined with the mutual interest of managers and workers in an efficient and consensual chain of command, led workers' and officers' organizations to assert a degree of control over their industry and everyday affairs that was unimaginable in a factory setting.[24] The syndicalist FORA-IX praised the outcome as a textbook triumph of solidarity in which differences in hierarchy, skill, and category of employment were undermined by a mutual recognition of the preeminence of "class struggle."[25] Throughout the river and sea ports of the coastline, traveling crew members, delegates, and inspectors became the symbols of the FOM's tentacular presence in the most remote areas of the country. Effective trade-union solidarity became a realizable endeavor which the revolutionary syndicalist leadership used to hold Argentina's shipping firms to collective agreements, raising expectations among the broader working-class that their success could be emulated.

Against the backdrop of a 450 percent rise in the number of striking workers in Buenos Aires in 1917, the FORA-IX grew ten times in size (with 530 member unions) by 1920; during the same period membership in the anarchist FORA-V burgeoned from twenty-one craft-based societies to well over two hundred.[26] The FOM and SROPC figured prominently in the leadership of both federations and continued to assert the locational strength which had made the early organizational achievements of the anarchist heyday possible. The radicalism of these movements is evident in their practice of solidarity, both local and transnational. Mariners' assemblies in 1917 decried the plight of the largely foreign-born work

24 Prefectura General de Puertos, *Copiador de Notas* no. 9, April 28, 1918; *La Organización Obrera* May 13, 1918.

25 Niklison, "La Federación Obrera Marítima," 72–74.

26 José Elias Niklison, "La Federación Obrera Regional Argentina," *Boletín del DNT* 41 (April 1919): 37; Policía Federal, Sección Orden Social, *Memoria de investigaciones, 1918* (Buenos Aires: n. ed., 1919).

force in the tightly controlled industrial setting of meatpacking plants in Berisso and Avellaneda, where "husbands, wives and even children work like slaves slaughtering and processing beasts in an atmosphere of darkness and putrefaction."[27] The FOM held back crews for the tugboats which towed foreign ships to the plant wharves to load frozen meat, and its members refrained from contracting work aboard the foreign ships themselves, boycotting all local vessels that did business with the plants. Concerted solidarity was extended to a major conflict of industrial workers for the first time in the history of Argentine mariners' unionism.[28] Later that year, by declaring a national general solidarity strike to strengthen the impact of a major railway workers' movement against foreign-owned companies, the FOM caused a quasi-total paralyzation of transport activities throughout the country.[29] The following year in the remote province of Misiones, the FOM supported rural plantation workers in their struggle against in the age-old system of tyrannical debt peonage that held them virtually prisoners of their contractors.[30] By suspending all traffic of Argentine ships to Montevideo the FOM also assured the success of a general strike in neighboring Uruguay.[31] In 1919, when an Armour packinghouse-subsidiary in Asunción, Paraguay, switched flags and requested Argentine navy conscripts to man its vessels in Barranqueras, its British management caved to a FOM boycott and agreed to pay the mariners' full back wages, plus their trip back to Buenos Aires and all costs incurred by the inconvenience.[32]

Further evidence of the radicalism of the syndicalist FOM was its repeated rehearsals of public solidarity and resistance to capitalist counteroffensives, on the stage of the local community in La Boca. For example, during a lockout decreed by ship owners in early 1919 to achieve free trade, free labor, and free transit, the prohibition of boycotts, and the abolition of union control, the federation and its allies threw their weight behind campaigns to provide idle seamen with emergency housing and once again sustained an *olla popular*, or public cafeteria staffed by volunteers of the maritime cooks' and stewards' union. It fed an average of 1,700 strikers daily and rationed food supplies for seamen's families according to need. The syndicalist press elevated such solidarity to the rank of "experiment in working-class empowerment," describing the self-managed cafeteria as

27 *La Organización Obrera*, December 15, 1917; "Lucha de los obreros de la carne," pamphlet edited by the FOM, 1917.
28 *La Organización Obrera*, February 22 and 23, 1918.
29 Niklison, "La Federación Obrera Regional Argentina," 47–53.
30 Cf. Rafael Barrett, "Lo que son los yerbales," in *Obras completas* (Montevideo: Ediciones Populares para América Latina, 1988), 115–26.
31 Prefectura General de Puertos, *Copiador de Notas* no. 13, September 1, 1918.
32 *La Unión del Marino*, August 1919.

a lesson in the "rights and duties of the struggle for free and unsubjugated labor."[33] Friendly allies such as the barbers and flour millmen donated free haircuts and their workers' pay on the site, local grocers donated food, and free cultural activities were staged; executives of the popular *Boca Juniors* soccer stadium even lent their stadium for massive workers' assemblies.[34] These and other examples of the mobilization of *boquense* society in favor of solidarity with idle port workers gave substance to revolutionary syndicalist claims that a social awakening could only result from the emancipatory breakthroughs of sustained class struggle. The insurgency could not be portrayed as the work of isolated foreign subversives bent on dissolving the fabric of Argentine society.

The good fortunes of the FOM stood in sharp contrast to the renewed mass arrests and deportations which befell organized labor general in 1919 in the wake of the "Tragic Week." The longshoremen's resistance society, which had spearheaded the revival of the anarchist FORA-V from its headquarters in La Boca, had to contend with autonomous rivals in other sections of the port, which invoked "revolutionary trade-union struggle" in formalizing a solidarity pact with the powerful maritime workers' federation to strengthen their hand against blackleg agencies.[35] Animosity toward their powerful syndicalist competitors ran high, and turf wars often escalated into violence.[36] When it came to workplace activism, however, the tacit solidarity pacts of the past tended to revive cooperation between different sectors of dockside labor, in spite of the ideological and organizational quarrels which plagued their unions. Shared community ties and common strategic objectives at the level of everyday class conflict, rather than the simple fact of doctrinal compromise, explain why in mid-November of 1920 the two most antagonistic branches of longshoremen's unionism formed a Pro-Unification Committee during a massive anarchist assembly in La Boca. In defiance of directives by the leadership of the FORA-V, the resistance society voted to join a single autonomous union that dropped its "resistance society" denomination, but preserved such anarchist trademarks as the refusal of compulsory arbitration, the defense of informality in the formation and placement of work gangs, and the commitment to strikes and boycotts. Accordingly, its appearance was viewed by the authorities as a major threat to the stability of labor relations in the port.[37] Once again, ideological "purity" and institutional

33 *La Organización Obrera*, February 15 and March 1, 1919.
34 *La Organización Obrera*, March 1 and 8, 1919.
35 *La Unión del Marino*, August 1919.
36 Policía de la Capital, sección 24, *Copiador* no. 216, March 3 and 5, 1920.
37 *La Vanguardia*, December 15, 1920; Prefectura General de Puertos, *Copiador de Notas* no. 3, January 12, 1921.

alignment with one of the larger FORAs fails to account for the complexities of real workers' responses to the circumstances of workplace struggle and community solidarity. The British *Review of the River Plate* and the conservative National Labor Association (Asociación Nacional del Trabajo, or ANT) gave voice to capitalists' assessment of the threat posed by these developments: both described the new longshoremen's alliance as nothing less than a "soviet."[38]

In April 1921, after the victory of an epic thirteen-month nationwide maritime workers' strike against the Mihánovich line which the unified longshoremen had supported, the SROPC and its allies affirmed their continued adherence to anarchism, notwithstanding their independence from the FORA-V. Their joint leadership ordered that all cartmen working in the port would have to be affiliated with the resistance society that housed the anarchist federation in the nearby neighborhood of Barracas, the *Sociedad de resistencia conductores de carros*. Cartmen who resisted their incorporation into an organization that symbolized the anarcho-communist insurgencies of the prewar period would now be faced with the systematic boycott of their vehicles by other workers on the docks. Since the syndicalist federation had resolved to promote cooperation between the two rival FORAs, the longshoremen were able to enlist tens of thousands of workers from the unions of maritime, shipyard, and flour mill workers, railway men, crane operators, and others in its support of their goals. This full-scale assertion of working-class control over the ports of the nation finally caused the Yrigoyen government to weigh in decisively on the side of the conservative ANT, the militaristic Argentine Patriotic League, and ship owners' lobbies in both the riverine and ocean liner sectors by ordering a full two-week shutdown of the port of Buenos Aires and sending in troops. Anarchist and syndicalist resiliency was again tested, this time by mass arrests and detentions of workers, Patriotic League assaults, and the forcing of union leaderships into clandestinity. The FOM's network of riverside organization facilitated the rapid paralyzation of port cities nationwide. Even organized agricultural workers in the northern provinces rallied the movement. Several captains of foreign steamers in the port of Buenos Aires refused to hire blacklegs for fear of reprisals from their labor organizations back home. The Customs Authority was effectively transformed into a direct contracting agency for the ANT. Police squads entered cafés, delis, and gambling halls in search of strikers, and established strict vigilance of streets and union halls in La Boca.[39]

38 *The Review of the River Plate*, January 28, 1921; *La Concordia*, May 5, 1921.

39 *La Organización Obrera*, June 1, 4, and 18, 1921; *La Vanguardia*, May 31 and June 1, 1921; *La Organización Obrera*, June 18, 1921.

In this context of widespread violence, terror, and economic emergency, García's hard-earned alliance of the FOM with officers' unions began to erode over the continued grass-roots cooperation of syndicalists and radicalized anarchist resistance societies.[40] In June, with the joint strike committee of the two FORAs dissolved and State-sponsored repression at its height, the leaderships of the unified longshoremen's unions met in a tenement in La Boca and resolved that anarchist directives to continue the movement were futile; shortly after conceding defeat, the committee—and the syndicalist/anarchist alliance—were effectively dissolved.[41] Although the first Yrigoyen administration would be remembered by later generations of labor activists in Buenos Aires as the first Argentine regime ever to open the floodgates of social reform, the collapse of anarchist resistance societies and syndicalist trade unions in 1921 ushered in an era of repression unseen since 1910. Only months after asserting its unprecedented omnipotence the Argentine labor movement was decimated by force. Sealing its fate was the bloodiest military crackdown in the history of the first half of the century, after a revolt of Argentine and Chilean agricultural laborers in distant Patagonia.[42] Yet while traditional accounts of the history of organized labor in Argentina correctly point to 1921 as the year that began the postwar labor movement's demise, neglect of its sequel is, in view of subsequent developments in the port of Buenos Aires, highly misleading. The close study of the 1920s is key to understanding the configuration of waterfront unionism on the eve of the Second World War, and provides a necessary caveat to the widely held notion that the working-class traditions upon which the "national-popular" paradigm of Peronism (and anti-Peronism) would later build emerged in an historical vacuum. "The ghosts of insurgencies past" haunted the next quarter century in ways that are seldom understood, and belie, once they are recognized, the notion that workers simply folded and moved on to more "modern" forms of labor organization. In fact, anarchist and syndicalist organizational forms, tactics, and cultures of solidarity, which were incubated in the first two decades of the century, were still present among longshoremen, maritime workers, and their local allies in the 1940s, as were many of the protagonists whose stories are chronicled here.

In a situation of scarce job opportunities and displacement by the ANT, Germán Malvido's Diques y Dársenas union accepted an invitation

40 *La Vanguardia*, June 4 and 6, 1921.

41 *La Vanguardia*, June 7 and 12, 1921.

42 See Osvaldo Bayer, *La Patagonia Rebelde* (Buenos Aires: Hyspamérica, 1980); Susana Fiorito, *Las Huelgas de Santa Cruz (1921–1922)* (Buenos Aires: Centro Editor de América Latina, 1985); Sandra McGee Deutsch, *Counterrevolution in Argentina, 1900–1932. The Argentine Patriotic League* (Lincoln: University of Nebraska Press, 1986); *La Organización Obrera*, April 2, 1921.

by José "Pepe" Damonte, a respected agitator in his fifties who would enshrine anarchist activism in La Boca for the next quarter century, to attend a large workers' assembly in the historic Verdi Theatre in early 1922. One month earlier, under Damonte's leadership, the anarchist longshoremen's union had reclaimed its resistance society denomination and formed an emergency committee for the purpose of reunifying all sections of dock labor under a single banner. A motion was approved by 453 votes to 4 to form a new Unified Port Workers' Union made up of five-member commissions representing four geographic zones, and which were to meet on a weekly basis in presence of a central commission dominated by the anarchist resistance society.[43] The resolution is important in that it reflects a resurgence of anarchist activity and underscores the prestige still enjoyed by historic activists of the resistance society. Its materialization, however, would remain elusive for years to come. The inability of the union to fully enforce respect of working conditions, and the impunity with which ANT inspectors enforced discriminatory labor policies, limited the effectiveness of organizational drives that had historically rested on the tangible effectiveness of direct action.[44]

In reality, anarchist labor organizers in La Boca had seldom been truly effective without the relay of maritime workers. The once-overpowering FOM had lost its alliance with the railway men's federation in 1920 and relied on the Federation of Shipyard Workers (Federación Obrera de Construcciones Navales, or FOCN) to reconstruct, after 1921, its authority within the larger syndicalist movement. It held a Unification Congress in La Boca in March of 1923 in which a combative revolutionary syndicalist orientation triumphed and ideological competitors were sidelined, culminating in the formation of the revolutionary syndicalist Union Sindical Argentina, or USA. Waterfront unions were prominent among founders of new labor federation; they collectively instilled the USA with a strong revolutionary orientation. Shipyard brazier Atilio Biondi, for example, was a member of the recently formed Argentine Libertarian Alliance (Alianza Libertaria Argentina, or ALA), an "anarcho-bolshevik" movement supportive of the Russian Revolution. Within the FOM, the ALA was active in the historically anarchist-influenced sailors' and firemen's sections. It would exert tangible influence in mariners' assemblies from 1924 onward, accompanying the ascendency to leadership rank of one of its most well-remembered activists, sailor Juan Antonio Morán. A small group of like-minded longshoremen formed the Anarcho-Communist Group of Port

43 *Boletín de Servicios de la ANT*, March 5, 1922; Policía de la Capital, sección 24, *Copiador de Notas* no. 233, February 24, 1922.

44 *Boletín de Servicios de la ANT*, June 20 and November 5, 1922; *La Vanguardia*, April 2, 1923.

Workers. The most visible impact of these groups in the port was the resurgence of the economic sabotage practiced by early resistance societies, particularly in the shipyard braziers' union, where the use of direct action tactics never wavered throughout the first half of the century.[45]

Another key development was the emergence of Gerónimo Schizzi, a raucous young man in his early twenties and a dedicated adversary of anarchist activism in the port, who two decades later would carry his union into the Peronist alliance. Schizzi secured the backing of reinvigorated syndicalist waterfront unions, strongly established in the social fabric of the quayside community, to marginalize Pepe Damonte and the SROPC.[46] In 1927 the FORA-V responded by reactivating the *gremios pactantes*, or "bonded unions," a system which had allowed the resistance societies to coordinate both work placement and solidarity strikes prior to 1921. The cartmen's, truckers', warehouse and Central Produce Market workers', crane operators', and carpenters' unions, all of varying ideological stripes, coordinated their efforts with the SROPC to rebuild the labor movement in the areas of the port it controlled, under the auspices of an anarchist leadership that still enjoyed widespread popularity in the community of La Boca. The results were encouraging. After six years of scarce activity and within six months of beginning its reorganization drive, the longshoremen's resistance society claimed two thousand affiliates. Its professed goal was to reunite the port workers of Buenos Aires under the banner of strict apoliticism and class solidarity, to dislodge the ANT, and to harass private contractors with frequent twenty-four-hour strikes.[47]

When the SROPC mobilized thousands of workers against a new law requiring longshoremen to carry an identification card while in the port, a measure designed to help contractors identify "disorderly" workers, it demanded that foremen be given full sovereignty in shape-ups and all representatives of State-sponsored "authority" be chased from the docks. Even the vehemently anti-anarchist Diques y Dársenas union participated in the quasi-total paralyzation of the entire Buenos Aires waterfront, from Barracas to Retiro, and thus a national crisis of commerce.[48] The momentum of this resurgence might have been sustained by the expulsion of the ANT and Patriotic League from the port (decreed in October 1929 by Yrigoyen's second administration), had the anarchist SROPC not

45 *La Antorcha*, February 1 and May 6, 1924; September 25 and October 16, 1925.

46 *La Vanguardia*, August 17, 1923, January 19, 1924; Policía de la Capital, sección 24, *Copiador de Notas* no. 270, May 3, 1923.

47 *La Protesta*, April 14, May 20, June 18, September 13, October 5, 25, and 26, 1927; *El Látigo del Carrero*, April 1928; *El Obrero Portuario*, September 15, 1927; *La Vanguardia*, October 25, 1927; AN, *Memoria y Balance, 1926–1927* (Buenos Aires: n.p., 1927).

48 *La Protesta*, November 29, December 21, 29, and 31, 1927, and January 21, 1928; Prefectura General Marítima, *Memoria 1927*, 60.

been mired in conflict with the syndicalist USA and ultraconservative nationalist political forces intent on locking anarchists and foreigners out of employment. Diques y Dársenas had roots in the mobilization of nativist themes against the alleged "foreign" agitators of the anarchist FORA-V based in cosmopolitan La Boca. During the 1920s the union had been through a unification process with the SROPC, a ruthless open-shop drive by the ANT and Patriotic League, and a period of reorganization by the syndicalist USA. Now and for years to come, the leaders of Diques y Dársenas would confront atavistic nativism with progressive-sounding nationalism, accusing foreign capital and foreign anarchists of plotting together to prevent the emergence of a strong industry-wide longshoremen's union. As for the resistance society, fully reorganized and ready for battle, it confidently set out to reconquer turf lost to blacklegs and fascists in the 1920s, undeterred by what it perceived as a recipe for working-class defeat: the shift of syndicalist discourse from revolution to nationalism.[49]

The result was a fierce outbreak of violence between the rival syndicalist and anarchist unions, neither of which acknowledged the other's zones of influence and control. Violence broke out on an almost daily basis as workers increasingly armed themselves in self-defense. Between January and September of 1930, the authorities recorded two dozen instances of armed confrontations between members of the two unions. The government responded by reinforcing Prefecture patrols and posting a navy regiment at the entrance of the southern pier linking La Boca to the modern port.[50] Syndicalists alleged that foreign shipping companies were conspiring to help the anarchists undermine their efforts to improve the workers' welfare; the *gremios pactantes* feared that the promotion of gun violence in lieu of working-class solidarity was certain to provoke the militarization of the port.[51] They were right. As the 1930 military coup approached, it appeared that three decades of anarchist activism on the docks and in La Boca, and fifteen years of ebbs and tides in their relationship with syndicalist rivals, were coming to an ominous and undignified end. Yet both leaders at the time of the SPROPC and Diques y Dársenas, Pepe Damonte and Gerónimo Schizzi, would remain the locally respected standard-bearers of their respective working-class traditions, at the helm of still-vigorous anarchist and syndicalist organizations, well into the

49 *La Protesta*, October 16 and December 29, 1929; *La Vanguardia*, February 19, 1930; *Diques y Dársenas*, July 1, 1930.

50 *La Protesta*, November 27; December 7 and October 27, 1929; *La Vanguardia*, January 5, 10, 11, 13, 17, 1930; April 8 and 11, 1930; Prefectura General Marítima, *Memoria 1929* & *Memoria 1930;* Policía de la Capital, *Copiador de Notas* no. 290, sección 24, (1930): 364–66.

51 *La Vanguardia*, April 6 and 29, May 10 and 14, 1930; *El Obrero Portuario*, June 1, 1930.

1940s when the bureaucratic and modernizing State finally lowered the coffin, by force, on the history and ideals they carried.

The military coup of General Félix Uriburu in September 1930 ushered in what both nationalists and revolutionaries in the labor movement would later call an "infamous decade." Infamy, however, had not been absent from the era of Radical Civic Union rule; and the threads of solidarity and resistance—as well as the fracturing impact of nativism and nationalism—that were woven over three decades did not suddenly unravel. During the nine-month state of martial law that followed the coup, rural migrants flooded the market for casual labor on the waterfront. The conflict between the SROPC and Diques y Dársenas had escalated into more than just than a turf war between anarchist and syndicalist rivals: it crystallized into a struggle over the bearings of civic and class identities forged over three decades of labor organization in the tightly knit community of quayside workers. Nationalists stigmatized the "foreignness" of contractors and ship owners who employed SROPC-affiliated workers in cosmopolitan La Boca, and the opposition of European-owned ocean liner companies to progressive labor legislation fueled rumors of their connivance with anarchists.[52] In fact it was the push of Schizzi's organization for "absolute control" over the port outside of the Riachuelo district, its advocacy of nonpartisan, moderate trade unionism, and its efforts to recruit among the pool of recently arrived rural migrants that determined its mobilization of nativist themes, rather than a clear line of ethnic demarcation between workers. Whereas the 50 percent preference for Argentine-born workers decreed by the military authorities was denounced as "fascist" by the SROPC, Diques y Dársenas hailed it as a just response to the unemployment crisis. Further contributing to the portrayal of anarchists as "foreigners" was the radicalization of underground SROPC activists, in particular their alleged use of economic sabotage (burning warehouses, destroying cargo, and slowing down the pace of work), which drew accusations of anti-patriotic subversion from the Prefecture.[53] The theme of nationalism thus provided the leadership of Diques y Dársenas with a convenient lever against both the anarchist resistance society and the foreign agro-export interests behind the 1920s-era union-breaking efforts of the State. But nationalism used ethnicity as a foil; although the rhetoric of Diques y Dársenas targeted the "foreign" anarchists of the SROPC leadership, ethnic heterogeneity characterized the membership of both unions. The two foremost leaders of the resistance society, Pepe Damonte and Florentino Carballo, both held Argentine

52 *Diques y Dársenas*, June 1 and August 1, 1931, January 1, 1932.

53 *Diques y Dársenas*, December 1, 1931; SROPC, *Libro de Actas 1933–1939*, 30; Prefectura General Marítima, *Copiador Especial. Seguridad y Accidentes, 1930–1934*, 13.

citizenship; only six of the eleven remaining members of the clandestine leadership fell under the threat of deportation under the terms of the Residency Law—a recently immigrated Yugoslav, two Italians, a Spaniard, a Bulgarian, and an Uruguayan. And while Gerónimo Schizzi was born in Argentina, eleven of the twenty-one Diques y Dársenas affiliates arrested between August 1931 and November 1932 were foreigners from Spain, Italy, the Levant, and the Philippines.[54]

After the lifting of the state of siege and the election of Agustín Justo, both dockworkers' unions were authorized to resume their activities openly. In 1933 Diques y Dársenas joined the new National Labor Confederation (Confederación General del Trabajo, or CGT), the result of a merger after the coup between the socialist Confraternidad Obrera Argentina (COA) and syndicalist USA. The CGT continued the syndicalist tradition of forbidding its members to hold public office. It distinguished itself from its revolutionary syndicalist predecessor, however, by a commitment to reformism and legislative lobbying by means of direct participation in State institutions. In reaction to the 1933 Roca-Runciman treaty conceding advantageous terms of trade to Great Britain, and in response to the beginnings of import-substitution industrialization, organized labor began to voice nationalist concerns which coincided neatly with those of Schizzi's longshoremen's union. Diques y Dársenas did not overtly discriminate between nationalities in its drive to unionize workers in Puerto Madero. Instead, it directed its nationalist vindications against the powerful foreign ocean liner shipping lobby and against the association of contractors with export interests or anarchist resistance societies. The strategic backing of the FOM allowed the union to forge its own alliances, at the workplace level, with foremen and employers' interests in the port, and to build bridges with other waterfront unions in along the littoral. Membership in the CGT also placed it at an advantage in the drive for protective legislation, and provided its leaders with legitimacy in broader movement of organized labor.

Further complicating this story is that as had been the case since the early 1900s, ideological rivalries and rhetorical loathing were not an absolute barrier against dialogue and tactical unity in the interests of the labor movement's survival. When on the first day of August 1933, Civic Legion groups formed a welcome committee for German embassy personnel scheduled to arrive on board the ship *Monte Oliva*, Schizzi's union participated in the anti-fascist demonstration staged by the anarchist's local federation in Buenos Aires. Ensuing riots resulted in numerous arrests of

54 Policía de la Capital, División de Investigaciones, sección 24, *Copiador de Notas* no. 290, 306, 314, and 321, February 6, 1930, August 28, 1931, June 10, 1932, May 2, 1933; sección 22, *Copiador de Notas* no. 302, 304, and 314, June 10, August 16, and November 29, 1932.

workers from both organizations.[55] That month the FOM invited both the SROPC and Diques y Dársenas to its congress in La Boca, where traditional assembly-based deliberations of the rank and file continued to air familiar syndicalist and anarchist themes. Schizzi enthusiastically backed the seamen's and railwaymen's project to create a "national transport and cargohandling federation." SROPC delegate Pepe Damonte defended a loose, less vertical form of coordination which would respect the sovereignty of local assemblies and allow the FORA to flourish.[56] Although Damonte and Schizzi would accuse each other mutually, during the next two decades, of furthering the goals of capitalism in the port, both unions represented the interests and ideals of groups of experienced longshoremen, or, at the very least drew their membership from the influence they enjoyed with foremen and contracting firms in the local community. From 1934 onward each union settled into a segmented labor market, and gradually shed its inclination for violent reprisals against the other. Both continued to denounce gangsterism, Prefecture patrols, and fascist Civic Legion paramilitary troops. Both also resisted the infiltration of Communist Party cells which, from 1932 onward, lobbied for their unification by distributing flyers throughout the port and speaking out during assemblies.[57]

The experiences of maritime workers organized by the FOM in the 1920s also prefigured developments that would shape the contours of labor organization in La Boca and its environs through the 1940s. New forces in the maritime transportation industry generated realignments within Argentine syndicalism that would draw workers with a strong tradition of trade-union independence and direct action first into the Laborist alliance that handed Juan Perón power, then into the defense, against the national-popular State, of a half century of working-class radicalism in the community of La Boca and the country's ports. Paralleling the longshoremen's saga, organizations were drawn into rhetorical standoffs regarding how best to defend their constituents' lot—through nationalism or cosmopolitanism, via government and legislative intervention or the principled defense of autonomy and worker control; in the end anarchist forebodings were vindicated, as the suspension of trade union independence and democratic traditions accompanied the nationalization and bureaucratization of their industry and labor process. Here too historical perspective is warranted, for the offensive against revolutionary syndicalism and the FOM's powerful allure among workers began under Yrigoyen, not Perón,

55 *La Vanguardia*, August 1 and 3, 1933; Policía de la Capital, sección 22, *Copiador de Notas* no. 190, August 8, 1933.

56 *La Vanguardia*, August 25, 1933; SROPC, *Libro de Actas 1933–1939*, 57.

57 *La Vanguardia*, July 2, 1933; March 8, July 21 and 30, 1934.

and gained momentum under the Radical Civic Union administration of Marcelo de Alvear (1924–1928), which abandoned all pretense of State neutrality in conflicts opposing maritime workers to shipping capital and the ANT.

The popular García, whose resignation in the wake of the 1921 defeat had been refused by a clamorous assembly vote, had come to lose faith in the durable efficiency of federalist trade union organization. When in 1924 the union of captains on ocean liners, the Centro de Capitanes de Ultramar, broke with the FOM and established its own government-sponsored recruiting agency, his legacy of unifying all categories of seafaring labor was shattered.[58] The background to this crisis was the passing in parliament, in November 1923, of a controversial retirement pension law for workers. The law stipulated that 5 percent of each worker's earnings and 8 percent of the total wages paid by employers would be withheld for pension funds. In retrospect, it was the first broad-ranging attempt by an Argentine government to establish a national welfare system. The influential shipping and export interests behind the ANT feared that the inevitable decasualization of seafaring trades would inhibit the association's open-shop drive and increase the authority of unions among workers.[59] On this occasion, the owners found an inconspicuous ally in the FOM, which considered the law to be simply inapplicable in the context of the merchant marine. Lorenzo Gasparini, addressing the Chamber of Deputies on behalf of the union, explained that any pension law requiring thirty years of service in the profession would necessarily penalize mariners and seamen forced to undergo prolonged periods of unemployment. No fireman, he argued, could survive more than fifteen years of service in the engines; fatigue, tuberculosis, and rheumatisms among sailors, cooks, and other categories inevitably shortened these men's careers.[60]

The vast majority of labor unions belonging to the anarchist FORA and syndicalist USA contested the imposition of the State-sponsored measure, and flatly rejected the principle of withholding sums from workers' wages. Within the USA, a long-standing syndicalist conception held that a system of retirement pension funds should be directly administered by the unions, rather than by the State.[61] The Union's founders were eager to assert their revolutionary credentials—a mixture of direct-action anarchist tactics and revolutionary syndicalist principles anchoring emancipatory working-class consciousness in the everyday defense of organizational independence and labor market control. The leadership of the

58 Prefectura General Marítima, *Memoria 1924*, 22–25

59 *La Vanguardia*, May 11, 1924; *Boletín de Servicios de la ANT*, March 5, 1924.

60 *La Unión del Marino*, February 1924.

61 *Bandera Proletaria*, January 19, 1924; *La Acción Socialista*, June 16, 1906.

FOM cautioned against resorting to a general strike on the grounds that certain officers' had manifested their staunch advocacy of the reform.[62] Their reluctance did not deter the rank and file, however, and in assembly debates which evidenced the revolutionary syndicalist adherence to direct democracy, member unions overwhelmingly favored a show of force. On May 3 the USA and anarchist FORA-V declared a nationwide general strike to demand the law's abrogation. Two days later, much to the embarrassment of labor organizers, the ANT, a loathed symbol of oligarchical arrogance, locked out industrial and commercial establishments in Buenos Aires "in sympathy" with the strike's objectives. The government invoked nationalism and pro-welfare principles in exploiting the paradox. All remaining doubts were lifted on its intentions: no longer would trade unions be allowed to paralyze the export economy in pursuit of their goals.[63]

At the initiative of its director Alberto Dodero, the Mihánovich line opened a labor exchange in its offices and called upon idle workers to sever their ties with both the officers' unions and the FOM, in order to avoid deskilling on a massive scale. From 1924 onward Dodero, the only prominent owner to support the retirement pension law, would implement a policy of company paternalism designed to stabilize a sizeable contingent of the work force on his ships, and take advantage of the deregulation of FOM control over job placement to roll back union gains. All of this was accompanied by a nationalist discourse of benevolence toward workers that appealed to their patriotism against disloyal foreign interests and so-called "anti-national" agitators whose ideologies were perceived as colluding with anti-government export firms. Even through Alvear postponed the law's implementation, the FOM was now faced with a charm offensive by the employer of two-thirds of the nation's maritime workers and owner of virtually all of its coastwise fleet. Just as the SROPC had encountered a true rival in the Diques y Dársenas union, the federation found itself enmeshed in a turf war for workers' allegiances with a formidable foe. During a massive two-month general strike in August 1924, reminiscent of past labor insurgencies throughout the nation's ports and which mobilized even the solidarity of anarchist resistance societies, the maritime workers faced accusations of treason ("*vendepatrias*" or traitors to the nation) for soliciting the support of the International Transport Workers' Federation. When it was defeated the entire Federal Council of the FOM resigned under criticism from the rank and file.[64]

62 *Bandera Proletaria*, January 26, 1924.

63 *Bandera Proletaria*, May 11, 1924; Sebastián Marotta, *El movimiento sindical argentino: su génesis y desarrollo, t.III, 1920–1935* (Buenos Aires: Editorial Calomino, 1970), 153–66.

64 Prefectura General Marítima, *Memoria 1924*, 35–50.

For the first time in a quarter century, sections of the maritime workers' federation in Buenos Aires and the river ports operated without a coordinating body. They were unprepared, however, to forsake two decades of proven strength and bargaining power in the labor process. Given the prevailing atmosphere of counterrevolution and intimidation no attempt to resurrect the legitimacy and effectiveness of workplace cooperation seemed likely to succeed without experienced leadership. As García sought to rebuild the alliance with officers through an informal "Council of Relations," he solicited the backing of the Socialist Maritime Workers' Group (Agrupación Socialista Marítima). Led by Yugoslav immigrant Welko Denda, the group had waged an internal battle against the revolutionary syndicalist, "apolitical," and federalist orientation of the FOM during and after the 1923 congress, relayed by the socialist electoral machine in La Boca.[65] Juan Antonio Morán, a revolutionary from the ranks of anarcho-bolshevism who acted as interim secretary of the FOM, mobilized the sailors' and firemen's sections against García's centralizing plans. The Alvear government, for its part, promoted legislation that would allow maritime prefect Hermelo to preside over a joint committee of workers and ship owners, with subaltern workers reorganized under the authority of officers' unions. According to this scheme, designed to institutionalize peaceful collective bargaining under the auspices of the government, work-related conflicts would be resolved by an arbitration tribunal charged with enforcing a new labor code for the merchant marine, which legally curbed the workers' right to strike. In pursuit of its plans to form a company union, the Mihánovich line supported the plan.[66] In alliance with the Officers' Circle (Círculo Naval), a club created by the paternalist-minded Dodero, in 1924 the socialists established a new Union of Maritime Workers (Unión Obrera Marítima, or UOM).[67] It rapidly earned the derogatory label by which workers designated the ANT: *la patronal* (the bosses' union). Before long its centralized organizational scheme, which thwarted the assembly-based deliberative tradition of both officers and mariners' unions, came under fire. It undermined informal arrangements which had hitherto ensured the practical and consensual enforcement of rules, regulations, and standards on board the ships—one of the dull, everyday consequences of syndicalist power that is critical but usually overlooked by enthusiasts of revolutionary movements.

In 1927 García brought the recently created Federation of Officers' Unions to the table of a new provisional leadership body which, this time,

65 *La Vanguardia*, January 10, 1925; *Bandera Proletaria*, March 21, 1925; *La Unión del Marino*, November 1925.

66 *La Internacional*, September 24, 1925; Prefectura General Marítima, *Memoria 1925*, 69–71.

67 *La Vanguardia*, August 9, 1925.

coalesced the FOM and the officers' union against the policies of the State and capital. On November 23, nearly three thousand mariners and seamen packed an assembly in the Verdi Theatre in La Boca, the scene of countless historical landmarks in local labor history, during which in the presence of USA secretary Pascual Plescia, revolutionary syndicalist Antonio Morán, the officers' leader José Segade, and García himself renewed with syndicalist federalism and sealed a formal solidarity pact. The FOM was reorganized and reactivated its interior branches.[68] This renewal of a movement which many had thought defeated three years earlier embarrassed the Alvear administration, and began, it should be noted, well before Hipólito Yrigoyen, remembered as the "benefactor" of the FOM for his defense of government neutrality, recaptured the reins of power. During 1927 and 1928, the picture of the quayside community provided by contemporary accounts is one of relative openness and political pluralism, an environment in which the FOM, which ignored political sirens, could conceivably renew with the organization and proselytism of its glorious past.[69] When the government withdrew its support for the ANT, thereby allowing FOM unionization efforts to go unhindered, the syndicalist press hailed the event as a sensational capitulation of State resolve in the face of trade union unity. The pro-anarchist *gremios pactantes* in the cargohandling sector denounced the move as treason: freed of ANT control as a concession to the FOM, much of the port was likely to fall into the hands of their syndicalist rivals.

Strong affinities and convergences still existed, though, between rank-and-file supporters of these two iconic symbols of anarchist and syndicalist memory—the SROPC and the FOM—in the Riachuleo district; many activists had been involved in one or the other, and sometimes in both. When in September and October a series of boycotts to prevent the Mihánovich line from disembarking FOM-allied officers escalated into a major strike, old reflexes of industry-wide, community-supported, transnational, and cross-ideological solidarity kicked in. Crews of incoming coastwise vessels walked out, the mooring of tugboats in La Boca interrupted overseas shipping, Uruguayan mariners stalled the movement of passenger ferries, and FOM sections in Rosario, Santa Fé, and smaller ports along the Paraná River, aided by the Paraguayan Maritime League in Asunción, interrupted the company's upriver operations. Anarchist leaders emerged from hiding and resumed their community activism, using a

68 *La Vanguardia*, April 5, June 24, September 2, and December 1, 1927; *La Unión del Marino*, August 1927; *Bandera Proletaria*, October 8 and November 26, 1927.

69 *La Protesta*, October 24, 1926; and April 10, 1927; *La Vanguardia*, October 14, 1927; *La Prensa*, January–June 1927; *Libertad*, January 9, 1928; Prefectura General Marítima, *Memoria 1927*, 54.

large women's rally in La Boca in memory of Luisa Lallana, a martyred FORA activist, to generate support for the seamen's cause. Even communists, in particular the Yugoslav Communist Group in La Boca which channeled recent Mihánovich hires from Europe into the FOM, joined the mobilization, as did their comrades from Paraguay.[70] By the time of Yrigoyen's second inauguration as president in mid-October, the FOM had regained its renegade status: a shootout between its leader Antonio Morán and strikebreakers in a bar in La Boca left a Paraguayan sailor dead and sent Morán to jail for several months.[71] Morán was a seasoned revolutionary and no friend of reformism or moderation; he was a member of the famed *anarquistas expropiadores*, advocates of armed retaliation against State-sponsored violence led by the famed Severino Di Giovanni.[72]

The wide array of support networks and alliances evidenced in 1928 were made possible by the syndicalist-inspired federalist statutes of the FOM and participatory democracy fomented by its sections and assemblies in periods of conflict. As had periodically occurred since the epic rise of the federation in 1916, that same diversity and pluralism also drew in "establishment" sympathies. In addition to the syndicalist USA, anarchist FORA, and Communist Party cells, the striking maritime workers enjoyed the support of Yrigoyenist figures in the Radical Civic Union, who had held former Alvearist maritime prefect Ricardo Hermelo and his ANT allies in high contempt. The strike ended on October 29 in a resounding victory for the unions. Even the anti-strike UOM joined the concert of cries for improving the seamen's lot. It settled into welfare-related activities such as the promotion of public baths and low-cost housing for seamen, using the Mihánovich line's connections in parliament to lobby for decasualization and a new retirement pension law.[73] Later in the 1930s, following the eviction in of its socialist founder, the union under the leadership of Daniel Alvaredo embarked on an aggressive unionization drive designed to enhance its credibility among workers throughout the merchant marine, and secured a closed shop clause to control hiring on the Mihánovich fleet.[74] It demanded an industry-wide pay raise and denounced the disloyal competition of foreign railway companies which

70 *Bandera proletaria*, September 27, 1928; *La Internacional* March 26, 1927; October 20 and 27, 1928; and April 20, 1929; *El Marino Rojo*, October 15 and November 13, 1928; *La Voz del Marino*, October 21, 1928; *Boletín de Servicios de la ANT*, October 20, 1928.

71 *La Protesta*, May 18, 1928; *Bandera Proletaria*, May 26, September 1, 22, and 28, 1928; *La Internacional*, October 13, 1928; Policía de la Capital, sección 24, *Copiador de Notas* no. 290, October 1, 1928.

72 Osvaldo Bayer, *Los anarquistas expropiadores y otros ensayos* (Buenos Aires: Editorial Legasa, 1986), 86–87.

73 *La Vanguardia*, April 17 and 18, July 11, and September 18, 1929; *Crónica mensual del DNT*, September 1929.

74 *El Marino*, August 1938, July 1939, and June 1946.

were held responsible for the economic difficulties of shipping companies. Between July 1937 and July 1938, membership grew from 1,798 to 4,102, and a section was organized in the upriver port of Concordia. Others would follow in the historic FOM bastions of the interior. The new statutes adopted in February 1938 continued to define the union as mutualist, exclusively concerned with the material betterment of its members and their families. In an important departure from the past, however, officers were excluded from the ranks of the UOM, allowing the conservative union to compete with the FOM as a representative organization of "subaltern" workers. Within five years the UOM would claim a membership of ten thousand, on par with that of its syndicalist rival.[75]

The most important factor behind this impressive evolution, however, was the inauguration of a conservative president, Roberto Ortiz, in February 1938. Under Ortiz the government would pursue the acquisition of vessels, reform Argentine legislation to foment coastal shipping, and actively support the international expansion of the Mihánovich line. While UOM leaders cultivated an image of independence from the company, their much-clamored loyalty to President Ortiz earned the union national status as the promoter of progressive legislation for workers in the merchant marine. It advocated the stabilization of seamen's lives through family improvement, responsible no-strike trade unionism, and the defense of Argentine sovereignty.[76] It would be too simple to attribute this sudden expansion of a conservative trade union solely to compulsory affiliation of seamen employed in the Mihánovich fleet. Many of the themes developed by the UOM, in particular the need for a labor code, annual paid vacations, and a retirement pension law, were also articulated in the form of demands by the FOM. The syndicalist union also promoted sobriety, discouraged gambling, and addressed the issue of family life in its defense of the working man's right to rest. Individual insubordination to ship captains' orders was punished by expulsion, wildcat strikes were described as violations of "trade-union democracy," and the use of violent methods of direct action, such as economic sabotage or physical attacks on unaffiliated crews, was actively discouraged. This quest for respectability, while derided in anarchist circles and often at odds with the tumultuous realities of sailors' lives, nonetheless reflected widely shared aspirations for stability and social improvement among workers who enjoyed little of either. Demands for the redistribution of wealth accompanied industrialization and economic recovery.[77]

75 *El Marino*, December 1937, February and April, 1938; *Orientación*, March 26, 1942.
76 *El Marino*, July, August, September, October, and December 1938; February 1939.
77 *USA*, March 3, 1938; *La Unión del Marino*, May 15 and November 1, 1938, and January 1, 1939; SROPC, *Libro de Actas 1933–1939*, 399–401.

On a broader level, the conservative government's alignment with the interests of the Mihánovich line made an objective FOM ally of several competing ship owners' lobbies. Employers' organizations representing smaller upriver lines and Atlantic coastwise traffic supported the FOM and officers' unions in their battle against the UOM. This "turf war" drew the syndicalist unions, which professed goals of working-class emancipation, defended federalism, and held ship owners at the mercy of strikes and boycotts, into a gradual process of emulation with the conservative UOM. Conversely, when it came to weighing in on government policy, the UOM rivaled with its syndicalist counterpart in the mobilization of anti-capitalist rhetoric. In an echo of past revolutionary campaigns, coastwise shipping firms were deemed guilty of shamelessly exploiting workers in the Upper Paraná and in Patagonia. The once-loathed company union, which continued to ban strike action from its program, also incorporated many communist mariners who had been expelled from the FOM for their involvement in partisan politics. From 1940 onward, the Communist Party newspaper *Orientación* presented the UOM as a modern industrial union destined to relegate anarcho-syndicalism in the merchant marine to the dustbins of history.[78]

If one were to simply read this vibrant and tangible, ongoing local history of class conflict and everyday militancy through the lens of the larger national labor movement, the continued radicalism of the FOM might be missed. It had entered the 1930s in a posture of revolutionary resistance to the dictatorship of General Uriburu after the death of García. Reorganized in 1933 under the leadership of veteran syndicalist sailor Fortunato Marinelli, the FOM joined the CGT; a sign that the "revolutionary" prefix to "syndicalism" was not—with 40 percent of the workforce in the merchant marine unemployed—as vital as the preservation of past gains and relationships with allies.[79] But the decision to join the mainstream national labor movement was short-lived; the federation would leave the CGT several years later when its politicization by socialists and communists ran counter to syndicalist traditions. Syndicalists would subsequently lead the Federation through the war and into the Peronist era, first as allies (during World War II), and then as foes (under Perón's government) of the "national-popular" State. In the mid-1930s strikes and boycotts continued successfully, particularly in three sectors—Atlantic coast shipping, traffic in the port of Buenos Aires, and large oil tankers—that formed the core of uncontested FOM authority throughout the decade. From 1934 onward the FOM partially recovered its

78 *El Marino*, July 1939–July 1940; *Orientación*, 1940–1943.

79 *La Vanguardia*, March 8, August 23, 24, and 25, September 14, 15, and 30, 1933; January 28 and 31, April 15 and 28, 1934; *CGT*, October 11, 1934, and September 20, 1935.

influence in the interior provinces through the Provincial Workers' Union of Entre Ríos, a regional federation based in Concepción del Uruguay of port, agricultural, and meatpacking workers as well as other craft unions in various areas of agro-export activity.[80] The FOM thus emerged from the Uriburu dictatorship and economic depression in a situation similar to that which had prevailed in the 1920s: it remained influential locally as well as nationally in the everyday management of work on the ships. The FOM, Provincial Union, and autonomous shipyard workers' FOCN resurrected the USA in 1937 and dominated its leadership; Fortunato Marinelli became general secretary and the revolutionary syndicalist shipyard brazier Atilio Biondi—a one-time anarchist FORA legend from the early 1900s—treasurer. Of the fifteen members elected to its leadership body, seven were members of the FOM or the shipyard workers' federation.[81] Numerically, the syndicalist USA and anarchist FORA-V no longer represented but a small fraction of the labor movement nationwide. In La Boca, however, the disproportionate weight of prominent traditional unions (SROPC, FOM, FOCN) in two "national" labor federations with professed revolutionary goals was a factor of local pride. The strategic location of waterfront workers made itself increasingly felt with the growth of the merchant marine, and the defense of these traditions, a matter of survival for the aforementioned unions, became increasingly intertwined with the memory of the local community, still the locus of continuous labor unrest.

This caused General Agustín Justo and Roberto Ortiz, Uriburu's conservative successors, to throw the State's support behind the national reorganization of maritime labor and standardization of its work norms. Longshoremen, who faced challenges due to growing internal migration trends and employer impunity throughout the depression years, also factored in the equation. In 1938 Gerónimo Schizzi, Félix Romero, Bartolomé Moreira, and Francisco Gaona left Diques y Dársenas and formed the Unified Port Workers' Union of Buenos Aires, which revived syndicalist rhetoric of class struggle.[82] Schizzi was not an unknown figure to the police; he had been arrested on numerous occasions for his involvement in canteen brawls, contempt of authority, or armed assault, and had even been investigated in a murder case. Yet after his defection from Diques y Dársenas, Schizzi seemed to puzzle everyone around him. To the police he

80 Laura Kalmanowiecki, "La Union Sindical Argentina: de la revolución prometida a la incorporación al sistema politico: in Torcuato S. Di Tella, ed., *Sindicatos como los de antes* (Buenos Aires: Biblos/Fundación Simón Rodríguez, 1993), 138–39.

81 Hiroshi Matsushita, *Movimiento obrero argentino, 1930–1945: sus proyecciones en los orígenes del peronismo* (Buenos Aires: Siglo Veinte, 1983), 171–79.

82 *La Vanguardia*, September 15, 1934, and May 12, 1935; *Diques y dársenas,* July 15, 1936; SROPC, *Libro de Actas 1933–1939,* 202, 255, and 261; Prefectura General Marítima, *Copiador Especial. Seguridad y Accidentes, 1935–1937*, 20–25.

was an anarchist, to the resistance society a right-wing nationalist, to the communists a communist. Whatever political ties may have incited him to reembark on a new unionization drive, the belligerence of his union alarmed the authorities as well as the anarchist SROPC, which deplored a growing number of defections to Schizzi's reunification movement.[83]

In the summer of 1939, the advent of the Second World War brought activities in the port to a sudden halt.[84] Schizzi's union invoked the national economic interest in defense of Argentina's neutrality in the war, blaming unemployment on foreign imperialists. It also solicited the recognition of veteran longshoremen as rightful claimants of labor legislation, a position which amounted to defending their rights against *golondrinas*, or migrant laborers, in the context of a depressed job market. The union also requested State intervention in the enforcement of work norms and wage scales, and prefecture support in its efforts to dislodge the SROPC and Diques y Dársenas from their respective closed shops. Schizzi succeeded in carrying his union's cause to parliament, and positioned himself as the champion of social reform on the docks; he now needed the backing of the larger labor movement. Such support came from the FOM, which was eager to win worker control over the administration of a new proposed pension fund system. A new alliance between longshoremen and maritime workers took form. Finally, in June 1940, Schizzi's union demanded the creation of a labor exchange to rationalize the distribution of jobs in the port, and resolved to join the CGT. A conjunction of seemingly unrelated factors had united communists, socialists, and syndicalists behind the policies of a conservative government to grant welfare rights to port workers, against the will of shipping and contracting concerns.[85]

Above all, the interests of the State, maritime workers', and the longshoremen's union converged on what had become an issue of national emergency: the need for a strong merchant marine capable of protecting Argentine economic sovereignty in situations of war. Syndicalist unions gradually shed their principled opposition to political activism, joining

83 *Lo que anhela el Consejo pro Federacion Argentina de Portuarios y Estibadores*, Buenos Aires, flyer dated 1940; SROPC, *Libro de Actas 1933–1939*, 354; "*La unidad de los obreros portuarios*," flyer of the Regional Committee of the Communist Party dated January 1939; *El Marino*, December 1937; *La Vanguardia*, July 28 and August 15, 1939; Policía de la Capital, División de Investigaciones, Sección 22. *Copiador de Notas* no. 324, October 10, 1936; Sección 24, *Copiador de Notas* no. 374 & 379, August 31, 1938 and March 25, 1939; Policía Federal, *Copiador Sección Especial 1932/1934, Extractos y Diligencias, Informe* no. 458, October 15, 1933, and *Copiador Sección Especial 1934/1935, Extractos y Diligencias, Informe* no. 314, November 12, 1934.

84 *Orientación*, November 30, 1939, and May 30, 1940.

85 *La Vanguardia*, November 30, 1939; March 12, May 23, and June 11, 1940; *El Marino*, November and December 1939, February and December, 1940, and February and October 1941.

with communists and socialists in local anti-war groups and lobbying the Ortiz government for protective labor legislation, the defense of working-class living standards, and nationalist economic policies. During its September 1940 congress, the FOM issued an unprecedented declaration of support for a State commission that advocated the promotion of an independent merchant marine through the investment of Argentine capital in the acquisition of ships. The union also resolved to apply for legal recognition, a major departure from the syndicalist orientation of the past, as part of its campaign to secure union control over the administration retirement pensions.[86] What these trends reveal is a recognition by unions of the inevitability of State-sponsored reforms, and of the advantages they might obtain from incorporation into the political system. Three years prior to the emergence of Juan Perón, the economic nationalism of communists, syndicalists, and conservatives had already set the stage for the increased cooperation of waterfront unions with State agencies.

When conservative President Ramón Castillo replaced the ailing Ortiz in 1941, both the FOM and the UOM were inclined to work with the government. They regularly sent delegations to meet with the president, and applauded his decision to acquire the first vessels of the State merchant fleet. The syndicalist FOM still used strikes and boycotts for wage increases and leveled attacks against leaders of the rival union for their opposition to strikes and unfailing loyalty to the directors of the Mihánovich line. Meanwhile, local sections of the FOM mobilized their influence in the community to encourage voter registration in the headquarters of the local fire station, where elections were scheduled in April 1942 to designate the workers' representatives in the administration of the new pension fund.[87] For the first time, mariners and seamen, regardless of their nationality, were solicited as citizens to elect their representatives in a public institution devoted to their welfare; and the FOM, more than at any time during the two Yrigoyen presidencies, was able to capitalize on State neutrality in its conflicts with the shipowners to reassert the effectiveness of direct action in improving the workers' lot. The result was an overwhelming electoral victory: the FOM defeated the UOM by 8,782 votes to 2,454. Despite its decision to join the CGT one month prior to the vote, the UOM, which had negotiated the retirement pension law with the Ortiz government, suffered from a severe loss of credibility: its secretary Daniel Alvaredo resigned in May 1941 amid accusations of pro-Axis lean-

86 *Orientación*, August 8 and 23, 1940; *La Vanguardia*, September 8, 1940; FOM, *Memoria al congreso a realizarse de septiembre de 1942 en adelante* (Buenos Aires: Imprenta Minerva, 1942), 8–10.

87 *La Vanguardia*, October 26, 1941; March 5 and 29, 1942; *Orientación*, March 26, 1942.

ings in the war. Fortunato Marinelli became the elected representative of all of the nation's mariners and seamen, including those employed by the Mihánovich fleet, in the first welfare institution ever to directly address their future; he was seconded by Atilio Biondi. In La Boca, the event was celebrated by thousands of men and women in front of the new three-story union building overlooking Necochea Street, which donned red flags and Argentine national banners for the occasion. Three decades of revolutionary syndicalist struggle had culminated in the official recognition of workers' rights, and of the union's right to represent them.[88]

The FOM remained firmly in the hands of syndicalists for whom the reinforcement of trade union control and influence took priority over parliamentarism and politics. Paradoxically, this stance converged with that of the military regime that toppled Ramón Castillo in June 1943. Colonel Juan Domingo Perón became the head of a new Labor and Welfare Secretariat, a government arbitration body which centralized all labor and welfare-related issues in the hands of a single authority. From that position he inaugurated a policy of calculated concessions to the noncommunist trade union movement in an effort to rally working-class support for the regime.[89] Antonio Aguilar, a veteran syndicalist sailor since 1914 who replaced Marinelli at the helm of the FOM in November 1943, began frequently soliciting the arbitration of the Secretariat in conflicts with ship owners while invoking time-tested syndicalist precepts of political neutrality. This pragmatic approach to the government received the approval of a majority of the rank and file in 1944. The union never came out openly in favor of the regime, except to applaud the promulgation, in October of the same year, of the Peonage Statute (Estatuto del Peón) which for the first time in history extended organizational rights and welfare policies to casual agricultural laborers. In the two years preceding Perón's accession to the presidency, however, the FOM, which expressed sympathies for the allied cause in the war, did nothing to pressure the regime to change its course and refrained from participation in the broad political alliance formed by the opposition.[90]

---

88 *El Marino*, May 1941; May and March 1942; FOM, *Memoria al congreso a realizarse* de septiembre de 1942 en adelante, 83–88; FOM, *La Caja de jubilaciones maritimas y el control obrero* (Buenos Aires: n.ed., 1942).

89 *Boletín Oficial*, July 24, September 13 and 15, November 15, and December 4, 1943; República Argentina. Ministerio de Trabajo y Previsión de la Nación, *Memoria Junio 1946–Diciembre 1951*, Buenos Aires: División de Publicaciones del Ministerio de Trabajo y Previsión, 1953; 7–8; Matsushita, *Movimiento obrero argentina, 1930–1945*, 260–61; Juan Carlos Torre, *La vieja guardia sindical y Perón. Sobre los orígenes del peronismo* (Buenos Aires: Editorial Sudamericana/Instituto Torcuato Di Tella, 1990), 60–61.

90 *La Unión del Marino*, November 1944–September 1945 and December 1946; República Argentina. Ministerio de Trabajo y Previsión, *Estatuto del Peon*, Buenos Aires: 1944.

Pepe Damonte's anarchist longshoremen's resistance society, on the other hand, had fomented a strike against the "fascist dictatorship" in September 1943 and its leaders were ruthlessly persecuted. As it had in past periods semiclandestinely, the SROPC was poised to mobilize its symbolic capital among local quayside workers against the growing influence of the State in their everyday lives. The Riachuelo district became a focal point of resistance to the new regime, and of repression against real or perceived "foreign" agitators of all persuasions. A radical anarchist group, the Federación Anarco-Comunista de Argentina (FACA) led by Ángel Borda and Laureano Riera, was hunted down by the police for planting explosives and engaging in economic sabotage against port and railway infrastructures. The shipyard workers' federation—nominally pro-FOM—would also, throughout the following decade, wage an all-out war against the Peronist State, and coordinate direct action campaigns against it with the "*gremios pactantes*" of the anarchist FORA-V. The FOM itself, firmly established in the community as a symbol of revolutionary achievement and working-class citizenship and a tapestry of anarchist, communist, socialist, and Radical Civic Union sympathies, entered the Peronist era both firmly committed to trade union independence and inclined to support the nationalist and pro-labor inclinations of the controversial colonel.

On the docks the fierce opposition of the SROPC to the June 1943 coup had resurrected the turf war between the two longshoremen's unions, and an alliance with the military authorities was certain to help Schizzi's union expand its influence over the anarchist-controlled areas of the port. After the military coup Schizzi became an assiduous visitor to the Labor and Welfare Secretariat, and in August 1944 he formed the Union of Longshoremen and Related Workers (Sindicato Unión Portuarios y Afines, or SUPA) with Perón's support.[91] From the perspective of the anarchist resistance society, Schizzi was "a cameleon, an illiterate, reactionary agent of employers who dipped his hand in every stew, from syndicalism to communism and fascism."[92] For many workers in the port, however, he was a charismatic trade unionist who led the SUPA into the laborist movement and obtained Perón's support for material improvements in their working conditions and everyday lives. For the first time in history, longshoremen throughout the country were durably organized into a national trade union movement other than the anarchist FORA-V. Still, the 1940s would be marked by a resurgence of the anarchist resistance society in the port of Buenos Aires and by a conflictual relationship between the Peronist union and the State.

91 "A todos los obreros estibadores del pais," SUPA flyer dated December 1946; FOM, *Los trabajadores del transporte marítimo y fluvial* (Buenos Aires: n.ed., 1946), 5–8.

92 Interview with Victorio Fiorito, March 5, 1991.

In a world of work characterized by insecurity, exhaustion, safety hazards, and widespread abuses of authority, the attraction of genuine citizenship rights and the exaltation of pride in one's work, regardless of education, skill, or personal wealth—which had been constant themes of the anarchist predicament for three decades—and the promise of their translation into fact was an important source of legitimacy for Schizzi's union. Not surprisingly, longshoremen poured into the downtown Plaza de Mayo at the end of the afternoon work shift on October 17, 1945, on the day of the cathartic popular mobilization which culminated in the defeat of the military faction responsible for Perón's forced renunciation a week earlier.[93] Perón went on to defend the "national revolution," emphasizing the need for State-promoted industrialization and the importance of national sovereignty, and warning that "if we don't undertake a peaceful revolution, the people will resort to violent revolution." While stigmatizing, to the delight of syndicalists, the corruption and selfishness of professional politicians, he argued that the army was fundamentally concerned with eliminating the illnesses and malnutrition that "rendered 40 to 50% of the population useless" to the nation. For him the "authentic interests" of the working class would no longer be "held at the mercy of shameless employers or venal agitators."[94] To the trade unions and to broad sectors of the working class, the language and symbolism of the "national revolution" rang true, and was supported by concrete measures. The "constitutional freedom march" organized on September 19, 1945, by the entire political opposition—from the communist and socialist Left to political parties of the right—was closely followed by the single most empowering measure—from the perspective of organized labor—ever taken by an Argentine government: the promulgation by decree of the "Law of Professional Associations," a veritable charter of industrial citizenship which promised unions full legal rights, representative autonomy, arbitration tribunals, and even co-participation in management decisions.

Subsequently the SROPC and FORA-V, as well as a new federation that resulted from the triumphant merger of the FOM and UOM, would spend the entire first presidential term of Perón vigorously defending, from the streets of La Boca and through their still vibrant networks of

93 Sub-Prefectura de la zona del Río de la Plata y del Puerto de Buenos Aires, *El órden social en el puerto*, Buenos Aires, 1946, 189–90. On the events and interpretation of this foundational moment of Peronist political history, cf. "La CGT y el 17 de octubre" in Juan Carlos Torre, ed., *La formación del sindicalismo peronista* Buenos Aires: Editorial Legasa, 1988, 122–27; Daniel James, "October 17th and 18th, 1945: Mass Protest, Peronism and the Argentine Working Class," *Journal of Social History* 21 (Spring 1988): 441–61.

94 Luis B. Cerrutti Costa, *El sindicalismo, las masas y el poder* Buenos Aires: Editorial Trafac, 1957; 149–56; editorial by Juan Perón in *Revista de Trabajo y Previsión* 1, no. 1 (January–March 1944): iii.

activists throughout the nation's ports and rivers, deep-seated traditions of federalist solidarity, working-class-control, direct democracy, trade-union independence, and the right to strike, even drawing Schizzi's powerful longshoremen's union into a mortal conflict with the State and its bureaucratic proclivities for direct intervention in, and repression of, organized labor. When they were defeated, it was by the force of a fierce State-sponsored crackdown. Nationalism, and the concessions made by labor to government overtures of progressive welfare reform, erased not just their hard-won organizations, but a half-century history of epic anarchist and revolutionary syndicalist aspirations for an empowering grassroots citizenship rooted in direct action and cosmopolitan community solidarity, against the State, bureaucratic control, political parties, vigilante justice, atavistic nativism, and capitalist impunity. Freed from the atrophies of academic generalization, selective partisan judgment, and teleological rewritings grounded in the assumed inevitability of its outcomes, their story—replete with dreams, illusions, triumphs, and reversals—is a thread that deserves to be woven into the collective memory of the workers whose emancipation they envisioned. The tight-knit working-class communities along the southern quays of the port of Buenos Aires witnessed the birth and apogee of anarchist resistance societies in the 1890s and early 1900s; those epic labor insurgencies, and the violent backlash they invited from the State, police, and ruling classes, shaped local memories in ways that informed the choices of others who faced similar challenges in subsequent decades. And if at times this militancy of resistance to government and political intervention in the lives of workers gathered strength, or left traces, the sources of its effectiveness raise at least as legitimate an historical question as the reasons for its eclipse (the finality of which, incidentally, historians are poorly qualified to predict).

ANARCHISM, THE SUBALTERN, AND REPERTOIRES OF RESISTANCE IN NORTHERN PERU, 1898–1922

Steven J. Hirsch

Carlos Rama, the late Uruguayan historical sociologist, once noted, "The 'anarchisms,' just like the 'socialisms,' are varied and, in Latin America, don't lack for different variations."[1] This astute observation, so often ignored or downplayed in nation-centered treatments of anarchist movements, aptly fits the case of Peru. Anarchism in Peru was never a monolith or a strictly self-contained national movement. It can be described more accurately as a set of diverse, multiple, and overlapping regional and local anarchist movements, which in turn were interlinked with transnational anarchist movements by formal networks and informal webs of exchange. These movements, comprising press organs, activist groups, educational and cultural associations, and labor organizations were manifest in Peru from the 1890s through the 1920s. They tended to adapt anarchist ideology and praxis to the specificities of regional and local power relations, geography, and demographic characteristics. Such was the case in northern Peru where a distinctive anarchist movement developed in response to land concentration, peasant proletarianization, and coercive labor practices brought on by the formation of sugar export enclaves in the departments of La Libertad and Lambayeque. It also was animated by a principled determination to contest the authoritarian rule of national and regional oligarchs and the vestiges of colonialism. Focusing on the anarchist movement in northern Peru, I intend to elucidate how it transcended urban/rural spatial divisions, ethnic differences, and parochialism to forge a multiethnic subaltern resistance movement.

1 Carlos M. Rama, "Los intelectuales y el anarquismo latinoamericano," *Cuadernos Americanos* 227, no. 6, (November–December 1979), 135.

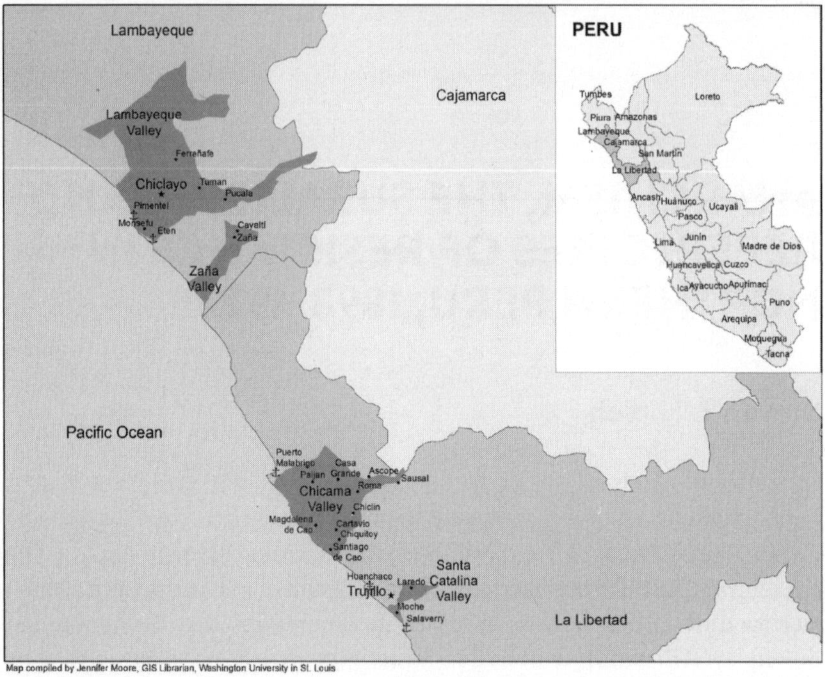

Map compiled by Jennifer Moore, GIS Librarian, Washington University in St. Louis

Contesting Oligarchic Rule: The Anarchist Struggle for Urban and Rural Worker Solidarity

The system of domination in northern Peru between 1890 and the early 1920s was predicated on the rule of a small group of sugar planters with access to foreign capital and markets. Composed of unassimilated foreign immigrants (Italian, German, Spanish, Irish-American) and Peruvian creoles, the sugar planter class appropriated and reorganized land, water, and labor resources in the fertile valleys of La Libertad and Lambayeque. During the first two decades of the twentieth century, sugar plantations expanded rapidly at the expense of small estates and Indian communities. For example, Casa Grande, the largest sugar plantation in the Chicama Valley in La Libertad, absorbed twenty-five estates and numerous small plots of Indian land. A relatively modest estate in 1850 with 724 hectares, by 1927 Casa Grande had grown to nearly 41,000 hectares with large, technologically advanced processing mills.[2] On a smaller scale, a similar process of land consolidation occurred in the valleys of Lambayeque and Saña in Lambayeque department. Cayaltí emerged as the dominant sugar plantation in Lambayeque after acquiring nine estates and gaining control over land and water resources belonging to small communities in the

---

2 Michael J. Gonzales, *Plantation Agriculture and Social Control in Northern Peru, 1875–1933* (Austin: University of Texas Press, 1985), 44.

Saña Valley.[3] Preeminent political power accompanied the growth and capital accumulation of the sugar plantations. Not only would planters hold important political and economic posts in their own departments, they also exercised power at the national level. Two sugar planters held the presidency for a total of twelve years between 1899 and 1919, and others served as cabinet ministers and congressmen.[4] With the active collaboration of national and local governments, sugar planters established a modern enclave economy in the region.[5]

The sugar enclaves in La Libertad and Lambayeque were characterized by an integrated production and infrastructure complex and a system of social control. As a result of government concessions, sugar planters in the Chicama and Lambayeque valleys were permitted to use or build railway lines linking plantations to the ports of Salaverry, Malabrigo, Pimentel, and Eten.[6] In addition, they were allowed to modernize port facilities. Government support for the enclaves included insuring an adequate labor supply and security. Labor scarcity on the coast was a chronic problem. After some initial experiments with State-sanctioned importation of Chinese (1870s) and Japanese (1898–1910s) laborers, planters turned to the coercive recruitment of indigenous peasants from the highland areas of La Libertad, Lambayeque, and Cajamarca.[7] To secure indigenous labor, planters utilized debt entrapment or *enganche* contracts which the State condoned and enforced.[8] Planters could also count on State interventions to maintain order and security in the enclaves. When the private police force on the plantations could not contain labor agitation, the State intervened with the *guardia civil* (national police) and the regular army. Sealing the enclaves off from urban-based agitators and

3 Ibid., 52.

4 Peter Klaren, "The Sugar Industry in Peru," *Revista de Indias* 65, no. 233 (2005): 39.

5 On the origins and dynamics of the sugar enclaves in northern Peru, see Julio Cotler, "State and Regime: Comparative Notes on the Southern Cone and the "Enclave" Societies," in David Collier, ed., *The New Authoritarianism in Latin America* (Princeton, NJ: Princeton University Press, 1979), 274–75.

6 Gonzalez, *Plantation Agriculture and Social Control in Northern Peru*, 53–54; Peter K. Klarén, *Modernization, Dislocation, and Aprismo: Origins of the Peruvian Aprista Party, 1870–1932* (Austin: University of Texas Press, 1973), 70–71.

7 Nearly eighteen thousand Japanese laborers were imported to work on Peru's coastal estates. The presence of Japanese workers on the sugar plantations in northern Peru was relatively insignificant and declined rapidly. By 1920 only twenty Japanese peons remained on the haciendas in Lambayeque, See, Gonzales, *Plantation Agriculture and Social Control in Northern Peru*, 119–23.

8 For an analysis of *enganche* labor in northern Peru, see, Inés Bazán y José Gómez Cumpa, "Enganche y formación de espacios regionals en el Perú: Lambayeque 1860–1930," in Humberto Rodríguez Pastor, ed., *Congreso Nacional de Investigación Histórica*, Vol. 1, (Lima: Concytec, 1991), 249–67, and Peter Blanchard, "The Recruitment of Workers in the Peruvian Sierra at the Turn of the Century: The Enganche System," *Inter-American Economic Affairs* 33, no. 3 (Winter 1979): 63–83.

labor organizers and preventing peasant and *bracero* (plantation laborers) mobilizations were hallmarks of planter rule.

For anarchists in Trujillo and Chiclayo, the coastal capitals of the La Libertad and Lambayeque respectively, the sugar export enclaves were an affront to their sensibilities and cherished ideals. They profoundly resented the superexploitation of indigenous braceros, the dispossession of peasant smallholders, and denial of basic rights of organization, free movement, and education to workers and peasants. With the aim of combatting these abuses, anarchist activists sought to promote solidarity between the incipient urban working class in Trujillo and Chiclayo and subaltern groups within the sugar enclaves. Initially this entailed organizing and politically educating the craftsmen, service employees, and factory workers in the fledgling consumer goods industries.[9] Though the number of urban workers was never large, it rose with the growth of Trujillo and Chiclayo. Between 1908 and 1920 the population of Trujillo doubled from ten to twenty thousand, while Chiclayo's grew from fourteen thousand in 1907 to nearly twenty-eight thousand in 1921.[10] Only after anarchist activists founded urban labor organizations and a vibrant anarchist press did they turn their attention to building bonds of solidarity among urban and rural workers.

The principal figures behind the formation of an anarchist movement encompassing urban and rural workers in northern Peru were Julio Reynaga Matute and Manuel Uchofen Patazca. Reynaga, a mulatto, former stevedore, and autodidact, resided in Trujillo. A dedicated anarcho-syndicalist, he was a founding member of the Liga de Artesanos y Obreros del Perú (League of Artisans and Workers of Peru, LAOP), Trujillo's first class-oriented labor organization in 1898. In accord with anarchist precepts, LAOP adopted an open membership policy that included artisans and workers of all races and nationalities and emphasized worker self-emancipation.[11] Devoted to the propagation of anarchist ideas, Reynaga also established an anarchist study center, Centro de Estudios Sociales

---

9 In Chiclayo urban-industrial workers were employed in furniture, soap, candy, candle, beer, leather, and textile workshops and factories. They also worked as chauffeurs and railwaymen. See Carlos J. Bachmann, *Departamento de Lambayeque: Monografía Histórico Geográfica*, Lima: Imprenta Torres Aguirre, 1921, 272–73. Similarly, in Trujillo, urban-industrial workers held jobs as mechanics, carpenters, bakers, weavers, typographers, chauffeurs, railwaymen, and construction laborers. See, Demetrio Ramos Rau, *Mensaje de Trujillo—del anarquismo al aprismo* (Trujillo, Peru: Instituto Nor Peruano de Desarrollo Economico Social, 1987), 49.

10 Peter Blanchard, *The Origins of the Peruvian Labor Movement, 1883–1919* (Pittsburgh: University of Pittsburgh Press), 1982, 11; Bachmann, *Departamento de Lambayeque*, 258.

11 Initially membership was restricted to Peruvian nationals, but this was changed at the behest of Reynaga at an extraordinary session of the LAOP in 1902. See, *Libro de Actas de la Liga de Artesanos y Obreros del Perú* (hereafter LALAOP), Vol. 1, April 24, 1902.

"Unión y Energía" (Center for Social Studies Union and Energy, CESUE) in 1906 and two anarchist newspapers, *La Antorcha* (The Torch, 1903–1907) and *El Jornalero* (The Day Laborer, 1906–1915). Both anarchist publications were distributed widely throughout the coastal, valley, and highland areas of La Libertad. Uchofen's actions in Chiclayo paralleled Reynaga's. A self-educated carpenter and print worker of mestizo descent, Uchofen labored tirelessly to spread the idea of anarchy and to promote anarcho-syndicalist organization. In doing so, he founded and directed the anarchist newspapers, *La Protesta Libre* (The Free Protest, 1906–1909) and *La Abeja* (The Bee, 1909–1922). Together with Reynaga's anarchist newspapers, they formed a regional anarchist press network that routinely shared information on workers' social conditions and struggles in the sugar export enclaves. Uchofen also assisted in the foundation of Chiclayo's main labor organization, the anarcho-syndicalist Confederación de Obreros de 1 de Mayo (May 1st Workers' Confederation) in 1907. Membership in this organization, like the LAOP and the CESUE, was open to urban and rural workers of all ethnic, racial, and national backgrounds.

To understand the nature of the anarchist project in northern Peru one must first consider the role of Reynaga and Uchofen as anarchist "popular intellectuals." Both Reynaga and Uchofen fit Baud and Rutten's definition of popular intellectuals, that is, individuals who "seek to define the problems of subaltern groups, articulate their grievances, and frame their social and political demands."[12] Indeed, they articulated a trenchant critique of the sugar enclaves as centers of capitalist exploitation and colonial forms of racial/ethnic oppression and power. Under their direction the anarchist press repeatedly denounced the use of *enganche* labor, the enslavement of *braceros*, and the collusion of sugar planters and state authorities in the dispossession of peasants and the exploitation of both urban and rural workers. By detailing the daily abuses suffered by indigenous braceros, the anarchist press sought to engender sympathy and solidarity among urban workers for their rural counterparts. *La Antorcha*, for example, in an article titled "The Modern Slavery on the Haciendas of the Valley of Chicama," decried how indigenous "beings of our species" were subject to dehumanizing treatment and called on urban workers to "gaze on those [haciendas] and contemplate the heartbreaking scene," and to recognize "that the vision that must be seen is the braceros and their rights."[13] *El Jornalero*, in a regularly featured column titled "Echoes of the Haciendas," described the sugar plantations as "not centers of work" but "prisons of torment, where the workers, principally the Indians . . .

12 Michiel Baud and Rosanne Rutten, "Introduction," *International Review of Social History*, Supplement, 49 (2004): 2.

13 *La Antorcha*, May 20, 1905; See also, May 1, 1907.

are exploited in a thousand ways."[14] *La Protesta Libre* and *La Abeja* likewise railed against sugar planters for perpetrating all manner of depredations against *braceros* and the indigenous peasantry. In particular, they denounced the systematic theft of indigenous lands and waters. Manuel Bancayán, a member of the *La Abeja* directorate, accused the hacendado class and the Regional Administration of Water in Lambayeque of robbing indigenous peasant communities of land and water and creating conditions for "modern feudalism." "It causes me great indignation," he declared, "when I see in every part of this department an outrage. . . . I see the indigenous race exploited and without protection."[15] For Reynaga, Uchofen, and the anarchist press the subjugation of braceros and indigenous peasants necessitated an emancipatory struggle. They would frame this struggle as a revolutionary project involving urban and rural subaltern groups.

The most articulate and fervent proponent of this revolutionary project was Manuel Uchofen. Only a movement composed of the totality of the region's subordinate, exploited, and oppressed laborers, he insisted, would be capable of opposing the sugar planters and their allies. Invoking the trope of a hierarchical and oppressive beehive, Uchofen urged his readers to think of Peruvian society in terms of a mass of worker bees locked in mortal combat with a small number of lazy parasites or "zánganos."[16] Undoubtedly inspired by the First International's official organ, *The Bee-Hive*, and its dictum of workers' self-emancipation, he exhorted urban and rural workers from all ethnic and racial backgrounds to rise up against the dominant parasites of the Peruvian beehive. In an editorial titled "*Las Abejas y Los Zánganos*" (The Bees and the Parasites), published in *La Protesta Libre* in 1909, Uchofen issued his anarchist call to arms:

> We have in every society without exception two classes of people: those characterized by idleness and those that perform labor. It is the great beehive composed of bees and parasites. By natural law and for the convenience of the working classes, it is necessary to separate from the parasites and to scream out this warning. It is the holy anarchist law to bring an end to the assassins of humanity, to liberate the thousands of victims of oppression and of so much tyranny brought about by the zánganos.[17]

14 *El Jornalero*, November 17, 1906.
15 *La Abeja*, September 3, 1910.
16 To my knowledge only anarchists in northern Peru consistently used the trope of a beehive and worker bees. The one exception was in central Peru. Adolfo Vienrich, an anarchist intellectual based in the highland town of Tarma, occasionally referred to worker bees in connection to local urban and indigenous subaltern groups.
17 *La Protesta Libre*, March 1909.

A year later in *La Abeja*, Uchofen reiterated that anarchism was the antidote to a social order composed of parasites and worker bees. He editorialized, "We are anarchist socialists; we love this great doctrine because it will abolish the chain of miseries and shame that weighs on the working classes and will purify the real conditions of the zánganos [who are] nourished by the producers."[18] Given this formulation, Uchofen, not surprisingly, viewed solidarity between urban workers, braceros, and peasants as central to the anarchist revolutionary project in northern Peru, a perspective shared by anarchists in Trujillo.

Building bonds of solidarity between urban and rural workers however was not an easy task. Anarchists in Trujillo and Chiclayo had to overcome worker apathy, logistical problems related to spatial distances, bracero and peasant illiteracy, and planter hostility. Undeterred by these imposing obstacles, anarchists made a concerted effort to establish lines of communication between the coastal urban centers and the sugar plantations and rural towns. From its inception in 1903, *La Antorcha* made contact with rural workers in the Chicama and Moche Valleys. Despite what it characterized as a "silent, surreptitious, and active war" against it by "bigwigs and hacendados," *La Antorcha* managed to place agents on plantations in Chicama, in the town of Ascope, and other points within the sugar enclave.[19] *El Jornalero* would also develop a wide network of agents and subscribers in Trujillo and the surrounding valleys, though not without difficulty. It acknowledged as much in an editorial in 1907 that complained of "the impossibility of its free introduction on the haciendas" owing to planter intimidation and the cowardice of some its agents.[20] It had more success delivering its publications using the railway lines that linked Trujillo with the port of Salaverry, the town of Ascope, and the Laredo sugar plantation.[21] *La Protesta Libre* and *La Abeja* developed a similar communication and distribution network from Chiclayo to the plantations and rural communities. In 1912 *La Abeja* informed braceros and workers that they could obtain copies of the newspaper from representatives on the haciendas Tumán and Pucalá and in the town of Ferreñafe, assuring them that "all of these persons are well related to the working class."[22]

As far as can be discerned, anarchists adopted a three-pronged strategy to address the formidable barrier of illiteracy among braceros and

18 *La Abeja*, 1st week of November, 1910.
19 M. Vargas Morales to Y.Y. Lombardzi [*sic*], January 3, 1905; Julio Rodríguez to Teodoro Moreno Machado, January 13, 1905, LAOP Correspondence Collection. See, also, Ramos Rau, *Mensaje de Trujillo*, 65–66.
20 *El Jornalero*, January 26, 1907.
21 *El Jornalero*, May 9, 1913.
22 *La Abeja*, 1st week of August, 1912.

indigenous peasants.[23] First, anarchists organized clandestine propaganda tours of the sugar plantations. Between 1899 and 1902, for example, Reynaga infiltrated the sugar plantations and delivered a series of lectures promoting some braceros to become members of LAOP and laid the groundwork for future urban worker–bracero solidarity.[24] The second strategy entailed encouraging braceros, rural workers, and indigenous peasants to submit their complaints to the anarchist press rather than government officials. In this way anarchists opened spaces for rural subaltern groups to express their views about mistreatment at the hands of *enganchadores*, landlords, priests, mayors, and governors and facilitated mutual understanding.[25] The third strategy centered on the foundation of anarchist study centers, schools, and libraries on haciendas and in rural towns. For example, anarchists organized a Centro de Estudios Pomalca (Pomalca Study Center), a library, and a night school on the hacienda Pomalca (Lambayeque) in 1906–1907, and a Centro de Estudios Sociales Labor y Luz (Labor and Light Social Studies Center), an anarchist study center in the indigenous community of Moche (La Libertad) in 1911.[26] Taken together these strategies contributed to the spread of libertarian ideas and the promotion of bonds of friendship and solidarity between urban and rural subalterns.

Constructing an Anarchist International Imaginary in Northern Peru

The political outlook and actions of the anarchist movement in northern Peru were shaped in large part by Reynaga and Uchofen. Both figures were self-identified anarchists imbued with a cosmopolitan sensibility, internationalist worldview, and a commitment to international social revolution. This was reflected in the content of their anarchist presses and their personal statements. In the pages of *El Jornalero* Reynaga published articles calling for free peoples to erase national borders to hasten the social revolution.[27] For his part Uchofen openly declared that "although I am Peruvian, I don't belong to [Peru], I am of the world—that is my country."[28] Flowing from their shared internationalist outlook was a mutual determination to engender an anarchist international imaginary among the subaltern in La Libertad and Lambayeque. By developing webs of exchange and solidarity with anarchist movements worldwide, they sought to break workers' sense of isolation and parochialism. They also endeavored to

23 Peru's indigenous population was effectively disenfranchised in 1896 when Spanish literacy became a requirement to vote.
24 LALAOP, Vol. 1, February 23, 1900; June 12, September 19, and October 15, 1902.
25 *La Antorcha*, May 20, 1905; *El Jornalero*, January 26, 1907, July 25, 1912.
26 *El Oprimido-Lima*, April 1908, number 8; *El Jornalero*, June 15, 1911.
27 *El Jornalero*, December 1, 1906.
28 *El Hambriento* 54, September 1909.

draw on the cultural and political expressions of international anarchism to unify the region's diverse subaltern groups.

Fostering an anarchist international imaginary fell primarily to the anarchist press. Reynaga and Uchofen wasted no time in forging webs of exchange between *La Antorcha*, *El Jornalero*, *La Protesta Libre*, and *La Abeja* and more than a score of Spanish-language anarchist newspapers based in Spain, Argentina, Chile, Cuba, and Mexico.[29] The steady import of foreign anarchist newspapers, owing to the fortuitous proximity of Trujillo and Chiclayo to the Pacific Ocean and to international maritime lines, allowed Reynaga and Uchofen to publish frequent reports on the anarchist and worker movements in Latin America, Europe, and the United States. News and communiques from foreign anarchist movements were also transmitted via the vibrant anarchist press in Lima, which maintained close ties to the anarchist press in Trujillo and Chiclayo. Inveterate or casual readers of the anarchist press in northern Peru could easily imagine that they formed part of a much larger and more robust international anarchist movement. As if to further reinforce this perception, *La Protesta Libre* published correspondences with the Anarchist International in Amsterdam.[30] In addition, Reynaga and Uchofen routinely allocated space in their anarchist newspapers to the publication of doctrinal essays by prominent international anarchist thinkers and activists such as Errico Malatesta, Peter Kropotkin, Elisée Reclus, Rudolph Rocker, Pietro Gori, Antonio Pellicer Paraire, Enrique Flores Magón, and Maximiliano Olay.

The intentional cultivation of an anarchist international imaginary by the anarchist movement in northern Peru manifest itself in public rituals, visual icons, slogans, music, and theater. May Day demonstrations and tributes were *de rigueur* in Trujillo and Chiclayo during the first two decades of the twentieth century. Replete with red flags and solemn tributes to Chicago's martyrs, May Day formed part of a regional anarchist ritual calendar of events. The commemoration of May Day in Trujillo and Chiclayo, sponsored by LAOP and *La Abeja* group respectively, served to underscore international anarchist and worker solidarity. Pascual Meza Veliz, an anarchist worker, for example, stressed this very point in a lecture on the origins of May Day and its celebration around the world to LAOP members.[31] May Day also was imbued with local meanings. In 1907 *La Antorcha* used the occasion of May Day to equate the victims of sugar planters in

29 Among the foreign anarchist newspapers that had *canje* (exchange) arrangements with the anarchist press in Trujillo and Chiclayo were *Tierra y Libertad* and *La Escuela Moderna* from Spain, *La Protesta*, *El Proletario*, and *Espiritu Libre* from Argentina, *Luz y Vida* and *Tribuna Libre* from Chile, *¡Tierra!* from Cuba, and *Regeneración* and *Reforma Libertad y Justicia* from México.

30 *La Protesta Libre*, 3rd week of August, 1909.

31 LALAOP, Vol. 2, March 30, 1907.

Chicama with the Chicago martyrs and to agitate for revenge. It declared "because [of] the blood spilled in Chicago and that of the neglected victims of our valleys, which are rife with martyrs, we ask for vengeance!"[32]

Tributes to international anarchist martyrs and commemorations of worker massacres in Chile and Argentina were also held regularly by anarchist groups and workers' organizations in Trujillo and Chiclayo. Foremost among the tributes was the homage paid to Francisco Ferrer i Guàrdia shortly after his assassination in 1909. Ferrer's conception of the modern school had served as a model for Reynaga and Uchofen's organization of rationalist workers' schools. Not surprisingly, LAOP and the *La Protesta Libre* group organized an annual event in honor of Ferrer.[33] Ritualized public protests and expressions of worker solidarity were also organized by anarchists in northern Peru. In particular, they protested the massacre of Chilean mine workers in Iquique in November 1907 and the brutal state repression of workers in Buenos Aires in May 1909. Given the presence of Inocencio Lombardozzi, an Argentine anarchist, and his significant influence in the anarchist movement in northern Peru, this was to be expected. Before escaping persecution in Buenos Aires and Santiago, Lombardozzi had been involved with the Argentine and Chilean labor movements and maintained close ties to them while in political exile in Peru.[34] Another contributing factor was LAOP's informal ties to these labor movements. In fact, on the basis of these ties LAOP had been issued invitations to send delegates to workers' congresses in Buenos Aires and Santiago.[35]

Adopting slogans, symbols, music, and works of theater associated with international anarchism was also used to unify artisans, workers, braceros, and peasants in northern Peru. In addition to reciting the First International's slogan "that workers' emancipation is the task of workers themselves" and using the red flag, anarchists also encouraged workers to recall the Paris Commune, embrace the slogan of "Liberty, Equality, and Fraternity," and to memorize and sing "La Marsellesa."[36] *La Antorcha* and

32 *La Antorcha*, May 1, 1907, number 83.

33 LALAOP, Vol. 2, October 16, 1909, Extraordinary Session; *La Protesta Libre*, 3rd week of October 1909, 3rd week of December 1909.

34 On Lombardozzi's ties with the Chilean labor movement while in Trujillo, see, Sergio Grez Toso, *Los anarquistas y el movimiento obrero: La alborada de "la idea" en Chile, 1893–1915* (Santiago, Chile: LOM Ediciones, 2007), 314n314.

35 State repression in Argentina prevented the realization of the South American Workers Congress scheduled for 1910. On the solicitations for LAOP send a worker representative to Buenos Aires, see, LALAOP, Vol. 1, August 8 and September 17, 1906; and LALAOP, Vol. 2, November 24, 1908. LAOP selected and sent a representative to the Chilean Workers' Congress. See LALAOP, Vol. 2, August 30, 1913.

36 On the call for workers to replicate the Paris Commune, see, *La Antorcha*, December 1, 1906.

El Jornalero urged workers to contemplate the meaning of "Free Humanity, equality, fraternity, and love of the land."[37] In 1905 LAOP formally adopted the "La Marsellesa" as its anthem and the red flag with a white triangle in the middle symbolizing liberty, equality, and fraternity as its official banner.[38] Similarly, in 1913 the Confederation of First of May in Chiclayo officially proclaimed its adherence to the "principles of Liberty, Equality, and Fraternity" to the applause and vivas of assembled workers.[39] Staging international anarchist theatrical works like A. Mario Lazzoni's *¡Martir!*, written in Montevideo in 1901, was also employed to inculcate anarchist beliefs and working-class unity. Described as a "completely libertarian drama" that explores the meaning of "bread and work" and the significance of "proletarian blood," it was performed in Chiclayo's workers' theater "2 de Mayo" in November 1911.[40] For those unable to attend the performances, *La Abeja* printed the play in serial form in its pages.

Anarchism and Subaltern Resistance in the Sugar Enclaves

To what extent did the anarchist movement in northern Peru succeed in fostering worker and peasant solidarity and resistance in the sugar enclaves?[41] If one defines solidarity as "an experience of willed affiliation," "conscious commitment," and a "performative" act, then it would appear there is ample evidence of some success.[42] And, if one considers the role of the anarchist movement in several multiethnic subaltern rebellions and the organization of "unions of resistance," in the enclaves, again, the evidence points to considerable anarchist influence. The following section examines the anarchist movement's relationship to the Chumán insurgency (1910) and Zaña revolt (1913) in Lambayeque and the Chicama Valley rebellions (1912, 1921–1922) in La Libertad.

The indigenous peasant insurgency that broke out in Ferreñafe in November 1910 had the support of the anarchist movement. Led by Manuel Casimiro Chumán Velásquez, a mestizo priest and fierce critic of *latifundismo* (large landed estates), the insurgent movement called for the restitution of usurped Indian lands and water, "the redemption of the Lambayecano Indian," and the replacement of oligarchic rule with a "true

37 *La Antorcha*, September 20, 1906; *El Jornalero*, November 17, 1906.

38 LALAOP, Vol. 1, April 21, 1905. Ytalto Martín Chihuala Peche, ex-president of LAOP, suggested that the three sides of the triangle symbolized liberty, equality, fraternity. Personal communication, February 9, 2012.

39 *La Abeja*, May 11, 1913.

40 *La Protesta Libre*, 3rd week of October 1909; *La Abeja*, 2nd week of November 1911.

41 This is a slightly revised section that appears in my chapter on "Anarchist Visions of Race and Space in Northern Peru, 1898–1922," in Kirwin Shaffer and Geoffroy de Laforcade, ed., *In Defiance of Boundaries: Anarchism in Latin American History* (Gainesville: University of Florida Press, forthcoming).

42 David A. Hollinger, "From Identity to Solidarity," *Daedalus* 135, no. 4 (Fall 2006): 23–24.

democracy." The anarchist press in northern Peru endorsed the insurgents' revolutionary program.[43] This is not surprising given its contact with the Mexican anarchist press and its subsequent full-throated support for the Mexican Revolution. *La Abeja* asserted that the proposition of "Land and Liberty" and "bread for all" formulated by "our compañeros in Mexico is ours."[44] *El Jornalero* likewise would express admiration for the Mexican Revolution's goal to "abolish the State and to redistribute the land."[45]Although the Chumán insurgency would be suppressed within a few months, Uchofen and La Abeja would continue to laud the insurgency and its sacrifices in defense of Ferreñafe's indigenous community and support the political aspirations of Chumán.[46]

Following the Chumán insurgency, anarchists in Chiclayo turned their attention to the peasant community of Zaña and its conflict with Cayaltí, a sugar plantation owned by the powerful Aspíllaga family. On January 1, 1913, Zaneros of indigenous, African, Chinese, and mixed race descent destroyed the barriers that Cayalti had erected to enclose its lands and water and reclaimed lands they asserted rightfully belonged to the community.[47] Four days later *La Abeja* sanctioned the land seizures and opined that Zaneros "should be left in peace on the lands that they had worked for so long."[48] As the conflict dragged on into March and April, *La Abeja* repeatedly published open letters from Zaneros as well as sympathetic interviews with José Mercedes Cachay, their mixed race leader.[49] One letter pointedly protested the contemptuous attitude of Lambayeque's political elite and Cayalti's landowners toward Zaña and its inhabitants. It stated, "Zaña doesn't have its own life, its sons are day laborers that imitate parasites, but on the other hand, they know THEY ARE NOT SLAVES . . . the sons of Zaña are not savages and they demand what is counseled by the love of their rights."[50] After soldiers attacked Zanero protesters and squatters on May 4, leaving four dead and twelve wounded, the anarchist movements in Lambayeque and La Libertad roundly condemned the "massacre." *La Abeja* and *El Jornalero*

43 Julio César Sevilla Exebio, "La montonera del cura Chumán, Ferreñafe 1910," *Utopía Norteña* 1 (1995): 148, 150.

44 *La Abeja*, 2nd week of November 1911.

45 *El Jornalero*, June 1, 1911.

46 *La Abeja*, October 27 and November 17, 1912.

47 For a discussion of the ethnic and racial composition of Zaña in the early twentieth century, see Luis Rocca Torres, *De la multitud a la soledad: La vida de José Mercedes Cachay, Líder Popular Lambayecano* (Chiclayo, Peru: Centro de Estudios Sociales Solidaridad, 1993), 32–34.

48 *La Abeja*, January 5, 1913.

49 José Mercedes Cachay is described by his biographer as having the features of a "mestizo-yuna-hispano." See note 46.

50 *La Abeja*, March 9, 1913.

circulated a special bulletin with the victims' names and demanded punishment for the military authorities and hacendados responsible for the bloodshed.[51] Echoing this sentiment the Workers Confederation First of May in Chiclayo sent a letter of protest with two hundred signatures, including Uchofen's, to the president of the republic. It also collected and sent funds to aid the victims and their families.[52]

Despite the anarchist press and labor movement's support for the Zaneros, no official action was taken to restore Zaña's lands or to punish the perpetrators. On the contrary, the Prefecture of Lambayeque ordered the arrest of Mercedes Cachay, Zaña's leader, and the continuation of repression as long as the Zaneros maintained "their rebellious attitude."[53] In January 1914 authorities imprisoned Mercedes Cachay and several Zaneros on charges of destruction of property. *El Jornalero* decried their unjust imprisonment and expressed outrage at the absence of liberty and rights for the poor in Peru. To remedy all of these wrongs, *El Jornalero* editorialized, "the Peruvian proletariat only needs [to apply] large doses of blood."[54] Aimed at the diverse urban and rural workers in the enclaves, this anarchist clarion call for workers' self-emancipation would ultimately reverberate in a region-wide strike wave in the early 1920s.

In April 1912, a mass bracero rebellion broke out in the Chicama and Moche Valleys prompting anarchists to engage in propaganda and solidarity actions on behalf of sugar workers. The conflict began on April 8 when upward of five thousand rural workers armed with hatchets and machetes converged on hacienda Casa Grande and demanded an increase in wages and a reduction in work loads. Guards stationed on the hacienda clashed with strikers after the braceros occupied the sugar mill and attacked a company store. Fifteen workers were killed.[55] Protests and work stoppages soon spread to the other sugar plantations in the Chicama and Moche Valleys. To prevent further destruction to plantation installations and the burning of cane fields, Lima sent 300 troops to bolster the rural police, and the military prefect of La Libertad declared a state of siege.[56] Anarchist propaganda in support of the braceros led the prefect to imprison Reynaga and shutter *El Jornalero*.[57] By mid-May the uprising was suppressed, but not before it had claimed the lives of 150 workers. After his release from prison in June, Reynaga continued to defend the braceros and to vent his ire on the planter class. *El Jornalero* harshly criticized

51 *La Abeja*, May 8, 1913; *El Jornalero*, May 16, 1913.
52 *La Abeja*, June 29, 1913.
53 Prefect of Lambayeque to Director of Government, January 15, 1914, AGN, Folder 164.
54 *El Jornalero*, July 15, 1914.
55 *La Industria*, April 9, 1912.
56 Ramos Rau, *Mensaje de Trujillo*, 53.
57 *La Industria*, April 16, 1912.

the owners of Casa Grande for firing "countless employees and braceros without any justification" and for evicting them from plantation quarters without notice.[58] In addition to propaganda, anarchists intervened with the authorities on behalf of the braceros. On June 13, 1913, the CESUE in Trujillo convened delegates from anarchist groups and worker organizations in La Libertad to form a commission to secure the release of jailed braceros. Meanwhile *El Jornalero* continued to bring public pressure to bear by publishing poignant articles on the imprisoned braceros. On June 20, one article observed that "seven miserable indigenous braceros" had already been subject to more than a year in the Trujillo jail. The mother of Francisco Huamán, one of these braceros, had implored the editorial staff at *El Jornalero* to intercede on his behalf. The article concluded with an appeal to the Trujillo public:

> Is it possible for the people of Trujillo to consent and support [this situation], knowing that this old and sad woman is dying of pain and hunger, only to keep the feudal lords content and free from strikes and workers' demands in Chicama Valley? No and a thousand times no. It's necessary for the working class and all the people to raise their voice in defense of those poor workers, for humanity, for comradeship, and for our own preservation.[59]

The very next day the prefect and the presiding criminal judge bowed to the commission and public pressure and released the prisoners.

In the years following the first Chicama rebellion in 1912, the anarchist movement laid the groundwork for a more concerted and extensive assault on oligarchic rule and capitalist exploitation in the sugar export enclave. LAOP continued to reach out to rural peons and offer succor and financial aid.[60] Meanwhile anarchist workers circulated widely throughout the enclave promoting a counter-hegemonic perspective, worker unity, and syndicalist organization. Driven by the desire for better job prospects or compelled to move by employers' hostility, they migrated frequently from rural to urban and urban to rural settings. In the process of traversing the department and spreading anarcho-syndicalist ideas and organization, they created what Andrew Herod would call a "subversive geography of mobility and solidarity" in La Libertad.[61] By 1921 it would result in a major anarchist-influenced workers' insurgency that engulfed the entire sugar enclave.

58 *El Jornalero*, June 11, 1912.
59 *El Jornalero*, June 20, 1913.
60 *La Opinión Pública*, June 3, 1917.
61 See Andrew Herod, ed., *Organizing the Landscape: Geographical Perspectives on Unionism* (Minneapolis: University of Minnesota Press, 1998), 123.

Several young radical mestizo workers played an instrumental role in the spread of anarcho-syndicalist ideas, organization, and labor militancy in La Libertad. These were Manuel Arévalo Cáceres, Eduardo Chávez Terrazas, Artemio Zavala Paredes, and Leopoldo Pita Verde. Arévalo migrated from his native province of Ascope to the Chicama Valley to work as a rural laborer and a mechanic on various sugar plantations. At the age of fourteen he worked alongside Chávez Terrazas as a mechanic's assistant on the Cartavio plantation. Both had contact with Julio Reynaga and were exposed to anarcho-syndicalist ideas disseminated by *El Jornalero*.[62] In 1917 Chávez founded the first workers' resistance society at Cartavio, called Sociedad Obrera de Auxilios Mutuos y Caja de Ahorros. Subsequently, Arévalo went to work at Casa Grande and formed a Workers' Committee to press for the eight-hour day. For his temerity, Arévalo would be arrested and transported to Lima in August 1920. Before returning to Trujillo and the sugar enclave in 1921, he formed relationships with anarcho-syndicalists in Lima-Callao.[63] On the eve of the 1921 worker insurgency, he promoted syndical organization and workers' cultural associations named for Manuel González Prada, the renowned Limeño anarchist thinker, on the haciendas Chiclín, Chiquitoy, and Casa Grande.[64]

Zavala Paredes became an influential proponent of syndicalism after migrating from the sierra town of Santiago de Chuco to work as a mechanic at the Roma plantation. There he befriended Joaquín Díaz Ahumada, another worker autodidact, and together they read publications by Malatesta, Kropotkin, and other revolutionary socialists.[65] He also had contact with Chávez Terrazas and drew on his advice to found Roma's first union organization, the Sociedad Obrera de Auxilios y Caja de Ahorras de Roma in March 1921.[66] Shortly thereafter, as the union's leader, he drafted a list of demands that challenged the system of domination on the hacienda. Among other demands it called for the abolition of *enganche* contracts and corporal punishment, removal of the civil guard, and the implementation of an eight-hour workday and minimum wages. Amid the ensuing strike action in April, Zavala teamed with Leopoldo Pita, a worker on hacienda Chiclín, to colligate worker organizations in

62 Arévalo delivered the eulogy at Reynaga's funeral in July 1923. José Daniel Hidalgo Gamarra, *Arévalo. El Hombre Completo* (Trujillo, Peru: Servicios Gráficos Litton's EIRL, 2004), 28, 41.

63 See, Juvenal Ñique Ríos, *Manuel Arévalo Cáceres: Apuntes Históricos* (Lima: Universidad de San Martín de Porres, 2007), 148.

64 On the influence of González Prada on Arévalo, see ibid., 158–59, 181–86.

65 Joaquín Díaz Ahumada, *Luchas sindicales en el valle de Chicama* (Trujillo, Peru: Libreria Star, n.d. 2nd edition), 52–53.

66 Zavala elected not to use the term "union" in order to avoid provoking the plantation administrators. See Javier Delgado Benites, *Artemio Zavala: Paladín del Sindicalismo Liberteño* (Trujillo, Peru: Impresos Gráficos Gutemberg, 2011), 45.

La Libertad into a single, departmental labor federation.[67] In August 1921 they founded the Regional Labor Union (Sindicato Regional del Trabajo, SRT), which claimed to represent twenty-eight thousand sugar, railway, port, and urban workers and two thousand employees.[68]

The anarcho-syndicalist propaganda and organizing activities of itinerant workers and anarchists in Trujillo profoundly influenced the mass mobilization and struggle of workers in Chicama in 1921. This can be seen in the use of solidarity and general strikes that converted what was originally a local conflict over wages at the Roma plantation into a broad working-class struggle against the dominant order in the sugar enclave. On April 6 and September 13, 1921, for example, workers in Trujillo engaged in general strikes with support from enclave transport and port workers. In addition, one can discern in this labor insurgency the realization, albeit temporary, of long-standing anarchist objectives, such as the formation of an urban and rural worker alliance, the organization of bracero unions, and the establishment of a powerful departmental labor federation. The SRT's strike demands also reflected anarcho-syndicalist formulations. Among its eighteen-point list of demands, the SRT insisted on the recognition of all workers' organizations, the abolition of *enganche* labor, and the adoption of the eight-hour workday.[69]

For the planter class there was little doubt that the escalation of worker militancy in the enclave was attributable to anarchist agitation. Rafael Larco Herrera, owner of the Chiclín plantation put it bluntly: "The recent workers' movements of this valley have been controlled by known elements of anarchist affiliation, that are easily identified in Trujillo at any time."[70] In Lima the business and mainstream press shared this view. *Variedades*, a popular high-society magazine, editorialized, for example, that provocateurs "have undermined the spirit of the workers of the valley with a bolshevist virus and with outdated Proudhonian theories and other nonsense" and "implanted in the heart of the laboring masses the most rebellious anarchist ideas."[71] The striking workers, it added, "were not strikers seeking redress for a violated right, but revolutionaries unfurling a banner of the destruction of property."[72] Sugar planters, likewise, considered SRT leaders to be recalcitrant revolutionaries and refused to recognize the legitimacy of the SRT or its affiliated worker organizations. To thwart initial government attempts to seek a negotiated solution

67 *La Industria*, August 11, 1921; see also Delgado Benites, *Artemio Zavala*, 62–63.
68 *La Industria*, August 15, 1921.
69 *La Industria*, December 12, 1921. Defense of the workers' press was another demand.
70 *La Industria*, August 23 and October 20, 1921.
71 *Variedades*, October 15, 1921, 1597–98; and October 22, 1921, 1669–70.
72 Ibid.

Zamalek underpass, *Tank vs. Biker* wall

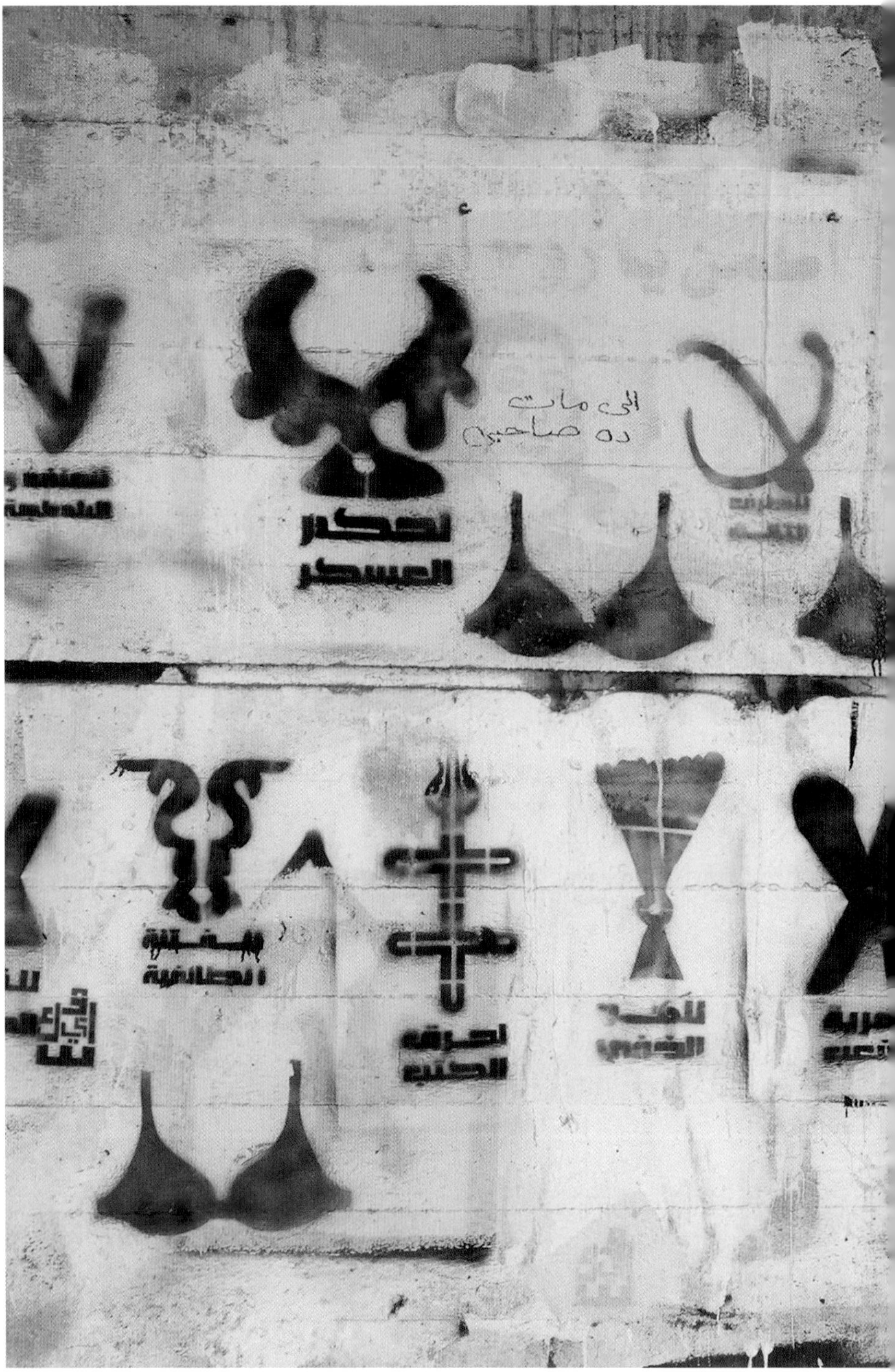

Various “No” stencils sprayed on the *Tank vs. Biker* wall in Zamalek

للحكم
العسكر
في ناس
انعمت
عشان انت
تتشوف

"You can step on the flowers, but you cannot postpone spring"

The No book

"No to infantilizing the people."

"No to sectarian divisions."

"No to the emergency law."

"No to the barricading walls."

"No to a new pharaoh."

"No to sniper pashas."

"No to burning of books."

"No to killing Azhari sheikhs."

"No to military rule."

"No to violence."

"No to stripping the people."

"No to stealing the revolution."

Rafael Larco sent a memo to the Ministry of Development (*Ministerio de Fomento*), characterizing the SRT as a sinister, confrontational organization with an unstable rotating leadership bent on the creation of "soviets" in the Chicama and Santa Catalina valleys.[73] Fearing that the SRT posed a real threat to the sugar industry and Peru's national economic interests, the Leguía government, acting at the behest of the planter class, forcibly dismantled the SRT in 1922. Pita, Zavala, and other SRT leaders were arrested and transported to Lima aboard a naval warship while army troops suppressed the strikes at the cost of one hundred workers killed and two hundred wounded. José Ignacio Chopitea, owner of hacienda Laredo, summed up the gratitude and relief of the sugar planters in a note to the military prefect of La Libertad. Comparing the SRT to France's anarcho-syndicalist General Confederation of Workers (CGT), he exclaimed, "You have saved Trujillo and the nation drowning in its cradle this poor imitation of that confederation, which here calls itself the Regional Labor Union."[74]

Conclusion

The formation of the anarchist movement in northern Peru coincided with the expansion of the sugar export enclaves from the 1890s to the early 1920s. Centered in the coastal cities of Trujillo and Chiclayo, it sought to unite urban and rural workers and peasants to resist land and water usurpation, the dispossession of peasant communities, and the imposition of coercive and exploitative labor practices in La Libertad and Lambayeque. To counter the designs and pretensions of sugar planters and state authorities, it formulated an emancipatory project predicated on urban and rural worker solidarity and an inclusive subaltern resistance movement. To overcome ethnic differences and parochialism and to unify the region's diverse subaltern groups, it assiduously promoted an anarchist international imaginary. This anarchist internationalist identification and worldview were bolstered by transnational anarchist networks and the adoption and adaptation of slogans, icons, and cultural forms linked to international anarchism. Between 1912 and 1921, the anarchist movement achieved a significant degree of organization and resistance capabilities. This was reflected in the series of rebellions that nearly upended oligarchic rule in the enclaves.

Despite the repression of the anarchist movement in the northern Peru in the early 1920s, it did not eradicate a vital legacy of urban-rural worker solidarity and resistance. Indeed, throughout the 1920s and the

73 Reprinted in Rafael Larco Herrera, *Memorias* (n.p., 1947), 66.

74 *La Industria*, January 14, 1922.

early 1930s new anarchist groups and workers' movements emerged to carry on the struggle for land and liberty and social revolution. These ideas and goals were articulated by anarchist groups and labor organizations such as Chiclayanos Concientes, the anarcho-syndicalist Land and Maritime Workers Federation of the Port of Eten (1926), the bracero organization on hacienda Cartavio (1922), and the Syndicalist Solidarity Group (1928) in Trujillo. They also resonated with and informed the mass-based Trujillo rebellion of July 1932, led by the American Popular Revolutionary Alliance (APRA). Among the leaders of this rebellion were Juan Delfín Montoya, a veteran peasant activist, and Manuel Barreto Risco, who learned the tenets of anarcho-syndicalism at the side of Leopoldo Pita Verde.[75] Today the history of the anarchist movement and its struggles in northern Peru continues to be a vital legacy for future workers' movements in the region.

75 Margarita Giesecke characterizes the Trujillo rebellion as a "social revolution" based on the massive participation of urban and port workers, and braceros. She also notes the conspicuous leadership role of former anarcho-syndicalist activists. See Margarita Giesecke, "The Trujillo Insurrection, the Apra Party, and the Making of Modern Peruvian Politics," (PhD dissertation, University of London, Birkbeck College, 1993).

SPRAYING NO

Bahia Shehab
Cairo, April 2013

Spraying NO

I was recruited to the revolution by images and sounds that I saw in my newsfeed. I have never belonged to a political party and I was never in my life interested in politics. I spray messages on the streets of Cairo because I simply want to see the country where my daughters and their children will live in the future a better place. I want them to find happiness here on their land and not seek it on the lands of others because their government is corrupt, and for that idea I am willing to face whatever fate decides to throw my way.

My story started with a book. In 2010, I was invited as an artist to produce an installation for The Future of Tradition—The Tradition of Future, an exhibition at the Haus Der Kunst in Munich, produced by the Khatt Foundation in Amsterdam. The foundation is concerned with the development of Arabic script, and the exhibition was to showcase works by female Arab artists and designers. The curator had only one condition: I had to use Arabic script for my artwork. As a human being living in the world at that moment—as an artist, an Arab, a woman—I decided I only had one thing to say: NO. There were a thousand things I wanted to say no to. In Arabic, to confirm and stress the no, we say, "No, and a thousand times no." So I decided to look for a thousand different no's. I found characters from Spain, Afghanistan, Iran, China, and all the countries where Arabic was used, on everything ever produced—buildings, mosques, architecture, plates, textiles, pottery, books. I examined all of these artifacts, and it was very easy to find the "no" character in Arabic because the Islamic Shahadah starts with, "There is no God but Allah." So the word "no" was easy to spot because it was everywhere. With the thousand no's, I created a plexiglass curtain, 3.5 by 7 meters.[1] I compiled my findings in a book, placing the no's chronologically, stating the places I found them, the medium, and the patron that commissioned the work and the date.

When the revolution started in January 2011, I forgot completely about the artwork and the book and became very immersed in the unfolding events of the revolution. Nine months into the revolution, I realized that every no has a reason. They are not a thousand general no's. I could assign a purpose, a message, to each one of these no's. So I started using the no's like ammunition. I designed stencils with them, and sprayed them on the walls and streets of Cairo. At the same time, I was taking these characters out of their historic context and assigning them a new context—a modern context—giving them new life. So many of these no's are resurrected historic graphic forms coming back to life.

1 "A Thousand Times NO," The Khatt Foundation Center for Arabic Typography, last modified March 14, 2014, http://www.khtt.net/page/25951/en.

The first "no" I ever sprayed on the streets of Cairo was "*No to military rule.*" The image of dead people thrown and piled like garbage on the street was too painful for my conscience to accept. I later discovered that an NGO called Mosireen was behind the circulation of that image.[2] It was nine months into the revolution and the military was in control of the country. This was November, 2011; Egyptians were afraid of the void on the chair; the man on the street wanted to feel that there was someone in control, and the talk and preparations for the first presidential election campaigns were still corridor chats in ministries, private clubs, and several Egyptian mansions. Marshal Tantawi came out with a speech confirming that the military was not interested in running the country and Egypt would have a new president by the end of June 2012. It was clearly communicated to me through my newsfeed that under military rule in Egypt people were still being shot and gassed on the street, thus my simple expression "No to military rule." This is what my mind at the time could process.

But I later discovered that what was happening on the street was not caused by the military alone, but rather by a regime that was still in place using the same apparatuses to deal with the demands of protesters. So I started looking at the products of this regime and I started spraying "no" to them. "*No to violence*" because activists were and are still sharing images of brutality against them online. Rami Essam is a young man who came from Mansoura, a small city in a province in Egypt, to Tahrir Square a few days into the revolution with nothing but his guitar and a dream for a better Egypt. Rami shared an image of his bruised and beaten body on March 10, 2011,[3] but I was too taken with the dream of the revolution and too naive to believe that the rotten system of governance was still there. So after the series of severe street brutalities in November 2011, I started to look again at the events of the past nine months and I started rejecting them, spraying no to them on the streets. "*No to blinding heroes*" was sprayed for Ahmad Harara and the hundreds of protesters who were specifically being targeted and shot in the eye. Ahmad was shot in his right eye on January 28 and in his left eye on November 19, 2011. He appeared in a TV interview smiling and saying that if the price of freedom and dignity for a better Egypt is losing the light of his eyes then he is willingly giving them both, but we want a better country.[4] On the same topic, "*No*

2 Mosireen, last modified March 19, 2014, http://mosireen.org/.

3 "URGENT: Rami Essam testimony about his torture at the Hands of the Army Yesterday, قطر الندى (Dewdrops), last modified March 10, 2011, http://atralnada.wordpress.com/2011/03/10/ramy/.

4 "Akhir Kalam: Ahmad Harara Gave the Light of His Eyes as a Free Man," Akhir Kalam: Ahmad Harara qadam nour 'ainaih hurran, YouTube, last modified November 21, 2011, http://www.youtube.com/watch?v=m5YSdredAJg.

to sniper pashas" was sprayed in reference to a video that was circulating in November of 2011 of a police lieutenant called Mahmoud Sobhy el-Shinawy who was caught on video shooting at protesters and being saluted by one of his assistants saying to him, "You are so strong, Pasha, you got the boy's eye."[5] That sentence initiated a wave of anger against the Egyptian police forces; it stood as proof that the police are responsible for shooting at the protesters and more specifically that they meant to shoot at the eyes of protesters and police officers salute each other when they get someone's eyes. How far can their sadism go? We have the hard fact in video circulating and thousands of people watching it. Now what happens when thousands of people view something online is that the people in the mainstream media start picking up on it, so the video was also shared on TV, creating an even bigger schism between the police and the people. I wanted to honor in the same stencil Ahmad Harara again, for the second eye he lost, so I added a salute to him on the top of the "*No to sniper pashas*" stencil.

The physical violence that is inflicted on protesters is no longer hidden behind prison walls; it is taking place on the street and it could happen to anyone now. What is different is that we are very aware of this fact. How do you react to such an idea? Someone wants to kill you because you have an opinion different from theirs. I spray for myself and for the others around me who are suffering, and I can see and hear their suffering. Their news does not come to me two months later in a dead letter from the fronts, it comes to me in real time and in full color with sound and movement. Their suffering is real and tangible and it projects on me as a human being, because I can see their cuts and their bruises, I can see their bullet wounds and hear their screams. I do not need to be on the street to see their suffering; they have brought their suffering to me, to my house, to my room, to my screen. I am their fellow human and I feel that I need to act accordingly. So I don't stop. I spray some more.

"*No to stripping the people*" was sprayed for the veiled lady with the blue bra whose video was circulated on social media and went on to travel the world on the front pages and major news networks around the globe.[6] She was captured on video as three soldiers dragged her to the ground, stripping her clothes off her body, revealing her now famous blue bra. She never came out; we will never know who she is; she is too afraid or too

5 "Mahmoud Sobhy el-Shinawy an Egyptian Officer Targeting the Eyes of Protesters," Mahmoud Sobhy el-Shinawy zabit masry yastahdif a'yin al-mutathahirin, YouTube, last modified November 21, 2011, http://www.youtube.com/watch?v=tuXxVw4xTlo.

6 "Image of Unknown Woman Beaten by Egypt's Military Echoes around the World," *Guardian*, last modified December 18, 2011, http://www.guardian.co.uk/commentisfree/2011/dec/18/egypt-military-beating-female-protester-tahrir-square.

ashamed. But stripping her on the streets of Cairo on December 17, 2011, stripped the army of any respect the people had for them. Now the police and the army have both been labeled as corrupt in the eyes of the people. We have hard proof, we have videos, pictures, and sound bites, all we need now is justice. I sprayed a blue bra with "*No to stripping the people*" and a footprint, the footprint of the soldier who stomped on her stomach with his boots. The footprint reads "Long live a peaceful revolution" because we would not like to retaliate with violence, a very difficult sentiment to keep up after the brutality that you see and that makes us closely understand the greatness of a character like Gandhi.

Activists who are being gassed on the street collect the empty shells that are fired at them and they look at the place of manufacturing and post photos of the different kinds of tear gas being sprayed. They circulate these when a new shipment of tear gas arrives from its destination, and they share articles in foreign newspapers that detail how much tear gas was bought and for how much money it was bought. We know the evil and its sources and we know it is going to be used on peaceful protesters and we just want a better country. "*No to tear gas*" was sprayed after seeing the many images of empty tear gas shells from the United States and the UK. There are even jokes about it. One activist who found an empty gas shell shared its expiry date online with a caption that read, "The people want fresh tear gas. This one has expired five years ago." A couple went down to the street to get married wearing their wedding clothes and their tear gas masks. The tear gas mask became a fashion statement in post-revolution Egyptian society, and there has been tremendous compilation of gas mask inventions and design solutions documented in photos from different protests on the streets of Egypt in the past two years.

So these stencils that are directly related to the safety of people found their way from my studio to the streets of Cairo. But once I started thinking further, beyond the man on the street, I thought of the cause of the actions against the man on the street and "*No to emergency law*" was born. We have been living under emergency law since the assassination of Sadat. On May 31, 2012, under the reign of President Mursi, the cancellation of the emergency law in Egypt was declared. But people are still being arrested on the streets sometimes for no charges and demonstrators are still being asked to provide details of their protests to the government before they go down to the streets. The police still have access to our houses and our offices when they want to. I still do not feel safe in my country and I do not feel that my government has my or my daughters' best interests in mind, so I spray some more.

Images of Salma Said circulated on February 5, 2012. She had bullet wounds in her face with blood running down from a wound so close to her eye that it was evident her eye was almost going to meet the same fate that both eyes of Ahamd Harara have met. Her images look like the images you would see of the statue of the Virgin Mary crying blood. The difference now is that Salma is not a religious character. She is real and she lives in the now and that bullet could have hit anyone, anyone who would dare to walk the streets of Cairo and voice their opinion. No one is safe anymore. X-ray shots of tens of small bullets that were fired at her body by the police were circulated by activists on Flickr. I sprayed "*No to bullets*" because of the hundreds of photos I saw of activists with bullet wounds in their body.

Sheikh Imad elDine Effat was shot during a demonstration on December 16, 2011, leaving behind two orphans and a widow. I use his name as an example of the thousands of people who were shot and are still disappearing off the streets of Cairo. "*No to killing men of religion*" was sprayed on the streets to highlight how blind the regime is, that it does not differentiate between good and bad, that its killing machines are working brutally and randomly on the street without differentiating a thug from a peaceful protester, in this case a man of religion. I will not write about the young men, the teenagers who are still currently being killed on the streets because they are admins on Facebook pages that are opposing the regime, I will merely mention Sheikh Imad as an example. For the no of this stencil I took a ligature off a tombstone at the Islamic museum in Cairo. I thought that since the topic is death I might as well use a symbol from history that also belonged to death.[7]

On December 17, 2011, the Institute of Egypt was burned. I thought it was a painful strike to intellectuals inside the country and outside. A recent post by Khaled Fahmy, a prominent local historian, on his social site mentions the fact that this building has been dead for a very long time because nobody used to visit it anyway. He blames the Egyptian intellectuals for deserting governmental institutions. I guess thirty years can take their toll on anyone, even intellectuals.

Among the thousands of important books burned on that December night was copy of the *Description de l'Égypte*. It is not a catastrophic problem in the sense that there are several copies of the same sort in and out of Egypt, but the message that even our history is being erased became even more depressing. It also became more and more evident what a crumbling, useless regime had been ruling the country for the past thirty years. An institution as valuable as this one was left with no proper security or protection. But we knew that all along, and that is part of why the revolution started. The management of cultural heritage is a

7 Mubarak al-Mekki, Tombstone, inventory #3904, Islamic Museum in Cairo.

concept very foreign to the previous regime and the current one alike. "*No to burning books*" came to life in this context, and we were able to come out with something very valuable from this tragic event. When the books were burning, all of the conservationists came together for the rescue, so people from different institutions who were concerned collaborated on salvaging whatever was left. That event introduced people to each other who were operating in the same field of conservation in the same city and they have devised plans for the process of rescuing books, so that in case another unfortunate event takes place, they now know how to address the problem efficiently. We should always look for anything positive in the darkest of moments.

I saw images of the barrier walls that were set up in downtown Cairo all around the Ministry of Interior to protect the building against protesters on February 5, 2012. One street artist, Ammar Abou-Bakr, wrote a Quranic verse in big bright fluorescent colors on one of these walls. A total of seven walls were set up at the time, and the number increased up to twelve walls under Mursi's rule. The wall where Ammar wrote his verse was blocking the street that lead to my old school where I studied for my master's degree for four years. I considered that building home because it housed the rare books library of the American University in Cairo. The idea that I could not have easy access to that building was a disturbing thought for me. "*No to barrier walls*" was sprayed on that wall, and on the same night I sprayed it along with many other no's on the barrier walls that were right in front of the Ministry of Interior. Behind that wall was where the government keeps its guns and tanks that are used to kill protesters, snipe their eyes out and mutilate their bodies. It was the first full wall I sprayed. I met random people at the Buras Café, a place downtown where the rebels meet after demonstrations to discuss plans and remeet after they have been gassed down by the government. It is a good meeting spot and very central. The people who came to help me were from different walks of life, some of them university professors and others shop owners. They were mostly young, with ages ranging from seventeen to forty, but they all helped and they all sprayed and I never saw some of them again.

On the February 1, seventy-four young men who went to Port Said to watch a football match were killed in the stadium. The match was being broadcast live on TV to the horror of the millions of people watching. One of the young men killed was a student at the university where I taught. His name was Omar Mohsen and he was graduating that spring. I found a poem by Pablo Neruda scribbled on a piece of paper in a field hospital in Tahrir Square. The poem read, "you can cut down the flowers but you can't delay the spring." It was the first time I went down to the street to spray a stencil in broad daylight. It did not matter anymore whether I got caught or not. I was very angry and I felt sorry for the mothers who thought that they sent their children off to a peaceful recreational football match and they welcomed them back as corpses. I did not feel that I deserved to live anymore. I sprayed the poem all around Tahrir and all around al-Ahli Club.

"*No to a new Pharaoh*" was sprayed on May 28, 2012. Ahmad Shafik and Mohamed Morsi were the finalists in the first "democratic" presidential elections in Egypt. Shafik belonged to Mubarak's old regime and Mursi belonged to the Muslim Brotherhood. Neither option represented the aspirations of the revolution. I went down to Mohamad Mahmoud Street in Tahrir to pay tribute to the portraits of the martyrs that are painted on the AUC walls in downtown. I discovered a huge painting by Ammar Abou-Bakr lamenting the results of the elections. He had worked all of the night before. I cried for half an hour on the street when I saw his work at 5:00 a.m. on the sidewalk. I knew that we are connected. I have never met him in my life, but when the result was announced we all hit the streets at the same time to protest for the same reason, without any previous plan. This is the mass subconscious that everyone keeps talking about. I was living it and it was painful and beautiful at the same time. Finding each other on the streets of Cairo, this is the real revolution.

We learnt a great lesson in May. We learnt that our actions on the street are not reflected in the ballots, and until we organize and unify we will not be able to take this country to the better place we want it to be. We learnt that democracy needs tools that we still have not acquired. We learnt that we are taking baby steps toward a new future, but the most important part of this whole process is that we learnt.

More no's flowed afterward: no to postponing trials, no to military trials, no to a constitution before the president, no to sectarian divisions, no to external agendas, no to third parties, no to conspiracy theories, no to aliens, no to the infiltrating minority, no to stealing the revolution, no and a thousand times no.

In November of 2012, I sprayed one more no, "*No to Mursi.*" He had just given himself new dictatorship authorities and he deserved one of my no's with flying colors. After that no, I studied and counted the 970 remaining ones in my book. I know I will need them in the days, months, and years to come. I know I have more than enough ammunition. The Egyptian revolution is not dead. This is not the end, this is only the beginning.

Author's Note

In the past three years I have sprayed many campaigns after the thousand times no on the streets of Cairo. On June 30, 2013, we went down again to demonstrate against Muslim Brotherhood rule. Egyptian law scholar and diplomat Mohamed ElBaradei along with national religious figures, General AbdulFattah al-Sisi, and several other army generals, all appeared on TV on July 3, 2013, to announce the ousting of Mohamed Morsi from his post as president and declare a new road map for Egypt.[8] We refused to belive that that was a military coup because it was also the will of the people; we did go down in the millions demonstrating against the Brotherhood regime. A video circulated of General al-Sisi saying that he has no interest in anything except seeing Egypt as the best country in the world and that the army has no intentions of running the country and they are only concerned with realizing the will of the people, and the people believed.

General AbdulFattah al-Sisi resigned from his post as head of Egypt's armed forces in March of 2014 to announce that he will be running for the presidency.[9] In May 2014, al-Sisi was elected president with the overwhelming majority of votes in his favor. As I write these words, police brutality, activist imprisonment and assassinations, and the silencing of opposition has intensified. The examples are too many to be ignored. Will we go down to the streets again? I do not know, so far the people are still happy with their newly elected president, but the torture machine is alive and kicking. A part of society chose to ignore the fact that injustice is being practiced against people who have different views than theirs, but for how long can this be sustained? The road to justice is still young and the biggest battles are yet to be fought. They might not be fought in big numbers on the streets anymore, but they will be fought. We planted the seeds, but whether we will live to see them grow is a different question.

Cairo, July 4, 2014

8 See the following videos of this event: "Dr Mohammad al-Baradie's Word at the Armed Forces Conference 3/7/2013," Kalimat al-doctor Mohammad al-Baradie fi moutamar al-quwat al-musallaha 3/7/2013, https://www.youtube.com/watch?v=Wu1A79IpogA/; "Statement of the army's general leadership and Egyptian Armed Forces and the excommunication of President Mohammad Mursi," Bayan al-qiyada al-'ammah liljaysh wal quwwat al musallaha al-masriya wa 'azl al-rais Mohammad Mursi 3/7/2013, https://www.youtube.com/watch?v=dAssiYJLfL4/; "The word of the Sheikh of al-Azhar 3/7/2013 Excommunicating Mursi from rule," Kalimat Sheikh al-Azhar 3/7/2013 'azl Mursi 'an al-Hukim, https://www.youtube.com/watch?v=UbAY5gvnXzU.

9 "Sisi: I swear by Allah that I will not run for the presidency," al-Sisi aqsum billah ma hartashah lilriasa. https://www.youtube.com/watch?v=AhXZKNWG5jo.

The Destruction of Maps
Haifa Zangana

THE BLACK MIRROR: ANARCHISM, SURREALISM, AND THE SITUATIONISTS

It was in the black mirror of anarchism that surrealism first recognized itself.

André Breton

SURREALISM AND SITUATIONISM:

An attempt at a comparison and critique by an Admirer and Participant, including a brief look at a seemingly faraway place in space and time; or, King Kong meets Godzilla . . . How New Thoughts are let loose in the World

Penelope Rosemont

> Young people everywhere have been allowed to choose between love and a garbage disposal unit. Everywhere they have chosen the garbage disposal unit.
>
> —Gilles Ivain (Ivan Chtcheglov)

> When it comes to revolt, none of us need ancestors.
>
> —André Breton

> Without Contraries is no progression.
>
> —William Blake

This is an attempt at the impossible, that is to sum up *briefly* the interactions, the concepts, and the importance of two of the most significant and most radical movements of the twentieth century, movements that have not only shaped the thoughts and actions of radical thought and alternative media but have found their way into the mainstream, for better or for worse, and changed in major ways how we see and interpret our world. The Chicago Surrealist group which Franklin Rosemont and I helped found from an outpost of the Industrial Workers of the World (IWW), the Solidarity Bookshop, was in contact with the situationists and their writings, with anarchists Fredy and Lorraine Perlman in Detroit, and also with André Breton and the French surrealist group. There were significant points of rupture between the surrealists and the situationists, but they shared a narrative history and an analysis of both is needed so that we may determine what has been surpassed, make decisions about the nature of the society we live in, and create new possibilities for the emergence of another, hopefully improved, version.

In 1965, my arrival in Paris was an accident. I was with Franklin Rosemont and we had just been deported from England as undesirables. A large black "x" was impressed with a pen in our passports and we were given a special security guard escort to our plane. Perhaps this was the best accident, or objective chance experience as surrealists label it, of our entire lives. It's true we had gone to Europe looking for surrealists, for anarchists, and for adventure . . . and we found all of them.

Not far from the hotel we found in Paris at Rue Dauphine and Rue de Buci, an international surrealist exhibition had just opened. It was called *L'Ecart absolu*, absolute divergence, and it was dedicated to and being held in celebration of the utopian socialist thinker Charles Fourier, inventor of the Phalanstery and the Butterfly Passion.

At the very center of the exhibition was a giant piece, a "monster" fifteen feet tall—made up of a huge pink mattress, with mattress head and mattress arms extended. It had one eye—a television set; from its head sprouted the sirens of a police van; its stomach consisted of an automatic washer with a window; its contents, the wash (daily newspapers), tumbled over each other hypnotically. And then on a label we found its name; it was called *The Consumer* and it exemplified that great bloated *monster* of contemporary society.

The café where the surrealists met in 1965 was Le Promenade de Venus and it was located in the old central market district Les Halles, where in the middle of the night and all night long, trucks still rumbled over the cobble-stoned streets bringing vegetables, cheeses, and meats. Workingmen transported sides of beef on their shoulders and rolled giant cheeses to the covered market area in wheelbarrows. The sweet smell of onion soup pervaded everywhere. Fairly large and well lit, the café was filled with mirrors, but definitely it was a working-class café. The surrealists gathered daily, arriving one by one after the end of their workday. This meeting seemed the highlight of their day. Perhaps it was the elation that the *L'ecart absolu* exhibition had created, but each strode in boldly, smiling, and shook hands all around.

Across the Seine, near the Sorbonne, was a small bookstore, La Vieille taupe, the old mole. That is where I found the Situationist International (SI) literature in March 1966. I brought the flashy journal *Internationale Situationiste* and the "Address to Revolutionaries of Algeria and All Countries," the SI statement on the Algerian war, back to our hotel and both Franklin and I thought it excellent.

A surrealist group-initiated statement, the "Declaration of the 121" in 1960, had been the first issued against the vicious Algerian war. In 1966 the war dragged on, so it was important to see such a militant statement as the one the SI had issued. It seemed to signal that an entire new generation was not going to tolerate war and was ready to take a stand against oppression everywhere.

Later, at La Vieille taupe we bought more SI literature, and talked with the person who ran the store. He inquired, "Would you like to meet the situationists?" And indeed we did want to meet them, in part because calling ourselves revolutionaries then, when we were living the "best of all possible lives" in the "best of all possible worlds," seemed totally out of place, impossible, crazy. And what we hoped for was to meet people who besides ourselves were intransigent insurrectionists, implacable enemies of the stale social order.

A few days later, we met representatives of the SI at a small café on a second floor, plain white walls, nobody there but us four: Guy Debord, Alice Becker Ho, Franklin Rosemont, and I. Our meeting with Debord went well. We liked him very much, he smiled often, had a lively intelligence, good sense of humor, and was well acquainted with surrealism and its ideas. He admitted a fondness for surrealism and said, "If this were the 1930s, I'd be a surrealist!" But he considered that surrealism had been absorbed: "They teach it in the grade schools. Now one must be a situationist!"

We commented that we thought conditions were different in the United States, that people there really didn't know what surrealism was since so very little was available in translation—the surrealist images had moved with the speed of light compared to its theory and politics. And we thought a better understanding of surrealism would create an understanding and a necessity that would push beyond stale and rigid Marxism, that our group in making a specifically surrealist intervention in the United States would certainly add a new dynamic to the growing revolutionary consciousness. A more difficult task than we imagined, but surrealism never aspired to be a mass political movement in itself, it didn't plan to issue membership cards. The same was true with the SI—they were after a fashion what could be called "influencing machines" or "viruses of the mind," using one of today's modern expressions from the popular writer Richard Brodie. Surrealism has always considered itself a choice, a way of life. Both of these groups, surrealists and SI—admirers of Sade, Rimbaud, and Lautréamont—would be well-pleased to be considered "viruses of the mind."

Much of what is still "in the air" today, imprinted in our consciousness from the 1960s, are remnants, the few words, the slogans that were put together to fit on buttons or to be quickly painted on walls. One can't remember May '68 or situationists without remembering, "Be Realistic,

Demand the Impossible" or "All Power to the Imagination!"—very surrealist-inspired slogans. And when we remember the anti-war movement, a slogan that comes to mind is the phrase our Solidarity Bookshop group invented in 1965 for a spring demonstration, "Make Love, Not War!" (Recently seen at a San Francisco bakery, transformed yet again to "Make Loaves, Not War!") These compact and closely fitted together words unfold into entire worlds. Worlds that are still in the making. I recall when we put the phrase together, giving a new twist to the old War Resisters League slogan, "Make Peace, Not War!" Too dull, we thought. The '60s were all about love and sexual freedom, we wanted to celebrate it. And in this day of computers, it is amusing to think about the way I had to physically arrange the letters on a circle drawn from a coin to put together the badge layout. To our great astonishment, demand was such that we needed to have the button printed and reprinted many times.

At our meeting with Debord, we were able to understand his French and he could understand our English, so our conversation ranged far and wide. We told about our Solidarity Bookshop in Chicago and our mimeoed journal, *Rebel Worker*. We had a lot in common with the SI, including being convinced of the importance of workers' councils. Also, we made a point to recommend Paul Cardan's *Modern Capitalism*. We planned to visit the London Solidarity group, Cardan followers, in the coming weeks.

We asked if we could bring some SI literature back with us to Chicago. This meeting was near the end of our sojourn in Paris so the exchange had to be arranged quickly. Debord was glad to supply us with SI literature free of charge. He liked us, otherwise why would he have spent so long with two kids? He was ten years older, in his thirties, with quite a few accomplishments. (We were twenty-two, and when I look at our photos I'm surprised anybody took us seriously.) Not eager to end the meeting, he seemed a bit disappointed that we didn't want to follow up on joining the SI . . . so, for better or for worse, we missed our chance to be the American section.

A couple of days later, Mustapha Khayati brought the SI publications Debord had promised. He didn't seem very familiar with surrealism or especially friendly. We did ask him about how one went about joining the SI and what the requirements were, but were told abruptly that we couldn't "dabble" in surrealism, too—dual memberships were not tolerated. We brought up Benjamin Péret, probably a mistake. Péret had written an attack on the SI published in *Le Surréalisme même*. Khayati gave us a stack of assorted pamphlets for our bookshop and at least three hundred copies of *The Decline and Fall of the Spectacular Commodity Economy*. These we sold in Chicago at Solidarity Bookshop, across the country though our journal *Rebel Worker*, through our mail order catalogue, and at Barbara's Bookstore, then on Wells Street. It is an honor to have had a role in spreading these ideas and to have been part of that network of new thought.

For us to whom history played an important role in understanding daily life, it was frustrating when we brought up the situationists to the surrealists. We got a scowl from Radovan Ivšić and simply, "They are not our friends." Nothing further. Breton was not present at that meeting. This response was not unusual; they didn't like to talk about splits and it was hard to pry this information out of any of them.

Before we left I suggested that we needed to write an essay or a manifesto, something to give to the surrealist group to explain at least in part why we had come, what we were doing there, and what our future intentions were. Our piece that we left with them, "The Situation of Surrealism in the United States," was translated and published the next year in *L'Archibras 2*, October 1967. It was later published in Franklin's book, *The Morning of a Machine Gun*, in May 1968 (just as things were heating up in Paris and Chicago). Liberation Press at the SDS headquarters in Chicago was the printer. I was working there at the time. In our essay, we brought Herbert Marcuse's importance to the attention of the Paris group.

*

There is a considerable tangled and knotted web of history behind the relationship between the surrealist group and the SI group. Quite a few of the persons who played important roles in one were also linked to the other, or were among the important players in surrealist groups or SI precursor groups or knew one another from those groups or were in contact with each other. Our friend Edouard Jaguer in Paris, who was very helpful on my book *Surrealist Women*, was part of a small group of young people who established the group Le Surréalisme révolutionnare toward the end of World War II. He was a member of Cobra (and also later part of the Paris surrealist group). Later, he established the surrealist-related journal *Phases*. Important Cobra members were Asger Jorn and also Pierre Aleshinsky, whose beautiful print *Central Park* was prominently displayed at the surrealist exhibition L'Ecart Absolu right next to the giant pink mattress of *The Consumer*. Both Jorn and Aleshinsky played significant roles in the SI.

*

One of the major theorists of surrealism today, Michael Löwy, writes in *Morning Star: Surrealism, Marxism, Anarchism, Situationism, Utopia* that surrealism is "the human spirit in revolt and an eminently subversive attempt to re-enchant the world. . . . to reestablish the 'enchanted' dimensions at the core of human existence—poetry, passion, mad love, imagination, magic, myth, the marvelous, dreams, revolt, utopian ideals—which have been eradicated by this civilization and its values.... surrealism is an adventure that is at once intellectual and passionate, political and magical, poetic and dreamlike."[1] Löwy's book also contains an essential article assessing the significance of Guy Debord and his thought, "Consumed by Night's Fire: The Dark Romanticism of Guy Debord."

Löwy evaluates the subversive implications of the concept of *dérive* and quotes Debord: "the future will speed up irreversible changes in behavior and the structure of society. One day, we'll build cities to practice dérive in" (*Morning Star*, 2009). Löwy considers Debord and the SI, if not belonging directly to surrealism, to have drawn a considerable part of their subversive force from it and to be linked to it by "elective affinity."

At the beginning of *Arsenal 4* (1989), Franklin Rosemont wrote, "Surrealism began, point blank, with life-and-death questions that everyone else ignored or pretended to ignore: questions of everyday life, suicide, madness, nature, poetry, love, language and absolute revolt. The most audacious dreams of centuries suddenly were dreamed anew and brought to fruition in this new and unexpected 'communism of genius' that plunged its roots deep in the manifold forms of outlawed subjectivity. Here was a dialectical *leap* of world-historical implications, transforming once and for all the conditions of thought, art, poetry and life itself."

"The situationist encounter with surrealism," Ron Sakolsky commented, "in spite of the Oedipal denial of the many connections between the two on the part of the situationists, can better be seen as a dialogue between 'specialists in revolt.' In regard to anarchy, surrealist Benjamin Péret's writings on worker self-management can be seen as congenial to the tentative anarcho-communism of the situationists' emphasis on workers councils." Sakolsky's essay "Surrealist Desire, Anarchy & the Poetry of Revolt" is an important discussion of surrealism and its political evolution. It contains a lengthy discussion of the politics of surrealism and situationism and is included in his book *Creating Anarchy*.[2]

Bernard Marszalek, a Chicago anarchist, *Rebel Worker* writer, and part of our Solidarity Bookshop staff, considering our days working together in the '60s, comments:

> The SI and Surrealism are complementary. Where the surrealists lacked a political program in the narrow sense the SI supplied one, generalized self-management, not simply worker-councils though that was the core of the historic thrust for a world based on popular desire. But the SI lacked the wider vision that the Surrealists

1 Michael Löwy, *Morning Star: Surrealism, Marxism, Anarchism, Situationism, Utopia*, introduction by Don LaCoss (Austin: University of Texas Press, 2009), 116.

2 Ron Sakolsky, *Creating Anarchy* (Liberty, TN: Fifth Estate Books, 2005).

> provided, encapsulated by the concept of the marvelous in everyday life. These two elements really need each other. And lastly, the anarchist example of melding these two aspects into a practical utopianism informs both while lacking their depth. We anarchists *did* live differently (proto-surrealism) and had a generalized critique of power on all levels (the SI's contribution). I think this is the real contribution of Chicago's *Rebel Worker* group, connecting these all together.[3]

*

Surrealists and situationists do have significant differences, however—an especially basic one is their disagreement on the unconscious mind, its existence, its importance in everyday life, in history. The situationists tended to side with bourgeois rationalists and dismiss the importance of the Unconscious, while the surrealists found in the Unconscious—the very font of creativity—those uncensored mental processes found in dreams and thoughts, those desires that are beyond our control which the Society of the Spectacle tries to either exploit or condition, to use for its own ends, basically to sell a product or to sell an ideology or a bankrupt social system. The SI attacked the importance of art but for a while at least promoted thinking about city design and architecture.

Both the surrealists and the SI venerated the liberated sexuality of de Sade, but the SI criticized surrealism for what it considered a bourgeois attitude toward love. On the other hand, existentialist Simone de Beauvoir didn't like the surrealist attitude on love either. Those involved in surrealism have championed the feminine, voiced the idea of love, and encouraged women. There have been many women theorists and creative artists among surrealists, more than any previous art movement. Surrealist sex rebel Claude Cahun is finally getting a share of the attention her work deserves. Annie LeBrun, Nancy Joyce Peters, and Nora Mitrani are important among surrealist theorists. Leonora Carrington, Mimi Parent, and Toyen have contributed masterpieces as surrealist painters. Suzanne Césaire, Jayne Cortez, and Carmen Bruna are startling and wonderful surrealist poets. Surrealists have often called attention to the idea that the progress of a civilization could be judged by the way it treats its women and upheld a belief in Mad Love and sexual experimentation, even pushing further considered concepts such as the androgyne and the Egregore. Women and sexuality is a major area in which SI thinking should have been and needs to be developed.

---

3 Bernard Marszalek, e-mail message to author, 2012.

Though the SI was fascinated with dérive, something one might consider applicable to a stroll through the forest, their thinking was divorced from the natural world. Like the old-line Marxists, they were oriented toward cities, work, and technology. One is hard-pressed to find even a passing reference to, much less any concern for, the earth or its creatures. Surrealists, as poets influenced by Lautréamont and thinkers influenced by Darwin, were sensitive to the natural world and exalted the wonders of the shark, the octopus, the luna moth. Some of the first militancy concerning the environment was ours in Chicago with our often quoted and reprinted anti-zoo leaflet issued in 1971, "The Anteater's Umbrella," and later involvement with other defenders of nature, especially Earth First! Though even before that, in 1966 our "Theses on Vision, X-Ray and Otherwise" ended with "the forest is deep and the night is long, but now we know the wolves are on our side."[4]

*

Historically, both the SI (actually in this case its precursor the Letterist International, or LI) and the surrealists appreciated the value of scandal and were both extremely anti-religious. The surrealist group had issued a passionate anti-religious statement, "To Your Kennels, Curs of God," on June 14, 1948. And so the surrealists did not overlook but roundly applauded the Letterist International disruption of Easter Sunday Mass at Notre Dame Cathedral on April 9, 1950. LI member Michel Mourre began his speech by announcing to a packed High Mass crowd,

> I accuse the Catholic Church of infecting the world with its funereal morality,
> Of being the running sore on the decomposed body of the West.
> We proclaim the death of the Christ-god, so that Man may live at last.

This disruption (on live TV yet) went on for several minutes before worshipers realized that it was a hoax, not part of the program at all. Mourre fled but he was caught and almost lynched. In this case, the police arrived in time to *save* him from an angry mob.

André Breton was the first to come to Mourre's defense. His letter to the journal *Combat*, whose editor, Louis Pawels, had denounced the action, was published April 12, 1950. It provoked a raging eight-day debate. Surrealist Benjamin Péret, in a letter published on April 14, called the Notre Dame action, "perfectly justified." Among the reasons he gave was

4 Franklin Rosemont, Penelope Rosemont, and Paul Garon, *The Forecast Is Hot!: Tracts & Other Collective Declarations of the Surrealist Movement in the United States* (Chicago: Black Swan Press, 1997), 9.

the fact that the Catholic Church still supported Franco's fascism in Spain. But the church and the French state wished to avoid further scandal and a public trial *at all costs*, so in spite of all, Mourre ended up in a mental institution for only a short time.

It was the next year, in October 1951, that Guy Debord, who was to become the major theorist of situationism, joined the LI, having met them in April at the Cannes Film Festival. They were screening their new film, titled *Treatise on Slime & Eternity*.

So it is not entirely surprising to find that in October 1954, the surrealists and Letterist International decided to work together on a manifesto/disruption of the hundredth anniversary of the birth of the poet Arthur Rimbaud to be hosted by the bourgeois powers that be. Both loved and held as a motto to live by Rimbaud's often quoted words, "Never Work!"

In 1954 there were several meetings of representatives of the two groups. The surrealists included several I knew—Bedouin, Benayoun, Goldfayn, Légrand, Pierre, Schuster, and Toyen. Breton did not attend these meetings, due to illness. The resulting text was far less exciting than the earlier surrealist statement, "Permittez," that denounced a 1927 Rimbaud celebration. This time, they chose to point to a fraud—a poem falsely attributed to Rimbaud. Breton had exposed this false poem in a pamphlet, *Flagrant Délit*, in 1949.

The signers for the LI included Debord, Bernstein, Dahou, Fillon, and Wolman. There seemed to be agreement and they gathered signers. This statement is found under the title "*Ça commence bien.*" But before the Rimbaud event took place, there was a split. The LI angrily denounced the surrealists in a text, "Et ça finit mal." The surrealists replied by denouncing the LI as Stalinist, but that wasn't the entirety of the exchange; accusations flew back and forth. A lengthy account can be found in *Tracts Surréalistes et Déclarations Collectives 2*, edited by José Pierre.

When the former LI, now situationists (SI), brought out their lavishly printed magazine in June 1958, they continued their critique of surrealism in this, their very first issue, in the essay "The Bitter Victory of Surrealism." In fact, this was their opening article, so it is obvious they attached great importance to surrealism and thought it necessary to make a clear distinction between themselves and it.

For surrealists such as André Breton, who had hoped to see an end to war, a revolution that surpassed the one in Russia in 1917, and a transformation of the daily life—to have friends such as Leon Trotsky assassinated, to experience yet another world war, to have ex-members such as sellout Salvador Dalí use surrealism to find fame and fortune was indeed a "bitter victory." But this was a too-narrow view of the accomplishments of surrealism. Surrealism had a wide influence; it made permanent changes in our perception of reality. Our world never really has been quite the same after surrealism.

The second article of that issue, "Sound and the Fury," also concerns surrealism. Péret criticized the SI briefly in "Poetry Above All" in *Bief* 1 (November 15, 1958); the SI replied with "Nostalgia Beneath Contempt" in *IS 2* in December 1958. Of course, this kind of exchange among radicals, especially among young radicals, provides a kind of reality testing—if it is rotten it will fall.

The SI continued its obsession with surrealism, but at the same time expanded its view and its theory to encompass more surrealist concerns. Eventually, in 1970 (though only published in 1977), an entire book was tossed together by Raoul Vaneigem, *A Cavalier History of Surrealism*. For a fine critique of this book, see Don LaCoss's "Conflicting Views of Surrealism and Revolution: Raoul Vaneigem vs. Robin D.G. Kelley," published in Noel Ignatiev's *Race Traitor.*

While there are certainly things to criticize about situationism, the SI's work has a powerful relevance for today. The structure of the world remains politically and socially much the same as it then was, but at the same time the pressures that induce change are much greater. Social formations have not kept pace with technology or human needs. *Whole worlds are in transition*. One only needs to glance at the headlines.

The development of the SI in the 1950s and '60s benefitted from several important French currents of thought: the College of Sociology, especially Bataille, Caillois, Kojève, and Leiris; the Annales group of historians that included Fernand Braudel; the Philosophies group, critical theory, Lukács, but especially Henri Lefebvre. The SI method of digesting ideas completely, modifying them and presenting them seamlessly, appropriating the ideas rather than the tedious quoting and acknowledging that is the more academic way, brought them a new immediacy. They sought and developed a critical theory which expanded on many of the favorite themes of surrealism, interested in Sade, in Fourier, in Cardinal de Retz, in play, in dérive, but they dismissed art and poetry and gave a *new immediacy to ideas of political revolution*. The SI itself is being a bit recuperated today; the emphasis seems to fall on their anti-art analysis of the spectacle, ignoring that very political immediacy that was so crucial to the time.

My article "Berkeley Was Only the Beginning" appeared in the July 1965 issue of *Rebel Worker*. This was before we went to Paris. At that time we considered that students had no power over the productive forces; our basic thinking was very anarcho-syndicalist and IWW-influenced. We believed there were more revolutionary possibilities in young workers and the jobless. There could be a revolutionary youth movement of dropouts. One of our more scandalous leaflets, one that moved neighborhood parents to despair, called for students at a local high school to "Drop out of school and join the revolution!"

It was written up in the local paper as yet another problem for the embattled school district, and IWW General Secretary-Treasurer Walter Westman reported that the IWW headquarters was flooded with complaints.

In 1966, a little over a year after the Berkeley Uprising, the situationist-influenced students at Strasbourg took over the student government. They put the budget of the student government to good use, printing situationist material to the chagrin of the university administration. In fact, one of Debord's professors and friends, Henri Lefebvre, taught there. The SI's excellent pamphlet on the poverty of student life put them on the leading edge of the rapidly building student movement. This put the SI in a relationship to young people similar to SDS in the U.S. but with considerably more theoretical development. Carl Davidson's 1967 pamphlet on student syndicalism, *The New Radicals in the Multiversity*, crystalized the U.S. view of student radicalism and the creation of student militancy.

*

To trace contacts between the two groups back a little further, we find that twenty-two-year-old Asger Jorn (b. 1914) from Denmark (later a supporter and financial backer of the SI) was in an exhibition with Léger in Paris, and that Christian Dotremont (b. 1922) from Belgium participated in the group Abstrait-Surréaliste in 1937 at age fifteen. The group published a review, *Linein*. Among his friends were surrealists Magritte, Marien, and Ubac. During World War II, daring young radicals published several surrealist journals, first *La Main à plume* (1941–1945). This group included Regine Raufast, Tita, Vulliamy, and Jaguer, and it paid dearly for its courage and intransigence with eight deaths and many deportations at the hands of the Nazis.

Other surrealist- and SI-related journals included: *La Révolution la nuit*, published in 1945–46; *Surrealisme Révolutionnaire*, founded by Christian Dotremont in 1947 in Brussels; also, *Les deux soeurs* (1946–47). Participant Constant Nieuwenhuys (b. 1920) was a figure related later to Amsterdam's Provo movement. It was Dotremont who introduced the work of Henri Lefebvre to the pre-Cobra Surrealisme Révolutionnaire group in the 1940s; especially interesting was Lefebvre's idea that everyday life should "become a work of art!" and that every technical means should be applied toward the goal of the "transformation of everyday life!"

The Cobra group (founded in 1948 with members from Copenhagen, Brussels, and Amsterdam) had as its principle figures Jorn, Dotremont, and Constant. There is plenty of fascinating information available on this in the Situationist International online or Jean-Jacques Raspaud and Jean-Pierre Voyer's *L'Internationale Situationniste: Chronologie, bibliographie, protagonistes (avec un index des noms insulté)*, 1972; Christophe Bourseiller's *Vie et mort de Guy Debord*; and Guy Debord's *Correspondance*.

*

In spring 1966 we left Paris for London where we met Charles Radcliffe, who we knew through his writings in *Anarchy*, edited by Colin Ward. We immediately developed an electrical sympathy with Radcliffe, and found we were operating on the same wavelength. As we were staying with him and Diana Shelly, discussions could and did go on nonstop for a month. In a matter of days we wrote, typed onto stencils, and printed on a mimeograph an issue of the *Rebel Worker* in time for May Day, 1966. We went down to Hyde Park for the big May Day march and sold all of them. The enthusiasm for new revolutionary ideas was astonishing.

In that issue of *Rebel Worker*, Radcliffe wrote with fire, "The new revolution may be obscene and blasphemous; it must deface the power structure when it cannot destroy it; the criterion is defiance not discipline. The new revolution must support every last insurrection of the mind and body against this bloodfed society—our movement is symbolized by the bomb-thrower, the deserter, the delinquent, the hitch-hiker, the mad lover, the school dropout, the wildcat striker, the rioter and the saboteur."

Our brains felt alive, ignited by our encounters in Paris and London; back in the United States we put out the statement "The Forecast Is Hot!" (July 10, 1966) and distributed it at a gigantic civil rights march led by Martin Luther King. Meanwhile, Charles, too, was still on fire and put out the first issue of his journal *Heatwave*, reporting on the Provo riots: "As this first issue of *Heatwave* goes to press the Dutch capital of Amsterdam is still in a state of uneasy peace after a series of youth riots. *Heatwave* reprints extracts from various newspapers which present the outlines of the explosion and leave a clear impression of the seriousness with which the Dutch authorities are treating their youth revolt. We think these extracts will interest our readers, provide a basis for further thinking on the 'World Revolution of Youth' and also indicate that Holland, for many years regarded as being asleep, is gradually producing a wide-awake resistance to contemporary society."

The next issue of *Rebel Worker* (number 7), produced in 1967 in Chicago, saw surrealist André Breton and situationist Jean Garnault in the same issue—this didn't please either group. In fact, Garnault was expelled before the *Rebel Worker* even got to France, another factor that did not endear us to the SI. Garnault's "Elementary Structures of Reification" was the first translation of situationist material to appear in the United States.

Solidarity Bookshop collective member Bernard Marszalek put together an article commenting on the war and the Society of the Spectacle titled, "I Saw It on TV and Then We Proved It at Home." He wrote, "The obfuscating complexity of the War in Vietnam, so carefully fostered by our well-suited war-lords, to induce apathy on the citizenry, has engendered an unexpected popular reaction. . . . Television especially has contributed positively in this respect, for every news program carries quite candid coverage of the war in progress, with each report adding more evidence to the belief that there is absolutely nothing in South Vietnam worth sacrificing the lives of American youth for."

Truth is we didn't have time then to translate SI works or criticize them in any detail. We assimilated them by a kind of osmosis as we discussed them at Solidarity Bookshop with those attempting translations of unitary urbanism, détournement, psychogeography, etc. We were inspired by what the SI wrote and considered whether the world needed psychozoology, too. (We did, in fact, put together something of the sort with our "Anteater's Umbrella" leaflet.) But after all, in 1967, things were heating up fast, our statement "The Forecast Is Hot!" indeed timely. I got a job at Students for a Democratic Society (SDS) and it paid $20 per week—a bit more than the bus fare. We were spending our time doing wall posters, leaflets, the *Rebel Worker*, in the streets at anti-war demonstrations being chased by cops. Soon it was 1968.

*

In London, Charles Radcliffe met Chris Grey and the two of them couldn't wait to give this rotten civilization its final kick. They came out with *Heatwave* 2 in October 1966. In their editorial "All or Nothing at All!" the two of them declared war:

> We are living through the break-up of an entire civilization. Contemporary society has only one foundation—its own inertia—the last vestiges of religion and ideology cannot conceal the extent of our mass-alienation. Nothing means anything anymore. There seems to be no escape from the isolation and senselessness of our lives. For all of us the abyss seems likely to open at any moment. We are all alone in a world that has become one huge madhouse.

Rebel Worker and *Heatwave* were among the major proponents of the World Revolution of Youth. The idea seems to have originated in the United States with Jonathan Leake and Walter Caughey in New York. They formed the Resurgence Youth Movement (RYM) and published their first issues of *Resurgence* in 1964, though the ideas connecting rock 'n' roll and revolution were published earlier in "Pop Goes the Beatle," written by Radcliffe in *Anarchy* magazine in 1963. And in 1965 Franklin Rosemont published his pamphlet "Mods, Rockers and the Revolution."

In Chicago we published, in a stapled, mimeographed edition, long excerpts from *The Decline and Fall of the Spectacular Commodity Economy* (1967) with Bernard Marszalek's introduction.

We welcomed Fredy Perlman's pamphlet, "The Reproduction of Everyday Life," in 1969 when we found it at Solidarity Bookshop. We had just missed his visit. His *Against His-story, Against Leviathan* is one of the best anarchist books that period produced. The Detroit collective Black and Red, together with *Radical America*, published the first translation of Debord's *Society of the Spectacle* (1970). This anarchist activity begun by Fredy and Lorraine Perlman led to the long-lasting journal *Fifth Estate* and a dynamic group including Peter Werbe and David Watson.

*

Surrealist activity in Paris in May 1968 is discussed by Don LaCoss in *Surrealism in '68: Paris, Prague & Chicago—Dreams of Arson & the Arson of Dreams*. Our surrealist friends in Paris covered the walls with slogans, took to the barricades, put out statements including "Long Live Adventurism!"—provocative enough to have them placed under indictment, though charges were later dropped.

Our activity in the United States was formed by how we saw our own situation, the possibilities of resistance, and the hopes of liberation. One of the problems we faced was the annihilation of our own working-class history by the ruling class and its replacement by bourgeois history. We lived in the same neighborhood that the Haymarket martyrs had lived and met in, and no one knew it. So part of our mission, for better or for worse, was the recovery of that history of revolt, the consideration of the possibilities of another society, and the discovery of other societies that existed in parallel time, especially those of Native Americans and African Americans. Paul Garon, who joined us in 1967, explored the expression of black revolt through jazz and blues in his book, *Blues and the Poetic Spirit*.

Our approach to revolt was more historical than philosophical. Philosophy too easily became the intricate domain of specialists and we aspired like the early surrealists to be only "Specialists in Revolt."

*

Historian Robin D.G. Kelley, writing in *Freedom Dreams*, comments, "Surrealism may have originated in the West, but it is rooted in a conspiracy against Western Civilization. Surrealists frequently looked outside Europe for ideas and inspiration . . . in tracts like 'Revolution Now and

Forever!' the surrealists actively called for the overthrow of French Colonial rule."[5]

One of the significant developments of surrealism that the SI did not consider in its various critiques was the influence of surrealism on Pan-Africanism, especially through Martinique, and Aimé and Suzanne Césaire in particular. In *Freedom Dreams*, Robin D.G. Kelley writes, "Aimé Césaire, after all, has never denied his surrealist leanings. As he explains: 'surrealism provided me what I had been confusingly searching for. I have accepted it joyfully because in it I have found more of a confirmation than a revelation.'"[6] Kelley explains that Césaire's *Discourse on Colonialism* (1950) "was indisputably one of the key texts in a tidal wave of anti-colonial literature produced during the post war period—works that include . . . Frantz Fanon's *Black Skin, White Mask* (1952) [and] George Padmore's *Pan-Africanism or Communism? The Coming Struggle for Africa* (1956)."[7]

In 2009, Robin D.G. Kelley and Franklin Rosemont edited a substantial book, really only a sampling of surrealism's expression in the Pan-African world, *Black, Brown & Beige: Surrealist Writings from Africa and the Diaspora.* There is no doubt that the African revolutions changed the face of the planet and that liberation inspired a great optimism. So much of the last few decades have been attempts through corruption or military interference to get Africa back under one form or another of imperialist domination.

U.S. surrealists were fortunate to be joined by historian David Roediger. When L.A.'s Watts area went up in smoke again in 1992, Roediger and Rosemont put out a statement for the surrealist group in support of that uprising, "Three Days That Shook the New World Order," inspired by the critique the SI had put together on the Watts Revolt of 1965.

Rosemont and Roediger also edited two issues of Noel Ignatiev's journal *Race Traitor.* From the very beginning, surrealists, with their anti-colonial attacks and the inspiration they found in Africa and other world cultures, have seen themselves as enemies of Western civilization, as race traitors.

Besides editing the largest work so far on the U.S. surrealist movement, Ron Sakolsky has long been active as an anarchist. In *Swift Winds* he considers that, "From an anarcho-surrealist perspective, moving toward a world in which we can lead more poetic lives involves restoring the insurrectionary power of the imagination and unleashing it to create an anarchy that is not afraid to dream."[8]

---

5 Robin D.G. Kelley, *Freedom Dreams: The Black Radical Imagination* (Boston: Beacon Press, 2002), 159.
6 Ibid., 169.
7 Ibid., 174.
8 Ron Sakolsky, *Swift Winds* (Portland: Eberhardt Press, 2009), 30.

The SI and the 1968 uprisings may have shaken up surrealism and saved it from occultation, increasing mysticism, and commercialization, but what will save the SI's ideas from increasing abstraction and co-optation? The Occupy movement, which was influenced by SI thinking, came along at a fortunate time to pin radical theory back to practice, but at the same time it raises the stakes and also the question, what next?

*

Franklin Rosemont considered it necessary that a major focus of surrealist work should be poetry and with it, the restoration to language of the *real power of our own thought*. Rosemont wrote with a fascination for the history of the neglected, the forgotten, the repressed—the history of revolt and the urge for liberation that persists always in the human spirit. Among his writings are a book, *Joe Hill*, another on *Jacques Vaché and the Roots of Surrealism*, and an often reprinted pamphlet, "Karl Marx and the Iroquois." He pointed out that Debord incorrectly considered surrealism as *irrational*. But surrealism is not irrational, it is *anti-rational*.

Writing about surrealism, situationism, and anarchism continues to provoke heated discussion. Ron Sakolsky in *Creating Anarchy* begins, "The ongoing surrealist project is, at its core, an uprising against authoritarianism and alienation . . . surrealism's ultimate aim is the dissolution, synthesis, and supercession of the despotic binary contradictions that are used to suppress the most dazzling possibilities of thought and life."[9]

And more recently the discussion of situationism in Max Cafard's *Surregional Explorations* critiques and develops our understanding of those important concepts. He writes, "*The Society of the Spectacle* remains one of those few invaluable books that can begin to shake the reader's faith that a ludicrously absurd and criminally insane social order must be absolutely equivalent to the inherent and eternally ordained nature of things." Besides his assessment of the SI, Cafard also develops surrealist thought further when he advocates "mad love" with "the power to regenerate the world . . . And at the same time with the power to regenerate each other."

Radcliffe writes in *Dancin' in the Streets* (2004) that Debord in print is "undeniably magisterial. The lucid and imperious prose, the centimeter-perfect dialectical analysis and the sharp, witty, ice-cold, theoretical precision of *The Society of the Spectacle* builds its argument, interdependent paragraph by interdependent paragraph . . . still both challenging and thrilling." He also found Vaneigem's *Revolution of Everyday Life*, "an inspired, apocalyptic and passionate fusion of wisdom, madness and rage,

9 Sakolsky, *Creating Anarchy*, 111.

illuminated by the fires of destruction . . . a roller coaster ride of a book, written with the limitless expectation of those days."[10]

According to Rosemont, "the fact remains that the central elements of the situationist project—rejection of the pseudo-world of the spectacle; support for workers' self-emancipation, the passion for freedom and true community, revolt against work and affirmation of play, *détournement*, revolution as festival, 'consciousness of desire and desire for consciousness'—were all essentials of surrealism's project long before the S.I. existed. . . . I recall Guy Debord: In spite of himself—and above all in spite of the *myth* of himself—the most surrealist of anti-surrealists!"[11]

Debord's *The Society of the Spectacle* (1967), like Marx's *Communist Manifesto*, may prove to be one of the most influential and enduring documents of our time. It has provoked, and continues to provoke, critical thinking on how our world is structured, how it functions, its values, what is its future, and in this it surpasses any other theoretical work of the time. Of course, it was *part* of that time and "the developments of capitalism *have* speeded up." Now thanks to computers, the internet, and YouTube *everybody* can be part of the spectacle, *for better or for worse*, as is plain to see.

In 1981 Ken Knabb translated and edited the *Situationist International Anthology*, which has been printed and reprinted and remains in print as an essential book finally making many important texts available. Knabb himself has been active in applying SI thinking to a critique of today's world. It is astonishing that there are no Marxists or Marxist organizations interested in the SI (or surrealism for that matter). When I asked Knabb about this and about why he thought the SI was of interest to anarchists, he replied that "since most 'Marxist' currents are more or less Stalinist or Bolshevik, and since most people who know anything about Hegel are academics, the anarchists, who at least have some sort of antiauthoritarian practice, end up seeming more closely related." Also, possibly anarchists are more open to new ideas and seek more creative paths toward social change.

None of what I have been able to discuss here has considered the major contributions by surrealists worldwide from Cairo to Buenos Aires, from Tokyo to Prague, who have been active theoretically, creatively, and politically and put out numerous books, journals, exhibitions, and so forth in a continuing effort to develop and expand surrealism. Surrealism has been a movement with an experimental and international focus from its very beginning.

10 Franklin Rosemont and Charles Radcliffe, eds., *Dancin' in the Streets: Anarchists, IWWs, Surrealists, Situationists & Provos in the 1960s as Recorded in the Pages of the Rebel Worker & Heatwave* (Chicago: Charles H. Kerr Publishing Company, 2005), 63–64.

11 Ibid., 63.

My own interests these days lead me toward a critique of everyday life, the deconditioning necessary for us to accomplish a liberated future: what is work and what is play and what *could* they be? And how can we transform our relationship to the natural world and to each other . . . how will our acts influence events? For that matter, I also like to play with "what is history?" And to play with "what is identity?" Who do we think we are anyway, what validates our idea of self and gives it a social value? Especially in these days of no jobs and uncertain futures.

I recently corresponded with Arturo Schwarz, who has written the major study of Marcel Duchamp as well as other major books on surrealism and who, at ninety, has lived through so much of the twentieth century and known so many of those involved in surrealism and situationism. Arturo mentioned in closing that though "Debord interested me, I thought that Breton's Surrealism was an infinitely richer and more positive philosophy of life and I still remain a staunch promoter and supporter of his ideas." Surrealism began as and remains a great experiment in human freedom. I too feel that you cannot surpass surrealism for its experience, for its sheer exhilaration, for its exuberance of life.

Part of our work as surrealists attempted to understand and put together a critique of the new myths in formation: advertising, science, pop culture. We saw as important, new mythological figures that harbor the seeds of liberation such as Bugs Bunny—especially Bugs Bunny—as Groucho Marx, as King Kong, as Godzilla. Sometimes my brain entertaining itself visualizes King Kong or Godzilla confronting the gigantic pink mattress of *The Consumer*. Who will be the winner in this colossal confrontation?

And speaking of King Kong and Godzilla, surrealism and situationism, these two heroes/anti-heroes, creations born of dream/nightmare, filling our ears with cries/roars, these two *enraged* escapees from cultural conditioning—still today—these two *Monsters of Consciousness* remain most certainly . . . "At Large!"

Selected Bibliography

Biro, Adam, and René Passeron. *Dictionnaire Général du surréalisme et ses environs.* Fribourg: Office du Livre, 1982.

Bourseiller, Christophe. *Vie et mort de Guy Debord, 1931–1994*. Paris: Plon, 1999.

Cafard, Max. *Surregional Explorations.* Illustrations by Stephen Duplantier. Chicago: Charles H. Kerr, 2012.

Debord, Guy. *Society of the Spectacle*. Detroit: Red & Black, 1970.

———. *Correspondence*. 3 vols. Paris: Arthème Fayard, 1999–2003.

Ducornet, Guy. *Surréalisme & athéisme: "A la niche les glapisseurs de dieu!"* Lassay-les-Châteaux: Ginkgo, 2007.

Duwa, Jerome. *Surréalists et situationnistes vies paralleles*. Paris: Editions Dilecta, 2008.

Garon, Paul. *Blues and the Poetic Spirit*. London: Eddison Press, 1975.

Ignatiev, Noel, ed. "Surrealism in the USA." Special issue, *Race Traitor* 13–14 (Summer 2001).

Jappe, Anselm. *Guy Debord*. Translated by Donald Nicholson-Smith. Berkeley: University of California Press, 1999.

Kelley, Robin D.G. *Freedom Dreams: The Black Radical Imagination*. Boston: Beacon Press, 2002.

Knabb, Ken. *Situationist International Anthology, Revised and Expanded Edition*. Berkeley: Bureau of Public Secrets, 2006.

LaCoss, Don. *Surrealism in '68: Paris, Prague, Chicago—Dreams of Arson & the Arson of Dreams*. Chicago: Surrealist Research & Development Monograph Series, 2008.

Löwy, Michael. *Morning Star: Surrealism, Marxism, Anarchism, Situationism, Utopia*. Introduction by Don LaCoss. Austin: University of Texas Press, 2009.

Raspaud, Jean-Jacques, and Jean-Pierre Voyer. *L'Internationale Situationniste: Chronologie, bibliographie, protagonistes (avec un index des noms insulté)*. Paris: Champ Libre, 1972.

Roediger, David. *History Against Misery*. Chicago: Charles H. Kerr Publishing Company, 2006.

Rosemont, Franklin, Penelope Rosemont, and Paul Garon. *The Forecast Is Hot! Tracts & Other Collective Declarations of the Surrealist Movement in the United States*. Chicago: Black Swan Press, 1997.

———, and Charles Radcliffe. *Dancin' in the Streets: Anarchists, IWWs, Surrealists, Situationists & Provos in the 1960s as Recorded in the Pages of the Rebel Worker & Heatwave*. Chicago: Charles H. Kerr Publishing Company, 2005.

Rosemont, Penelope. *Dreams & Everyday Life: André Breton, Surrealism, Rebel Worker, SDS & the Seven Cities of Cibola*. Chicago: Charles H. Kerr Publishing Company, 2008.

Rosemont, Penelope, Dennis Cunningham, and Winston Smith. *Insect Music: Surrealism, Alchemy, and the Image*. San Francisco: Grant's Tomb, 2012.

Rosemont, Penelope. *Surrealist Women: An International Anthology*. Austin: University of Texas Press, 1998.

———. *Surrealist Experiences—1001 Dawns, 221 Midnights*. Chicago: Black Swan Press, 2000.

———. *Lost Worlds, Forgotten Futures, Undreamed Ecstasies: Some Thoughts on the Relationship of Surrealism to the Mayan Millennium & to Each his Own Pluriverse*. Surrealist Research & Development Monograph Series. Chicago: Charles H. Kerr Publishing Company, 2012.

Sakolsky, Ron. *Surrealist Subversions: Rants, Writings & Images by the Surrealist Movement in the United States*. Brooklyn: Autonomedia, 2002.

———. *Creating Anarchy*. Liberty, TN: Fifth Estate Books, 2005.

———. *Swift Winds*. Portland: Eberhardt Press, 2009.

Schuster, Jean and José Pierre. *Tracts Surréalistes et déclarations collectives, 1940–1969*. Paris: Le Terrain vague, 1982.

Schwarz, Arturo. *I Surrealisti*. Milan: Mazzotta, 1989.

Wark, McKenzie. *50 Years of Recuperation*. New York: Buell Center, 2008.

BLACKENED SYLLABUS: WILL ALEXANDER'S FIGURE OF THE KING

Barry Maxwell

> This flagrant negation of humanity which constitutes the very essense of the State is, from the standpoint of the State, its supreme duty and its greatest virtue. . . . This explains why the entire history of ancient and modern states is merely a series of revolting crimes; why kings and ministers, past and present, of all times and of all countries—statesmen, diplomats, bureaucrats, and warriors—if judged from the standpoint of simple humanity and human justice, have a hundred, a thousand times over earned their sentence to hard labor or to the gallows.
>
> —Mikhail Bakunin, *Federalism, Socialism, Anti-Theologism*

> If in order to win it were necessary to erect the gallows in the public square, then I would prefer to lose.
>
> —Errico Malatesta, *Pensiero e Volontà*, October 1, 1924

> The poet . . . has had to surmount the power of tyrants and magicians, and has had to take on the authority of a phantom egret ruling from a transparent throne of sound.
>
> —Will Alexander, "Alchemy as Poetic Kindling"

The harsh and vengeful judgment of Bakunin; Malatesta's measured, resolute, but melancholy refusal of violence: the poles of these positions have strung anarchism painfully between them. Will Alexander's assertion, enigmatic at first hearing, points beyond both the murderous justice of Bakunin and, equally, what Malatesta might be accused of, at least at this moment: defeatism. My subject in this paper is, in general terms, the relations between power, political power, and poetic language—poetic power, if you will. By attending to the work of Will Alexander, a contemporary African American surrealist poet,[1] I hope to get at the ways in which this writer has understood the dimensions of the atrocity of the sovereign, the king, the monarch, the ruler *as such*, and has worked in language to refine, in the alchemical sense, the fearsome meanings of the words sovereign; king; monarch; and, by extension, patriarch, husband, emperor, president-for-life, *duce*; Führer—the whole dishonorable lexical and historical host. I also want to clarify what I see as the particular nature of Alexander's poetics in relation to his dramatization—a monodrama—of the self-unmooring of his figure of the sovereign, that is, the imagistic conceiving of a new kind of power, at an absolute distance from violence, a new dimension of power, which shines through his imagined king's renunciation of domination. At work in Alexander's writing, then, is what Walter Benjamin, in another context, called the "true politics" of "the demolition of violence," a politics, in Aimé Césaire's words, of "the miraculous weapons" of undomesticated language.[2]

To speak to these questions, I will draw from several sources in Alexander's writing: the long poem "Haiti," which is the second half of his 1995 poetic diptych *Asia & Haiti*; "The Whirling King in the Runic Psychic Theatre," which appears in his 1998 book *Towards the Primeval Lightning Field*; his book of prose texts gathered under the title *Singing in Magnetic Hoofbeat* (2012); and an essay from *The Brimstone Boat* (2012) titled "Escaping Mass Seduction."[3] Later, the work of political anthropologist Pierre Clastres comes briefly to the fore.

---

1 Will Alexander is not much taken with conventional (auto)biographical summaries, so I will forebear. See, though, "My Interior Vita" in *Compression and Purity* (San Francisco: City Lights, 2011), 65–70. I thank Will Alexander and Nick Nesbitt for their help with this work, and, for his encouragement, John Holloway. I thank Gavin Arnall and Maria Giulia Fabi for providing occasions in Princeton and Trieste for the presentation of early versions of this essay.

2 For "Die wahre Politik" and "Abbau der Gewalt" see Walter Benjamin, *Briefe*, Vol. 1, ed. Gershom Scholem and Theodor W. Adorno (Frankfurt am Main: Suhrkamp Verlag, 1966), 247. *The Correspondence of Walter Benjamin, 1910–1940*, edited and annotated by Gershom Scholem and Theodor W. Adorno; trans. Manfred R. Jacobson and Evelyn M. Jacobson (Chicago: University of Chicago Press, 1994), 168–69; Aimé Césaire, "The Miraculous Weapons," in *The Collected Poetry*, trans. Clayton Eshleman and Annette Smith (Berkeley: University of California Press, 1983), 116–19.

3 *Asia & Haiti* (Los Angeles: Sun & Moon, 1995), hereafter *A&H*. "The Whirling King in the Runic Psychic Theatre," in *Towards the Primeval Lightning Field* (Oakland: O Books, 1998; reissued by Litmus Press, 2014), hereafter *WK*. *Singing in Magnetic Hoofbeat: Essays, Prose Texts, Interviews and a Lecture, 1991–2007*, ed. and intro. Taylor Brady, afterword Andrew Joron (Ithaca, NY: Essay Press, 2012), hereafter *SMH*. "Escaping Mass Seduction," *The Brimstone Boat: Poetry and Essays* (Los Angeles: Rêve à Deux, 2012), hereafter *EMS*.

I am mindful, as I begin, of three issues. The first has to do with Alexander's syntactically complex, forbiddingly learned, referentially daunting, and imagistically startling language. To put it plainly, the writing is very difficult. In "Haiti," Alexander offers a compression of his poetic:

> here
> we've shattered
> inoperable plain song
> therefore
> we speak with the same incessant elusives
> with riddling poltergeist connectives
> with the maturated scarring
> with the ceaseless untenable bone grafts
> blurred between albescence & crow (*A&H*, 129–30)

The second and third matters are surrealism and alchemical thought. Alexander, recognizing kindred spirits in André Breton, Philip Lamantia, and, particularly, Aimé Césaire, has characterized surrealism as the imagination able "to fly without pedestrian manacles" (*SMH* 195). Again, the poet in modernity has had "to surmount the power of tyrants and magicians, and has had to take on the authority of a phantom egret ruling from a transparent throne of sound" (*SMH* 146). This synaesthetic image of authority refigured as if by a dream, made not the positive of a negative, but the movement beyond those contradictory states, instances the surrealist and alchemical achievement of making words new. "The reality now accrues concerning the poet's leap beyond marred verbal zones of pedestrian psychic levels, beyond their antitransgressives, beyond their skittish colloquial internment" (*SMH* 113). What does this mean, in practice? In the following passage, I have substituted the word "sovereignty" for the phrase "the constellation Dorado," and made other corresponding changes:

> If I name "sovereignty," it is not the same sovereignty of the [political theorists], nor does it carry the same set of values when placed within a page of rigorously balanced [biopolitical] theory. It is a new sovereignty, capable at one touch of expansion and Utopia. It automatically becomes an enemy of the quotidian, an enemy of fixation and separation. It burns, it takes up the incandescence which the civil systems shun. It becomes a rich imaginal shadow flowing through a verbal lens of miracles. Then there is no longer the dried eradicated stanchion of word as use, of word as measuring rod, of word as rational entrapment. The voice then ceases to conclude on a point, or stare at surrounding virtues for approval. (*SMH* 153)

We have the following from André Breton on the matter of alchemy:

> I would appreciate your noting the remarkable analogy, insofar as their goals are concerned, between the Surrealist efforts and those of the alchemists: the philosopher's stone is nothing more or less than that which was to enable man's imagination to take a stunning revenge on all things, which brings us once again, after centuries of the mind's domestication and insane resignation, to the attempt to liberate once and for all the imagination . . . [4]

Let me turn to the ground of the historical relations of surrealism and revolutionary thought by mentioning only two of many intersections at which surrealism understood itself, and was understood by others who had standing to judge, as at one with revolutionary conviction. Walter Benjamin's 1929 evaluation of the movement stands:

> Since Bakunin, Europe has lacked a radical concept of freedom. The Surrealists have one. They are the first to liquidate the sclerotic liberal-moral-humanistic ideal of freedom, because they are convinced that [here Benjamin quotes André Breton] "mankind's struggle for liberation in its simplest revolutionary form (which is, nevertheless, liberation in every respect) remains the only cause worth serving."[5]

Another moment: Breton and Leon Trotsky, both in exile in 1938, wrote while together in Mexico the "Manifesto for an Independent Revolutionary Art," in which we read:

> If, for the better development of the forces of material production, the revolution must build a socialist regime with centralised control, to develop intellectual creation an anarchist regime of individual liberty should from the first be established. No authority, no dictation, not the least trace of orders from above![6]

In practice, we should note, surrealism has had nothing but trouble with "centralised control," even as intermittently and contradictorily embodied in the person of André Breton himself. That said, Breton's lengthy 1934 address to a public meeting in Brussels, published as *What Is Surrealism?*

4 André Breton, *Second Manifesto of Surrealism*, in *Manifestoes of Surrealism*, trans. Richard Seaver and Helen Lane (Ann Arbor: University of Michigan Press, 1972), 174–75.

5 Walter Benjamin, "Surrealism: The Last Snapshot of the European Intelligentsia," in Michael Jennings, Howard Eiland, and Gary Smith, eds., trans. Rodney Livingstone et al., *Walter Benjamin, Selected Writings, Vol. 2: 1927–1934.*, (Cambridge, MA: Harvard University Press, 1999), 215.

6 André Breton, Diego Rivera, [Leon Trotsky], *Manifesto for an Independent Revolutionary Art*, trans. Dwight Macdonald, in Franklin Rosemont, ed., *What Is Surrealism?* (New York: Monad, 1978), 185.

is necessary as a record of a changing understanding of the movement's definition and commitments.[7] If we are looking for a short definition of surrealism, though, this one by the Czech woman artist Toyen won't be bettered soon: surrealism is "a community of ethical views."[8] Note, and this is crucial, that surrealism has never been, except in the mouths of mercantilists, an artistic style. Surrealism is a name not for a dripping watch franchise operation run by Avida Dollars, nor for a set of aesthetic prescriptions to fill, but for the point of refusal of the breviary, of the prescription, of the role of the trained animal or animal trainer: that is its ethic. How does Alexander see his relations with surrealism? "I understand that surrealism is a great energizer," he has said, "but it has never been a theoretical or abstract circumference inside of which I was buried . . . it is an energy, and I think I have discovered something that is unique and invincible in the realm of its ubiquitous waters" (*SMH* 227).

Everywhere in his work, the poet provokes the questions of domination and freedom, but no place more explicitly than in his placing of the passage from Bakunin that appears at the head of this essay as an epigraph to his own essay "Against the State and Its Future as a Homicidal Enclave."[9] Its first paragraph gives the temperature of Alexander's understanding of

7 Breton, "What Is Surrealism?," in *What Is Surrealism?*, 112–41.

8 Toyen, "A Community of Ethical Views," in Penelope Rosemont, ed., *Surrealist Women: An International Anthology*, (Austin: University of Texas Press, 1998), 81.

9 *SMH* 31–36. Alexander's epigraph to this chapter comes from the following passage of Bakunin's *Federalism, Socialism, Anti-Theologism*. The entire passage follows.

This flagrant negation of humanity which constitutes the very essence of the State is, from the standpoint of the State, its supreme duty and its greatest virtue. It bears the name patriotism, and it constitutes the entire transcendent morality of the State. We call it transcendent morality because it usually goes beyond the level of human morality and justice, either of the community or of the private individual, and by that same token often finds itself in contradiction with these. Thus, to offend, to oppress, to despoil, to plunder, to assassinate or enslave one's fellowman is ordinarily regarded as a crime. In public life, on the other hand, from the standpoint of patriotism, when these things are done for the greater glory of the State, for the preservation or the extension of its power, it is all transformed into duty and virtue. And this virtue, this duty, are obligatory for each patriotic citizen; everyone is supposed to exercise them not against foreigners only but against one's own fellow citizens, members or subjects of the State like himself, whenever the welfare of the State demands it.

This explains why, since the birth of the State, the world of politics has always been and continues to be the stage for unlimited rascality and brigandage, brigandage and rascality which, by the way, are held in high esteem, since they are sanctified by patriotism, by the transcendent morality and the supreme interest of the State. This explains why the entire history of ancient and modern states is merely a series of revolting crimes; why kings and ministers, past and present, of all times and all countries—statesmen, diplomats, bureaucrats, and warriors—if judged from the standpoint of simple morality and human justice, have a hundred, a thousand times over earned their sentence to hard labour or to the gallows. There is no horror, no cruelty, sacrilege, or perjury, no imposture, no infamous transaction, no cynical robbery, no bold plunder or shabby betrayal that has not been or is not daily being perpetrated by

the State form. He writes: "At its core the state has characterized its praxis as ballet by liquidation, as an injudicious social strife, as a dark microbial ballast, its itinerary being the scalding dust measured by the clockwork of mayhem. Its memoirs, more in keeping with microscopic rubellas, with politically allotted viral infections. And each survivor of such besiegement is alphabetic with maiming" (*SMH* 31). "Alphabetic with maiming"—we will return to that phrase.

The introduction of the matters of magic and esotericism into the committedly, if not necessarily, belligerently rationalist context of many of the other writings in this book needs a gloss. These twin operations are fundamental to Alexander's writing, but only through an anti-reactionary consciousness, that is, through poetic understanding of magic's resources and dangers. If fascism is psychoanalysis in reverse, then Alexander's flooding of his texts with alchemical lexicon—never prescriptive or orthodox, by the way—is Jung shifted out of reverse.[10] At least since 1935 and Ernst Bloch's *Heritage of Our Times*, we have been sensitized to the ways in which the most repellent and dangerous politics have fastened onto the charismatic functionality of certain mystery traditions, using them as brutal and cynical occultism. Hitler and Goering, shake hands with Papa Doc. Alexander knows about these traps, yes, but he is also deeply mindful at each moment that, as a poet of great importance to him, Friedrich Hölderlin, once wrote, "Wo aber Gefahr ist, wächst/ Das Rettende auch" (Yet where danger lies/ Grows that which saves).[11] A common mischar-

---

the representatives of the states, under no other pretext than those elastic words, so convenient and yet so terrible: "for reasons of state."

These are truly terrible words, for they have corrupted and dishonoured, within official ranks and in society's ruling classes, more men than has even Christianity itself. No sooner are these words uttered than all grows silent, and everything ceases; honesty, honour, justice, right, compassion itself ceases, and with it logic and good sense. Black turns white, and white turns black. The lowest human acts, the basest felonies, the most atrocious crimes become meritorious acts.

Mikhail Bakunin, *Federalism, Socialism, Anti-Theologism*, accessed April 14, 2014, http://www.marxists.org/reference/archive/bakunin/works/various/reasons-of-state.htm.

10 The phrase "psychoanalysis in reverse" was, according to T.W. Adorno, coined by his Frankfurt School colleague Leo Lowenthal. See "Television and the Patterns of Mass Culture" in *Mass Culture: The Popular Arts in America,* eds. Bernard Rosenberg and David Manning White (New York: The Free Press, 1957), 480. To establish a fuller context for Jung's writings on alchemy, the reader might consult Jung's 1936 essay "Wotan," with its extremely dubious address to a contemporary mythological revival, a revival that had its political dimension, as *Ergriffenheit* (possession; "being seized"). In a letter to Gershom Scholem in 1937, Walter Benjamin notes that he was "waging an onslaught on [Jung's] doctrines, especially those concerning archaic images and the collective unconscious," and that on the evidence of Jung's earlier essays, he found that Jung's "auxiliary services to National Socialism have been in the works for some time." *The Correspondence of Walter Benjamin, 1910–1940*, 540.

11 Friedrich Hölderlin, "Patmos," in Richard Sieburth, trans., *Hymns and Fragments*, (Princeton, NJ: Princeton University Press), 89.

acterization of surrealism presents it as an irrationalist movement *tout court*, as if it learned nothing from dialectical thought, as if it could not be other than "hysterical." Frequently passed over is Breton's 1934 assertion in the aforementioned Brussels talk that surrealism's initial emphasis was on gutting logic and cracking the manacles of instrumental reason; he calls this the movement's "intuitive epoch." That early emphasis, however, swung to fundamental engagement with questions of radical left politics as a matter of surrealist practice, and this began the "reasoning epoch." Alexander is the witting legatee of all of this gravid modernity—and we should not neglect invoking Césaire at this moment—but I also want to note here, for later development in remarks on Clastres's work, that surrealism's emphasis on magic, esotericism, and the dream have made common cause with an explicit articulation of primitivity.

In the pieces of his that I take up, and elsewhere, Alexander writes in three modes: the *apotropaic*, writing talismanically to ward off the worst; this motive uses the *homeopathic*, in the sense of methodologically setting certain mystery traditions *in opposition to* state power as violent mystification and the mystification of violence. These modes and procedures are most in evidence in "Haiti." When we turn to "The Whirling King in the Runic Psychic Theatre," though, a third mode is in play, the *heraldic*. And I mean by this not at all the herald as a sign of arrogant power, "an official employed to oversee state ceremony, precedence, and the use of armorial bearings, and to make proclamations, carry ceremonial messages, and oversee tournaments," but rather the heraldic as synaesthetic annunciation and greeting of the *Novum*.

1

Two gleams:
From Aimé Césaire's 1956 letter of resignation from the French Communist Party:

> The dead, the tortured, the executed . . . These are not the kind of ghosts that one can ward off with a mechanical phrase.[12]

And from the *Second Manifesto of Surrealism*:

> This question of malediction which till now has elicited only ironic and hare-brained comments, is more timely than ever. Surrealism has everything to lose by wanting to remove this course from itself.[13]

12 Aimé Césaire, "Letter to Maurice Thorez," trans. Chike Jeffers, 1956, *Social Text 103* 28, no. 2 (Summer 2010): 145–52.
13 Breton, *Second Manifesto of Surrealism*, 176–77.

A recondite yet clearly furious language of indictment ignites Alexander's long poem "Haiti," which speaks in the collective voice of "*les Morts*," those "undistinguished dead," in Maya Deren's words,[14] who were the victims of the hideous Duvalier regime, and the voice is scalding:

it is we who speak
with a sun of splinters spewing from our heart
from our thorax burning with intestinal moray explosion (72)

Do these lines help in gathering the senses of Alexander's phrase "alphabetic with maiming"? The formula invokes language taken to the particulate level; it registers:

a) damage to language, even to its smallest signs, as a legacy of Duvalier, such that to have to use the alphabet that he used is to again cause grotesque pain to the collective subject;
b) damage to *les Morts*, at each recurrence in the language of their murderers of alphabetic particles used to kill them, lie about them, forget them;
c) the unstemmable need of the undistinguished dead to retort, to use alphabetic particles as lethal projectiles, alphabetic with the desire to maim the torturer.

The language of the Dead marshals, then, for sixty unrelenting and tonally unmodulated pages, the form and power of the curse, directed against François Duvalier, dead for twenty-four years at the poem's publication in 1995, and his consort Simone, who was not to die until 1997. The poem curses the forever copulant bodies of dictator and consort, the one dead, the one still then living, after her fashion, both objects of unbounded collective hatred:

Papa Doc
with his rotted & greenish blood
with his consort
the Madame
ailing in her rubies & bones
we accuse them
with every quarter of their accursed mandibles
with every despicable vibration as owls
their gestures
their veins as leopards turned around in a mirror
grown from themselves lashing out as monsters

14 Maya Deren, *Divine Horsemen: The Living Gods of Haiti* (Kingston, NY: McPherson, 2004 [1953]), 28.

we see them now
throughout a wrenching prolapse through the kingdoms of hell
caged by the demons
within the macerated bones of mutual self-bleeding

she
in lacerated sullage
he
atop
her fly infested vulva
like a gargoyle
squandered in the wax of his miserable finality (*A&H* 74–75)

"Sullage" is wastewater, sewage. The *ethic* of what Alexander calls "maledictive withering" (*A&H* 126) strips off the fake sanctity of the ruler and the equally fake sacrality of the State, and this is the ethic that burns through the whole of his writing. And yet, the poet's relations to state power, for all of their astonishing verbal violence, do not cease with excoriation. While the curse is needful, as long as history stinks with atrocity, it is also only reactive, bound to the object of its hatred, unfree, and prey to despair. It is not, finally, the power that is most needful and elusive. And so, the *intent* of this "maledictive withering" is to ensure that the dead Papa Doc stays dead. This is to say, in the context of Haitian vodoun, of which he considered himself an adept, that he *not* be either brought back as a zombie, nor as a soul positively reclaimed from the waters of the abyss, as in the rite described by Maya Deren in *Divine Horsemen: The Living Gods of Haiti*, a book that Alexander has acknowledged as a source for his poem.[15] For Alexander's poem, it is as Deren says, notwithstanding the inversion of a reclamatory ceremony into an execration: "The living do not serve the dead; it is the dead who are made to serve the living" (28).

To deny the bad irrationality of Papa Doc's fearsome use of vodoun, is to reanimate the best of the Haitian revolution, which for Alexander "was a victory of Africa over the West . . . 1804 marked the year that the incumbent dermatology of the West was defeated" (*SMH* 126). Yet the suppurating deadness of the matter that is the copula FrançoisSimone will have no rest, no quiet, no end of pain in its damnation. The collective voice of the Dead sends against Papa Doc and Simone Promethean torturers, vultures to tear them into new shapes of agony:

we
the dead

15 Ibid., 46–53.

send against them plankton armies
empowered by anger with a special knowledge of torture
perhaps an eye taken out & put back at angles
or having the teeth tragically spilled into an open rectal furnace
this is the law that the vultures instinctively sculpt for us (*A&H* 76)
. . .
this is the gargoyle couple
living by torture
by each excruciating mental fatality
that they've rapturously inflicted
all the suffering returning like blackened starlight in their mouths
(*A&H* 78)

The "radium cage" that the Dead have made for the hideous pairing takes from them their language that once was lethally absolute:

. . . the gargoyle couple
mere trodden upon enclitics
who've lost the stress of their pouring murderer's grammar (*A&H* 78)

The boiling cataract of invective goes on and on, annihilating conventional historiography's pretense to adequacy in treating atrocity. It also defeats the reader longing for surcease or, less honorably even, "balanced judgment." It is as if Alexander were in strategic accord with Adorno's postulate in *Minima Moralia* that "history does not merely touch on language, but takes place in it."[16] The dictator, the President for Life, the sovereign ruler along with his baleful consort have *cursed from them*, if I can put it that way, their power over the grammar of murder and are made "mere trodden upon enclitics," pieces of subjacent and shortened language, not even full words, and certainly no longer the fearsome Word from the dictator that would mean torture and murder. And so, the voice of the Dead comes into its own power to change history:

first
a hot and unglistening wax
flung down the slopes of their temples
then the implantation of leeching sewers in the mounts of their throats
our alchemical understanding
to distill transparency from their sufferings
their heritage of stains

16 Theodor Adorno, *Minima Moralia: Reflections from Damaged Life*, trans. E.F.N. Jephcott (London: NLB, 1978), 219.

their winged & in-aerial stumbling in feces
their grotesquely spun inertia imprisoning their compounds
in blinding pulmonary thickets
in procedures dissected on burning chromium tables
near the crest of intensive scapular gyrals
their wounds stitched and re-stitched
with a calibrated voltage

François
Simone
you exist at our behest (*A&H* 88)

It would blunt the invective acuity of this poem to speak of resolution or "victory"; as a measure of its contempt, the poem simply drops its dishonored objects at its close. The Dead have taken to themselves, though, sway over the naming of what remains of Duvalier's legacy:

this was your keepsake Francois
the weird & topical befoulment that you rendered
the zodiac that you grew & peopled with despair (*A&H* 113)

The State, Duvalieriste or any other, provokes the curse because it is unalterably, essentially, a set of procedures to enact—and here Alexander quotes Bakunin again—"the most flagrant, the most cynical . . . the most complete negation of humanity. It shatters the universal solidarity of all men on the earth, and brings some of them into association only for the purpose of destroying and conquering, and enslaving all the rest" (*SMH* 34). This is the condition, Alexander insists along with Bakunin and Malatesta, of *all* states and state operations, not just the local instance of the Duvalier dictatorship, but of the pretended cosmos of each and every State apparatus. In this sense, "Haiti"'s curse is flung in the teeth of all rule. There is danger, here, however. A cardboard sign that the mob held up in 2008 before the New York Stock Exchange read, "JUMP! YOU FUCKERS!" Many an anarchist can quote the words "We won't be happy until the last bureaucrat is hung from a lamp post by the guts of the last capitalist." Others, perhaps recalling Malatesta, try to stay with, "We are not murderers."[17] Here we have come to Caliban's anguish: how not to lie, broken, in paralysis and defeat, tormented

17 Said without Chesterfield's tedious cynicism: "Comrade Gregory has told us, in only too apologetic a tone, that we are not the enemies of society. But I say that we are the enemies of society, and so much the worse for society. We are the enemies of society, for society is the enemy of humanity, its oldest and its most pitiless enemy (hear, hear). Comrade Gregory has told us (apologetically again) that we are not murderers. There I agree. We are not murderers, we are executioners (cheers)." G.K. Chesterfield, *The Man Who Was Thursday* (Oxford: Oxford University Press, 1908), 30–31.

by having learned from the experience of oppression only to curse, or to take action only by killing, that is, by blindly acting like a state.

The risk of despair, an artifact of what Alexander calls "the predatory stupor," does not have stranglehold centrality at every moment in his work. It *slackens*, and those alphabetic with maiming come to know the saving thing that grows with danger, and herald this in the language of the "stupefacient image," the image that operates surreally. It is as if, as Wilson Harris writes in his novel *Jonestown*, "The sickness of slaughter for slaughter's sake was subtly evolving beyond fixtures of cruelty into a net to save me and hold the Predator at bay."[18] Or, as Alexander writes of the poet's relation to the collective Dead: "our alchemical understanding/ to distill transparency from their sufferings/ their heritage of stains" (*A&H* 88). The requirement here is for what Alexander calls forth in "The Zone Above Hunger": "What I speak of is the imaginal power to leap beyond the brutally imposed confines to combat the bureaucracies with an elemental seismics, with a new and alien thinking" (*SMH* 174). Does a truly "elemental seismics," then, call us to the recombinant act of poetic thinking, "alphabetic with maiming," putting in array letters, words, phrases, sentences, and images that do not recapitulate the death sentence of hierarchical power? The "ballet by liquidation" that Alexander indicts produces its own destruction, occurring in history, to be sure, but the writers whom we most need are those, like Will Alexander, and Wilson Harris, and Kamau Brathwaite, and Jayne Cortez, and Nathaniel Mackey, who help this destruction along.[19] These are writers driven by what Harris has observed in his essay "Adversarial Contexts and Creativity": "My greatest difficulty in scanning the world of the present and the past was to determine the genuineness of moral conviction or action in humanity to transcend repetitive cycles of violence and greed." He continues:

> Wherever one looks, whether in the West or in the societies of the Third World, it would seem that moral being cannot be divorced from a deepened cycle of creativity through which we may visualise a breakthrough from absolute violence. Such a breakthrough requires us to accept the adversarial contexts in which cultures wrestle with each other but to descend as well into camouflages and masks as flexible frames within the mystery of genuine change. *The mystery of genuine change.*[20]

---

18 Wilson Harris, *Jonestown* (London: Faber and Faber, 1996), 98.

19 See the conclusion of Mackey's novel *Bass Cathedral*, Brathwaite's *Trench Town Rock*, and Harris's *Jonestown* and *The Dark Jester*. And listen to the remarkable series of LPs by Jayne Cortez released on her Bola Press label.

20 Wilson Harris, "Adversarial Contexts and Creativity," *New Left Review* 154 (November–December 1985), 125, 128.

"The Whirling King in the Runic Psychic Theatre" stages a breakthrough drama of sovereignty simultaneously self-unmoored from the throne of brutal power and reconfigured by imagination-as-language. As such, it answers Harris's call for a "deepened cycle of creativity" that does not simply abjure kingship, but descends into it as camouflage, as mask, as flexible frame. The goal is, in alchemical terms, to refine and sublimate any vestige of what the word "king" has, to the world's sorrow, meant; we are given the voice of the king in transformation: "This ignited imperator is one who spins within blankly inspired rulings, no longer an advocate of the regnant powers of iron, of weighted tourniquets of blood, of falsely embellished spasmodics" (WK 51). Structured as a narrative of "then" and "now," the king's voice traces his former state: "I secured the very essence of El Rey, The King at the very height of his predominance. I moved towards the founts of war and termination, and in the depths of my persona I was emblazoned with copper, my spears were flashes from previously slaughtered suns" (WK 63).

The sovereign's "self-induced dethroning" (WK 53) is a process that disavows the obligatory performance of state ritual as cruelty and spectacle, performance that the sovereign role constitutively entails:

> To chop off the heads of goats, to ornament state secrets with torture, no longer suffices as duty. And I mean duty as outward kinetic, concerning the drawing of human blood, concerning the murdering of monsters for prestigious display. (WK 53)

Turning away from and upward from the role of the sovereign brings "waves of oneiric potion, eclipsing the sands of parasitical foundries" (WK 58). The poet writes that "This is nobility as transmutation" (WK 68), not kingship as the rigidity of terror and the provocation of bloody countering acts, but "as transparent moraine, as upper habitation, where the waters and the suns are both kindled by splendour" (WK 54). *All* exercise of power-as-cruelty by the figure of the king, sovereign, ruler, monarch, overlord, master, owner, patriarch, suzerain, pope, priest, commander, boss, judge, jailer, torturer, rapist, and hangman is abjured in the "now" by the whirling king as he moves "in spontaneous rotation over and above a moonless burial law, roaming and escaping all my treaties with Saxon mensal incarceration" (WK 64). Elements of this range are a focus in Alexander's novels *Sunrise in Armageddon* and *Diary as Sin*, told through the voices of horrifically abused women of color, who nonetheless are not barred from "emerging from the mists of treason," as the title of a painting by Alexander has it.[21] We also

21 *Sunrise in Armageddon* (New York: Spuyten Duyvil, 2006); *Diary as Sin* (Cheltenham: Skylight Press, 2011). The painting is reproduced on the cover of the latter.

must remember Sara Nokomis Weir, a Blackfoot Indian, raped and murdered at age nineteen, to whom Alexander dedicates *Asia & Haiti*. Powers of memory, imagination, and ethics, *yes*, but, as the unrevisable pivot, *no* to power as constituted by the multiple series named by Kamau Brathwaite: "Slave servant overseer master: power. Money labor machines: power. Gun book cannon: power. God the Father, God the Son, God the White Holy Ghost: power."[22]

The *summa* of this drama arrives with the king's pronouncement that he has moved beyond kingship *as a power inimical to his own core* as well as to the lives of others:

> And I have withstood the forces which have dwelled upon my own extinction. . . . Cleansed of every form of dishonour . . . forms become sonic, like the sound of a second bell in a mirror. Therefore I remain invisibly inspired by the fact that the pivots of annihilation have never succeeded in ensnaring the fires of my central rootedness. Have never, despite attempts upon my shadow, inflicted a lasting penury upon my soul. I am of health . . . (WK 65)

Health, then, "the zone above hunger," "capable at one touch of expansion and Utopia," is the refinement issuing from "the authority of a phantom egret ruling from a transparent throne of sound." The fearsome central figure that arrogated to itself the most brutal operations of sovereignty becomes, in Alexander's work, "the centre as blackened syllabus" (WK 54), illegible, scratched out, disabled, disfigured, without wish or power to make edicts, to inflict violence or to provoke counterviolence. The figure of the king is supplanted by an image in which the words "authority" and "ruling" can maintain none of their former meanings, and the word "power" shatters through transmutation its own death grip. "We exist/ as other bodies of oxygen/ like a collective force/ of burning inks & kings" (*A&H* 119). That is at once a gain in intimacy with the undistinguished Dead, returning power to them, and at the greatest imaginal remove from their collective grave as a site of perpetual despair. "The poet," once again, "has had to surmount the power of tyrants and magicians, and has had to take on the authority of a phantom egret ruling from a transparent throne of sound." A phantom egret, albescence and crow, crow and transparence: incessant elusives, the most elusive of which is the emancipated world.

22 Edward [Kamau] Brathwaite, "Introduction," Melville J. Herskovits, *Life in a Haitian Valley* (Garden City, NY: Anchor Books, 1971), xv.

2

> The imagination can say that it is something other than an adjudicated diamond, or an orphan who smells hypnosis in his urine. (EMS, BB 164)

Yes. *Sí, se puede*. Yet the paradox of a truly anarchic poetic stands, and we are left to ask, with the political anthropologist Pierre Clastres in his *Society Against the State*, "from where does this institution without 'substance' derive its strength to endure? For what needs to be understood is the bizarre persistence of a 'power' that is practically powerless, of a chieftainship without authority, of a function operating in a void."[23]

I do not turn to Clastres for corroboration of what Will Alexander discloses through poetic thought. Rather than appealing to anthropological research and theorization as authoritative ballast, I would prefer to see in Clastres's essays an opening onto what he found in certain primitive societies, "primitive" meaning specifically in this instance a society without a State, "State" meaning in this instance the formal structure of coercive power.[24] Such an aperture can disclose a temporal imaginary in Alexander's work that might otherwise pass unremarked. Attending to Clastres and his particular definition of "the primitive"—no other gets or deserves our attention here—hooks us onto one of the most important of Alexander's outward vectors, outward from tedious and cruel rational everydayness. Movement beyond inert fact; disablement of language as instrumental rationality; exobiological excursion; restoration of the feral and the oneiric; and recovery of the better model of kingship in the primitive, the world before the dreamless misfortune of the State. Throughout his reports on what he found living among Amazonian indigenous peoples runs the assertion of a contrast of their society with that of western Europe and its tributaries.[25] His optic denies truth value to a fundamental reification of the West: "It is not evident to me that coercion and subordination constitute the essence of political power *in all times and in all places*" (*SAS* 13). Just as there no peoples without history, so, for Clastres, there are no societies without political power:

> Societies cannot be divided into two groups: societies with power and societies without power. On the contrary, it is our view (in

---

23 Pierre Clastres, "Exchange and Power: Philosophy of the Indian Chieftanship," in Robert Hurley and Abe Stein, trans,. *Society Against the State: Essays in Political Anthropology*, (New York: Zone Books, 1987), 29. Hereafter *SAS*.

24 Pierre Clastres, "Power in Primitive Societies," chap. 6 of *Archeology of Violence* (New York: Semiotext(e), 1994), 87.

25 Clastres's thought was decisively shaped by the Guayaki and Tupi-Guarani peoples, as well as the Mbya.

> complete conformity with ethnographic data) that political power is *universal*, immanent to social reality (whether the social is defined by "blood ties" or social classes); and that it manifests itself in two primary modes: coercive power and non-coercive power. (*SAS* 22)

Paradoxical seeming, if we have learned nothing but the equation of power with violence, Clastres insists that the equation of political power with domination is given the lie by noting a different kind of power, that founded in and expressed through language. The terrible, but, for colonizing States, usefully axiomatic misunderstanding is deaf to linguistic power, or, if not, can only imagine the power of language as the understrapper of force:

> From its beginnings our culture has conceived of political power in terms of hierarchized and authoritarian relations of command and obedience. Every real or possible form of power is consequently reducible to this privileged relation which a priori expresses the essence of power. If the reduction is not possible it is because one is on this side of the political, so that the absence of any command-obedience relationship ipso facto entails the absence of political power. (*SAS* 16)

Clastres points to the absence of chieftainship founded in domination, which unsurprisingly appears to the colonizer as a lack, a weak spot. The (mis)apprehension of primitive society's chief-without-power-to-command renders his language an aesthetic triviality, a mere social ornament. The *primary* and indispensable function of language for the colonizer *vis-à-vis* the conquered is the dyad command-obedience; absent this, the colonizer and the State or state capitalist enterprise that propels him out into the world cannot recognize a differing kind of power. "It is imperative," as Clastres then holds, "to accept the idea that negation [of power as domination] does not signify nothingness; that when the mirror does not reflect our own likeness, it does not prove there is nothing to perceive" (*SAS* 20). Counter to the restricted imagination of political power only as similitude, the primitive society, that is, the society without a State, exists and reproduces itself through a different imaginary mode of political power:

> The whole political philosophy of primitive society can be glimpsed in the obligation of the chief to be a man of speech. This is where the space occupied by power unfolds, *a space that is not as one might imagine it*. And it is the nature of this discourse whose repetition is scrupulously seen to by the tribe, it is the nature of this masterful speech that directs us to the real locus of power. (*SAS* 153; emphasis added)

The mastery of speech by the chief does not make him a master with the power to command. Instead, the chief, who would be chastised at the least, and banished at worst for attempting to use language or force to exact compliance, holds his position because of his issuance of a particular kind of language:

> Verbal invention, arising from the desire to name beings and things according to their hidden dimension, their divine essence, results in a linguistic transmutation of the everyday world, a noble style of speech sometimes mistaken for a secret language. In this way, the Mbya speak of "the flower of the bow" to designate the arrow, the "skeleton of the fog" in naming the pipe, and "flowery branches" to evoke the fingers of Ñamandu. An admirable transfiguration which puts an end to the confusion and *ressentiment* of the world of appearances where the passion of the *last men* does not wish to be detained.[26] (*SAS* 162)

Here we have come to the confluence of the imaginative reach of primitive man's language with the writing of Will Alexander. A community of ethical views, then, in which the indispensable is the "admirable transfiguration" by language of a shadow world that instills misapprehension, the symnecrosis of power and violence, for example. There is no wish to linger in what Jacques Camatte called "this world we must leave."[27] Speech that abjures command: if Clastres is correct in his assertion that, "In effect, each one of us carries within himself, internalized like the believer's faith, the certitude that society exists for the State" (*SAS* 189), wouldn't the imagination-in-language that transmutes and *clarifies* our certitude that a world without command has existed and can exist again help us toward health, toward "the zone above hunger"? The Whirling King makes a relation to language that is feral, well beyond his control, and in that relation realizes a new figuration of power.

New, at any rate, to the conventions of kingship, but with precedent in history. In *Universal Emancipation: The Haitian Revolution and the Radical Enlightenment*, Nick Nesbitt contrasts the emancipatory promise of the

26 However Nietzschean the language here, the "last men" is what, in Clastres's translation, the Guarani Indians choose to call themselves. See *SAS* 170. Clastres is compounding discourses here, and worrying through the indigenous language refracted through Nietzsche's ideas is work for another occasion.

27 "Even where an individual has attained a high degree of reification and has been transformed into an organic automaton of capital, there is still the possibility that the whole construction could break apart. Here, we would do well to follow an old piece of advice from Marx: It's not enough to make the chains visible, they must become shameful. Each individual should experience a crisis." Jacques Camatte, "Against Domestication," trans. David Loneragan, in *This World We Must Leave and Other Essays*, ed. Alex Trotter (New York: Autonomedia, 1995), 121.

1793 revolution to its later flattening, with Toussaint's 1801 Constitution, into "militaristic, antidemocratic, and paternalist authoritarianism."[28] Notwithstanding Toussaint's formidable skills at the imposition of his will, however, the Bossale community of African-born former slaves was strategically deaf to Toussaint's thunder heralding enlightenment maturity as submission to duty and obedience to the order of the State, and took to the hinterlands. "The Bossale community of Saint-Domingue clearly perceived the constitution of an autonomous transcendental state mechanism—so ardently sought after by the military elite from Toussaint to Christophe—to constitute a threat to be avoided at all costs" (*UE* 169).

Drawing on the work of Gérard Barthélemy, Nesbitt makes clear that the rural existence of the Bossale community functioned as an "'egalitarian system without a state,'" and did so from the late 1790s to the 1960s, "until the destruction of the Haitian (natural and social) environment under the regime of Papa Doc undermined its viability" (*UE* 171). While with the revenance of Papa Doc we are again in the pale of Will Alexander's "Haiti," we would do well to remember the length of the life made in opposition to Toussaint's state and its historical outgrowths, which so logically spawned King Christophe and President-for-Life Duvalier. The stakes couldn't be higher: in Nesbitt's understanding, "It is precisely this sustained construction of a large-scale *stateless* community that distinguishes Haitian Bossale society from all the major political forms of modernity, whether representative or monarchic democracy, fascist, or bureaucratic socialist" (*UE* 170). This is the lacuna in normative political theory, then, an instance "whose accomplishments are simply invisible or incomprehensible to the outside world" (*UE* 170). Unsurprisingly, in Barthélemy's view, the Bossale model aligns with Clastres's analysis of Amazonian lifeways: in the first instance deliberate *marronnage* from, and in the second, communal self-protection against authoritarian enclosure, proclaimed by whichever king.

3

Will Alexander's writing requires of its readers extended concentration. Here, then, is material for that faculty, in reply to the demand from some quarters for both a common language and a recognizable activist orientation. "Of course," writes the poet,

> one does need to make protest concerning a hectare of murdered Indians, or of the institutional mephitics advanced against biological-Africa. According to certain elements in reportage, such

28 Nick Nesbitt, *Universal Emancipation: The Haitian Revolution and the Radical Enlightenment* (Charlottesville: University of Virginia Press, 2008), 166. Hereafter *UE*.

behavior goes no deeper than the reprehensible mechanics of the capital economy.

But for the imagination another level of experience exists, which lurks beyond the in-nautical. The in-nautical, meaning prose, containment, contiguous aspiration. What is meant here is the imagination of spirit which organically supersedes damaged lightning as property, or strategic simulacra conditioned by Roman property as model. One can take, as example, Julius Caesar in Gaul. Destroy tribes, create treasonous conditions, subject whole zones to immolation. Of course, this being action as fear through vociferous means. This being the psychology of the ruined who project ruin upon the ruined. It is like an equation which galls through the superficial extent of its grasp. Its principle: protect at all costs the right to hostility; the prize, gold or land, plundered by predacity.

But what of interior damage?

Of maimed consciousness?

Of heritage through mental distortion?

This to the prosaic world remains the blinded experience, remains the occulted inner impairment. Which is something other than repression by scorpions. The inner balance lingers and dissolves by commandeering insult. Then the memory takes on the unwarranted slaughter, the labour in dazed tobacco fields. One then whispers by uncertainty, under laws of distilled enmity. Such is the environment of a ravenous moral foundation, fighting to gain one's strength through transmixing one's immediate oneiric vitality according to European superimposition. This being the damage culled from 2,000 years.

Now one faces a present circuitously ruled by such indelible stanchions. Yet the code of one's spontaneous firmament must be the exponential form of miraculous antidote. One can no longer be dispelled by horizontal deletion. By technical aims, by the onslaught of misguided popular incursion. One must remain feral. One must hold in one's feathers a glossary of teeth. Which is something other than a studied or philosophical circumstance, or the silhouette in the corporal lean-to. This is where the untameable resistance resides, rising from a rebellious mariner's coffin as a psychic territorial Hun. But one does not stop there.

Is suffering consequential? What constitutes evolution beyond it? We can name the structural mutilations to the hummingbird as immense as the world; what more, in the face of the undeniable historical structuration that hurts us, can language do? "So what is structure?" the poet asks, "Drafts of money? Owned trivia as property? One could say yes, both are central to the structure. Which extends to what Artaud once called the piling up of bodies" (EMS 168). This we can recognize: "nothing but a monochromatic litmus suffused with exhaustive terror . . . all forms of the irregular are lessened, then hauled up for elimination. Be they Arawaks, or Haitians, or Afghanis, or other nonspeaking flora or fauna—like limbs hacked off by the Dutch in the midst of the slave trade in order to maim captured African maroons" (EMS 169). The evolution that our most necessary poets speak of comes through "cosmogonic Surrealism"[29] and answers Wilson Harris's call for genuine change. Not gutting predation anymore, the malevolence and avarice that cause bleeding, but the free association of action that "takes on drift, floating through a mass of cryptic tenuosity. A tenuousness which spills into utopian disservice" (EMS 172–73). A program, or other, and better? What is the value of this poetry for anarchism? Do we find it of value to receive signals from places of life that we can hardly imagine exist? The mine has collapsed. It does no good now to say that the tunnels were poorly shored up from the beginning. With luck and good ears, we'll hear tapping from below. Let's get to it, then, and bring up the living.

29 Nick Nesbitt, *Caribbean Critique: Antillean Critical Theory from Toussaint to Glissant* (Liverpool: Liverpool University Press, 2013), 117.

MASTERS WITHOUT SLAVES: RAOUL VANEIGEM'S DÉTOURNEMENT OF NIETZSCHE

Gavin Arnall

> Each word, idea or symbol is a double agent. Some, like the word "fatherland" or the policeman's uniform, usually work for authority; but make no mistake, when ideologies clash or simply begin to wear out, the most mercenary sign can become a good anarchist.[1]
>
> —Raoul Vaneigem

> There are no forbidden words; in language, as it will soon be everywhere else, *everything is permitted*. To forbid the use of a word is to relinquish a weapon that our opponents will use.[2]
>
> —Mustapha Khayati

It would be imprecise to describe Raoul Vaneigem as committed to anarchism, since, for the former situationist, the suffix "-ism" signals the ossification of radical theory, its hardening into a generalized and generalizing ideology.[3] Vaneigem's commitment to total revolution, the end of hierarchy and the refusal of power, direct democracy and self-management,

1 Raoul Vaneigem, *The Revolution of Everyday Life*, trans. Donald Nicholson-Smith (Oakland: PM Press, 2012), 85.

2 Mustapha Khayati, "Captive Words (Preface to a Situationist Dictionary)," *Guy Debord and the Situationist International*, ed. Tom McDonough (Cambridge: MIT Press, 2004), 179.

3 For Vaneigem on "-isms," consider the following passage from *The Movement of the Free Spirits*: "All would-be universal ideologies—such as nationalism, socialism, fascism, communism—wear the withering skin of religion until they, too, begin to shrivel up, turning cancerous at the same uncontrollable rate at which capital proliferates." Raoul Vaneigem, *The Movement of the Free Spirits*, trans. Randall Cherry (New York: Zone Books, 1994), 45. Vaneigem extends this argument to situationism in a recent interview: Raoul Vaneigem and Hans Ulrich Obrist, *In Conversation with Raoul Vaneigem*, http://www.e-flux.com/journal/in-conversation-with-raoul-vaneigem/.

nonetheless exhibits his clear affinity with anarchist thought and forms of organization. Born in Lessines, Belgium, Vaneigem is best known for his participation, throughout the 1960s, in the Situationist International (SI), a group founded in 1957 by Guy Debord and other artists and thinkers formerly connected to the Letterist International, the Movement for an Imaginist Bauhaus, and the London Psychogeographical Society.[4] Vaneigem's most influential book, the *Traité de savoir-vivre à l'usage des jeunes générations* (1967), translated into English as *The Revolution of Everyday Life*, could be described as, among other things, a manifesto and compendium of hypotheses on how to construct a passionate life that would supersede the mediocrity of late capitalist consumer society. A number of sources inspire and inform the ideas and arguments expressed in these pages, ranging from the writings of Karl Marx, Charles Fourier, and Mikhail Bakunin to the aesthetic interventions of Dada, the Marquis de Sade, and the Comte de Lautréamont, from historical events like the Paris Commune and the Russian Revolution to everyday acts of creation, love,

4 Histories of the Situationist International generally underemphasize Vaneigem's role in the group despite his fundamental contributions to it. This may be because his ideas and style occasionally diverged significantly from Debord's, the main protagonist of most accounts of the SI. This divergence and the debates it sparked led to Vaneigem's resignation/expulsion from the group in 1970. One difference between Debord and Vaneigem is the latter's significant proximity to the anarchist tradition. Debord accordingly titled his account of the SI and its division *The Real Split in the International*, an allusion to Marx and Engels's "The Alleged Splits in the International," which presaged the expulsion of the anarchists from the First International. See: Situationist International, *The Real Split in the International*, trans. John McHale (London: Pluto Press, 2003). Along with underplaying Vaneigem's contributions, many histories of the SI reproduce this split and minimize or erase the anarchist tendencies within the group. Peter Wollen's extensive overview of the group, its history, and its influences symptomatically commits this error in the following passage: "If we can see the SI as the summation of the historic avant-gardes, we can equally view it as the summation of Western Marxism—and in neither case does the conclusion of an era mean that it need no longer be understood or its lessons learned and valued." Wollen privileges the influence of Marxism over anarchism instead of recognizing both political positions as equally relevant for the group. This skewed perspective of the SI is only possible because Wollen focuses on Debord and Asger Jorn while virtually ignoring Vaneigem. See: Peter Wollen, "Bitter Victory: The Art and Politics of the Situationist International," *On the Passage of a Few People through a Brief Moment in Time: The Situationist International 1957–1972* (Boston: MIT Press, 1989), 27. Two fundamental studies of the SI, remarkable for their range and depth but unremarkable in their treatment of Vaneigem's thought, include McKenzie Wark, *The Beach Beneath the Street: The Everyday Life and Glorious Times of the Situationist International* (London: Verso, 2011); and Vincent Kaufmann, *Guy Debord: Revolution in the Service of Poetry*, trans. Robert Bononno (Minneapolis: University of Minnesota Press, 2006). Wark's follow-up book is exceptional, especially regarding studies of the SI in English, because of its extended discussion of Vaneigem and his theoretical contributions before and after his split with Debord and the SI. See McKenzie Wark, *The Spectacle of Disintegration: Situationist Passages out of the 20th Century* (London: Verso, 2013), 49–84.

and play. A peculiar and unlikely interlocutor, given his consistent commitment to the (re)production of slavery and hierarchy, Friedrich Nietzsche also informs the ideas and terminology of *The Revolution of Everyday Life*. I argue, however, that Vaneigem converts Nietzsche's words and ideas into good anarchists, that he repurposes the mercenary's signs and symbols for an alternative project. This essay accordingly examines the translation of Nietzschean formulations into radical theory, the modification and reorganization of a preexisting vocabulary to construct a different language.[5]

Nietzsche's appearance in Vaneigem's seminal treatise is far from unprecedented. Numerous factions of the Left, particularly within the anarchist tradition, have championed Nietzsche and drawn extensively from his writings.[6] Emma Goldman, for example, gave many lectures on Nietzsche and his work while traveling throughout the United States and argued that, in a certain sense, Nietzsche was an anarchist.[7] In her autobiography, Goldman relates the following exchange at Justus Schwab's saloon in New York City:

> They began discussing Nietzsche. I took part, expressing my enthusiasm over the great poet-philosopher and dwelling on the impression of his works on me. [James] Huneker was surprised. "I did not know you were interested in anything outside of propaganda," he remarked. "That is because you don't know anything about anarchism," I replied, "else you would understand that it embraces every phase of life and effort and that it undermines the old, outlived values." [P.] Yelineck asserted that he was an anarchist because he

5 Consider Khayati on this point: "[N]othing is more obviously subject to dialectics than language, insofar as it is a living reality. Thus all criticism of the old world has been made through that world's language and yet against it, hence automatically in a *different* language. All revolutionary theory must invent its own words, destroy the prevailing meaning of other words, and provide new positions in the 'world of meanings' that correspond to the new reality under preparation, a reality that must be released from the prevailing muddle." Khayati, "Captive Words," 173.

6 See, for example: *I Am Not a Man, I Am Dynamite!: Friedrich Nietzsche and the Anarchist Tradition*, eds. John Moore and Spencer Sunshine (New York: Autonomedia, 2004). See also: Seth Taylor, *Left-Wing Nietzscheans: The Politics of German Expressionism, 1910–1920* (New York: Walter de Gruyter, 1990). Although with some significant gaps regarding anarchism's appropriation of Nietzsche, the most complete discussion of Left-Nietzscheanism, from its earliest instantiations to its presence in the works of Georges Bataille, Pierre Klossowski, Gilles Deleuze, Michel Foucault, and Jacques Derrida, is Geoff Waite's unparalleled study and critique of the phenomenon, *Nietzsche's Corps/e: Aesthetics, Politics, Prophecy, or, the Spectacular Technoculture of Everyday Life* (Durham, NC: Duke University Press, 1996). I offer a response to Waite's intervention in note 32.

7 These lectures have unfortunately been lost. For a speculative reconstruction of their contents, see Leigh Starcross, "'Nietzsche Was an Anarchist': Reconstructing Emma Goldman's Nietzsche Lectures," *I Am Not a Man, I Am Dynamite!: Friedrich Nietzsche and the Anarchist Tradition*, 29–39.

> was an artist; all creative people must be anarchists, he held, because they need scope and freedom for their expression. Huneker insisted that art has nothing to do with any ism. "Nietzsche himself is the proof of it," he argued; "he is an aristocrat, his ideal is the superman because he has no sympathy with or faith in the common herd." I pointed out that Nietzsche was not a social theorist but a poet, a rebel and innovator. His aristocracy was neither of birth nor of purse; it was of the spirit. In that respect Nietzsche was an anarchist, and all true anarchists were aristocrats, I said.[8]

Two important points from this striking passage are to be highlighted. First, Goldman maintains that anarchism's subversion of antiquated norms and beliefs coincides with Nietzsche's revaluation of values. Goldman also suggests that the affinity between Nietzsche and anarchism stems from their shared aristocratic spirit, their common will to live an exuberant life.

Goldman's perspective nevertheless disavows the relationship between Nietzsche's poetry and his social vision, between his aristocratic spirit and his steadfast opposition to all forms of egalitarianism.[9] This is especially disturbing because some of Nietzsche's most vitriolic critiques were directed at anarchists and anarchist ideals. Consider the following passage from *Beyond Good and Evil*, which Huneker may have been referring to at the New York saloon:

> Witness the ever madder howling of the anarchist dogs who are baring their fangs more and more obviously and roam through the alleys of European culture. They seem opposites of the peacefully industrious democrats and ideologists . . . but in fact they are at one with the lot in their thorough and instinctive hostility to every other form of society except the *autonomous* herd, even to the point of repudiating the very concepts of "master" and "servant"—*ni dieu ni maître*.[10]

Nietzsche's elitism and aristocratic individualism propels him to view both democratic movements and the anarchist call to end authority and

8 Emma Goldman, *Living My Life*, Vol. 1 (New York: Cosimo Books, 2008), 194.

9 For Waite, this disavowal is symptomatic of a much larger phenomenon: "Arguably *the* constitutive paradox of post/modern intellectual, artistic, and political life . . . is that Nietzsche seems to attack nothing more vehemently than democracy, feminism, popular culture, and the Left in general. Yet nowhere and at no other time has he enjoyed a warmer, more uncritical—hence more masochistic—welcome than today from precisely this same Left—warmer and more uncritically than ever even on the Center or the Right." Waite, *Nietzsche's Corps/e*, 75 (emphasis in original).

10 Friedrich Nietzsche, "Beyond Good and Evil," *Basic Writings of Nietzsche*, trans. Walter Kaufmann (New York: Random House, 2000), 306.

servitude, embodied in the popular slogan "no gods, no masters," as committed to "making [man] mediocre and lowering his value."[11] Nietzsche proposes instead that "every enhancement of the type 'man' has so far been the work of an aristocratic society—and it will be so again and again—a society that believes in the long ladder of an order and of rank and differences in value between man and man, and that needs slavery in some sense or other."[12]

Nietzsche holds that hierarchical forms of social organization are necessary for the enhancement of man because he rejects the notion that "to benefit humanity as a whole" means "to benefit all human beings."[13] Rather, the idea is to allow "a choice type" to flourish, while everyone else must sacrifice "*for [their] sake*, must be reduced and lowered to incomplete human beings, to instruments."[14] A "higher state of *being*" is to be reached by a select few who, like the "sun-seeking vines of Java," bathe in light while standing on the back of others.[15] Although Nietzsche's literary and aphoristic style, his use of rhetoric and vivid imagery, "the magic of his language," likely encouraged Goldman to read the author of *Beyond Good and Evil* figuratively or allegorically, the above passages unambiguously propose concrete positions against those who would challenge a social order founded on hierarchy and slavery.[16] Nietzsche's aristocratic spirit, in other words, is linked to a project that strives for the production and reproduction of aristocratic forms of social organization; his poetic revaluation of values inhibits the subversion of antiquated social norms of rank and order.

Vaneigem, like Goldman, draws from Nietzsche's thought, but he is more aware of the unity of Nietzsche's spirit and social vision and therefore approaches Nietzsche strategically and with caution. Vaneigem does not ignore or relativize Nietzsche's authoritarian social and political commitments but rather appropriates and manipulates Nietzschean formulations in order to invest them with a new, revolutionary content, thereby liberating them from their servitude as instruments of power. The situationists called this practice of resignification, of repurposing preexisting elements for the construction of a new ensemble, "détournement." The prehistory of détournement includes a number of recombinatory concepts and practices, such as Kierkegaard's recollections, Marx's inversions of the genitive, Lautréamont's creative plagiarisms, Dada's technique of

---

11 Ibid., 307

12 Ibid., 391.

13 Alexander Nehamas, "Who Are 'The Philosophers of the Future'? A Reading of *Beyond Good and Evil*," *Reading Nietzsche*, eds. Robert C. Solomon and Kathleen M. Higgins (Oxford: Oxford University Press, 1988), 58.

14 Nietzsche, "Beyond Good and Evil," 392 (emphasis in original).

15 Ibid. (emphasis in original).

16 Goldman, *Living My Life*, 172.

photomontage, the Letterist Isidore Isou's distinction between the amplic and the chiseled, and Bertolt Brecht's principle of *Umfunktionierung*.[17] According to the situationists, détournement's two fundamental laws include "the loss of importance of each détourned autonomous element—which may go so far as to completely lose its original sense—and at the same time the organization of another meaningful ensemble that confers on each element its new scope and effect."[18] In its basic structure, détournement is the playful desecration of existing meaning followed by the reorganization of the desecrated for the construction of new meaning. This formal description of the procedure is nonetheless insufficient, since détournement's conversion process is also a subversive form of political intervention. Détournement not only negates and constructs meaning but also liberates resources formerly frozen in the grip of authority.[19]

Although these aspects unite all of its forms, the practice of détournement is far from univocal. In the pre-situationist text "A User's Guide to Détournement" (1956), Debord and Gil Wolman distinguish between three forms of détournement: "minor détournements," "ultra-détournements," and "deceptive détournements."[20] While minor détournements appropriate forgotten or commonplace elements, like press clippings or discarded photographs, and place them in a new context from which they draw a heightened meaning, ultra-détournements modify everyday social life, ascribing new significance to common gestures, words, clothing, spaces, and situations. A minor détournement of press clippings could produce an agitational collage whereas an ultra-détournement of an everyday space might create "a fantastic fairground, a sunny pleasure dome, where the most exhilarating adventures would allow themselves to be directly experienced."[21]

---

17 Debord discusses how Marx and Kierkegaard use détournement in Guy Debord, *The Society of the Spectacle* (New York: Zone Books, 1995), 145. Anselm Jappe highlights Isou's contribution to détournement in Jappe, *Guy Debord* (Berkeley: University of California Press, 1999), 59, 60. Martin Jay offers a genealogy of détournement that includes the other elements listed above in Martin Jay, *Downcast Eyes: The Denigration of Vision in Twentieth-Century French Thought* (Berkeley: University of California Press, 1995), 424.

18 "Détournement as Negation and Prelude," *Situationist International Anthology*, ed. Ken Knabb (Berkeley: Bureau of Public Secrets, 2002), 67.

19 Given his excellent contributions to the study of Debord and the Situationist International, it is peculiar that Tom McDonough obscures this important aspect of détournement in a recent formalistic presentation of détournement and recuperation. See Tom McDonough, "Ideology and the Situationist Utopia," *Guy Debord and the Situationist International: Texts and Documents*, ed. Tom McDonough (Cambridge, MA: MIT Press, 2004), ix–xx.

20 See Guy Debord, "A User's Guide to Détournement," *Situationist International Anthology*, 14–21.

21 This is how Vaneigem describes the détournement of the Palais de Justice in Brussels. See Vaneigem, *The Revolution of Everyday Life*, 237.

Deceptive détournements, on the other hand, repurpose "an intrinsically significant element," such as an iconic artwork or a statement made by a famous historical figure, "which derives a different scope from the new context." This practice of détournement thus establishes a distance between an element's initial meaning and its new, altered signification; however, if deception is total, if the original and its distance from the new signification is unrecognizable, then the détournement becomes unreadable, appearing as a faithful repetition or a wholly new creation rather than a subversive appropriation. As Debord and Wolman assert, "*the main impact of a détournement is directly related to the conscious or semiconscious recollection of the original contexts of the elements.*"[22]

Included in the user's guide is this particularly relevant example of deceptive détournement:

> [D.W.] Griffith's *Birth of a Nation* is one of the most important films in the history of cinema because of its wealth of innovations. On the other hand, it is a racist film and therefore absolutely does not merit being shown in its present form. But its total prohibition could be seen as regrettable. . . . It would be better to détourn it as a whole, without necessarily even altering the montage, by adding a soundtrack that made a powerful denunciation of the horrors of imperialist war and the activities of the Ku Klux Klan.[23]

Neither cooperation nor purity, what Vaneigem describes as ineffectual refusal (reformism) and extreme refusal (nihilism), the practice of détournement presupposes that the elements already at hand need only be reorganized to release their revolutionary potential, "that a critique of the world of spectacle [can] only be articulated through the components of spectacle itself."[24] When confronted with the organizers of the spectacle, the situationists declare: "We are neither going to leave the present field of culture to them nor mix with them."[25] The third, situationist option is the individual and collective manipulation of that which manipulates the individual and the collective, the subversion and appropriation, in other words, of the entire field of culture.

There are some important variations of the practice of deceptive détournement. For example, the first thesis of Debord's *The Society of the*

22 Ibid., 17. Debord elaborates on this point in his discussion of "allusions" in, Guy Debord, *Panegyric: Volume 1 & 2* (London: Verso, 2004), 8 (emphasis in original).

23 Debord, "A User's Guide to Détournement," 19.

24 Tom McDonough, "Guy Debord, or the Revolutionary without a Halo," *October* 115 (Winter, 2006): 45. Vaneigem develops the distinction between ineffectual refusal/reformism and extreme refusal/nihilism here: Vaneigem, *The Revolution of Everyday Life*, 144, 145.

25 "Now, the SI," *Situationist International Anthology*, 175.

Spectacle (1967), which states that "the whole life of those societies in which modern conditions of production prevail presents itself as an immense accumulation of *spectacles*," is a deceptive détournement of the opening sentence of Marx's *Capital*.[26] By explicitly theorizing détournement while practicing it, Debord's text provides its own guide to any interpretation of its theses: "The device of *détournement* restores all their subversive qualities to past critical judgments that have congealed into respectable truths—or, in other words, that have been transformed into lies."[27] In contrast to the détournment of *Birth of a Nation*, which transforms the film's racist content into anti-racist propaganda, Debord's détournement of Marx is restorative, it reactualizes the once transgressive character of Marx's words, encased in falsity as a result of their spectacular co-optation. The implications of deceptive détournement's intervention thus depend, in part, on the former significance and context of the détourned element.

McKenzie Wark's *The Spectacle of Disintegration: Situationist Passages out of the 20th Century* offers an illuminating examination of Vaneigem's détournement of Charles Fourier that could be read, as he proposes, alongside Debord's détournement of Marx (and Hegel).[28] I would argue, however, that it would be a mistake to read Vaneigem's détournement of Nietzsche in the same vein, for Vaneigem does not restore Nietzsche's voice but rather makes his words and ideas recoil back at him, slashing vocal cords that vibrate on behalf of authority.[29] "Repurposing (*détournement*) is the only revolutionary use of the spiritual and material values promoted by consumer society," Vaneigem tells us in *The Revolution of Everyday Life*.[30] He continues: "The main tactical and strategic issue is how to turn the weapons that commercial pressures oblige the enemy to distribute against that enemy itself. A user's guide to repurposing should be available to all consumers who want to stop consuming."[31] As a defender of order and rank, indeed as someone who intended to use his writing to perpetuate hierarchical power and slavery, Nietzsche is a dangerous weapon.[32] And

26 Guy Debord, *The Society of the Spectacle* (New York: Zone Books, 1995), 12 (emphasis in original).

27 Ibid., 144, 145.

28 See: McKenzie Wark, *The Spectacle of Disintegration: Situationist Passages out of the 20th Century*, 49–84.

29 Greil Marcus defines détournement as "a politics of subversive quotation, of cutting the vocal cords of every empowered speaker, social symbols yanked through the looking glass, misappropriated words and pictures diverted into familiar scripts and blowing them up." Greil Marcus, *Lipstick Traces: A Secret History of the Twentieth Century* (Cambridge, MA: Harvard University Press, 2003), 179.

30 Vaneigem, *The Revolution of Everyday Life*, 230.

31 Ibid., 239.

32 Although far too rich and multilayered to summarize here, one of the main arguments of Waite's *Nietzsche's Corps/e* is that Nietzsche intended to "re/produce a viable

he admitted it: "I am not a human being, I am dynamite."[33] Rather than retreating from this weapon, which would amount to surrendering it without combat, Vaneigem appropriates and repurposes Nietzsche. The creative and playful spark of détournement lights the dynamite's fuse. Nietzsche's explosion is simultaneously a revelatory flash of truth—negation and prelude.

---

form of willing human slavery appropriate to post/modern conditions, and with it a small number of (male) geniuses equal only among themselves" by mobilizing an esoteric semiotics that would subrationally manipulate his readers (Waite, 232). Nietzsche's corpus, according to Waite, advances certain philosophical claims that have no ontological or esoteric existence but are nonetheless politically useful and therefore circulated exoterically for public consumption. Potential communists attempt to politically appropriate Nietzsche's exoteric claims for their own projects, but, like computer viruses, these claims sooner or later infect their hosts, transforming revolutionaries into Left-Nietzschoids "who are supposed to *believe* that they are opposing tyranny when *in fact* they are supporting its undergirding conceptual and economic system" (ibid., 225, emphasis in original). Left-Nietzscheanism, in other words, is always already manipulated by Nietzsche's esoteric messages, even as it attempts to creatively manipulate Nietzsche's exoteric themes; Left-Nietzschoids always already collaborate with Nietzsche's socioeconomic project of order and rank, even when deconstructing Nietzsche's texts. Although generally unflinching in his critique of the main currents of Left-Nietzscheanism, Waite is hesitant and ultimately inconclusive regarding his stance on the situationists. It is no surprise, given his critique of the leftist appropriation of Nietzsche, that Waite explicitly mentions "situationist activism" (ibid., 119) and détournement (ibid., 171) as strategies that are ultimately infected by Nietzsche's esotericism. However, he does not offer a sustained critique of the situationists, instead admitting "a certain solidarity with what remains of international situationism" (ibid., 116) and drawing heavily on situationist ideas throughout the book, as evinced most obviously by the title: *Nietzsche's Corps/e: Aesthetics, Politics, Prophecy, or, the Spectacular Technoculture of Everyday Life*. Indeed, Waite's defense of his method and style of writing, of long endnotes, pastiche, and the use of dashes, implicitly evokes the practice of détournement: "If all these might appear in the abstract to be 'Nietzschean' strategies, now they are turned against Nietzsche's corps/e. There are several important *formal-technological* as well as *politico-ideological* aspects of endnote-pastiche" (ibid., 77, emphasis in original). This ambivalent passage suggests that repurposing Nietzschean strategies can aid in combating Nietzsche and his corps while also doubly qualifying this statement with the phrase "in the abstract" and the scare quotes around "Nietzschean," suggesting doubt about the truly Nietzschean quality of these strategies. This ambivalence is significant because the situationists may offer the strongest challenge to Waite's argument regarding appropriation. When faced with Nietzsche, the Left has to ask itself the following question: Is it possible to wrest certain elements of Nietzsche's corpus from his cold, dead hands, from his corpse, without becoming a part of his corps? For Waite, the answer is consistently no, whereas Vaneigem's *The Revolution of Everyday Life* suggests that there is no other way to get beyond Nietzsche. If Nietzscheanism "is isomorphic with the Society of the Spectacle," as Waite argues, then the best weapon against it is détournement (364). Cooptation is always a risk, but it is an even greater risk to relinquish a weapon that the organizers of the spectacle will use.

33 Friedrich Nietzsche, "Ecce Homo," *The Anti-Christ, Ecce Homo, Twilight of the Idols and Other Writings*, eds. Aaron Ridley and Judith Norman, trans. Judith Norman (Cambridge: Cambridge University Press, 2005), 143, 144.

As we saw in the case of Marx, however, critical judgments can always suffer spectacular recuperation. "Power creates nothing; it coopts."[34] Yet power cannot harness the creativity of détournement; the gold of détournement's revolutionary alchemy turns to coal when it touches enemy hands.[35] Once recuperated, further détournement is required, lest radical propositions of the past are to remain black stones of carbon. As Vaneigem asserts, "the watchword 'Workers of the World Unite!' may have helped construct the Stalinist state, yet one day it will underpin the classless society. No poetic sign is ever definitively commandeered by ideology."[36] Debord similarly posits that détournement is "the fluid language of anti-ideology. It occurs within a type of communication aware of its inability to enshrine any inherent and definitive certainty."[37] Détournement and recuperation, in other words, are dialectically antagonistic practices mobilized in a continuous war of position and maneuver.[38]

The practice of détournement may itself sound Nietzschean. While explaining the genealogical principle of the discontinuity between the origin of some thing or practice and its local usefulness in a specific situation, Nietzsche posits the following in *On the Genealogy of Morality*:

> Something extant, something that has somehow or other come into being, is again and again interpreted according to new views, monopolized in a new way, transformed and rearranged for a new use by a power superior to it; that all happening in the organic world is an *over-powering, a becoming-lord-over*; and that, in turn all overpowering and becoming-lord-over is a new interpreting, an arranging by means of which the previous "meaning" and "purpose" must of necessity become obscured or entirely extinguished.[39]

Nietzsche's notion of interpretation, as a practice that rearranges and transforms meaning for a new use or purpose, appears closely related to the situationist practice of détournement.[40] But the aim of détournement

34 "All the King's Men," *Situationist International Anthology*, 150.
35 See Vaneigem, *The Revolution of Everyday Life*, 169.
36 Ibid., 84.
37 Debord, *The Society of the Spectacle*, 146.
38 A helpful discussion of the dialectical relationship between détournement and recuperation can be found in Karen Kurczynsi, "Expression as Vandalism: Asger Jorn's 'Modifications,'" *RES: Anthropology and Aesthetics* 53–54 (Spring–Autumn, 2008), 293–313.
39 Friedrich Nietzsche, *On the Genealogy of Morality*, trans. Maudemarie Clark and Alan J. Swensen (Indianapolis: Hackett Publishing Company, 1998), 50, 51 (emphasis in original).
40 Gilles Deleuze's interpretation of Nietzsche on interpretation, itself a creative manipulation of the philosopher's thought, resonates with the practice of détournement insofar as it highlights interpretation's (mis)appropriation of its object: "Interpretation reveals its complexity when we realize that a new force can only appear and appropriate

is not to seize power, to become-lord-over—this is the objective of recuperation. Détournement, on the contrary, rattles the very structure of power in order to contribute to its ultimate supersession. Insofar as Nietzsche interprets the act of interpretation as an expression of the will to power, we could say that the practice of détournement is itself a détournement of Nietzsche's interpretation, for détournement is interpretation as the refusal of power.[41] Détournement enacts this refusal not only at the level of content, by transforming the political valence of a given element of the spectacle, but also at the level of form, by appropriating without formal citation, by expressly undermining any claim of authority or property.

Given its architectonic nature and its emphasis on historical periodization, it will be helpful to review the basic structure and historical arch of *The Revolution of Everyday Life* before considering further examples of the détournement of Nietzsche. The first part of the book, titled "Part One: Power's Perspective," is divided into three sections that theorize Power as a form of social organization whereby masters (e.g., feudal lords and bourgeois capitalists) mobilize certain constraints, mediations, and seductions in order to maintain and reproduce conditions of servitude. In the first section, Vaneigem explores Power's mechanisms of *constraint*, which include humiliation, isolation, suffering, labor, and decompression (i.e., the weakening of antagonisms). Next, Vaneigem argues that, under Power's perspective, *mediations* can become alienated and alienating and that aspects of everyday life augment this estrangement, such as the dictatorship of consumption, the prevalence of economies based on exchange, the use of technology as a mechanism of control, and the dominance of the quantitative over the qualitative. The third section exposes how Power's *seductions* make wretchedness attractive. Examples include the seduction of causes that entail self-sacrifice, illusory forms of unity that obscure actual separation, appearances that hide the reality of our choices, roles that suffocate our identity with identification, and obsession with time experienced as constantly slipping away. The first part of the book concludes by exploring survival sickness, an affliction that plagues those

an object by first of all putting on the mask of the forces which are already in possession of the object." Gilles Deleuze, *Nietzsche and Philosophy*, trans. Hugh Tomlinson (New York: Columbia University Press, 2006), 5.

41 Christopher Janaway points out that Nietzsche's "revaluation of all values," in the original German (*Umwertung aller Werte*), "carries a sense of values being reversed or turned on their head, not merely examined afresh, as may be connoted by the 'critique' or 'calling into question' of the *Genealogy*'s Preface." This may sound very much like détournement, but it equally evokes spectacular recuperation. Without reference to the political implications of the practice, Nietzschean formulations easily, which is to say superficially, resonate with one of the SI's central practices. See Christopher Janaway, *Beyond Selflessness: Reading Nietzsche's* Genealogy (Oxford: Oxford University Press, 2009), 13.

who wallow in the passionless mediocrity of everyday life, and two spurious responses to this malady, namely *ressentiment* and nihilism. "Part Two: Reversal of Perspective" closes the book by envisioning a revolutionary chain reaction that begins with individual creativity and the construction of nonhierarchical microsocieties and ends with a new form of consciousness, a new way of life, and a new mode of social organization that would entail not only economic emancipation but also freedom from all forms of hierarchy and domination, the unity and mutual enrichment of the individual and the collective, the flourishing of the passions of play, love, and creation through projects of participation, communication, and self-fulfillment—in short, the revolution of everyday life.

Vaneigem repeatedly returns to a periodization of historical development in order to show how humanity arrives at the preconditions for the possibility of this complete transformation of quotidian experience. His periodization begins with the state of nature from which tribal social bonds emerge, followed by three modes of social organization—aristocratic feudalism, bourgeois free market capitalism, and the cybernetic welfare state. For Vaneigem, the struggle against natural alienation (e.g., death, disease, suffering) drives humankind to construct hierarchical communities, founded on pacts, contracts, and exchange, in order to increase the probability of survival.[42] This account of society's genesis distances Vaneigem from Nietzsche insofar as the latter rejects the "humanitarian illusion" of the social contract and proposes instead that the birth of social organization stems from the collective decision of "some blond beasts of prey, a race of conquerors and lords," to abandon their isolation in order to more effectively target the weak.[43] Whether the origin of society is sparked by the struggle for survival or by the struggle for power, this divergence in perspective stems from opposing valuations of hierarchy. Whereas Nietzsche's conception of higher and lower human types, of the strong and the weak, leads him to celebrate hierarchical social organization as life-affirming, Vaneigem historicizes hierarchical social forms so as to envision their eventual twilight.

In order to manage and regulate order and rank, feudal forms of social organization deploy what Vaneigem calls a "unitary myth" that connects lords and servants through a shared relationship to God. Vaneigem's most succinct description of this mythical bond follows:

> To the landowners the excluded made a *real* sacrifice of a significant part of their lives, accepting the owners' authority and laboring for

42 For Vaneigem on this transition from the state of nature to human societies, see, for example, Vaneigem, *The Revolution of Everyday Life*, 29, 30, 60, 61.

43 Nietzsche, "Beyond Good and Evil," 391. Nietzsche, *On the Genealogy of Morality*, 58.

> them. To the dominated group the masters for their part made a *mystical* sacrifice of their authority and their power as owners: they were ready to pay for the well-being of their people. God was the underwriter of the transaction and the guardian of the myth. He punished those who broke the contract, while those who kept to it he rewarded with power: mythical power for those who *really* sacrificed themselves, real power for those who did so *mythically*.[44]

The social pyramid, held together by the mortar of myth and sacrifice *qua* exchange, alleviates natural alienation; however, natural alienation is exchanged for a generalized state of social alienation. Although the feudal lords, unlike their servants, enjoy an aristocratic life of adventure and exuberance, they cannot escape alienation, for "the lord's subjectivity is fulfilled only through the denial of the subjectivity of others; in this way it chains itself up, for by shackling others it shackles itself."[45] In good Hegelian fashion, Vaneigem construes the master-slave opposition dialectically, asserting that the master enslaves himself *qua* master and that only the slave can achieve self-mastery, that "it is only from the negative starting-point that thoroughgoing revolt can make the project of absolute mastery feasible. It is slaves, struggling to throw off their chains, who unleash the movement whereby history abolishes masters."[46] Although Nietzsche may have had recourse to dialectical thinking, his thought is generally understood as opposed to Hegelian and dialectical reason.[47] As Gilles Deleuze asserts, Nietzsche conceives of dialectical reason "as the speculation of the pleb, as the way of thinking of the slave: the abstract thought of contradiction then prevails over the concrete feeling of positive difference, reaction over action, revenge and *ressentiment* take the place of aggression."[48] Accordingly, if Vaneigem wishes to release the affirmative from the death grip of Nietzsche's master, he will have to show how the struggle to throw off the chains of slavery is an active process not reducible to an expression of *ressentiment*.

Vaneigem maintains that the bourgeois revolution, capitalist industrialization, and the death of God do not really signal the overthrow of feudalism and the unitary myth but rather its mechanization, secularization, and fragmentation. In the shift from aristocratic domination and the qualitative tripartite separation between lord, servant, and God

44 Vaneigem, *The Revolution of Everyday Life*, 62 (emphasis in original).
45 Ibid., 191.
46 Ibid., 182. For Hegel's discussion of the master/slave dialectic, see the "Lordship and Bondage" section in: G.W.F. Hegel, *Phenomenology of Spirit*, trans. A.V. Miller (Oxford: Oxford University Press, 1977), 111–19.
47 Waite offers a provocative reading of Nietzsche's dialectic in *Nietzsche's Corps/e*, 238, 239.
48 Deleuze, *Nietzsche and Philosophy*, 10.

to bourgeois exploitation and the dualistic distinction of quantitative equivalence between capitalist and worker, disalienation coincides with a new form of alienation, hierarchy is challenged yet preserved, and the disenchantment of myth produces fragmentary ideologies. More changes occur as bourgeois exploitation incorporates automation and cybernetic programming. The mandates of production gradually give way to the dictatorship of consumption, the free market economy mutates into the welfare state, and the distinction between master and slave, those with power and those without it, begins to blur. As a result, master-slaves, competing for the consumption of crumbs of power, populate consumer society.[49] These historical processes coincide with what Vaneigem calls "the disintegration of the spectacle, the decomposition of all coherence, unity, myths, values, and even appearances."[50] What follows is the spectacle of disintegration, feeble replacements of previous values and myths that contribute to extending the life of commodity society.

Vaneigem postulates that the bourgeois era's victory over the forces of nature, its unparalleled advancements in production and technology, remove, at least *in potentia*, the originary justification for social alienation (i.e:, the struggle against scarcity, natural alienation). Hierarchical forms of social organization dig their own grave. The endless caricature of self-fulfillment, communication, and participation intensifies the thirst for the actual realization of these projects; the justification of exploitation and oppression in terms of the freedom to live a mediocre existence fosters the desire for a liberated, exuberant life. Vaneigem asserts that the proletariat in its new form, laborers who sell their labor power to consume, is driven by its passions, which the current system can only stifle, to close hierarchy's casket and emerge from the master-slave dialectic as free individuals, as masters without slaves. This is what Vaneigem calls "the aristocratic supersession of aristocracy," the overthrow of the last remnants of feudalism in order to make common an uncommon existence.[51]

Vaneigem characterizes the bourgeois era as an interregnum, "an intermediate stage between the life genuinely lived, if less than transparently, by the feudal masters and the life that will be constructed rationally and passionately by masters without slaves."[52] While he recognizes

49 Vaneigem recognizes that there are parts of the world that do not follow this general historical trajectory, thereby demarcating the limits of his periodization, but he also maintains, unapologetically, that the demands of affluent societies will be the global *minimum* program, that poorer countries will likewise strive for total revolution rather than accept mere ameliorations to their impoverished conditions. For Vaneigem's discussion of this issue, see Vaneigem, *The Revolution of Everyday Life*, 20–22.

50 Ibid., 143.

51 Ibid., 186.

52 Ibid., 54.

this intermediate moment as instrumental in establishing the material preconditions for the elimination of natural and social alienation, his account of historical development is neither positivist nor progressivist. He asserts in an extremely Nietzschean-sounding passage that the bourgeois revolution is also a counterrevolution, that it sets the stage not only for the massive production of wealth but also for the disintegration of values, for their conversion into values contrary to life:

> From the point of view of everyday life, the bourgeois revolution has not a few counterrevolutionary aspects. Rarely, on the market of human values, has the conception of existence suffered such a sharp devaluation. Proclaimed so defiantly to the whole universe, the bourgeoisie's pledge to usher in the reign of liberty and well-being served merely to underscore the mediocrity of a life which the aristocracy had managed to fill with passion and adventure but which, once made accessible to all, resembled nothing so much as a palace split up into servants' quarters. Thereafter hate would give way to contempt, love to attachment, the ridiculous to the stupid, passion to sentimentality, desire to envy, reason to calculation, and lust for life to desperation to survive.[53]

Just as Nietzsche critiques democratic (and anarchist) movements for devaluing man, attempting to convert great individuals into mediocre herd animals, Vaneigem asserts that the bourgeois revolution's redistribution and democratization of power is also the redistribution and democratization of servitude. Formerly experienced, at least by some, as a passionate and adventurous life, existence is impoverished, reduced to the boredom of affluent survival. Channeling Nietzsche's phobia of the mediocre and his attention to the value of values, Vaneigem succinctly asserts that the bourgeois revolution led to "the devaluation of aristocratic values, replaced not by superior values but by mediocrity."[54] The bourgeois interregnum is therefore "the perfect dwelling-place for Nietzsche's 'little man,'" the accuser of life who wallows in the shallow depths of the prosaic and trivial.[55]

If Nietzsche despises anything that would lower aristocratic individuals to a state of mediocrity, it is not because he is against mediocrity in all of its forms: "It would be completely unworthy of a more profound spirit to have any objection to mediocrity as such. Mediocrity is needed

53 Ibid.
54 Ibid., 74.
55 Ibid., 55. For Nietzsche's discussion of the little man, see Nietzsche, *Thus Spoke Zarathustra*, ed. Adrian Del Caro and Robert Pippin (Cambridge: Cambridge University Press, 2006), 176, 177.

before there can be exceptions: it is the condition for a high culture."[56] Nietzsche's pyramidal vision of a healthy society requires as its foundation a mediocre base of inhuman humans, of individuals as slaves and instruments. It is no wonder that he is equally against democratic and anarchist movements in Europe. Vaneigem, on the other hand, insists that history shatters the false choice between the democratic generalization of mediocrity known as late capitalism, a putrid flower that blooms from seeds planted by the bourgeois revolution, and a Nietzschean aristocracy, in which a choice type may rule above everyone else but neither side can escape the mutual alienation of the master-slave dialectic. For Vaneigem, a radical alternative that would resolve the dialectic by abolishing mediocrity and hierarchy alike is a real historical possibility. Vaneigem's analysis of the bourgeois era is thus a creative plagiarism of Nietzsche's ideas and symbols that places them within a nonhierarchical perspective. Repetition with difference.

To fully appreciate the presence and détournement of Nietzschean elements in Vaneigem's account of the bourgeois era and its late instantiation as consumer society, it is important to recall, telegraphically, Nietzsche's famous critique of the slave revolt in morality, which starts with the Jews' devaluation of knightly-aristocratic values prior to the birth of Jesus of Nazareth and extends to the French Revolution's struggle against the last of the European nobility.[57] In the first essay of *On the Genealogy of Morality*, Nietzsche introduces two human types—the strong and the noble, on the one hand, and the weak and the slavish, on the other. The former type, characterized as creative and active, deploys an "aristocratic manner of valuation" that affirms the self and all other manifestations of strength and creativity as good and then only retrospectively, as an afterthought, apprehends the weak, the incapable, and the subservient as bad. The weak, on the other hand, are filled with hatred and *ressentiment*, with jealousy and negativity, and seek to blame their suffering on others. Their slave revolt in morality rejects "the aristocratic value equation (good = noble = powerful = beautiful = happy = blessed)" and creates instead an alternative set of values. As Nietzsche posits: "The slave revolt in morality begins when *ressentiment* itself becomes creative and gives birth to values. . . . Whereas all noble morality grows out of a triumphant yes-saying to oneself, from the outset the slave morality says 'no' to an 'outside,' to a 'different,' to a 'not-self': and *this* 'no' is its creative

56 Friedrich Nietzsche, "The Anti-Christ," *The Anti-Christ, Ecce Homo, Twilight of the Idols and Other Writings*, 59.

57 For Nietzsche on the French Revolution, see Nietzsche, *On the Genealogy of Morality*, 32. For its role in the slave revolt, see Nietzsche, "Beyond Good and Evil," 251, 392.

deed."[58] While the noble begins with self-glorification, the slavish method of valuation starts with contempt for an other, for those individuals who are unlike the weak. The weak type consequently interprets all manifestations of strength and power as evil and then conceives of its opposite, powerlessness, as good.

While Nietzsche recognizes with fascination the sublimity of the "ideal-creating, value-reshaping hate" of the slave revolt, especially since the creation of values is typically associated with the noble, *On the Genealogy of Morality* is dedicated precisely to the critique of the slave revolt's values insofar as they are contrary to life and human flourishing and therefore constitute "a sign of distress, of impoverishment, of the degeneration of life."[59] What motivates Nietzsche's critique, in other words, is a very specific interpretation of life, a revaluation of existence. Nietzsche maintains, in an implicit polemic with Darwinism, that physiologists wrongly reduce existence to the struggle for survival: "A living thing seeks above all to *discharge* its strength—life itself is *will to power*; self-preservation is only one of the indirect and most frequent *results*."[60] Similarly, Nietzsche argues that "the wish to preserve oneself is the symptom of a condition of distress, of a limitation of the really fundamental instinct of life which aims at *the expansion of power*."[61] To affirm life would therefore mean to affirm power's expression and extension. Self-preservation may be a result of the will to power, but those who seek self-preservation *over* suppression and exploitation betray their own sickness, their weakened nature, and live impoverished lives.

Attuned to Nietzsche's diagnosis of self-preservation as pathological, Vaneigem terms the experience of living a passionless and mediocre existence under consumer society's rule "survival sickness."[62] "We must handle survival cautiously," Vaneigem writes, "for it wears us down; live it as little as possible, for it belongs to death."[63] Yet there are always those who cannot see beyond their sickness and may even fight for its intensification, for more survival. Vaneigem calls such an individual, evoking simultaneously Nietzsche and Max Scheler, the "man of *ressentiment*," the "perfect survivor, completely unconscious of the possible supersession."[64]

58 Nietzsche, *On the Genealogy of Morality*, 19 (emphasis in original).
59 Ibid., 3, 17. Nietzsche discusses noble value creation here: Nietzsche, "Beyond Good and Evil," 394–98.
60 Nietzsche, "Beyond Good and Evil," 211 (emphasis in original).
61 Nietzsche, *The Gay Science*, trans. Walter Kaufmann (New York: Vintage Books, 1974), 291 (emphasis in original).
62 Vaneigem offers an extended discussion of survival sickness in the chapter dedicated to diagnosing the malady (*The Revolution of Everyday Life*, 138–42).
63 Ibid., 140.
64 Ibid., 143, 152. Vaneigem explicitly refers to Scheler in his discussion of the man of *ressentiment*, but Nietzsche is so obviously in the background that it is unnecessary to

The man of *ressentiment* lives unhappily within Power's perspective yet cannot see beyond it, unable to grasp the historical possibility of another form of existence.

Accordingly, the man of *ressentiment*, "eaten up by jealousy, spite and despair, tries to turn these feelings into weapons against a world perfectly designed to oppress him."[65] Like the perpetrators of the slave revolt, this individual slavishly and reactively discharges his hatred outward toward that which is powerful and strong. Consider the following passage:

> A reformist trapped between total rejection and absolute acceptance of Power. The man of *ressentiment* rejects hierarchy out of umbrage at not having a place therein, and this makes him, as a rebel, an ideal slave to the designs of his masters of the moment. Power has no firmer support than thwarted ambition, which is why it takes every effort to console losers in its rat race by tossing them the privileged as a target for their hate. Short of a reversal in perspective, therefore, hatred of Power is merely a form of obeisance to Power's ascendancy.[66]

Power's chains are like arbor knots; they are tied such that they tighten around the resentful reformist as he despairingly struggles against them. This figure is the perfect survivor because his ineffectual gestures of refusal ensure the survival of survival sickness by perpetuating the source of the disease, namely the hierarchical social organization that inhibits living an authentic life. Vaneigem's manipulation of the Nietzschean motifs of survival and *ressentiment* thus exposes the limits of reformism. Insofar as his critique of reformism contributes to the articulation of an alternative that would constitute the total supersession of Power, the abolition of hierarchy as such, Vaneigem again creatively plagiarizes Nietzsche, placing his words in a new context so that they may serve a project contrary to his own.

If the man of *ressentiment* "becomes aware that survival is a losing proposition," he develops into a nihilist.[67] As is well known, Nietzsche characterizes European culture and its Judeo-Christian tradition as undergoing a crisis of nihilism, in which all values are devalued and life becomes meaningless. As a value-creating immoralist, Nietzsche's perspective on this crisis is necessarily qualified. Consider the following passage from *The*

invoke him by name.

65 Ibid., 152.

66 Ibid. Although Vaneigem does not ascribe to perspectivism, his persistent recourse to the language of perspective in order to describe changes in consciousness *and* in forms of social organization is a simple détournement of Nietzsche. For Vaneigem's most extended reflection on perspective, see ibid., 162–65.

67 Ibid., 156

Will to Power: "What does nihilism mean? *That the highest values devaluate themselves*. The aim is lacking; 'why?' finds no answer."[68] Nietzsche expands upon this definition by describing nihilism as that which appears "because one has come to mistrust any 'meaning' in suffering, indeed in existence. One interpretation has collapsed; but because it was considered *the* interpretation it now seems as if there were no meaning at all in existence, as if everything were in vain."[69] Nihilism forms when the value system that imbued things with meaning suddenly looks hollow. Nietzsche maintains, nevertheless, that there are different responses to meaninglessness, that there are active and passive forms of nihilism. Active nihilism is "a violent force of destruction" that energetically participates in the devaluation of values whereas passive nihilism is "the weary nihilism that no longer attacks; its most famous form, Buddhism; . . . a sign of weakness."[70] While passive nihilism wallows in nothingness, active nihilism hastens destruction; it is a Dionysian "expression of an overflowing energy that is pregnant with future."[71] This is why Nietzsche describes nihilism as a "transitional stage" that clears the way for the creation of new, nobler values that affirm rather than deny life.[72]

Likely alluding to how Nietzsche introduces the crisis of nihilism in *The Will to Power*, Vaneigem responds to an opening question on the subject with a scene of confusion and loss:

> What is nihilism? Rozanov's definition is perfect: "The show is over. The audience gets up to leave their seats. Time to collect their coats and go home. They turn round. No more coats and no more home." As soon as a mythical system enters into contradiction with economic and social reality, a chasm opens between the way people live and the prevailing explanation of the world, which is suddenly inadequate, completely surpassed.[73]

For Vaneigem, the unitary myth of the feudal aristocracy was the predominant interpretation or way of explaining the world, since it provided meaning to the suffering and sacrifice, both real and symbolic, of masters and slaves alike. As the unitary myth is fragmented by the bourgeois revolution, capitalist industrialization, and the death of God, traditional values begin to appear empty and artificial. In consumer society, the disintegration of the spectacle intensifies this crisis, releasing a sea of nihilism

68 Nietzsche, *The Will to Power*, trans. Walter Kaufmann and R.J. Hollingdale (New York: Vintage House, 1968), 9 (emphasis in original).
69 Ibid., 35 (emphasis in original).
70 Ibid., 46, 47.
71 Nietzsche, *The Gay Science*, 329.
72 Nietzsche, *The Will to Power*, 14.
73 Vaneigem, *The Revolution of Everyday Life*, 154.

that drowns all values in meaninglessness. The nihilist is thus someone aware of this process of disintegration, conscious of the hollowness of existence-as-survival.

Like Nietzsche, Vaneigem conceives of nihilism as "a sort of chrysalis stage of consciousness," a transitory moment straddling the reactive and the affirmative, and he likewise distinguishes between active and passive forms of nihilism.[74] For Vaneigem, passive nihilists defend decayed values despite the apprehension of the general decay of all values; they do not believe in anything but they act as if they really believed. Vaneigem cryptically evokes Blaise Pascal in this context, suggesting that passive nihilists make an empty wager by repeating the ritual of belief even in utter disbelief.[75] As with the man of *ressentiment*, Vaneigem repurposes Nietzsche's notion of passive nihilism to diagnose a political stance in relation to Power. If the disposition of the man of *ressentiment* is reformist, Vaneigem's passive nihilist cynically submits to the status quo.[76] As Nietzsche would say, the passive nihilist is too weary to attack. Active nihilists, on the other hand, counter the ineffectual refusal of *ressentiment* and the submission and subservience of passive nihilism with extreme refusal. For Vaneigem, "*Active* nihilism combines consciousness of disintegration with a desire to expose its causes by speeding up the process. The disorder thus fomented is merely a reflection of the chaos ruling the world. Active nihilism is prerevolutionary; passive nihilism is counterrevolutionary."[77] The extreme refusal of active nihilism ultimately swims with the current of meaninglessness by replicating what has already become a general condition, a basic banality. This form of nihilism is nevertheless prerevolutionary because it has surpassed the *ressentiment* of reformism without capitulating to Power.

Before distinguishing between active and passive nihilism, between its prerevolutionary and counterrevolutionary manifestations, Vaneigem lists "the fruit of free experimentation in the field of destroyed values.

74 Ibid.

75 Ibid., 155–57.

76 Vaneigem's characterization of passive nihilism resonates with Slavoj Žižek's theorization of cynicism as a form of ideology. In dialogue with Peter Sloterdijk, Žižek argues that it is no longer helpful to conceive of ideology as false consciousness, as a veil that hides the true meaning of one's actions. Instead, cynical ideology entails preserving the illusion even as it is revealed, acting as if the illusion were true while completely aware of its status as illusion. In other words, ironic distance, insofar as it fails to change how one thinks and acts, ultimately reproduces the current social reality. See Slavoj Žižek, *The Sublime Object of Ideology* (London: Verso, 1999), 28–30. Žižek also suggests that Pascal's wager is at bottom cynical: Ibid., 83, 84. For Sloterdijk's discussion of cynical reason, see: Peter Sloterdijk, *Critique of Cynical Reason* (Minneapolis: University of Minnesota Press, 1989).

77 Vaneigem, *The Revolution of Everyday Life*, 157 (emphasis in original).

Sade's passionate rationalism, Kierkegaard's sarcasm, Nietzsche's havering irony, the violence of Maldoror, Mallarmé's icy dispassion, Jarry's *Umor*, Dada's negativism."[78] The list is diverse and the descriptions are ambivalent; it is not clear where Vaneigem locates these outgrowths of nihilism on the political spectrum. What unites them, however is that they all lack something essential, namely a "sense of historical reality." The nihilist's consciousness of disintegration, in other words, is divorced from a consciousness of the historical possibility that shines through the cracks of this disintegration, from a "consciousness of the possibility of supersession."[79] Vaneigem contrasts the nihilists to the "greatest *makers* of history," figures like Marx and Lenin who *are* conscious of the movement of history yet lack what the nihilists embody—"a sharp awareness of history's immense destructive power in the bourgeois era."[80] While the extreme refusal of the nihilists limits their ability to actively and constructively redirect the course of history, the makers of history fail to grasp the historic forces of annihilation that accompany total revolution.

As his account of the bourgeois interregnum suggests, Vaneigem seeks to manipulate nihilism in the service of supersession. The revolution of everyday life requires it: "An alliance between nihilism and the forces of supersession means that supersession will be total. Herein without doubt lies the only wealth to be found in the affluent society."[81] Rather than mimicking the destructive power of the bourgeois era, nihilism's violent flame of refusal, repurposed, can reduce Power to ashes. The elements for this historic transformation are already at hand in the sparse wealth of affluent society, but they have to be reorganized, détourned. As Vaneigem explains: "Although [the nihilists] now suffer the despair of nonsupersession, a coherent theory may be expected, by demonstrating the mistakenness of their viewpoint, to place all the potential energy of their accumulated rancor at the service of their will to live. . . . *Nihilists*, as Sade would have said, *one more effort if you would be revolutionaries*."[82] In a moment of subtle reflexivity, Vaneigem performs what he prescribes by diagnosing the limits of nihilism through the détournement of Sade's words. A détourned Sade, in other words, is made to articulate the path through which he would arrive at his own self-negation *qua* nihilist.

This is precisely what Vaneigem does with Nietzsche throughout *The Revolution of Everyday Life*, détourning his ideological formulations to construct a radical theory that demonstrates the mistakenness of the

78 Ibid., 155.
79 Ibid., 159.
80 Ibid., 155 (emphasis in original).
81 Ibid., 156.
82 Ibid., 160 (emphasis in original).

philosopher's perspective by underscoring historical reality and the possibility of supersession. Détournement is accordingly the effort that converts the words of the nihilist into his own undoing, that harnesses and redirects nihilism's violent force of destruction, now pregnant with the future.

Vaneigem finds Nietzsche's theorization of the will to power to be the most mistaken notion within his conceptual apparatus. Nietzsche equates life, or sometimes the will to life, with the will to power; he argues in *Beyond Good and Evil* that "life itself is *essentially* appropriation, injury, overpowering of what is alien and weaker; suppression, hardness, imposition of one's own forms, incorporation and at least, at its mildest, exploitation . . . life *is* will to power."[83] Exploitation, he continues, "belongs to the *essence* of what lives, as a basic organic function; it is a consequence of the will to power, which is after all the will to life."[84] Vaneigem, on the other hand, contends that the passions of creation, love, and play are the fundamental elements of life. These passions correspond to three projects, the will to self-fulfillment, the will to communication, and the will to participation, which form the unitary triad of the will to life. The will to power is not absent from Vaneigem's view of life but rather is conceptualized as the latter's perversion: "The will to power is the project of fulfillment travestied, cut off from communication and participation. It is the passion for creation—and for self-creation—entangled in the hierarchical system, condemned to drive the mill of repression and appearances. Status and humiliation, authority and submission—such is the quick march of the will to power."[85] Nietzsche is misguided, Vaneigem asserts, when he reduces life to the will to power. The exploitation Nietzsche sees everywhere is simply the historically determinate distortion of individual creativity. It belittles life to equate it with such mediocrity and ennui.

In a chapter titled "The Organization of Appearances," Vaneigem lifts a passage from the preface of *Ecce Homo* that implicitly responds to Nietzsche's faulty revaluation of life:

> According to Nietzsche, the "ideal world" is a construct based on a lie: "Reality has been deprived of its value, its meaning, its veracity to the same degree as an ideal world has been *fabricated* . . . the *lie* of the ideal has hitherto been the curse of reality; through it mankind itself has become mendacious and false down to its deepest instincts—to the point of worshipping the *inverse* values to those which alone could guarantee its prosperity and a future,

83 Nietzsche, "Beyond Good and Evil," 393 (emphasis in original).

84 Ibid. (emphasis in original).

85 Vaneigem, *The Revolution of Everyday Life*, 213.

> the exalted *right* to a future." What can the lie of the ideal be if not the truth of the masters? When theft needs legal justification, when authority waves the banner of the general interest in order to pursue private ends with impunity, is it any wonder that the lie captures minds, so distorting people by shaping them to its "laws" that their very deformity comes to resemble a natural human attitude?[86]

While Nietzsche's perspectivism undermines the distinction between truth and falsity, the thing-in-itself and appearances, he nonetheless mobilizes these categories to critique the naysayers of life who invent an ideal world in opposition to the world as it exists. Vaneigem détourns Nietzsche by asserting that the lie of the ideal world is the fragmentary ideology of the master, what the latter peddle as truth. The naturalized utopia of the masters is familiar, stale: this is as good as it gets, there's no better system than capitalism, it's for the benefit of everyone that someone polices everyone else. These variations of the master's truth constitute the organized appearances that obscure the reality of exploitation and the possibility of supersession, justifying a form of social organization that can no longer be justified. Vaneigem turns Nietzsche's words into a denunciation of the master's ideal, a denunciation of the mystification of hierarchy and oppression. Yet this is exactly what Nietzsche achieves with his call to say yes to life defined as the will to power; his affirmations of exploitation and becoming-lord-over function the same way. Wasn't Nietzsche's truth that "caste-order, *order of rank*, is just a formula for the supreme law of life itself"?[87] Vaneigem's détournement of Nietzsche thus shows Nietzsche to be a fabricator of ideals, an organizer of appearances. Nietzsche's words are made to speak otherly, exposing the truth of their flawed utterer.

Vaneigem also pauses his détournement of Nietzsche to critique explicitly the latter's adoration of the will to power and order and rank:

> All the same, beneath its protective wrapping, the will to power does harbor traces of an authentic will to life. Think of the *virtù* of the *condottiere*, the exuberance of the giants of the Renaissance. But today the *condottieri* are no more. At best we have captains of industry, gangsters, arms dealers and art dealers—mercenaries all. For an adventurer, Tintin; for an explorer, Albert Schweitzer. Yet it is with such people that Zarathustra dreams of peopling the heights of Sils-Maria—in these runts that he claims to discern the lineaments of a future race! Truth to tell, Nietzsche was the last master, crucified

86 Ibid., 106. For the original passage, see Nietzsche, "Ecce Homo," 71.
87 Nietzsche, "The Anti-Christ," 59 (emphasis in original).

> by his own illusions. . . . As prone to disgust as he was, Nietzsche had no difficulty breathing in Christianity's ignoble stench by the lungful. By affecting not to understand that Christianity, for all its stated contempt for the will to power, was in reality its best shield, its most faithful henchman, stoutly opposed to the emergence of masters without slaves, Nietzsche gave his blessing to the permanence of a hierarchical world where the will to life dooms itself to be nothing more than the will to power.[88]

As its travestied form, the will to power during aristocratic feudalism contained remnants of the will to life, but its instantiations during the bourgeois era are mere shadows of these remnants, pale appearances of creativity and fulfillment that could not possibly portend Zarathustra's Übermensch. If *ressentiment* perpetuates rather that supersedes Power, Christianity ultimately protects the will to power even as it rebuffs it. By sanctifying hierarchy, Nietzsche acts like a good Christian, shielding weak and feeble distortions of the will to life.[89]

If historical conditions within bourgeois capitalism set the stage for the supersession of hierarchy, how might these conditions affect the historical realization of Nietzsche's social vision? Vaneigem suggests that humankind has already witnessed one historical manifestation of Nietzsche's vision, stating unequivocally that

> Nazism is Nietzschean logic called to order by history. The question was: what is the fate of the last masters in a society whence all true masters have vanished? And the answer: they become superslaves. Even the superman as conceived by Nietzsche, as weak as this figure may be, is obviously far superior to the flunkeys who ran the Third Reich. Fascism knows only one superman: the State. The State as superman is the strength of the weak.[90]

Nazism is the historical exemplification of the will to power during the bourgeois interregnum, and it shows itself to be "a will to passive

---

88 Vaneigem, *The Revolution of Everyday Life*, 214. This passage could be read as a détournement of Nietzsche insofar as it seems to evoke Nietzsche's screed against Wagner: "Richard Wagner, seemingly the all-conquering, actually a decaying, despairing decadent, suddenly sank down helpless and shattered before the Christian cross." Friedrich Nietzsche, "Nietzsche contra Wagner: From the Files of a Psychologist," *The Anti-Christ, Ecce Homo, Twilight of the Idols and Other Writings*, 276.

89 Nietzsche was of course aware of religion's usefulness, of its status as "one more means for overcoming resistances, for the ability to rule," but Vaneigem's point is that Nietzsche's own position regarding hierarchy is Christian. Nietzsche became Christianity's accomplice and, in his own words, "preserved too much of *what ought to perish*." See Nietzsche, "Beyond Good and Evil," 262, 264, 265 (emphasis in original).

90 Ibid., 214.

obedience" to the State.[91] Nevertheless, like Debord and Wolman with *Birth of a Nation*, Vaneigem does not leave Nietzsche, that stick of dynamite, to the Nazis. Instead, he appropriates and repurposes Nietzsche's ideas for the unified tripartite will to life. The stakes are high:

> Woe betide those who abandon their violence and their radical demands along the way. As Nietzsche noted, murdered truths become poisonous. If we do not reverse perspective, Power's perspective will succeed in turning us against ourselves once and for all. German Fascism was spawned in the blood of Spartakus. Our everyday renunciations—no matter how trivial—lend fuel to our foe, who seeks nothing short of our complete destruction.[92]

While Zarathustra urges the wisest to speak of the will to power and its expression in the annihilation and creation of values, lest these truths become poisonous, Vaneigem paraphrases Nietzsche's *Thus Spoke Zarathustra* to warn against abdicating to Power, lest more Nietzschean poison spill, destroying the possibility of practically realizing radical demands in everyday life.[93]

Vaneigem gleans the most light from the explosive détournement of Nietzschean formulations during his discussion of the proletariat and the future society of masters without slaves. As discussed above, Vaneigem frames the proletariat's overthrow of Power as a moment in the Hegelian master-slave dialectic. Since the master is dependent on his slaves *qua* master and therefore cannot escape the positive pole of alienation, Vaneigem draws the Hegelian conclusion that "it is only from the negative starting-point that thoroughgoing revolt can make the project of absolute mastery feasible. It is slaves, struggling to throw off their chains, who unleash the movement whereby history abolishes masters."[94] Given Nietzsche's subtle appropriation and critique of the master-slave dialectic, most visible in his analysis of the slave revolt in morality, it may seem as though Vaneigem's proletariat, struggling to throw off its chains, is simply another outgrowth of *ressentiment*, another instance of the weak reactively lashing out against that which is different.

---

91 Ibid., 149.

92 Ibid., 165.

93 "Only where life is, is there also will; but not will to life, instead—thus I teach you—will to power! . . . And whoever must be a creator in good and evil—truly, he must first be an annihilator and break values. Thus the highest evil belongs to the highest goodness, but this is the creative one. Let us speak of this, you wisest ones, even if it is bad to do so. Keeping silent is worse; all truths that are kept silent become poisonous." Nietzsche, *Thus Spoke Zarathustra*, 90

94 Vaneigem, *The Revolution of Everyday Life*, 182.

The quality of the proletariat's struggle, however, permits it to avoid entangling itself in its own chains:

> In contrast to the bourgeoisie, the proletariat is not defined in terms of its class opponent, but heralds the end of class distinctions and of hierarchy per se. . . . Whereas the bourgeoisie was content to forge arms against the feudal system—arms that one day will be turned against the bourgeoisie itself—the proletariat carries within itself the possibility of its own supersession. The proletariat is poetry, momentarily alienated by the ruling class or by technocratic organization, but ever apt to burst out of its bondage. As the sole depository of the will to life—for it alone has experienced in its full force the intolerable pressure of mere survival—the proletariat is destined to demolish the walls of constraint in the whirlwind of its pleasure and the spontaneous violence of its creative energy. All the joy and laughter that this will release the proletariat already possesses, for its strength and passion are drawn from within. What it is preparing to build will, in addition, destroy whatever stands in its way, like a fresh tape-recording automatically erasing the previous one. The power of things will be abolished by a proletariat in the act of abolishing itself, by virtue of a luxurious, nonchalant afterthought, by virtue of the sort of grace displayed by someone calmly manifesting their superiority. From the new proletariat will emerge, not the robotic humanists dreamt of by the onanists of the supposedly revolutionary Left, but masters without slaves.[95]

In this passage, Vaneigem releases the affirmation of life from the death grip of Nietzsche's masters. The endeavor is reminiscent of Marx's insurrectionary inversion of the genitive insofar as it accomplishes "the *reversal* of established relationships between concepts," revealing the master to be reactive and the slave to be life-affirming.[96] Although the establishment of a classless society will require significant confrontation and violence, the proletariat's revolution of everyday life is not a resentful revolt against its class opponent but rather a Dionysian affirmation of the will to life, an exuberant, even aristocratic, expression and satisfaction of its passions, a revolution in the service of poetry. Rather than "Death to the Exploiters," the proletariat's slogan is "Life First!"[97] The proletariat sheds its status as

95 Ibid., 187.

96 Debord, *The Society of the Spectacle*, 144 (emphasis in original).

97 Ibid., 254. Georges Bataille expresses a similar, although politically more ambivalent, idea when he asserts that "the positive practice of freedom, not the negative struggle against a particular opposition . . . has lifted me above a mutilated existence." George Bataille, *On Nietzsche*, trans. Bruce Boone (St. Paul: Paragon House, 1994), xxvii. Although beyond the scope of this essay, it is worth nothing that there are

slaves and in so doing also abolishes masters. The result is not a society of slavish herd animals, as Nietzsche would have it, but rather the emergence of a new kind of mastery that does not entail the enslavement of others and consequently self-enslavement. Vaneigem names the aristocratic figure that supersedes all hierarchical forms of social organization the master without slaves.

Prior to the revolution of everyday life, the aristocratic masters of old live on in their decrepit contemporary form as bourgeois master-slaves, little men peddling shards of fragmentary power for consumption ("Would you like to work for us?" "Can I interest you in a brand new car?"). The proletariat's aristocratic struggle accordingly represents "the aristocratic supersession of the aristocracy," the total abolition of all vestiges of feudalism left over after the failure of history's partial revolutions, bourgeois or otherwise.[98] Vaneigem identifies three passions as predominantly active in this endeavor to revolutionize everyday life. As reformulations of the passions of creation, love, and play, Vaneigem lists the passion for absolute power, the passion for smashing constraints, and the passion for rectifying an unhappy past. As with the basic passions of the will to life, these passions correspond to three projects—the supersession of patriarchal social organization, the supersession of hierarchical power, and the supersession of authoritarian caprice.[99]

Vaneigem predictably mobilizes Nietzsche to shine light on the passion for absolute power: "*The passion for absolute power*, a passion for placing objects directly in the service of human beings without the mediation of human beings themselves; and the consequent destruction of those who cleave to the order of things, slaves who possess crumbs of power. 'Because we cannot stand the sight of them, we shall abolish slaves,' says Nietzsche."[100] Absolute power entails the abolition of one form of power (power *over* others) and the liberation of another form of power (power *to* create without human mediation, without slaves). Establishing the conditions necessary for the expression of absolute power "opens up a unique opportunity for the will to reign over the world with no restrictions save those imposed by a finally reinvented nature and by

a number of resonances, as well as significant divergences, between *On Nietzsche* and *The Revolution of Everyday Life*. Given Bataille's role in the French reception of Nietzsche, this may not be a coincidence. Although *The Revolution of Everyday Life* does not explicitly mention Bataille, he is alluded to occasionally here: Raoul Vaneigem (J.-F. Dupuis), *A Cavalier History of Surrealism*, trans. Donald Nicholson-Smith (San Francisco: AK Press, 1999).

98 Vaneigem, *The Revolution of Everyday Life*, 186.

99 Ibid., 186–92.

100 Ibid., 188 (emphasis in original).

the resistance of things to being transformed."[101] Vaneigem mentions a number of failed attempts to satisfy this passion, from noble serial killers (e.g., Heliogabalus, Gilles de Rais, Elizabeth Báthory) to lords massacring their servants in Sade's *120 Days of Sodom*.[102] Although they unsuccessfully attempt to escape alienation through the intensification of alienation, to arrive at total humanity through total inhumanity, these figures fascinate Vaneigem insofar as they express in distorted form a genuine passion for uninhibited creative expression.

Vaneigem repurposes a fragment from Nietzsche's unpublished notes to locate the philosopher within this tradition of masters attempting to liberate themselves from their slaves.[103] A similar sentiment is expressed during the exchange between the Wanderer and the Shadow in *Human, All Too Human*: "For the sight of one unfree would embitter for me all my joy; I would find even the best things repulsive if someone *had* to share them with me—I want no slaves around me."[104] No matter how much disgust and loathing the sight of slaves provokes in Nietzsche, he cannot envision a world without them, going so far as to postulate in *Beyond Good and Evil* that every advancement of humanity has been and will be the result of "a society that believes in the long ladder of an order of rank and differences in value between man and man, and that needs slavery in some sense or other."[105] Due to the placement of Nietzsche's passage, Vaneigem nonetheless makes the evangelist priest of hierarchy utter, despite his blindness to historical possibility, a call for the abolition of slaves, for a world composed solely of masters, free to revel in the absolute power of creation.[106]

---

101 Ibid., 181. It is important to note that Vaneigem is not against mediation as such but rather against its alienated form. For this distinction, see the chapter "Mediated Abstraction and Abstracted Mediation," in ibid., 77–87.

102 Ibid., 180, 182.

103 Nietzsche's fragment in the original German reads: "wir ertragen den Anblick nicht mehr, folglich schaffen wir die Sclaven ab." Friedrich Nietzsche, "Nachgelassene Fragmente Herbst 1885 Frühjahr 1886," *Digitale Kritische Gesamtausgabe Werke und Briefe*, accessible at http://www.nietzschesource.org/#eKGWB/NF-1885,1[41].

104 Friedrich Nietzsche, *Human, All Too Human*, trans. R.J. Hollingdale (Cambridge: Cambridge University Press, 1986), 394. Many thanks to Tanya Rawal-Jindia for pointing me to this passage.

105 Nietzsche, "Beyond Good and Evil," 391.

106 Goldman likewise evokes Nietzsche in order to imagine a world of masters without slaves; however, while Vaneigem subverts Nietzsche by making him speak otherly, Goldman whitewashes one of Nietzsche's most abhorrent ideas in order to protect a "giant mind": "It does not occur to the shallow interpreters of that giant mind that this vision of the *Übermensch* also called for a state of society which will not give birth to a race of weaklings or slaves." Emma Goldman, *Anarchism and Other Essays* (New York: Dover Publications, 1969), 44.

Because Vaneigem conceives of the proletariat's passions as playing a major role in the overthrow of the existing social order, his starting point for the revolution of everyday life is not communitarianism but rather individual subjectivity. As long as society is structured hierarchically, the individual can only be opposed to other individuals and the collective in a relationship of mutual impoverishment of the passions and their satisfaction: "Individual survival-lines collide and cut one another off. Each imposes its limits on the freedom of others; projects cancel one another out in the name of their autonomy. Such is the basis of the geometry of fragmentary power."[107] Vaneigem accordingly suggests that establishing a federation of nonhierarchical and self-managed microsocieties, "protected areas where the intensity of conditioning tends towards zero," would reate the conditions of possibility for a new geometrical perspective to emerge, "which is neither a reflection nor an inversion of the earlier one. Rather, it is an ensemble of harmonized individual perspectives which never clash but which successfully construct a coherent and collective world. All these angles, though different, open in the same direction, as individual will and collective will gradually become one."[108] The alternative geometry of federated microsocieties prefigures the social organization needed to sustain a world of masters without slaves, of "free individuals, irreducible to one another."[109]

This alternative geometry has profound implications for Vaneigem's notion of revolutionary equality, which he arrives at by repurposing Nietzsche's aristocratic individualism and anti-egalitarianism:

> The viewpoint of altruism—or of solidarity, which is what the Left calls it—turns the meaning of equality on its head. Equality becomes nothing but the common distress of social isolates humiliated, fucked over, beaten down, betrayed—and contented: the distress of monads aspiring to join together not in reality but in a mystical unity. Anything will do: Nation, the workers' movement—no matter what, so long as it purveys that drunk-Saturday-night feeling of "we are all brothers and sisters". Equality in the great family of man reeks of incense, of religious mystification. You would need a

107 Ibid., 76.

108 Ibid., 164, 175. Félix Guattari and Antonio Negri define communism in similar terms, no doubt as a result of their own creative interpretation and manipulation of Nietzsche: "[C]ommunism is the establishment of a communal life style in which individuality is recognized and truly liberated, not merely opposed to the collective. That's the most important lesson: that the construction of healthy communities begins and ends with unique personalities, that the collective potential is realized only when the singular is free." Félix Guattari and Toni Negri, *Communists Like Us*, trans. Michael Ryan (New York: Semiotext(e), 1990), 16, 17.

109 Vaneigem, *The Revolution of Everyday Life*, 65.

> stuffed-up nose not to be sickened by it. For myself, I recognize no equality except that which my will to life according to my desires recognizes in the will to life of others. Revolutionary equality will be inseparably individual and collective.[110]

Although opening with an allusion to Hegel's idealist inversion of the dialectic, this passage contains subtle references to Nietzsche throughout, including an overt reference to Nietzsche's delicate sense of smell—"Bad air! Bad air!"[111] Nietzsche cannot stand to sniff "[t]he poisonous doctrine '*equal* rights for everyone'—Christianity disseminated this the most thoroughly"—because its abstract universalism erases difference, including distinctions of rank and order.[112] Nietzsche proposes, alternatively, "equality for the equal, inequality for the unequal" and advises those who wish to help others to only help their friends (i.e., equals) and to "make them bolder, more persevering, simpler, gayer . . . *to share not suffering but joy*."[113] Clearly drawing from Nietzsche, Vaneigem critiques the perspective of altruism/solidarity insofar as the individual connects with others based on their suffering, thereby sharing it with them, and that this connection is ultimately sustained by the abstractly universalist and religious sentiment that all men are created equal. Yet Vaneigem repurposes these Nietzschean formulations by subtracting a commitment to difference from its Nietzschean use as a justification of hierarchy. The point is not to oppose difference to equality, the individual to the collective, but to recognize their inextricable linkedness. This allows Vaneigem to place equality back on its feet, to envision a revolutionary equality in which irreducible individuals are bound together not by suffering but by the joy of their shared will to life.

For Vaneigem, "*savoir-vivre* means knowing how not to give an inch in the struggle against renunciation. Let nobody underestimate Power's ability to force-feed its slaves with words to the point where they become slaves to those words themselves."[114] If Nietzsche is not a man but dynamite then it is important to remember that the word dynamite comes from the Greek *dynamis* meaning power. To end the forced consumption of dynamite packed with words that serve authority, to struggle against the renunciation of individual and collective freedom, Vaneigem's *The Revolution of Everyday Life* repurposes Nietzsche's ideas and vocabulary for

110 Ibid., 34.

111 Nietzsche, *On the Genealogy of Morality*, 24. For Marx's discussion of Hegel's idealist inversion of the dialectic, see: Marx, *Capital*, 103.

112 Nietzsche, "The Anti-Christ," 40.

113 Nietzsche, "Twilight of the Idols," *The Anti-Christ, Ecce Homo, Twilight of the Idols and Other Writings*, 222. Nietzsche, *The Gay Science*, 271.

114 Vaneigem, *The Revolution of Everyday Life*, 85.

the creation of a radical theory.[115] The untimeliness of this endeavor, when much of today's Left eagerly consumes dynamite as though it were an addiction, underscores the book's significance and revolutionary potential. Indeed, *The Revolution of Everyday Life* is also a kind of user's guide to the future repurposing of Nietzsche. It therefore calls to be read by anti-readers that will concretely realize its propositions, starting with the construction of an anarchist language from the détournement of mercenary signs, a language that would communicate the everyday passion for a world of masters without slaves.[116]

115 Since virtually every page of *The Revolution of Everyday Life* is composed of détourned Nietzschean elements, this essay cannot possibly address all of them. Further examination could investigate how Vaneigem repurposes Nietzsche's ideas about roles, gifts, sacrifice, and suffering, as well as the philosopher's discussion of the relationship between art and life, during which he states that "we want to be the poets of our life—first of all in the smallest, most everyday matters." Nietzsche, *The Gay Science*, 240.

116 I would like to thank Barry Maxwell and Raymond Craib for their generous invitation to present a shorter version of this text at Cornell University's Institute for Comparative Modernities 2012 Annual Conference "Global Anarchisms: No Gods, No Masters, No Peripheries." I am also very grateful to Michael Arnall, Lital Levy, Alexander Nehamas, Bécquer Seguín, and the participants of Princeton University's 2013–2014 Comparative Literature Dissertation Colloquium for their extensive and helpful comments on earlier drafts of this article.

Clifford Harper

BLACK, RED, AND GREY: ANARCHISM, COMMUNISM, AND POLITICAL THEORY

All theory is grey.

the Devil

ANARCHIST METHOD, LIBERAL INTENTION, AUTHORITARIAN LESSON: THE ARAB SPRING BETWEEN THREE ENLIGHTENMENTS

Mohammed A. Bamyeh

What do social and scientific revolutions have in common?* Those who study scientific revolutions have been familiar enough, at least since Thomas Kuhn's *The Structure of Scientific Revolutions*, with the proposition that a revolution is a new paradigm displacing an old one. In other words, a revolution is a radical transformation in world perspective. More pointedly: a revolution is an experience of *enlightenment*. It is at this level that I wish to explore one aspect of the ongoing social revolutions that we have come to know as the Arab Spring. In the process, I hope that something more may be learned about the relationship of revolution to enlightenment, that is to say, to a *gnosis* of a new type.

In what follows, I would like to illustrate the proposition of revolution as enlightenment with specific emphasis on the Arab revolutions. The argument is made in three steps. First, I want to stress the notion of revolution as a product of *decisions* made in environments that spontaneously produce the knowledge needed to make such a decision—in other words, how revolutionary decisions are themselves means to new knowledge, rather than products of old knowledge. Second, I ask how this new knowledge emerges out of pure presence, which is to say, an unwavering mental focus, that characterizes the revolutionary climate, on the present *alone*—not the future, the past, the consequences of one's actions, or any other distracting thought. Third, I reverse course at the end and ask how this knowledge, however new it may appear to be, has been born out of the past, that is to say, how previous experiments in enlightenment have

* This article was originally published in *Constellations* 20, no. 2 (June 2013). A highly condensed, earlier version of this article appeared in the online magazine *Jadaliyya*, titled "Anarchist, Liberal, and Authoritarian Enlightenments: Notes From the Arab Spring" (2011).

deposited their lessons into memory, so much so that the "new" knowledge appeared so intuitively true and immediately accessible, without authorities, leaders, organizations, mediators, or complex intellectual work. This latter mode of knowledge may be defined as an anarchist path to enlightenment. This anarchist enlightenment is contrasted to an older authoritarian enlightenment, although the former possesses unexplored affinities to a third path that is also part of the character of the current moment: the liberal enlightenment.

How Revolutions Decide?

A revolution is produced by countless decisions made by millions of individuals. Wherever one is able to identify key leaders or organizations, the equation appears simpler, since analyzing decisions could largely be an analysis of the decisions that such identifiable agents make. But when we encounter, as in the Arab Spring, largely leaderless, loosely structured movements in which spontaneity and lightness are important features, and where even after initial revolutionary success, as in Tunisia, Egypt, Libya, and to an extent Yemen, no leaders or parties could be identified as standing in for the revolution as whole, discovering how revolutions have "decided" what to do next becomes quite an analytic challenge. Does it even make sense to speak of a revolution deciding? Does it matter? The question is difficult, but unavoidable. Outlining how a largely spontaneous revolution[1] decides where to go next may help us understand *part* of the dynamics of transitional, post-revolutionary periods, where a new system is not yet in place even though much of the old system has crumbled; where earlier revolutionary unity gives rise to multiple agendas; where the possibility of "losing" the revolution or having it "stolen" surround the environment with a sense of anticipation, danger, and dynamism; and where the revolution itself appears frequently to be on the verge of producing nightmarish sectarian or other kinds of civil strife

1 Since the beginning of these revolts, I have heard several commentators argue, often with highly partial evidence or with the aid of an inattentive social science, that the Arab revolutions were not spontaneous or at least more organized than suspected. Examining all these claims, which I think are profoundly mistaken, requires a separate article. Here, I only want to point out that viewpoints dismissing spontaneity seem to be based largely on a profound misunderstanding of what spontaneity means. For me, spontaneity does not imply the absence of any organizations whatever. Rather, spontaneity becomes a necessary dynamic whenever existing organizations are too weak, small, or reformist in character to be capable of engendering a revolution by themselves. This point is not contested by any pre-revolutionary organization. The one exception is Bahrain, where the continuing debacle of revolutionary effort may be traced precisely to the *existence* of an organization (Wefaq) that has become identified with the upheavals. I have argued this point in a different context elsewhere; see Mohammed Bamyeh, "The Arab Revolutions and the Making of a New Patriotism," *Orient* 52, no. 3 (2011).

worse than the old dictatorship. Those are all moments of decision. And in many cases, these issues appear even before revolutionary triumph and appear to threaten the entire revolution—as when the revolutionary military commander in Libya, Abdul Fattah Yunus, was assassinated by his own comrades or, more generally, when a morally pure revolutionary climate begins to be contaminated with intimation of civil war, as in Yemen or Syria. How do revolutions decide at those junctures, how do they respond to dangerous moments?

One of the most fundamental characteristics of a revolutionary decision is that it is the sort of decision that most clearly foregrounds human agency and creativity. No revolution was ever predicted and nothing in a previous oppression prepares one for revolution by any force of necessity. The fact that one is oppressed or has great grievances does not in itself lead to a revolution and, as we know, oppressive conditions may be tolerated for decades, even for life, without protest, without hope in the possibility of an alternative, with belief in fate, or in oppressive life as being the nature of the world, or with the aid of mind altering substances, thoughts and rituals. Before January 25, 2011, few expected change of any kind in Egypt, including the hardcore revolutionaries themselves, even though a wish for a revolution could be easily documented now throughout prerevolutionary literature. When the Tunisian revolution began five weeks before, the initial goals were not to unseat an entrenched regime but to protest a gruesome local event. The first revolutionary tremors in Libya, beginning three weeks after Egypt, took first not the form of a revolution but that of a local gathering in Benghazi that protested the arrest of a popular lawyer. The genesis of the revolution in Syria, shortly afterward, again first appeared not as a revolution but as local elders protesting the arrest of their children in the marginal town of Der'a. And for historical comparison with an earlier revolt with similar spontaneous dynamics, namely the first Palestinian intifada beginning in 1987, that too was triggered and became relentless following a traffic incident that, while fatal to four Palestinian workers, would on another day have been swallowed up as yet another proof of unassailability by a mighty regime of occupation.

That massive revolutions broke out so quickly from such innocuous beginnings belies the fact that the indignities suffered or witnessed in Sidi Bouzid or Der'a somehow seemed to require extraordinary decisions, decisions that differed substantially enough from how one had responded to similar incidents in the past—after all, Mohamed Boazizi was not the first person to immolate himself in Tunisia and arresting children and adults at will and without any charge had been little more than a mundane activity for the Syrian regime. There was no force of necessity that mandated that, when a popular lawyer is arrested, for example, a collective street protest would ensue nor that, when one's children are arrested, the best course of action was to storm the police station. In all these cases, however, there seems to be a common psychological thread: revolutions were caused not by an act of tyranny, since such acts were common enough and quite expected. Rather, they began by an unusual *reaction* to such acts, a reaction that itself gave participants a sense that what they were doing as a reaction (and not the original event itself) was *extraordinary*. Extraordinary, that is, in the sense that it expressed a decision to respond to an insult in a different way than had been customary. The fact that one does not today simply swallow up an indignity the same way one had done for decades, means that a subject of a new type has emerged. That emergence is experienced as such an extraordinary event that it greatly discourages stepping away from it afterward; to the contrary, it encourages most further exploring the new revolutionary possibilities unveiled by its very emergence.

The moment of a revolutionary decision thus mark the emergence of a new subjectivity at some locality, which then replicates like a virus throughout the country.[2] This subject feels like an agent of revolution because he is not an "individual," but a particular expression of the general will, and a personal condensation of "the people"—an otherwise abstract and rarely felt concept. A revolutionary subject of this nature is not simply an "individual"—expressing only a private will, acting alone, or with a specific group that cannot be imagined as coterminous with "the people."

While a revolutionary subjectivity in this form acts as a new form of self-disciplining that sets one up as the appropriate recipient of revolutionary, that is, extraordinary, knowledge, we cannot speak of any "completed" subjects with final shape, so long as the revolutionary process is underway. The revolution itself, in fact, can only be experienced as such only to the extent that this revolutionary subject is constantly looking for and acquiring extraordinary new stimuli, so that she could go on. The revolution is over, psychologically speaking, when this emerging revolutionary subject realizes that she has sufficiently mastered the general guiding principles of the new paradigm and determined that no substantially new knowledge is forthcoming for the time being. She may be said to be a more complete subject at that point, albeit of a new type. And like all completed subjects, she feels free to base her new world perspective, even her identity, on an event that is now perceived to have been concluded

2 The emergence of a new subjectivity has been noted by other observers, who highlight its tentative though reflexive and anti-neoliberal character. See Benoît Challand, "The Counter-Power of Civil Society and the Emergence of a New Political Imaginary in the Arab World," *Constellations* 18, no. 3 (2011): 271–83; and Sari Hanafi, "The Arab Revolutions; the Emergence of a New Political Subjectivity," *Contemporary Arab Affairs* 5, no. 2 (2012), 198–213.

successfully enough: the revolution slowly transforms from an extraordinary experience into an ordinary heritage, from acts of shattering an old paradigm into routines of familiarizing oneself with the contours of the new paradigm.

But in the heat of the revolutionary moment itself, when a new paradigm is not yet in place, one can only make situational decisions with little guidance, from either old or new paradigms: the old paradigm has just been demolished, but not yet replaced with anything other than one's own revolutionary activity. And the outcome of this activity lacks any guarantees; it possesses no support mechanism other than the evident will of so many others to go along. Thus it is easy to understand why the decisions that bring out and propel this subjectivity forward follow a nondeterministic path, since all decisions in the revolutionary climate have to be *original*, in the sense that no prior script exists that tells one how to revolt if one has never personally done it before.

The notion of a nondeterministic path to new subjectivity in general and a revolutionary decision in particular explains perhaps why revolutions have never been expected and why no theory has ever successfully predicted them. For a revolutionary decision consists precisely in rejecting what is offered up as immutable and unchanging reality, that is, the world that has been *determined* for the person confronting it. And the greatest proof of the completely subjective and creative, that is, undetermined, logic that makes all revolutions possible is precisely that one decides to embark on a revolution before one knows whether it has any chance of success at all. After all, none of the revolutions of the Arab Spring were premised on any guarantees of success. Quite the opposite, the obstacles facing them seemed so gargantuan, that the least credible story that one participant could tell another on the very eve of all these revolutions was that a revolution would happen the following day.

It is especially evident in spontaneous uprisings that the most fundamental decision out of which the entire uprising begins concerns rejecting the very idea of a determined reality, even as the alternative is not yet obvious and where no known dynamic has offered an *assurance* of revolutionary success. Such revolutions could not therefore be borne out of any "rational" calculation, which discourages the very idea of a revolution without clear prospects and in the face of a determined and powerful tyranny. To the contrary, spontaneous uprisings arise precisely out of a large number of individuals reinforcing each other's subjective *decision to ignore realism*. How "realistic," for instance, was the revolution in Syria? In its first seven months, between March and mid-autumn of 2011, demonstrators throughout the country have known that they would be met with live fire, yet they continued to turn up *every day* for what they knew to be a potentially deadly encounter with a verifiably murderous regime apparatus. One can do so only if the revolutionary decision is experienced as such an extraordinary epiphany that all seemingly solid, immobilizing realities in the world disappear from view, revealing a far more interesting feature of one's humanity—that is, the capacity to become a revolutionary subject—a feature rarely encountered in pre-revolutionary decisions.

This new humanity, experienced first at personal and local levels, gives birth to revolution when it is assumed, with some evidence, to be capable of being the property of ordinary persons. The emerging conviction, which characterizes revolutionary consciousness, of the ordinary and thus broadly distributed nature of this hitherto unseen humanity, makes it the basis of a new collective subjectivity—although, as I will explore later, a collective of a more anarchist than fascist character in this case.

The consequences of this epiphany are immeasurable. An oppression under which one has been languishing without a tremor for decades suddenly appears so thoroughly undeserved and intolerable at a moment when a small local confrontation with the old authority, common as it may be, is experienced as a profound revelation: "the people" are infinitely more noble than their government and that unaccountable thuggery and grand theft, the only consistent attributes of the pre-revolutionary Arab governmental order, are no longer accepted as simply mirror images of a peoplehood defined by its weakness, fragmentation, and dysfunctionality (and thus *deserving* the system of rule under which it languishes). In this refashioned (and usually temporary) iteration, the idea of "the people," *al-sha'b*, again becomes proper material for revolution. "The people" was therefore quickly elevated to ever higher realms in Arab revolutionary discourse and acquired more significant agency that ever before since it registered a discovery of profound self-worth that stood in sharp contrast to underserved rule by petty thieves, dour autocrats, and visionless, ineffective functionaries. More remarkably still, the idea of "the people" never seemed to require being embodied in a charismatic leader, vanguard party, or any grand structure that would stand in for peoplehood as a whole. Even where elements of such structures have emerged before revolutionary success, as in Libya, Syria, or Yemen, the structures remained diffuse and minimally coordinated.

In that way, the revolutions drew sustenance, energy, determination, and the will to sacrifice largely out of a broadly distributed moral fire in individual psyches than out of organizational or hierarchical command structures. For "the people" appeared as a macrocosm of the single revolutionary person, who then experienced herself *directly* as the agent of a grand moment in history. And once that standpoint was arrived at through a single action of protest, it could not be abandoned, just as one who had been forced to live under refuse for life cannot imagine leaving the summit of the world after he had suddenly realized that it had always been much closer at hand than ever thought before. So one has to stay there, since one has to understand more what this precious perspective was revealing to one's sensibilities and intellect. The Arab revolutions seem to have emerged, at least in so far as the dynamics of this new subjectivity is concerned, out of this will to understand the world as it appeared from an unusual location: a world that appeared unexpectedly open to grand human action rather than closed off by immutable laws of nature and garrisoned by brute force. In that way, the revolutions became the means for further ascertaining one's worthiness for this grand mission against an erstwhile closed and immobile system. This ascertainment could be accomplished only in constant action. The largely amateurish nature of the Libyan revolutionary military campaigns, which were one reason why the war lasted as long as it did, was itself the point: "the people" learned who they were and what they were doing, as they were doing it, and the revolutionary process was something to be learned by experiencing it—there was no manual on how to do it, and certainly no prior plan to guarantee success. But in the process of doing it, one learned what the revolution meant: the revolution, above all, was a *decision* without guarantees of success. And as such it could happen only because knowledge of a new type replaced old, "realistic" ways of thinking. The new knowledge informed the little person that he was the agent of history, but also that in being so he was not alone. It created him out of equal doses of heroic thoughts and modest sensibilities. In other words, it was an anarchist *gnosis*.

Knowledge out of Presence

It could easily be said that these revolutions captivated the imaginations of the millions of actors who made them because their goals were so sensible. But more interesting is how the revolutions themselves became tools of discovery, of both new knowledge and new sensibilities. These novelties appear to me at least as significant, in terms of generating mobilization and energy, than well-known grievances that had been festering for decades.

Concepts that had been previously unimaginable or abstract became in the revolutionary climate concrete. That which was immeasurable as the manifestation of a collective became felt as the property of the person. One of the those concepts, "the people," was used so profusely in ways that suggest that it was felt to be a natural and organic extension of one's own sense of truth and justice. The novelty (as well as rarity and passing nature) of *feeling* an abstraction as "the people" was evident in how it was used everywhere and without compulsion as a namesake of what everyone assumed to be intuitively true: "the people have decided . . . ," "the people want . . . ," "the people will not be humiliated . . . ," "the will of the people is . . . ," and so on. These usages were never expressed in terms of any precise mechanisms—that is, *how* the people might translate its will into a policy, or even whether a revolutionary committee ought to be formed, somehow, so as to express this peoplehood efficiently. In Tahir Square, where I spent the majority of my time during the first five weeks of the Egyptian revolution, I saw that peoplehood was usually used to express what were commonly regarded as intuitive propositions about which there existed a presumed social consensus. It was never used to express complex or presumably divisive theories of social order. Even "Islam" was never used *then* in any way that was synonymous with peoplehood.

The concept of the "civic state," for example, emerged precisely in that way, as a new popular concept expressing popular unity. The first usages I saw of the notion of a "civic state" in Tahrir Square were not vague, but explicitly explained what it meant by stating what it was *not*. The first sign I saw in Tahrir Square about the concept, explained that a "civic state" was one that was neither religious nor military. In other words, it was a state not ruled by *identifiable* agents known to be likely candidates for ruling the post-revolutionary state.[3]

Only in excluding such identifiable agents could the future state assume a "civic" character, expressing peoplehood *as the concept felt during the revolutionary moment. Al-sha'b*, an abstract formulation, did not appear to require being made concrete by being embodied in a savior leader, an organized party, or any concretely identifiable entity, since *al-sha'b*, at that rare revolutionary moment, felt so concretely close to earth, so directly present: "the people" was experienced as a direct outgrowth of what the little person was doing.

If a revolution of this kind could not be abandoned after it began, one likely reason is that it became an appealing form of life that was exceptionally effective in revealing the hitherto unsuspected sources of self and others, sources that in the revolutionary climate appeared infinite. In that light, pre-revolutionary life appeared to mimic death, frozenness, separation from others, and suspicion of all—the exact counter-ethics of

3 The principle of "civic state" was so broadly accepted that even the Muslim Brotherhood adopted it, precisely in the form it was formulated in Tahrir. In the debates leading to the final text of the Egyptian Constitution ratified in December 2012, the group continued to endorse that vision, refusing to support calls for defining the state as "Islamic," as well as other calls to designate "God" as the ultimate source of sovereignty (in the preamble and Article 5, ultimate sovereignty belongs to "the people").

"How may the occupation [of Tahrir] develop so as to have a [greater] effect? Let's talk to each other and think," Tahrir Square, Cairo, early February 2011 (image by author)

Conversation on the principles of the revolution, Tahrir Square, Cairo, early February 2011 (image by author)

the revolutionary moment. Much clearer to the revolutionaries than to outside observers was how the revolution itself was lived as such a profound experience in its own right, *rather than simply as means to an end.*

Nothing illustrates this disjuncture between how the revolution was lived and how the outside world perceived it better than how each sphere experienced the *relevance* of the question "what will come next?" When I was back in Europe and the United States, I was initially surprised by this question, even though it was to be expected. I realized only outside of the revolution that I rarely heard anyone asking the question as to what would come next in the middle of the revolution (apart from various utopias, none of which answered a question to which outsiders sought more precise and definite answers). The revolutionary perspective then seemed entirely fixated on the present, which appeared as such an exceptionally rich moment that one could not look away from it, without a sense of betraying the present, which completely saturated all senses. This observation seemed to me to justify a strict separation, in terms of social analysis, between the revolutionary moment proper and the post-revolutionary or transitional period. The psychology of the one is not that of the other. The proportion of practical, everyday political calculus to a sense of world transformation is not the same across the two periods, neither is the degree of social consensus. Most importantly, knowledge in the revolutionary moment is produced by an unwavering fixation on the present moment, which in transitional or post-revolutionary climate is replaced by a more normal orientation to the future and to the calculus of likely consequences of each action.

The focus on the present was evident in a number of dynamics that are probably typical of many other revolutionary moments in history, especially where there is no leading vanguard, no hierarchical guidance, and no plan as to what to do next when the "regime" refuses to step down. None of the Arab revolutions had any "plan B" or a clear road map as to how, exactly, the revolution would compel a regime to fall when that regime resisted the initial waves of the uprising. The Libyan revolution was certainly not intended at first to become the bloodbath it became, and the large defections by senior officials and ambassadors in that case may suggest that they had thought the task to be easier than it turned out to be. The revolutionaries in Yemen did not anticipate they would need an entire year of occupying public places, immobilizing the entire country, and bringing it to the brink of civil war before Saleh's regime would very reluctantly agree to a transitional period governed by a compromise. Nor is it clear at all that the Syrian revolution would have even been attempted had its horrible human price, complexity, and duration been known in advance. And even the relatively faster paced Egyptian and Tunisian revolutions had no clear prospects at the beginning: before February 11, 2011, no one in Egypt was certain how long it was going to take for the revolution to compel Mubarak to fall, and there was no plan to do much else in case he refused to do so other than more of the same. Even proposals to do something beyond occupying Tahrir Square–for example, marching on the presidential palace (as was eventually attempted in Yemen) could not materialize, since the absence of leadership favored occupation over marching as a style of physical protest.

In that case, like Yemen, occupation was the favored strategy not simply because it better expressed realities such as the lack of an alternative plan or absence of strong or unified leadership. More than anything, the tactic of occupation highlighted *presence* as something to be contemplated and in a way that delivered the greatest possible epiphanies out of the focus on the present moment. One did not move from either space or time because presence revealed itself to be the greatest means of discovery.[4] Life in Tahrir Square during the first weeks of the revolution, for

4 It is possible to trace these arts of presence to earlier experiences or traditions of resistance, although that requires a more extended treatment than is possible here. Asef Bayat had earlier described what he called the arts and politics of presence as he explored contemporary Muslim intellectual thought and movement practices during the pre-revolutionary period. He also described more general tactics of establishing presence, "quiet encroachment," that were the tools by which new urban poor managed to carve for themselves a permanent space, in spite of legal prohibition and in a way that did not require forming any formal organizations or movements with explicit goals. See Asef Bayat, *Making Islam Democratic: Social Movements and the Post-Islamist Turn* (Stanford: Stanford University Press, 2007); and *Life as Politics: How Ordinary People Change the Middle East* (Stanford: Stanford University Press, 2009).

example, was characterized by debating circles everywhere, and it was virtually impossible to be left alone, to not be talking to someone else, usually a complete stranger, for a significant amount of time. Talk was in fact the most frequent social activity and it was reinforced by countless other communicative attempts in that space, such as handmade signs, impromptu theater performances, songs, mini demonstrations, and humor.

These communicative acts were aimed in one part at generating new meanings, in another at performing an erotics of agreement. The two are not necessarily different activities, but if we focus on the meaning-generating part of the equation for now, it is easy enough to document how a vast amount of conversation went into elucidating the meaning of unclear concepts, advancing new ones, testing conspiracy theories, exchanging stories of personal encounter with the regime, lessons from tactics practiced the day before, and generally testing ways to systematize knowledge about the general structures of politics and society. Everything required a meaning, including, as I frequently saw in debating circles, defining what a "regime" was, since that was what "the people" wanted to topple.[5] For example, the "regime" was for some mainly the *head* of the regime, a position supported by the proposition that if the head was rotten it will corrupt everything else in the body.[6] For others, the "regime" was a small circle of high officials and rich businessmen, who colluded in order to plunder the country and for whom the head of the regime only offered coordinating services. But others defined the "regime" in vastly broader terms that included lower officials, the vast security apparatus, municipal and village councils, many intellectuals and artists, and virtually everyone associated with the quite common practices of patronage and corruption that had become a way of life for millions through the decades of dictatorship.

Debates on meanings of other relevant terms (for example, "civic state," "liberalism," "revolutionary legitimacy," and so on) rarely, as far as I could see, required consensus on a single definition. In any case, there was no one who could enforce consensus on any meaning or define a certain debate to be more worthy of being pursued than another.[7] Knowledge was solicited and produced anarchically, and debates lasted as long as there seemed to be a reason for them to last. New knowledge appeared more

5 Interestingly, I never saw a debate on the meaning of "the people," which may have to do with the fact that this abstraction was actually felt for the duration of the social consensus that defined the revolution in its early phase.

6 That proposition seems quite easy to believe in when one confronts a personalistic and dyanstic dictatorship ("sultanistic" as it is sometimes called).

7 Except for circles that formed around specific intellectuals who visited the crowds occasionally and around whom a temporary circle was formed for the duration of their visit.

significant than final conclusions or the imperatives of consensus. This anarchist type of knowledge flowed most effortlessly out of a fixation on the present, which typifies the revolutionary period itself; in the post-revolutionary or transitional periods, this type of knowledge require an extra effort.

Dialectics of Three Enlightenments

A revolution as described above may be regarded as an experiment in enlightenment. By this I mean that a revolution is a name we give to an environment in which radical new knowledge appears, usually in the form of a revelation or epiphany, and then gradually becomes established as a form of political or social culture during the post-revolutionary phase. Experiencing "enlightenment" is an indispensable attribute of any revolutionary culture, since without this experience it is impossible for a revolutionary subject to feel entitled enough to alter the status quo, nor motivated enough to place oneself in conditions of danger and preparedness for sacrifice that could only be sustained by a *gnosis* of a new kind, that is, nontraditional and noncustomary *gnosis*.

Two provisos are needed here, however: first, "enlightenment" does not necessarily imply a radical break from past traditions or a complete discontinuity, but at least the *appearance* of such a radical break—so long as appearance is good enough for sustaining revolutionary mobilization. Second, and related to the above, "enlightenment" is knowledge experienced as such. This is to say, enlightenment is not merely a European philosophical tradition. Rather, what we call enlightenment may emerge out of radical reinterpretation of an already familiar tradition (as in religious hermeneutics): as a way of employing familiar social traditions (e.g., hospitality, solidarity, everyday spontaneity, and so on) for purposes of revolutionary activism rather than for maintaining social peace and stability; or as refocusing old practices of solidarity from the local kin or communal level to national or other macro levels (e.g., one defends a homeland with the same zeal and sense of duty that previously had been employed only in relation to one's local community).

The connection between enlightenment and revolution is a quite familiar theme in European revolutionary history[8] as is the connection between the European Enlightenment and revolutionary movements

8 See, for example, Eric Voegelin, *From Enlightenment to Revolution* (Durham, NC: Duke University Press, 1975); David W. Bates, *Enlightenment Aberrations: Error and Revolution in France* (Ithaca: Cornell University Press, 2002); Frederick C. Beiser, *Enlightenment, Revolution, and Romanticism: The Genesis of Modern German Political Thought, 1790–1800* (Cambridge, MA: Harvard University Press, 2005); Margaret C. Jacob, *The Radical Enlightenment: Pantheists, Freemasons and Republicans* (Lafayette, LA: Cornerstone Books, 2006).

elsewhere in the world.[9] Nineteenth-century revolutionary thought in Europe is often traced to the Enlightenment critique of the arbitrariness of absolute power, and to the Enlightenment's elaboration of the creative capacity of human will, reason, and freedom. Since these philosophical propositions were social in their implications, they could only be verified (or amended, or abandoned) only with the aid of grand experiments in the political, cultural, and economic realms.

Those experiments have followed different techniques. In reflecting on the Arab revolts, I would like to propose three basic techniques of enlightenment, all implicated in different styles of revolution: 1) An authoritarian technique, in which a vanguard sees itself to be uniquely enlightened and, out of that feeling, entitles itself to eventually use the state to modernize an immobile, unruly mass presumed to be governed by arcane traditions; 2) a liberal technique, in which a modern state is seen to be crucial to engineer modern transformation but its elite is neither presumed to have monopoly over enlightenment nor the power to make such a claim; 3) an anarchist technique, in which enlightenment is seen to come most reliably from below, by discovering the revolutionary character of familiar civic traditions rather than through state power or social engineering.

The conception of three enlightenments here is not meant to describe the full scope of meanings and experiences of enlightenment, but only to sketch preliminary types of relations between strategies of enlightenment and revolutionary activity. The sketch above is based less on what enlightenment is supposed to accomplish than on the *identity* of its designated agent. In the history of Enlightenment, identifying its agent has often proved to be the most vexing question. For example, during the course of the nineteenth-century Islamic, Chinese, or Japanese Enlightenments, intellectual arguments in favor of "Enlightenment" were often couched in the language of anti-colonialism, even though colonial powers themselves were making all kinds of civilizational claims. This disjunture shows how it was important to not simply express Enlightenment's intellectual arguments in terms of logical coherence, but to identify clearly *who* was the right and wrong agent of Enlightenment. That had to be done since both colonial and anti-colonial powers could make the same claims.

But the colonial world was only an example of a larger modern global problem concerning the proper relation between authority of knowledge and that of power. Everywhere, the question of enlightenment became

9 For example, Nader Sohrabi, *Revolution and Constitutionalism in the Ottoman Empire and Iran* (Cambridge: Cambridge University Press, 2011); or Vera Schwarcz, *The Chinese Enlightenment: Intellectuals and the Legacy of the May Fourth Movement of 1919* (Berkeley: University of California Press, 1986).

a question of who had the legitimacy to make claims on its behalf. One approach to answering this question, which gave us the authoritarian enlightenment, highlighted the centrality of vanguardist power. The argument here posited as a central assumption the proposition that enlightenment signified something foreign to local or antecedent tradition, which meant that enlightenment required being introduced by a force that operated outside of such a tradition and had the power to overcome recalcitrant traditional preference for the old and familiar ways. Experiments along these lines cover the ideological gamut, from state socialism to European colonialism to Kemalism to Baathism, even though such ideologies seem to be so different from each other. But common to all was the centrality to social modernization of coercive power, usually represented in a modern state that intruded upon society in ways rarely seen before, even under the worst tyrannies.[10]

By the end of the twentieth century, this tradition of authoritarian enlightenment reached its limits, as it became increasingly clear how once youthful vanguardist powers, whether "free officers" or those who claimed to stand for a dictatorship of the proletariat, had given rise to increasingly frozen, exclusive kleptocracies whose elite ruled more and more openly on behalf of their own interests.

The liberal enlightenment represented an alternative solution to the problem of identifying the agent of enlightenment, a solution that has enjoyed more longevity than the authoritarian enlightenment, although it too had lost much credibility by the end of the last millennium. Michel Foucault's extensive critique of the power/knowledge alliance may be said to apply specifically to the liberal genealogy of the enlightenment, in which knowledge complements the otherwise partial power of the state. Indeed, it is noteworthy that Foucault addressed primarily post-revolutionary transformations of state science in Europe, where revolutions had delegitimized authoritarian structures and also undermined the prospects of an enlightened despotism. Central to the project of the liberal enlightenment was how knowledge may organize a civic link between state and society and in the process reduce the costs of policing and repressive needs, increasingly prohibitive in light of nineteenth-century revolutionary history, for the liberal order.[11]

---

10 On the decreasing ability of modern authoritarian regimes to use enlightenment discourse effectively, see Mona Abaza's highly useful study of this theme in pre-revolutionary Egypt, "Social Sciences in Egypt: The Swinging Pendulum between Commodification and Criminalization," in Michael Burawoy, Mau-kuei Chang, and Michelle Fei-yu Hsieh, eds., *Facing an Unequal World: Challenges for a Global Sociology*, Vol. 1, (Taiwan: Academia Sinica, 2010), 187–212.

11 Nineteenth-century Islamic enlightenment may be seen as a variation of the liberal genealogy, at least according to some interpretations. In more recent times, Rachid

To simplify, whereas the liberal enlightenment takes the position that power and knowledge ought to be natural allies and specifically in such a way as to reduce the cost of power while maximizing the *instrumental* benefit of knowledge, the authoritarian and anarchist enlightenments tend to set power and knowledge as opposites rather than allies. The authoritarian technique is premised on the Hobbesian presumption that since power is the best means to accomplish any goal, the more one has of it the less compelling need there is for knowledge, since power alone will do. Moreover, power will transform any existing social knowledge in any desired direction. The anarchist technique, by contrast, is defined by suspicion of the merit of power as means to ends. This standpoint highlights the compensatory value of knowledge alone as the best means. I have explored this idea at length elsewhere,[12] here I would like to focus on its reemergence in the context of the Arab Spring.

In the current Arab context, one dimension of the contemporary revolutions consists of them serving as means of testing, once more, the philosophical propositions of the Enlightenment. As such, these revolutions constitute part of the Enlightenment's ongoing global history. They are certainly not the Arab's first encounter with Enlightenment propositions; the story of such propositions themselves is indeed very old, and much of their underlying bases can in fact be found in indigenous philosophical and social traditions, rather than simply as recent importations from Europe.[13] As critiques of despotism, as enactments of popular will, as acts of liberation, as progressive demolitions of frozen reality, these revolutions express the failure of an earlier, authoritarian experiment. From a contemporary revolutionary perspective, it is easy enough to recognize the two basic failures of the now exhausted authoritarian path to enlightenment: 1) that path has more magnified the authoritarian than the enlightened aspect of the state; 2) the authoritarian path hid from view a crucial social fact being asserted now openly in Arab streets everywhere, namely that enlightenment comes from below, not from above;

Ghannoushi, one of the main contemporary progenies of that tradition, explicitly argued that claims to local rootedness of any enlightenment reduce the authoritarian impulse of its undertaker. He was trying to explain why modern secular forces in the Arab World had to be authoritarian, since they were weakly rooted in the societies they ruled.

12 I have addressed these transformations at length in my *Anarchy as Order: The History and Future of Civic Humanity* (Lanham, MD: Rowman & Littlefield, 2009), esp. 71–117.

13 See, for example, Albert Hourani, *Arabic Thought in the Liberal Age 1798–1939* (Cambridge: Cambridge University Press, 1983); Mustafa al-Tuwati, Muhammad ben Ahmouda, and Sadiq Jalal al-Azm, *Athar al-Thawrah al-Faransiyyah fi Fikr al-Nahda* (Beirut: Dar al-Farabi, 1991); and, most originally, Abd al-Rahman al-Kawakibi, *Taba'i al-Istibdad* (Beirut: Dar al-Nafaes, 2006 [1899]).

that society has already become more saturated with ethos of enlightenment than has its government.

The Arab revolutionary experiments seem to be based on several newly shared presumptions. First, that ordinary individuals are capable of new *gnosis* without leadership or guardianship, without even organizations in the common sense of the word. Second, that their enlightenment entitles them to undo the tyrannies under which they have languished in recent decades. Third, that acts of enlightenment are practical and not simply contemplative, world transformative rather than narrowly pragmatic. The agent of this revolutionary enlightenment is the little person, not the historical figure, the hero, or the savior. In an earlier article, I identified three features of this anarchist *gnosis* as evident in the Arab revolutions: 1) emphasis on the simple and intuitive nature of truth, which in a revolutionary climate appears as "revelation"; 2) conversation and debating circles alone as means of discovery, rather than hierarchical guidance; and 3) a notion of peoplehood devoid—*in spite of its abstract nature*—of any demand for it being embodied in a charismatic or other type of leadership.[14]

It is in this sense that the current Arab revolutionary wave is closest to anarchist ideals, which highlight spontaneous order and posit the principle of unimposed order as the highest form of a rational society and which, like all revolutionary currents in nineteenth-century Europe, had clear roots in Enlightenment thought. Obviously, few of the current Arab revolutionaries call themselves "anarchists." And in any case, none of the revolutions so far intend to replace the state itself with a self-governed civic order. They want only to modernize the state so that it respects citizen's rights and becomes more accountable.

Thus in these revolutionary experiments we encounter a rare combination of an anarchist method and a liberal intention. The revolutionary style is anarchist, in the sense that it requires little organization, leadership, or even coordination; tends to be suspicious of parties and hierarchies even after revolutionary success; and relies on spontaneity, minimal planning, local initiative, and individual will much more than on any other factors. On the other hand, the explicit goal of all Arab revolutions is the establishment of a liberal state—a *civic* state[15]—not an anarchist society.

14 See my "Anarchist Philosophy, Civic Traditions and the Culture of Arab Revolutions," *Middle East Journal of Culture and Communication* 5, no. 1 (2012): 32–41.

15 It is noteworthy that the "civic state" (*dawla madaniyya*) has been endorsed even by the religious parties that had won the elections in post-revolutionary Tunisia (Nahda) and Egypt (Freedom and Justice Party). Even where a religious interpretation of this concept has been given (e.g., civic state as the goal of Islam), the notion of a civic state represents a broader social consensus on the desired character of the post-revolutionary state.

It is not unusual in revolutionary histories for revolutions to produce an unintended result. Max Weber already suggested that this disjuncture between the intention and result of revolutions was inevitable when, in the midst of the 1919 revolution, he gave his famous lecture *Politik als Beruf*. But in the case of the Arab Spring, we witness a rare likelihood that revolutions are reaching precisely their intention: old Arab orders that have survived the revolts thus far, as in Jordan, Algeria, or Morocco, and *even* Syria, now officially agree with virtually all revolutionary demands, *except* moving out of the way of the revolution. The intention is so widely shared in society, and so simple, that no organization at all is required to express it.

A revolution here is an expression of social consensus: consensus on *both* method and intention. The liberal outcome is promised precisely by the anarchist method. Neither is a product of any party plan, but both are the foundation of the social consensus out of which the revolutions emerged. So here the entire revolution is rational, from beginning to end, since intention and result seem to cohere, even though method (anarchy) and theory (liberal) appear to have no connection at all.

Yet they are connected in at least two ways. First, both anarchism and liberalism are part of the heritage of the Enlightenment and describe related though different principles within it. Second, this relationship precedes the Enlightenment and expresses facets of older, less controlled but quite orderly and very old social realities. This symbiosis becomes more obvious if we do not confine our perspective to European history. For example, while "anarchism" or "liberalism" are traceable to the intellectual history of the Enlightenment, part of what they express may already be rooted in older pluralist communal traditions and customs of local governance and autonomy. These customs and traditions themselves facilitate the emergence of a distinctly self-conscious intellectual experience ("Enlightenment") as a means of systematizing or "bringing reason to" an older *gnosis*. Indeed, rather than invent it *ex nihilo*, one may find it much easier to intellectualize an idea that one has already sensed in some concrete social experience. One is more likely to accept an intellectual conception if one is already familiar with some living dimension of it. An idea becomes thinkable, and appears meaningful, to the extent that its author or audience has at least an empirical hint of its validity. And thus some connection between innovation and rootedness must be suspected even where it is emphatically denied.[16]

This consensus has itself compelled the broad-based religious parties to disavow any claim for an "Islamic state," which is no longer their expressed goal.

16 This point is explored in more details in my "The Social Dynamism of the Organic Intellectual," in Mohammed A. Bamyeh, ed., *Intellectuals and Civil Society in the Middle East* (London: I.B. Tauris, 2012).

The traditional systems of multiple loyalties (which integrated in practical and useful ways the multiple resources available though tribal belonging, guild membership, religious order affiliations, urban patronage, and mutual help networks) supplied the sufficient basis of a self-organized civic order for centuries, while insuring that no specific group intruded too much upon another—until the emergence of the modern state.[17] Elements of that old civic order appear to have sustained themselves even after modern, authoritarian states devoted all their resources to magnifying state power over society in the name of enlightenment. Yet, the persistence of elements of the old civic ethics can be evidenced in the revolutionary styles themselves: the spontaneity of the revolutions as an extension of the already familiar spontaneity of everyday life; revolutionary solidarity, out of which emerges the will to sacrifice and combat, as an extension of common, convivial solidarity in neighborhoods and towns; distrust of distant authorities as part of an old, rational and enlightened common attitude, based on the simple thesis that a claim to help or guide is unverifiable in proportion to the power and distance of the authority that makes it; and finally, nonviolence as a strategy learned not out of a manual written at Harvard, but as rooted in *familiar* and old habits of protest and conflict management. In recent years, we were made to forget the ordinary salience of those old traditions, as our attention was galvanized by spectacles of "terror" and "counterterror" (a game with no political result other than feeding the power hunger of the authoritarian order and serving as its last *raison d'être*).

The downfall of the authoritarian enlightenment can be traced to dynamics latent to it. One earlier proposition of such an enlightenment was based on a left vanguardist position that, as noted by Frantz Fanon long ago, usually expressed lack of knowledge by the vanguard of their own society. In its later phase, when this vanguard had long become accustomed to being the ruling elites, their vanguardism was transformed into pure paternalism: distance from the people became *lack of interest* in knowing the people. Amid this disinterest, the old vanguardist authoritarianism was expunged of its anti-colonial, progressive, Third Worldist claims and, out of its ashes there emerged a cold, paternal authoritarianism, disinterested in any form of peoplehood, and governed openly by an avowed marriage of business and state elites. Although it occurred

17 Few scholars have paid attention to elements of continuity in these civic traditions, and most preferred to explore their disintegration and replacement by statist logics, which are easier to document. For an example of the former, which shows how older civic traditions creatively adjust to more contemporary transformations in civic life, see Sheila Carapico, *Civil Society in Yemen: The Political Economy of Activism in Modern Arabia* (Cambridge: Cambridge University Press, 2007); as well as Asef Bayat, *Life as Politics*.

in many places earlier, this transformation was complete in most of the postcolonial Arab world (with the exception, of course, of Palestine[18]) by the mid-1990s.

The decomposition of this vanguardism revealed the dead end of the authoritarian approach to enlightenment. In pre-revolutionary literature, this dead end was invariably portrayed as some sort of impasse without end.[19] How such portrayals represented a broadly felt, pre-revolutionary search for an alternative path to the earlier promises of enlightenment can only be properly treated in a full-length exploration. But these portrayals were unquestionably part of a larger cultural project, in which a modern national memory was being formed, revised, and contested. The most important dynamic of this memory, sociologically speaking, was one in which collective lessons from recent historical experiences were distilled and deposited in *intuitive* forms into civic culture, whereafter they became organic to it. For example, the *intuitive* resistance to a unified or charismatic leadership in the Arab revolts must be rooted in recent adjustments in collective memory, since this resistance so clearly contradicts earlier experiences: revolutionary episodes in the colonial and postcolonial periods, from the Wafd Party to Nasser to Khomeini down to Nasrallah, have invariably highlighted the central role of the charismatic leaders and, more generally, presumed a central role, broadly accepted in society, for some unique vanguard group.

In other words, historical memory here is essentially a condensed verdict on the successes and failures of various experiments of a single enlightenment project. The contemporary revolutions express in their method the disastrous failure of the authoritarian technique and thus are intuitively suspicious of a method whereby a revolution produces leadership that is immediately prepared to take over when the head of the old regime falls. There was no Nasser or Khomeini to be seen anywhere in the Arab revolutionary landscape, in spite of the messianic, heroic, high emotional and sacrifice-laden environment of revolutions. Nor was there a unified or solid organization anywhere. The anarchist method has been at the very heart of these revolutions, even though anarchist society as such was not an expressed goal.

Enlightenment, whether conceived as an ultimate achievement or as already existing *gnosis*, could be approached using different techniques.

---

18 On the exceptional nature of the question of Palestine, see Mohammed A. Bamyeh, "On Humanizing Abstractions: The Path beyond Fanon," in *Theory, Culture and Society* 27, no. 7–8 (2010): 52–65.

19 Exemplary of that view were the damning series of the *Arab Human Development Report* (2002–2009), published under the auspices of the United Nations Development Program.

In the grand revolutions of the Arab Spring, the liberal interpretation of the enlightenment fought an authoritarian interpretation, with the aid of an anarchist method—that is to say, with the aid of familiar civic traditions, discovered again to be natural venues for expressing the organic and embedded nature of the enlightenment. That was why these revolts have been entirely against the authoritarian state, but not against any old cultural tradition.

The civic state that is now on the horizon is not the end of the story. Revolutions themselves establish new traditions. They provide a grand reservoir of memory of what is possible, and that memory tends to be employed in future contests. In the final analysis, the state itself is neither the most rational vehicle of any enlightenment nor even its necessary goal. But now that the authoritarian enlightenment is being demolished, enlightenment becomes everyone's business. The expectation from a liberal political order is that a relatively sovereign subject emerges, sometimes called "citizen," endowed with a confident sense of entitlement to be freed from state harassments, impositions, and irrationality; she sees herself to be the source of the state. But with the aid of this newly acquired sense of sovereignty, she confronts directly the question of overcoming one's own "self-imposed immaturity," as Immanuel Kant famously defined the condition of enlightenment.

But, in the revolutionary processes themselves, one demonstrates an accomplishment that required only a revolution to be experimentally verified. In overcoming not one's own but state-imposed immaturity, one demonstrates that the overcoming of a self-imposed immaturity has already taken place, inaudibly, and long before any revolution. The method of the revolution itself verifies the propositions of the enlightenment, now taken to earth and entrusted to ordinary mortals directly. These are now the custodians of this *gnosis*, until the next grand cultural experiment, whose shape will invariably have to flow in some way out of and in response to how the memory of the current moment will be deposited into civic culture.

NEITHER PROLETARIAN NOR VANGUARD: ON A CERTAIN UNDERGROUND CURRENT OF ANARCHIST SOCIALISM IN MEXICO

Bruno Bosteels

> Go to the struggle; strike firmly on the doors of the epoch. Glory awaits, impatient that you haven't already broken your chains into pieces over the heads of those who oppress you.
>
> —Ricardo Flores Magón, "To the Proletarians"

1

How can we conceive of the relationship between anarchism and socialism, or between anarchism and communism, both in general and more specifically in the context of Mexico? At first sight, it seems that we could distinguish two dominant articulations of this relationship, one negative and the other positive, depending on one's preferred point of reference.

The first, negative articulation looks at Mexican anarchism either from the point of view of international socialism and communism or from the point of view of anarchism on a global scale, only to find the Mexican cause to be wanting. The emphasis thus falls on elements of lack or absence: lack of organization, absence of knowledge from the theoretical tradition, and failure to develop a national political strategy, or at least one capable of outliving the local and spontaneous outbursts of violent insurrection. In fact, we can distinguish three levels or three forms of appearance of this structure of lack in anarchism when compared to socialism or communism, each level or form of which is only further compounded in the case of Mexico. First, in temporal or historical terms, the time of anarchist politics is seen as all too punctual, or devoid of duration; and closely tied to the so-called primitive or insufficiently modern, rooted in peasant traditions which have to do with land, rather than being connected with the modern experience of labor in the factory. Second, at the qualitative or developmental level, anarchism is associated with spontaneity rather than with organization; and with the intuitive or immediately present rather than with the conscious or scientific mediation of knowledge. Third and finally, in spatial or geographical terms, anarchism is seen as local and site-specific, as opposed to the scene of grand politics at the level of nation and State. In all three senses, anarchism appears as "mere" anarchism for lack of something else or something more—the more or else that would be deserving of the names of socialism or communism.

This negative evaluation, however, can easily be inverted or turned inside out. In Mexico, too, anarchism then becomes a positive, local or autochthonous and immanent ideology of the revolution. Precisely because of its roots in the agrarian, communal, and autonomous traditions of the peasant revolutionaries, anarchism thus would have to be seen as the proper expression of the spontaneous ideology of those loyal to Emiliano Zapata or Pancho Villa during the long cycle of the Mexican Revolution. Thus, in an older but still highly relevant article, the historian Barry Carr usefully insists that in each phase of this long cycle, going back to the first major wave of utopian socialism, from 1862 to 1882, via the radicalization of a more militant form of anarchism between 1900 and 1910 dominated by the figure of an exiled Ricardo Flores Magón, all the way to the heights of the Mexican Revolution proper, between 1910 and 1920, it was not Marxism or "scientific socialism" so much as anarchism or libertarianism that dominated the ideological landscape in Mexico: "Anarchist and libertarian precepts still dominated the most radical sector of a working class that was still only partially organized and in which liberalism and mutualism were still significant influences."[1] Taking such a view one step further and leaving behind the lingering pejorative connotations, many ideologues of the Mexican Revolution early on in fact made the image of spontaneous, popular, and often anti-intellectual revolutionary anarchism into the official dogma. As the Mexican novelist and autodidact José Revueltas writes in what in my eyes is still one of the best accounts of the Mexican Revolution, his 1961 *Ensayo sobre un proletariado sin cabeza* (Essay on a Headless Proletariat): "This is the point of departure for bourgeois-democratic ideologues to affirm the existence of some kind of immanent ideology, borne from the entrails of the revolution and belabored, not in theoretical thought but with the butt of a rifle, by the drama's very own protagonists and without the need for the latter to subject themselves to the indications of some libretto that would have been written out beforehand."[2] Now, the anarchist and lib-

1 Barry Carr, "Marxism and Anarchism in the Formation of the Mexican Communist Party, 1910–19," *Hispanic American Historical Review* 63, no. 2 (May 1983): 288.

2 José Revueltas, *Ensayo sobre un proletariado sin cabeza*, eds. Andrea Revueltas, Rodrigo Martínez and Philippe Cheron (Mexico City: Era, 1980), 114–15.

ertarian elements found among the followers of Zapata or Flores Magón no longer mark an absence or lack. Rather, they are supposed to be evidence of the absolute singularity of an unprecedented, incomparable, and strictly homegrown national ideology. What from the point of view of international socialism may be disparaged as an infantile deviation or leftist cult of spontaneity, now is worn as a badge of honor and praised in the highest possible terms as a local—even nationalist—rejection of all foreign-imposed models for the so-called fusion of theory and practice.

2

Regardless of the positive or negative evaluations, both of these answers to the question of the relationship between anarchism and socialism or communism suffer from similar limitations. In this respect I concur with my friend and colleague Ray Craib when, drawing inspiration from Roberto Schwarz's idea of "misplaced ideas," he observes that the nationalistic subtraction of all foreignness and the unreflective embrace of the international marketplace of ideas are mirroring and equally problematic extremes.[3] What is more, I would add that the point of departure is mistaken if we begin from a fixed idea of what constitutes anarchism or socialism and then go on to look for an articulation between the two, as if they had not been mixed and unevenly developed from the start in ideological formations alternatively described as libertarian or anti-authoritarian socialism or as socialist anarchism. In this sense I agree with Andrej Grubačić that the more urgent and important task today, rather than restore orthodoxies, consists in looking at the long twentieth century all the way to the present age of riots in light of what he calls the "Haymarket synthesis," obviously referring to the role of anarchists and Marxists in the incidents of 1886 in Chicago, or in terms of what I have elsewhere described as the lesson to be derived from those repeated historical experiences in which anarchists and communists as well as both utopian and scientific socialists—who had not yet split off into staunchly opposed camps—stood shoulder to shoulder on the barricades of the 1871 Paris Commune.[4] The methodological principle behind this proposal resides in the idea that the unevenness of such syntheses, which may well seem clearer in the so-called peripheries, should nonetheless also be seen as crucial to the so-called metropolis.

3 See Raymond Craib's "A Foreword" in this volume; referring to Roberto Schwarz, *Misplaced Ideas*, trans. John Gledson (London: Verso, 1992).

4 See Staughton Lynd and Andrej Grubačič, *Wobblies and Zapatistas: Conversations on Anarchism, Marxism and Radical History* (Oakland: PM Press, 2008), 11–14; and Bruno Bosteels, "The Mexican Commune," *Communism in the 21st Century*, Vol. 3, *The Future of Communism: Social Movements, Economic Crisis, and the Re-imagination of Communism*, ed. Shannon K. Brincat (Santa Barbara: Praeger, 2013), 161–89.

In other words, it is not just in the peripheries that the proper traditions of anarchism or socialism become watered down, eclectic, or heretical deviations. Rather, the process of the constitution of orthodoxies is no less convoluted in the center, so that in a sense what we must come to understand is how the heresies precede the orthodoxies. To be more precise, orthodoxy is constituted only retroactively as a result of the exclusion of heresy. Ideologies are rather like religions in this sense. What is labeled a deviation paradoxically is constitutive of the norm. But what exists before the long and often violent process of institutionalization that leads to the separation of a new norm is nothing more and also nothing less than a whole series of mixed constellations, intermittently punctuated by momentary crystallizations, from which only the official ideologues and all-knowing schoolmasters much later in the game can come and distill the textbook "isms" of socialism, communism, libertarianism, or anarchism.

The problem with any attempt at articulation is actually twofold. On one hand, any articulation presupposes that we have at our disposal a prior definition of what is anarchism, socialism, communism, or Marxism. On the other hand, in addition to the presumption of being clear and distinct entities, the historical development of such trends is typically assumed to follow a one-way path from center to periphery as if it were a single straight line or inexorable downward spiral from clarity to obscurantism, from orthodoxy to eclecticism, and from the rigors of consciousness to unreflective nonchalance. Indeed, what are the criteria invoked in the summary judgments about the ideology of the Mexican Revolution? Typically, they refer to the knowledge of the theory behind the ideologies in question, if not more narrowly to the books and pamphlets that have been read: Did Zapata know anything, for example, about the Marx/Bakunin debate? Had he or his close allies read any of the classical texts? Were they familiar with documents from the Paris Commune that had circulated in Mexico as early as in 1874 in periodicals such as *La Comuna* and *La Comuna Mexicana*? How much, if anything, did they know about the Bolshevik Revolution? About the Second International? And so on. Or else the criteria are more programmatic, so that the question will be asked whether the Ayala Plan, for instance, meets the presumed standards of a socialist program capable of grounding the formation of a political party with a national agenda at the level of the State.[5]

Surely, however, the lines of demarcation between all these political and ideological entities are more fluid—both structurally, or in principle, and historically, or in actual fact—than what the official ideologues and

5 This last one is the issue raised, for example, in Adolfo Gilly's canonical interpretation, *The Mexican Revolution*, trans. Patrice Camiller (New York: The New Press, 2006).

schoolmasterly analysts assume. And so, instead of seeking to bridge and articulate already separate and presumably distinct entities, the real task in my eyes consists in finding adequate ways to describe such a "mixed scene," to use a term dear to Jacques Rancière in *Proletarian Nights: The Workers' Dream in Nineteenth-Century France*, a book which itself serves as a model for the kind of historical analysis that I have in mind.[6]

3

In the specific case of Mexico, these questions of method only become more complicated due to yet another unfortunate split, namely, the division of labor among historians between those who study mainly the Mexican Revolution and are focused on the course of events between 1910 and 1920 as well as the ideological trends and so-called precursors related to them; and those historians of socialism and communism in Mexico who for the most part are focused on the official history of the Mexican Communist Party and its various outgrowths and alternatives, in relation to the destiny of the Comintern.[7]

The gap between anarchism and socialism or communism only grows wider as a result of this division of labor among historiographers of the Mexican Revolution. This is palpable even in the way news of the October

6 See Jacques Rancière, *Proletarian Nights: The Workers' Dream in Nineteenth-Century France*, trans. John Drury (London: Verso, 2012).

7 On anarchism and libertarian socialism in Mexico, see also José C. Valadés, *El socialismo libertario mexicano (siglo XIX)*, ed. Paco Ignacio Taibo II (Sinaloa: Universidad Autónoma de Sinaloa, 1984); Juan Felipe Leal, *Del mutualismo al sindicalismo en México: 1843–1910* (Mexico City: El Caballito, 1991); Carlos Illades, *Hacia la república del trabajo: La organización artesanal en la ciudad de México, 1853–1876* (Mexico City: Universidad Autónoma Metropolitana Iztapalapa/El Colegio de México, 1996); and Carlos Illades, *Las otras ideas: Estudios sobre el primer socialismo en México 1850–1935* (Mexico City: Era, 2008). Aside from Gilly's work, classic and best-selling interpretations of the Mexican Revolution include John Womack Jr, *Zapata and the Mexican Revolution* (New York: Vintage, 1968); and Friedich Katz, *The Life and Times of Pancho Villa* (Stanford: Stanford University Press, 1998). In Mexico, see among others Arnaldo Córdova, *La ideología de la Revolución Mexicana: La formación del nuevo régimen* (Mexico City: Era, 1973); Héctor Aguilar Camín and Lorenzo Meyer, *A la sombra de la Revolución Mexicana* (Mexico City: Cal y Arena, 1989); and Paco Ignacio Taibo II, *Pancho Villa: una biografía narrativa* (Mexico City: Planeta, 2006). On the history of communism in Mexico, see Karl M. Schmitt, *Communism in Mexico: A Study in Political Frustration* (Austin: University of Texas Press, 1965); Donald L. Herman, *The Comintern in Mexico* (Washington, DC: Public Affairs Press, 1974); Barry Carr, *Marxism and Communism in Twentieth-Century Mexico* (Lincoln: University of Nebraska Press, 1982); Paco Ignacio Taibo II, *Bolcheviques: Historia narrativa de los orígenes del comunismo en México (1919–1925)* (Mexico City: Ediciones B, 2008); Daniela Spenser, *Stumbling Its Way Through Mexico: The Early Years of the Communist International*, trans. Peter Gellert (Tuscaloosa: University of Alabama Press, 2011); Carlos Illades, *La inteligencia rebelde: La izquierda en el debate público en México 1968–1989* (Mexico City: Océano, 2001); and Barry Carr and Steve Ellner, eds, *The Latin American Left: From the Fall of Allende to Perestroika* (Boulder, CO: Westview Press, 1993).

Revolution was received in the land of Zapata. "The anarchist orientation of most of the radical workers did not at all dim enthusiasm for the momentous developments in the young Soviet state. The revolutionary events were simply given an interpretation that accorded with anarchist and syndicalist beliefs," as Barry Carr also observes. "For Mexican anarchists, the Russian Revolution was a magnificent example of 'direct action' (*acción directa*) carried out by an active minority with the familiar anarchist and libertarian slogans of antimilitarism, individual freedom, and the smashing of the state."[8] Conversely, the dominance of anarchist or libertarian elements within the ideology of the Mexican Revolution also represented a major obstacle for the newly formed Communist Party of Mexico (PCM), constituted only in November 1919, when the cycle of the Mexican Revolution was already winding down, Zapata having been murdered in April of that same year and Villa having retreated to the state of Chihuahua from where he could do no more than launch a series of desperate and bloody guerrilla attacks until finally laying down arms on June 26, 1920.

As a historian of Mexican communism, Barry Carr does offer us a hint of a different path, which I would like to follow in an attempt to cast new light on the role of anarchism in the mixed scene that is the history of contemporary Mexico. "The intriguing question with which the historian of Mexican communism is left is that of the periodization of this symbiotic relationship between Marxist and libertarian currents. At what point can we distinguish clearly between the two phenomena, and how many communists of the 1920s were in fact sympathizers with anarchist or syndicalist ideas?" Carr thus asks, before quoting the following observation from Revueltas's *Ensayo sobre un proletariado sin cabeza*: "The Communist party, reflecting the schematic mold in which it was formed, condemned anarcho-syndicalism in the name of Marx as being tainted by the abstract theory of the classical ideologues of anarchy. But it did not acknowledge the positive contribution the great anarcho-syndicalist mass movement made to the theme of working-class independence within bourgeois democratic struggle."[9] To come to understand this is all the more urgent today when the red and black specter of libertarian communism is once again roaming the streets of places like Ciudad Universitaria in Mexico City or establishing itself as the Commune of Oaxaca.

Ensayo sobre un proletariado sin cabeza, completed in 1961 and published in 1962, was meant as a founding text for the Liga Leninista Espartaco, the political organization with which Revueltas was seeking to overcome his ongoing problems with the PCM. Already the name of

8 Carr, "Marxism and Anarchism in the Formation of the Mexican Communist Party, 1910–19," 290.

9 Ibid., 305.

this new organization should serve as an indication of the Haymarket synthesis that is in gestation in these final years of Revueltas until his death in 1976.[10] The Leninist-Spartacist League was the author's answer to the absence of an authentic working-class party, or independent consciousness, in Mexico. The Mexican proletariat was "headless" precisely because no such class party in the Leninist sense had been able to develop in the aftermath of the complete "mediatization" of the Mexican revolution by the State. Instead, the new bourgeoisie had been able to establish a single-party rule under the PNR (Partido Nacional Revolucionario) and later the PRI (Partido Revolucionario Institucional), which was not broken until long after Revueltas's death, with the election in 2000 of Vicente Fox from the PAN (Partido de Acción Nacional). This phenomenon of "the revolution-turned-government" (*la revolución hecha gobierno*) is the prime target of Revueltas in his *Ensayo*. Claiming to be above all class interests, the government could pretend to represent the people beyond the class struggle, so that any opposition to the government meant opposition not only to the people but also to the very idea of the revolution. Consequently, any element of socialist or communist ideology was ipso facto absorbed into the dominant ideology of the bourgeois State:

> In our eyes the phenomenon consists in the following historical circumstance, which moreover constitutes a concrete reality to this day: the dominant bourgeois-democratic ideology that is in the process of development and, consequently, the ideology that is capable of proving itself as the most real and rational in the course of the practical and objective unfolding of this development insofar as it coincides with its own needs (and this coincidence occupies a prolonged period of time in the history of the Mexican reality), *assumes the socialist consciousness for itself*, makes it its own and reduces the proletarian ideology to converting itself, at best, in its most radical extreme, its *left wing*.[11]

As a result, the working class cannot realize its objective in the struggle for the establishment of socialism in Mexico.

---

10 In the 1960s "Leninist-Spartacist," however, did not necessarily mean a synthesis between V.I. Lenin and Rosa Luxemburg, between party vanguardism and social democracy, or between organization and spontaneity; it was also the name that at the time was beginning to be used as a code word for orthodox Marxism-Leninism. For Revueltas's subsequent changes, in which the Spartacist-Luxemburgian, councilist, and spontaneous elements will come to dominate the strict Leninist vanguardism, as witnessed especially in the novel *Los errores* and in the theoretical writings for *Dialéctica de la conciencia*, see chapters 2 and 3 in Bruno Bosteels, *Marx and Freud in Latin America: Politics, Psychoanalysis and Religion in Times of Terror* (London: Verso, 2012).

11 Revueltas, *Ensayo sobre un proletariado sin cabeza*, 177–78.

For Revueltas, at least at the time of his writing *Ensayo sobre un proletariado sin cabeza*, this historical impasse can be overcome only through the creation of an authentic working-class party, in which peasants and proletarians would have to join hands as was briefly the case during the episode of what Adolfo Gilly a few years later, writing from Lecumberri prison where he was jailed side by side with Revueltas, would label the Morelos Commune of 1914–1915, in the Zapata-controlled territory around Cuernavaca just south of Mexico City. In 1961, however, no prospect for such a "head" of the proletariat was anywhere near in sight:

> The working class in Mexico is like the enormous and impotent size of a colossal sculpture that is not yet finished. Marxism-Leninism will be the insuperable craftsman who will mold and sculpt the leading head of the proletariat. Then the giant will begin to march under the influence of the breath of life of history, so as to chase away with its steps the horrified shadows of the false working class ideologues, the political wheelers and dealers, the doctrinaire usurpers and all those who dreamt of keeping it subjugated to the chains of alienation, convinced as they were that it was merely a blind and vanquished titan.[12]

Because of the phenomenon of continued mediatization, the Mexican proletariat is headless, or carries on top of its colossal torso a head that is not its own but that of the newly formed, post-revolutionary bourgeoisie: "The Mexican working class, thus, projects itself in the history of the last fifty years of the country as a proletariat without a head, or that carries on its shoulders a head that is not its own."[13] What is worse, insofar as the PCM follows the disastrous political strategy of the Comintern to support the "progressive sectors" of the national bourgeoisie, the level of ideological alienation reaches deeply into the very core of the existing party structures that are supposed to organize a proletarian class consciousness. Revueltas thus proposes nothing less than to creating a genuine party as an alternative to the PCM. Such is the task ascribed to the fellow travelers in the Liga Leninista Espartaco: "It belongs to the proletarian ideologues to take up the task of giving the working class its consciousness in an organized form, that is to say, to organize this consciousness by instituting themselves as the *collective brain* that thinks *in the name of* the class, *for the class* and *with* the class."[14]

Put in these terms, the argument seems to be straightforwardly Leninist (albeit with the admixture of extraneous elements drawn from

12 Ibid., 46.
13 Ibid., 75.
14 Ibid., 194–95.

Jean-Paul Sartre) and a superficial reading of *Ensayo de un proletariado sin cabeza* could certainly be forgiven for failing to understand the need to add the Spartacist name to its proposed League. Anarchism and anarcho-syndicalism, moreover, appear as wholly separate from socialism properly speaking, along the lines of the pejorative evaluation mentioned above. In reality, however, the argument is far more mixed and ambivalent than appears at first. Revueltas is capable of suggesting as much, for example, when he writes: "Anarchism and anarcho-syndicalism by now have lost all influence in the working class movement of all countries and in fact have ceased to exist. But in the past they represented a considerable factor and, in spite of the misguided nature of their tactics and their perspectives, the great struggles led by them were evident expressions of the independence of the proletariat as a class."[15]

Sure, anarchism is described as an initial, still "primitive" phase or impulse, for which scientific socialism would represent the "superior form."[16] But Revueltas is also mindful of the fact that in the context of the complete alienation and mediatization of working-class consciousness, anarchism signals the only promise of genuine autonomy. This is nowhere more evident than in the portrait of one of the so-called ideological precursors of the Mexican Revolution: Ricardo Flores Magón.

4

Toward the end of *Ensayo sobre un proletariado sin cabeza* Revueltas indeed approvingly quotes the following portrait of Ricardo Flores Magón:

> Great is the guilt of the terrible agitator, but when one remembers his good faith, one thinks that whatever is good and bad in the revolution is owed to Magón and that those philosophies that people make up about Madero and Zapata are as unmotivated as they are meaningless. Madero sought to return to the family *clan*; Zapata wanted to bring back the indigenous *calpulli*; Magón had the vision of a red city of the future, which would be reached by wading through rivers of fire and blood. That is why he ended up blind in both eyes. His retina was burnt by that terrible bonfire that he had lighted up, just as his followers were devoured by the abyss of the past, which is more inexorable than the mysterious beetles that tradition has it kill all those who violate the Egyptian sarcophagus.[17]

15 Ibid., 198

16 Ibid., 198–99.

17 Quoted in Revueltas, ibid., 203 The portrait is taken from the memoirs of Victoriano Salado Álvarez, a diplomat in Washington, DC, for the old regime of Porfirio Díaz. Revueltas uses this portrait because for all its cynicism and superstitious fear before

Such a glowing portrait means that for Revueltas, the role of Flores Magón cannot be reduced to that of a mere "precursor" of the Mexican Revolution. Suffice it to think of the power of his words in "A los proletarios" ("To the Proletarians"), published in the famous *magonista* periodical *Regeneración* in September 1910 and likewise quoted extensively by Revueltas:

> Workers, my friends, listen: it's necessary, it's urgent that you carry the revolution to the point where it reflects the consciousness of the epoch; it's necessary, it's urgent that you incarnate the spirit of the century in the great battle. If not, the revolution which we look on lovingly while it takes shape is no different than the already nearly forgotten revolts fomented by the bourgeoisie and directed by the militarized leadership, in which your role will not be that of heroic, conscious liberators, but simply that of cannon fodder.[18]

Fifty years before Revueltas once again would find inspiration in these words to do the same, Flores Magón here is already pleading for the need for genuine autonomy in the struggle for radical emancipation:

> Take into account, laborers, that you are the only producers of wealth. Houses, palaces, railways, factories, cultivated fields—everything, absolutely everything is made by your creative hands, and nonetheless you lack everything. You weave the cloth, but you walk around almost naked; you harvest the grain, and you hardly have a miserable crumb to take home to your families; you build houses and palaces, and you inhabit huts and attics; the metals which you drag out of the earth only serve to make your bosses more powerful and your chains stronger and heavier. The more you produce the poorer and less free you become, for the simple reason that you make your bosses richer and freer, because only the rich can take advantage of political liberty. So then, if you revolt with the purpose of overthrowing the despotism of Porfirio Díaz, something which you will undoubtedly achieve, as that triumph is certain; if things go well for you after that victory you'll get a government that will put in

unknown historical forces, it speaks volumes about the real threat that Ricardo Flores Magón represented in the eyes of the dominant classes.

18 Quoted in Revueltas, *Ensayo sobre un proletariado sin cabeza*, 204. In English, see Ricardo Flores Magón, "To the Proletarians," trans. Chaz Bufe, *Dreams of Freedom: A Ricardo Flores Magón Reader*, eds. Chaz Bufe and Mitchell Cowen Verter (Oakland: AK Press, 2005), 161–62. For a broader contextualization, see James D. Cockcroft, *Intellectual Precursors of the Mexican Revolution 1900–1913* (Austin: University of Texas Press, 1968). Claudio Lomnitz's massive biography, *The Return of Comrade Ricardo Flores Magón* (New York: Zone Books, 2014) appeared too recently to be taken into account in the present study.

> effect the Constitution of 1857; and with that you'll have obtained, at least in writing, your political liberty. But in practice you'll be slaves every bit as much as you are today, and like today you'll have only one right: that of being worked to death.[19]

Revueltas's evaluation of the role of anarchism in this context certainly remains ambivalent. Thus, anarchism and anarcho-syndicalism are said to be part of the "deformed consciousness" of the working class in Mexico. Yet, at the same time, anarchism seems to be the only political wing during and after the Mexican Revolution capable of radicalizing the struggles and giving them a class character. Anarchism, in other words, is not just the symptomatic expression of the absence of an organized proletarian consciousness, due to the inexistence of a proper vanguard party; it is also the only genuine source of autonomous politics throughout the period dominated and coopted by the country's rising new bourgeoisie.

The dualism at the heart of the anarchist tradition in Mexico thus appears as an open-ended promise in the conclusion of *Ensayo sobre un proletariado sin cabeza*:

> Anarcho-syndicalism in Mexico (until the CGT becomes reformist and pro-government) is a-political as far as its traditional programmatic principles are concerned: the refusal to belong to any political party, electoral abstention, and so on. But Mexican anarcho-syndicalism moves within an essential contradiction, which is very characteristic and which we cannot fail to take into account. Within the circumstances of an absolute mediatization of the workers' movement by democratic-bourgeois ideology, which manages to keep the proletarian struggles within its purely and strictly trade-unionist frameworks, anarcho-syndicalism is the only workers' movement that in Mexico stamps the strikes with the character of veritable *class struggles*, that is, it *politicizes* them and gives them an autonomous proletarian nature—without, for that matter, adopting a negative attitude toward the democratic-bourgeois revolution, or without considering that it is a revolution that "finds itself in struggle with the interests of the proletariat."[20]

I cannot avoid the impression that anarcho-syndicalism appears twice in this account: first as one form of ideological deformation and the

19 Flores Magón, "To the Proletarians."

20 Revueltas, *Ensayo sobre un proletariado sin cabeza*, 214. The final quote within the quote is from Lenin's 1905 text "Two Tactics of Social Democracy in the Democratic Revolution."

second as the only form of authentic and independent working-class consciousness.

Thus, the final twist of the argument comes into view when we grasp the fact that the split between anarchism and socialism actually turns out to be an objective part of the ideological struggle on behalf of the bourgeoisie after the Mexican Revolution. A figure such as Ricardo Flores Magón, then, is seen as exclusively anarchistic in order to obscure his role as the bearer of an all too radical revolutionary agenda. "The point is that Flores Magón thus should appear before the eyes of the working masses, lorded over by governmentalism and by bourgeois democracy, as someone who opposed the struggle for the disappearance of the State to the historical struggles entrusted to the revolutionary movement of 1910–17," concludes Revueltas. "When the anarchist doctrinarian that was Flores Magón is thus confused with the proletarian ideologue *that he also was*, and whose mind echoed a historical need as basic and decisive as that of guaranteeing the independent participation of the working class in the bourgeois-democratic process, what ends up being covered up is not only this last aspect of Flores Magón's personal attitude but also *this very historical need or requirement* itself and therein consists, no doubt, the class tendency that inspires the representatives of democratic-bourgeois ideology to do so."[21] Are we not in similar situation worldwide? If not for the label of terrorism, all autonomous initiatives of protest and rebellion today are promptly labeled anarchist—even or especially within self-described leftist circles. Because of the generalized mediation of ideology as well as the collapse of the ideal of the vanguard party that traditionally was meant to overcome such cooptation and monopoly, we are now in a situation that is once again closer to the one described in Revueltas's essay with regard to Flores Magón than we are to the period in which Lenin first formulated his theory of the party. Neither God nor master: neither proletarian nor vanguard, but communist *and* anarchist. In other words, and to paraphrase Hegel, perhaps the obscure period in which we find ourselves at the beginning of this new millennium is the night in which all cows are not just black but red and black.

21 Revueltas, *Ensayo sobre un proletariado sin cabeza*, 206.

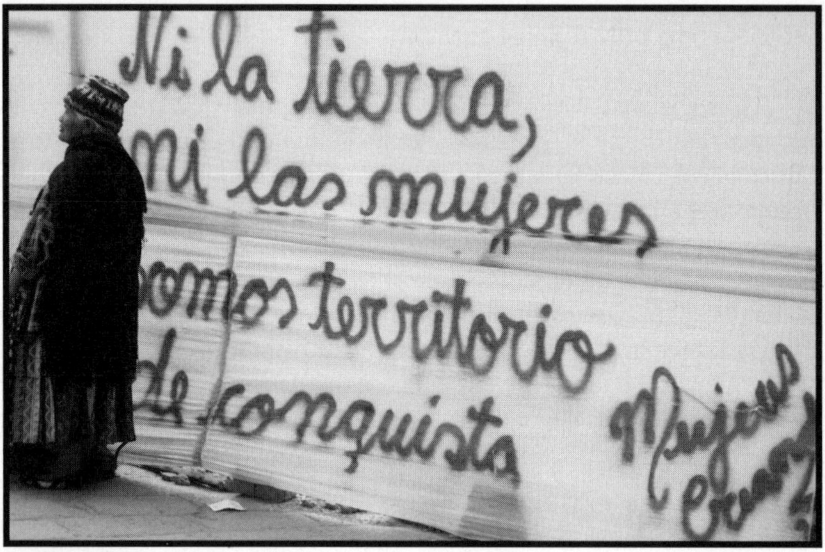

Neither earth,
nor women:
we are not territory
for conquest
—Mujeres Creando

GLOBAL ANARCHISM: PROVOCATIONS

Silvia Federici

> No boss, no god, no husband.[1]

> . . . fed up as we are with so many tears and so much misery; fed up with the never ending drudgery of children . . . fed up with asking and begging, or being a plaything for our infamous exploiters or vile husbands, we have decided to raise our voices and demand, yes, demand our bit of pleasure in the banquet of life.
>
> —From *La Voz de la Mujer*, first anarcha-feminist journal published in Argentina in the 1890s[2]

What do we learn by viewing anarchism as a "global phenomenon" with multiple origins and forms, rather than as a movement emanating from Europe and the United States? This question arises almost spontaneously from the trends that we observe in today's anarchist political movements that embody widespread aspirations to a world without states, without armies, without police forces, rather than a specific set of doctrines. As the image fades away of the stereotyped nineteenth-century anarchist—the bomb thrower, enemy of kings and queens, sacrificing his youth on the guillotine after taking a tyrant's life—different histories can be recognized as part of the anarchist world.

1 Maxine Molyneux, "No God, No Boss, No Husband: Anarchist Feminism in Nineteenth-Century Argentina," *Latin American Perspectives* 13, no. 1, Latin America's Nineteenth-Century History (Winter 1986).

2 All references to *Voz de la Mujer* are from Molyneux, "No God, No Boss, No Husband." http://libcom.org/history/no-god-no-boss-no-husband-world's first, posted by wojtek on Jan 3, 2012, accessed on August 6, 2013.

A first response, then, is that a non-Eurocentric perspective—as proposed by this conference—reveals the existence of non-European anarchist movements and the influence on them of local histories and cultures. It helps us discover new worlds, like that disclosed by Benedict Anderson's *Under Three Flags: Anarchism and the Anti-Colonial Imagination* (2005), which documents the presence of anarchists in the history of the anticolonial movement in the Philippines.[3] We learn from it of Jose Rizal, Mariano Ponce, and Isabelo de los Reyes—the protagonists of the resistance first to Spain and later to the United States in the 1890s, and with them, in the shadows, of the many others still waiting for historical recognition. We also learn that in the decade before World War I, Paris was the center of the Chinese anarchist movement, inspired by classic Chinese philosophers as much as from Kropotkin and Bakunin, that strongly influenced even Mao Zedong in his youth.[4] Again, a global perspective on anarchism leads us to discover that the first explicitly anarchist feminist group was created in the 1890s in Argentina, where it produced the anarcha-feminist newspaper *La Voz de la Mujer*, "one of the first recorded instances of the fusion of feminist ideas with a revolutionary and working-class orientation," all written by and for women, and challenging "the antifeminist attitudes prevalent among men in the movement."

But globalizing anarchism can achieve something more than finding non-European trajectories or "forerunners" in non-European cultural traditions, as Peter Marshall has done in tracing anarchism's origins in Taoism and Buddhism.[5] More important, it is to demonstrate that anarchism "as we have known it" is a principle that is present in every age and country, expressing an irrepressible desire for individual and collective self-determination, of which European anarchism is only *one embodiment* shaped by specific historical conditions. In other words, "global anarchism" can do more than displace the assumption of a centralized origin emanating its influence like a king his decrees. It can illuminate world history, showing, for example, as Sam Mbah and I.E. Igariwey have done in *African Anarchism* (1997), that, far from being a universal presence, states and governments and classes are recent historical formations, rarely found in much of pre-colonial Africa. Once we leave Europe, in fact, we discover that statelessness and the desire for self-government are not eternally

3 Republished under the title *The Age of Globalization: Anarchists and the Anticolonial Imagination* (London: Verso, 2013).

4 Robert A. Scalapino and George T. Yu, *The Chinese Anarchist Movement* (Berkeley: Center for Chinese Studies, Institute of International Studies, University of California, 1961).

5 Peter Marshall, *Demanding the Impossible: A History of Anarchism* (Oakland: PM Press, 2010), 53–65.

receding utopias, but are principles that for millennia have structured communities in every part of the world.

Anarchists, in this broader sense, were the inhabitants of the "New World," portrayed by the Italian humanist historian Peter Martyr (according to his English translator Richard Eden) as "the most happye of all men," living in a sort of golden age, free from toil and masters, not knowing "Myne" and "Thyne" and the struggle for gain.[6] So were the "Indians" that Amerigo Vespucci met in his voyages to the coast of South America, of whom he was to say that "they live amongst themselves without a king or ruler, each man being his own master."[7] So powerful was the influence of these reports from the "New World" that, according to Brandon, they not only radically changed the dominant account of the "golden age," but also gave us good reasons to believe that they brought the idea of "Liberty" as "masterlessness" into European political thought, where "liberty," until then, had only signified the right to free oneself from tyrannical rule.[8]

Communal structures, built on the principles of reciprocity and gift-exchange, like the *ayllu* system that still exists in the Andes, were also prominent in pre-conquest Bolivia and Peru, continuing to function even under the Inca and Spanish rule; and in this conference we have been reminded that the *potlatch* rituals practiced by indigenous communities in the region were in essence expressions of an anarchic principle, as a means of disaccumulation of material possessions and power.[9]

Knowledge of these realities is crucial for us, not because we can hope or wish to return to the past, but because we need to free our imagination from the assumption that we cannot organize our lives except through a central power, and that communal forms of existence are bound to remain small-scale formations unfit to provide the foundation for a new mode of production.[10] Highlighting the "positive" content of anarchism—"positive" in the sense of being positional or constituent in the autonomist sense—and stressing its political commitment to self-government and to the immediate liberation of everyday life, is especially crucial at a time when institutional politics is undergoing a historic crisis and, on the other hand, as a political philosophy, anarchism is veritably exploding. Anarchist

6 William Brandon, *New Worlds for Old. Reports from the New World and their Effect of the Development of Social Thought in Europe, 1500–1800* (Athens: Ohio University Press, 1986), 6.

7 Ibid., 38.

8 Ibid., 22–38, 122–25.

9 See Georges Bataille, *The Accursed Share*, Vol. 1, trans. Robert Hurley (New York: Zone Books, 1988) and Pierre Clastres, *Archeology of Violence*, trans. Jeanine Herman (New York: Semiotext(e), 1994).

10 On this topic, see George Caffentzis and Silvia Federici, "Commons Against and Beyond Capitalism." *Upping the Anti: A Journal of Theory and Action* (September 2013): 83–97.

or anarchist-inspired movements are growing everywhere, traditional anarchist principles—autonomy, common voluntary association, self-organization, mutual aid, and direct democracy—have gone from bases for organizing within the (anti)globalization movement to playing the same role in radical movements of all kinds everywhere.[11]

Undoubtedly, a crucial factor in the present popularity of anarchism, at least among younger generations, is the growing crisis of the state form. The dismantling of the welfare state—the policy the capitalist class reluctantly embraced in the post–World War II period for fear of communism—has in fact removed the last smokescreen behind which the state machine's repressive character could hide. By discarding its "welfare function" the state has certainly not vanished nor abolished itself, but it has renounced that element of its rule that could still provide a reason for allegiance and the basis for a social contract. All that remains of the state now is its gigantic repressive apparatus, including its codification of debt and debt repayment as one of the dominant social bonds, so that its identification with violence, the identification of the *state as violence*, has never been more evident.

On this basis, as Sasha Lilley pointed out in her introductory remarks to "Improvocations," the final session of the 2012 conference, a new relation is emerging between Marxism and anarchism which, in her words, are today, in the United States at least, more close than they have been since the time of World War I. As she put it, "with the emergence of non-statist Marxism" and the rise of grassroots movements not interested in doctrinal disputes, a convergence of these two political traditions is possible and already on the way. In invoking "anti-statist Marxism," I refer to the work of a variety of contemporary Marxist writers and activists—from John Holloway to Michael Hardt and Antonio Negri, Harry Cleaver, Peter Linebaugh, and George Caffentzis—who, while maintaining Marx's analysis of capitalist development and exploitation, reject Marx's assumption of a dictatorship of the proletariat as an intermediate state to the realization of communism. All these political theorists would agree (though perhaps for different reasons) with Negri's argument in *Marx beyond Marx* that to say "State" is to say "Capital."[12] That is, as John Holloway has put it, the state is not a neutral instrument tied to capitalism by purely external relations, transferable therefore into the hands of the working class, who presumably can "wield it for its own purpose." This, Holloway points out,

11 David Graeber, *Fragments of an Anarchist Anthropology* (Chicago: Prickly Paradigm Press, 2004), 2.

12 Antonio Negri, *Marx beyond Marx*, trans. Harry Cleaver, Michael Ryan, and Maurizio Viano, ed. Jim Fleming (Brooklyn: Autonomedia, 1991), 188.

is to attribute to the state an autonomy contemporary political economy belies.[13]

Most important, however, anti-statist Marxism shares the vision of the goal of "revolution" as a self-governed society: the free association of producers that Marx imagined as the foundation of communist society. Anarchism, however, must not only be globalized and expanded in its political reach. It must also be "de-masculinized," both to acknowledge the contribution that women have made to it and to extend the critique of authority and the state to a critique of patriarchal relations and, above all, a critique of the organization of social reproduction in capitalism—a theme underdeveloped in much of the history of the anarchist movement.

Opposed to all forms of authority, anarchists also rejected marriage and the family; some called for "free love." But with notable exceptions, their critiques remained at the level of abstract principle and many anarchist men denied the specificity of women's oppression and the legitimacy of a separate, autonomous organization to deal with it. As for the call for "free love," more than an assertion of equality between women and men and women's right to a sexual life, it often functioned as a justification for "free sex" with no responsibility attached to it. Thus, the women active in the movement learned from early on that their struggle would be on two fronts. Emma Goldman, who most coherently applied anarchist principles to the redefinition of male-female relations, campaigning against prostitution in marriage, unwanted pregnancies, and state control over love and sexuality, learned it when she took a stand against the repression of homosexuality and came under attack by her own male comrades.

The assumption of being involved in a "double struggle" was crucial also for Mujeres Libres, "the first autonomous proletarian women's organization in Spain," with approximately thirty thousand members, that formed in 1936 at the beginning of the Civil War. Convinced that women's specific forms of exploitation called for a particular form of struggle and that, despite their principles, their male comrades would resist "women's liberation," Mujeres Libres insisted on organizing independently of men, refusing the proposal of the Confederación Nacional del Trabajo (CNT)—a confederation of anarcho-syndicalist groups affiliated with the International—that they become part of the organization, calling themselves "free women" to stress their autonomy from men. This enabled them to engage in a variety of initiatives that would prepare

13 John Holloway, *Change the World Without Taking Power* (London: Pluto Press, 2002), 13–15.

women for social action taking into account their specific needs: literacy drives, discussion groups, day-care centers.[14]

It is thanks to these feminist strands within anarchism and their stress on autonomy and consciousness-raising that the movement exercised a significant influence on radical feminism in North America in the 1970s. As Alix Kates Shulman writes, by this time, the name of Emma Goldman was a "veritable password of radical feminism":

> Her face began appearing on T-shirts, her name on posters, her words on banners. An Emma Goldman Clinic for Women was founded in Iowa City, an Emma Goldman Brigade in Chicago, an Emmatroupe in New York City; screenplays, operas and stage plays were written about Goldman's life and produced in cities from Indianapolis to Denver to Hollywood and New York.[15]

Within today's feminisms as well there are strong anarchic strands. An example is the collective Mujeres Creando, an anarcha-feminist organization founded in 1992 in La Paz (Bolivia), which describes itself as "*indias, putas, y lesbianas*," committed to disobedience, creativity and the construction of a movement outside the state, political parties and NGOs.[16] Even the use by some feminists of nakedness as a political weapon can be seen as an anarchist tactic, in that nakedness has a leveling function, as a rejection of dress as instrument and symbol of authority and power.

There is a deep affinity between feminism and anarchism. Both are anti-hierarchical, anti-authoritarian, and "operate through loose, voluntary social organizations, relying on collective activity by small loosely connected groups."[17] Both favor direct action to promote change and use consensus as decision-making technique.[18] Both believe that social change begins with the transformation of everyday life and that political

14 M.A. Ackelsberg, "Separate and Equal?: Mujeres Libres and Anarchist Strategy for Women's Emancipation," *Feminist Studies* 11, no. 1 (1985): 4–5, accessed January 22, 2015, https://libcom.org/files/seperate%20and%20equal.pdf.

15 Alix Kates Shulman, ed., *Red Emma Speaks: An Emma Goldman Reader* (Amherst, NY: Humanities Books, 1996), 4,

16 See Mujeres Creando, *La Virgen de los Deseos* (Buenos Aires: Tinta Limon Ediciones, 2005); and *Mujeres Grafiteando* (La Paz: Compas, 2009). See also Martha A. Ackelsberg, *Free Women of Spain: Anarchism and the Struggle for the Emancipation of Women* (Oakland: AK Press, 2004).

17 Schulman, *Red Emma Speaks*, 17.

18 Women have discovered, however, that "consensus" techniques do not work in all situations and can actually have an exclusionary effect, especially with regards to women, who much less than men can afford the time-consuming process necessary to achieve consensus, as they often have to care for children and attend to other reproductive tasks. On the problematic and possible pitfalls of "consensus" as decision-making technique, see Amy Starecheski's discussion of its use in the self-governed community of Christiania, in Copenhagen. "Consensus and Strategy: Narratives of Naysaying and

work should stem from one's life experiences. As with any global form of anarchism, it has been claimed that feminism too has not only been influenced by the anarchist movement, but has *independently* gravitated toward "anarchist" organizational forms; "feminists—according to Penny Kornegger—have been unconscious anarchists in theory and practice for years."[19] More than that, as David Graeber has written in *The Democracy Project*, "[what] has now come to be called the 'Anarchist Process'—all those elaborate techniques of facilitation and consensus finding, the hand signals and the like—emerged from radical feminism, Quakerism and even North American traditions. In fact, the particular variety employed in North America should really be called "feminist process" rather than 'anarchist process.'"[20] Graeber is right, but the influence of feminism on anarchism exceeds the procedures of the decision-making process. Anarchists are incorporating in their perspectives feminist theories and methodologies that place the traditional anarchist critique of "patriarchy" on a new ground—one shaped not only by anti-authoritarian concerns, but rooted instead in an analysis of the capitalist organization of social reproduction and the sexual division of labor.

In this sense, feminism today is the theoretical and practical ground on which anarchism meets Marxism, in the common recognition of forms of work and exploitation—housework, reproductive work, the reproduction of labor-power—that both political traditions have ignored yet are central to their political perspective and struggle, if we accept that the transformation of everyday life is the ground zero of revolutionary change.[21] How will this recognition inform the future of the anarchist movement internationally? I think it will direct the movement's energies toward the creation of new "commons," alternative forms of reproduction functioning outside market and state, providing both a possibility of survival at a time when all means of reproduction—wages, welfare benefits, subsidies to health care, education, transport—are under attack, and a base from which to reclaim control of the determinants of everyday life and reclaim the "commonwealth."[22] In this case too, a global perspective on anarchism is essential, for it shows that internationally this process is already under way, though not under the insignia of a red and black flag. Anarchism as a principle of self-activity, self-organizing, and self-

Yeasaying in Christiania's Struggles over Legalization," in Håkan Thörn et al. eds., *Space for Urban Alternatives? Christiania 1971–2011* (Vilnius: Gidlunds Förlang, 2011), 263 ff.

19 Marshall, *Demanding the Impossible*, 557.

20 Graeber, *The Democracy Project* (New York: Spiegel & Grau, 2013), 194.

21 Silvia Federici, *Revolution at Point Zero: Housework, Reproduction, and Feminist Struggle* (Oakland: PM Press, 2012).

22 On the subject of the constitution of "commons," see Caffentzis and Federici, "Commons Against and Beyond Capitalism."

government shapes today not only social movements in different parts of the world, but that phenomenon Raúl Zibechi defines as "societies in movement," by which he refers to the emergence of grassroots struggles that are already producing "autonomous zones" and striving to achieve forms of territorial control:

> This means that the movements are now beginning to take the every day life of their people into their own hands. . . . The people do not only survive on the "leftovers" or "waste" of consumer society, but have also begun to produce their own food and other products for sale or exchange. They have become producers, which represents one of the movement's greatest achievements in recent decades, in terms of autonomy and self-esteem.[23]

A global perspective on anarchism today must turn to this reality, because it is in the *barrios*, in the *piquetes*, in the popular assemblies of the old and new world that a new type of anarchism is being formed, more cosmopolitan, more fluid in its contours, in which the influence of feminism, Marxism, Zapatism, and other "anti-systemic" social movements all play a part. This metamorphosis also stems from the awareness that none of these movements is self-subsistent, but all are necessary to an anticapitalist perspective.

From this recognition should issue the task that the Global Anarchisms conference began to outline. In the words of Sasha Lilley: investigating how a new anarchist politics can be and is being developed that constitutes a new political common, as the synthesis of these movements.

Selected Bibliography

Ackelsberg, Martha A. "Separate and Equal? Mujeres Libres and Anarchist Strategy for Women's Emancipation." *Feminist Studies* 11 no, 1 (1985): 63–83. https://libcom.org/files/seperate%20and%20equal.pdf. Accessed on January 22, 2015.

———. *Free Women of Spain: Anarchism and the Struggle for the Emancipation of Women.* Bloomington: Indiana University Press, 1991.

Anderson, Benedict. *The Age of Globalization: Anarchists and the Anti-Colonial Imagination*. London: Verso, 2013.

Bataille, Georges. *The Accursed Share*, Vol. 1. Translated by Robert Hurley. New York: Zone Books, 1988.

Brandon, William. *New Worlds for Old: Reports from the New World and Their Effect of the Development of Social Thought in Europe, 1500–1800*. Athens: Ohio University Press, 1986.

Caffentzis, George. *In Letters of Blood and Fire: Work, Machines, and the Crisis of Capitalism.* Oakland: PM Press, 2013.

23 Raúl Zibechi, *Territories in Resistance: A Cartography of Latin America Social Movements,* trans. Zamora Ryan (Oakland, AK Press, 2012), 37.

———, and Silvia Federici. "Commons Against and Beyond Capitalism." *Upping the Anti: A Journal of Theory and Action* 15 (September 2013).
Clastres, Pierre. *Archeology of Violence*. Translated by Jeanine Herman. New York: Semiotext(e), 1994.
Cleaver, Harry. *Reading Capital Politically.* San Francisco: AK Press, 2000.
Cohen, Mitchel. "What Is Direct Action?" Brooklyn: A Red Balloon Collective Publication, Zen-Marxism Series, 2013.
Federici, Silvia. *Revolution at Point Zero: Housework, Reproduction, and Feminist Struggle.* Oakland: PM Press, 2012.
Graeber, David. *Fragments of an Anarchist Anthropology*. Chicago: Prickly Paradigm Press, 2004.
———. *The Democracy Project: A History, A Crisis, A Movement*. New York: Random House, 2013.
Holloway, John. *Change the World Without Taking Power*. London: Pluto Press, 2002.
Hyde, Lewis. *The Gift: Imagination and the Erotic Life of Property*. New York: Vintage Books, 1983.
Lang, Olga. *Pa Chin and His Writings: Chinese Youth between the Wars.* Cambridge, MA: Harvard University Press, 1967.
Marshall, Peter. *Demanding the Impossible: A History of Anarchism.* Oakland: PM Press, 2010.
Mbah, Sam, and I.E. Igariwey. *African Anarchism. The History of a Movement.* Tucson: See Sharp Press, 1997.
Milstein, Cindy. *Anarchism and Its Aspirations*. Oakland: AK Press and the Institute for Anarchist Studies, 2010.
Molyneux, Maxine. "No God, No Boss, No Husband: Anarchist Feminism in Nineteenth-Century Argentina." *Latin American Perspectives* 13, no. 1,
Latin America's Nineteenth-Century History (Winter 1986): 119–45.
Mujeres Creando, *La Virgen de los Deseos*. Buenos Aires: Tinta Limon Ediciones, 2005.
———. *Mujeres Grafiteando*. La Paz: Compas, 2009.
Negri, Antonio. *Marx beyond Marx: Lessons on the Grundrisse.* London: Pluto and Autonomedia, 1991.
Scalapino, R. and G.T. Yu, "The Chinese Anarchist Movement." Berkeley Center for Chinese Studies, 1961. Accessed on August 1, 2013. http://dwardmac.pitzer.edu/Anarchist_Archives/worldwidemovements/scalapino.html.
Sears, Hal D. *The Sex Radicals: Free Love in High Victorian America.* Lawrence: Regents Press of Kansas, 1977.
Shulman, Alix Kates, ed. *Red Emma Speaks: An Emma Goldman Reader*. Amherst, New York: Humanities Books, 1996.
Starescheski, Amy. "Consensus and Strategy: Narratives of Naysaying and Yeasaying in Christiania's Struggles over Legalization." In *Space for Urban Alternatives? Christiania 1971–2011*, edited by Håkan Thörn et al. Vilnius: Gidlunds Förlang, 2011.
Stoehr, Taylor, ed. *Free Love in America: A Documentary History.* New York: AMS Press, 1977.
Zibechi, Raúl. *Territories in Resistance: A Cartography of Latin America Social Movements.* Translated by Zamora Ryan. Baltimore, AK Press, 2012.

AFTERWORD, BEGINNING WITH "A"

Barry Maxwell

A photograph of the skies above Ithaca, New York, taken by Shelley Wong just before the opening of the conference in Ithaca from which this book derives, records a nicely placed climatological encouragement. "Nicely placed": on the horizon. "Climatological": understood as political weather. "Our Ithaca lies below the horizon," wrote the German philospher Ernst Bloch, somewhere in *The Principle of Hope*, recalling the Odyssey while refusing its mythic strictures. Beyond the pitiful specter of a limp flag (it would be just as pitiful if stiff), beyond the bric-a-brac of law enforcement (traffic lights, license plates, parking spaces), beyond the pickup trucks and the power lines and the big blank big box stores of hamburger row, but *not* beyond the ancestral land of the Cayuga people, flares a world that says "tomorrow." An encircled "A" in the sky? Well, maybe. Maybe wishful seeing.

*

> Lewis Baltz, whose caustic but formally beautiful black-and-white images of parking lots, office parks, industrial garage doors and the backs of anonymous warehouses helped forge a new tradition of American landscape photography in an age of urban sprawl, died on Saturday in Paris. He was sixty-nine.[1]

Baltz, a minimalist, made "seemingly dispassionate, affectless" photographs, the obituary says. He knew what he was taking pictures of, though: the "ghastly transformation" inflicted on the land by "bulimic

1 Randy Kennedy, "Lewis Baltz, 69, Photographer of Urban Anomie," *New York Times*, November 27, 2014, B15.

Lewis Baltz, South Wall Unoccupied Industrial Structure 16812 Miliken Irvine, 1974

capitalism"—these are his words. "I used photography to distance myself from a world that I loathed and was powerless to improve." We need empty hopelessness as little as we need empty hopefulness. Baltz knew that in commodity culture the first comes wrapped inside the second, and he saw through the second. But not the first. Can I? Can we? I've had to caution myself against answering too quickly.

*

We do not wish to ignore the material determinants; a caution comes in a proverb from Egypt: "The hand in water is not the hand in fire." Nor do we ever wish to discount what the imagination shaping the future might help us toward. Mohammed Bamyeh has said it with precision: "learning proper to revolution is one that produces a new imagination, and not just tactical inventiveness."[2] In her 2012 video installation "Fight for the Line," Jolene Rickard of the Tuscarora Nation has made remarkably complex image convergences and overlays of history in the present, and as the future. The still image reproduced here is a moment from the installation, in which images were randomly projected onto a sign marking tribal land and onto the wall behind it. The land and the people who are part of it make a legitimate declaration in the familiar green-and-white form. Behind and upon the unalterable assertion of a people's homeland, the

2 Mohammed Bamyeh, "The June Rebellion in Egypt," http://www.jadaliyya.com/pages/index/12876/the-june-rebellion-in-egypt.

Jolene Rickard, "Fight for the Line" (2012)

image/nation moves and changes, calling the viewer into both variable relations and formulas in productive tension: "BREAK THE LAW!" and "TIME TO LET OUR 6 NATIONS LIVE IN PEACE." The artist has written: "Destabilizing and unpredictable, this piece responds to the duplicitous political and legal 'lines' between these nations as un-settled."[3]

Much of what the contributors do in this book grows from the need to *un-settle*, both materially, when and where possible, and imaginatively, when and where possible. Otherwise, *we can't breathe*. "Learning proper to revolution," then. And revolution proper to freedom.

---

3 Jolene Rickard, artist's statement in Iftikhar Dadi and Hammad Nasar, *Lines of Control: Partition as Productive Space* (London: Green Cardamom and Ithaca: Herbert F. Johnson Museum of Art, 2012), 202. See also, in the same volume, Rickard's detailed recounting of the history and issues informing her work: "Minds in Control," 78–85.

NOTES ON CONTRIBUTORS

Gavin Arnall is a PhD candidate in the Department of Comparative Literature at Princeton University writing a dissertation on the cultural translation of Marxism's abstractly universal categories in Latin America and the Caribbean. Gavin has published articles in journals such as *Critical Inquiry, Theory & Event*, and the *Journal of Latin American Cultural Studies.* He is the translator of the Argentine philosopher Emilio de Ípola's *Althusser: The Infinite Farewell* (Duke University Press, forthcoming) and the co-editor and co-translator of *Between Revolution and Democracy: José Aricó, Marxism, and Latin America* (Brill, forthcoming). He has also participated in the Occupy Wall Street movement and its afterlives, including the Free University experiments in radical education, and has taught courses on writing and literature at Garden State Penitentiary.

Mohammed Bamyeh is a professor of sociology at the University of Pittsburgh and Editor of *International Sociology Review of Books*. He is the author of *Anarchy as Order* (2009), *Of Death and Dominion* (2007), *The Ends of Globalization* (2000), and *The Social Origins of Islam* (1999). He has edited *Intellectuals and Civil Society in the Middle East* (2012) and *Palestine America* (2003).

Bruno Bosteels is professor in the Department of Romance Studies at Cornell University. He is the author of several books, including *The Actuality of Communism*, *Badiou and Politics*, and *Marx and Freud in Latin America*. He also translated numerous books by Alain Badiou, including *Theory of the Subject*, *Wittgenstein's Antiphilosophy*, *The Adventure of French Philosophy*, and *Philosophy for Militants*. He is currently working on a book on the Mexican Commune.

Raymond Craib teaches in the Department of History at Cornell University. He is the author of *Cartographic Mexico: A History of State Fixations and Fugitive Landscapes* (Durham, NC: Duke University Press, 2004; Spanish translation, UNAM, 2014) and the forthcoming *The Death of the Firecracker Poet: Subversive Santiago 1920*. Recent essays include "Sedentary Anarchists," in Bert Altena and Constance Bantman, eds., *Reassessing the Transnational Turn: Scales of Analysis in Anarchist and Syndicalist Studies* (London: Routledge, 2014) and "The Firecracker Poet: Three Poems of José Domingo Gómez Rojas" (with original translations of Gómez Rojas's poetry) in *New Letters: A Magazine of Writing & Art* 78: 1 (Fall 2011).

Silvia Rivera Cusicanqui, born in La Paz, Bolivia, in 1949 of Aymara descent, is a sociologist and activist linked with the katarista indigenous movement, the cocalero movement, and the libertarian movement. With other indigenous and mestizo intellectuals, she founded in 1983 the Taller de Historia Oral Andina (Andean Oral History Workshop), a self-managed group working on issues of orality, identity and indigenous and popular social movements, mainly in the Aymara region. She is the author of various books including: *"Oprimidos pero no vencidos": Luchas del campesinado aymara y qhichwa de Bolivia*, 1900–1980, (La Paz, 1984, translated in to English and Japonese); *Los Artesanos Libertarios y la Ética del Trabajo* (an oral history of La Paz's anarchist movement, in collaboration with Zulema Lehm); *Bircholas: Trabajo de Mujeres, explotación capitalista y opresión colonial entre las migrantes de La Paz y El Alto* (La Paz: Mama Huaco, 1996) and *Las Fronteras de la Coca: Epistemologías Coloniales y Circuitos Alternativos de la Hoja de Coca* (La Paz: ISIS/Aruwiyiri, 2003). Recently a new edition of a collection of her work from the 1990s has appeared under the title *Violencias (re)encubiertas en Bolivia* (La Paz: Mirada Salvaje, 2010). At the same time, Rivera Cusicanqui has produced videos and films, both documentary and fiction. These include a "docu-fiction" in video, *Khunuskiw, recuerdos del porvenir* (La Paz, 1993) and a 16mm fictional short, *Sueño en el cuarto rojo* (La Paz, 2000). Recently she has devoted herself to documentary work on agitation and cultural memory, including two videos connected with the book *Las Fronteras de la Coca: Junio 2001, La Retirada de los Yungas*, y *Viaje a la Frontera del Sur* (Jakima Producciones, 2003), and the short films *Fin de Fiesta* y *Sumaj Qhaniri, Chuyma Manqharu (Tú que iluminas el fondo oscuro del corazón)*, these last two co-directed by Marco Arnéz. For more than three decades she has been a professor at the Universidad Mayor de San Andrés (UMSA) in La Paz, in the field of Sociology. She has been a visiting professor at Columbia University, the University of Texas, University of Pittsburgh, New York University, La Rábida (Huelva), Jujuy,

FLACSO, the Universidad Andina Simón Bolívar in Quito and the École Pratique des Hautes Études, Paris. In 1990 she received a Guggenheim Fellowship and in 1993 was named Profesor Emerita of the UMSA. Since 2008 she has been part of the El Colectivo 2 group, which has published various books and five issues of the journal of the same name and in which a number of her works appear. With Rossana Barragán she has co-edited *Debates postcoloniales: Una introducción a los estudios de la Subalternidad* (Bogotá: Universidad Surcolombiana, 2007).

Geoffroy de Laforcade is an associate professor of Latin American and Caribbean History and the director of International Studies at Norfolk State University in Virginia. His research on Latin American anarchism has appeared in *In Defiance of Boundaries: Anarchism in Latin American History*, Geoffroy de Laforcade and Kirwin Shaffer, eds. (Gainesville: University of Florida Press, 2015); *Anarchism and Syndicalism in the Colonial and Post-Colonial World, 1870–1940*, Steven Hirsch and Lucien Van Der Walt, eds. (Leiden: Brill, 2010), *E.I.A.L.: Estudios Interdisciplinarios de América Latina y el Caribe*, and the *Revue d'Histoire du XIXe siècle*. He is also the lead author of *The How and Why of World History* (Dubuque, IA: Kendall Hunt, 2011) and co-editor of *Transculturality and Perceptions of the Immigrant Other*, Cathy Waegner, Page Laws, and Geoffroy de Laforcade, eds.: (Newcastle upon Tyne: Cambridge Scholars, 2011).

Silvia Federici is a feminist activist, teacher, and writer. She was a co-founder of the International Feminist Collective, the Committee for Academic Freedom in Africa, and the Radical Philosophy Association Anti-Death Penalty Project. She is Professor Emerita at Hofstra University. Her published work includes *Revolution at Point Zero: Housework, Reproduction and Feminist Struggle*; *Caliban and the Witch: Women, the Body and Primitive Accumulation*; *A Thousand Flowers: Social Struggles Against Structural Adjustment in African Universities* (co-editor); and *The Construction of the Concept of Western Civilization and Its Others* (editor).

Steven J. Hirsch is Professor of Practice in the Department of International and Area Studies at Washington University in St. Louis. He holds a PhD in Latin American History from The George Washington University and an MA in Latin American Studies from the University of Texas at Austin. His teaching and research interests focus on anarchism, Andean history, and Latin American populism. Currently he is working on a book manuscript titled *"Study, Organize, Rebel": The History of Anarchist Currents and the Struggle for Working-Class Emancipation in Peru, 1898–1932*. He is also the author of "Anarchist Visions of Race and Space in Northern Perú,

1898–1922," in Kirwin Shaffer and Geoffroy de Laforcade, eds., *In Defiance of Boundaries, Anarchism in Latin American History* (Gainesville: University Press of Florida, 2015); "Peru: 19th and 20th Century Historiography," *Handbook of Latin American Studies* 62 (July 2007) 268–81; "Peru: 19th and 20th Century Historiography," *Handbook of Latin American Studies* 60 (2005), 383–96; and co-editor with Lucien van der Walt, *Anarchism and Syndicalism in the Colonial and Postcolonial World, 1870–1940* (Leiden, The Netherlands: Brill Academic Publishers, 2010).

Adrienne Carey Hurley has taught East Asian Studies in California, Iowa, and Québec, served as an advocate for institutionalized youth, and been involved with a number of anarchist collectives, including the Montreal Anarchist Bookfair Collective. She translated Tomoyuki Hoshino's novel *Lonely Hearts Killer* (Oakland: PM Press, 2009) and is the author of *Revolutionary Suicide and Other Desperate Measures* (Durham, NC: Duke University Press, 2011); and "First They Came for Sherman Austin and the Anarchists of Color: New Fronts in the War on Critical Thinking and the Criminalization of Youth," *Left Curve* 28 (2004): 100–10.

Hilary Klein spent six years in Chiapas, Mexico, working with women's projects in Zapatista communities, and is the author of *Compañeras: Zapatista Women's Stories* (New York: Seven Stories Press, 2015). Originally from Washington, DC, Hilary has been engaged in social justice and community organizing work for more than twenty years, on issues such as affordable housing, immigrants' rights, workers' rights, and violence against women. She currently lives in Brooklyn and works at Make the Road New York, a membership-based community organization. She spent fall 2013 at Georgetown University as a Fellow at the Kalmanovitz Initiative for Labor and the Working Poor.

Peter Linebaugh is a child of empire, schooled in London, Cattaraugus, NY, Washington, DC, Bonn, and Karachi. He went to Swarthmore College during the civil rights days. He has taught at Harvard and Attica Penitentiary, at NYU, and the Federal Penitentiary in Marion, Illinois. He used to edit *Zerowork* and was a member of the Midnight Notes Collective. He wrote *The London Hanged* (London: Penguin, 1991), and, with Marcus Rediker, *The Many Headed Hydra* (Boston: Beacon Press, 2000), which has been translated into six languages. He wrote the *Magna Carta Manifesto*(Berkeley: University of California Press, 2008). He has written introductions to a book of Thomas Paine's writing (London: Verso, 2009) and to a new edition of E.P. Thompson, *William Morris: Romantic to Revolutionary* (Oakland: PM Press, 2011). His essays have been collected in

Stop, Thief! (Oakland: PM Press, 2011) and *The Incomplete, True, Authentic, and Wonderful History of May Day* (Oakland: PM Press, 2016). He is retired from the University of Toledo in Ohio. He lives in the Great Lakes region with a great crew, Michaela Brennan, his beautiful partner, and Kate, Riley, Alex, and Enzo.

Barry Maxwell teaches comparative literature and American studies at Cornell University, where he helped to put together the Institute for Comparative Modernities. He has written about Frederick Douglass, Walt Whitman, Kenneth Burke, Ernst Bloch, Walter Benjamin, David Hammons, Sun Ra, Miles Davis, Gwendolyn Brooks, and Nathaniel Mackey.

David Porter is a political science professor emeritus at SUNY/Empire State College, where he taught courses, among others, on comparative politics, revolution and modern Algeria. The 1960s inspired him toward anarchism especially through Algeria's huge *autogestion* effort, May '68 in France and various North American liberatory movements. Book publications include *Vision on Fire: Emma Goldman on the Spanish Revolution* (editor) (rev. ed., Oakland: AK Press, 2006) and *Eyes to the South: French Anarchists and Algeria* (Oakland: AK Press, 2011).

Maia Ramnath teaches history and Asian studies at Penn State University. She is a member of the Institute for Anarchist Studies board, South Asia Solidarity Initiative, Adalah-NY, and Historians Against War. Publications include *Decolonizing Anarchism: An Antiauthoritarian History of Indian Liberation Struggle* (Oakland: AK Press, 2012); *The Haj to Utopia: How the Ghadar Movement Charted Global Radicalism and Attempted to Overthrow the British Empire* (Berkeley: University of California Press, 2011); and the essays "Meeting the Rebel Girl: Narratives of Anticolonial Solidarity and Interracial Romance," in Benjamin Zachariah, Ali Raza, and Franziska Roy, eds., *The Internationalist Moment: South Asia, Worlds and World Views 1919–1939* (New Delhi: Sage Publications, 2014); and "Anarchism and Postcolonialism," in Carl Levy and Saul Newman, eds. *The Anarchist Imagination: Encounters with the Humanities and Social Sciences* (London: Routledge, 2015).

Penelope Rosemont: Long-time surrealist, in her charmed life she met many remarkable people, among them André Breton, Guy Debord, Aimé Césaire, and Leonora Carrington. She is the editor of *Surrealist Women: An International Anthology* (Austin: University of Texas Press, 1998) and currently secretary-treasurer of the Charles H. Kerr Publishing Company. Her publications include *Surrealist Experiences: 1001 Dawns, 221 Midnights*

(Chicago: Black Swan Press, 2000); *Dreams and Everyday Life: André Breton, Surrealism, Rebel Worker, SDS, and the Seven Cities of Cibola* (Chicago: Charles H. Kerr, 2008); and *Lost Worlds, Forgotten Futures, Undreamed Ecstasies: Some Thoughts on the Relationship of Surrealism to the Mayan Millennium* (Surrealist Research and Development Monograph Series, Number 2).

Bahia Shehab is associate professor of professional practice and director of the graphic design major at the American University in Cairo. She has developed and launched the new graphic design unit for the Department of the Arts with courses mainly focused on visual culture of the Arab world. Her artwork has been on display in exhibitions and galleries worldwide including China, Denmark, Germany, Italy, Lebanon, UAE, and the United States. Her book *A Thousand Times NO: The Visual History of Lam-Alif* was published in 2010. She is a 2012 TED Global Fellow and was included in the BBC's 100 Women 2014 list representing women of the world.

ICM THE INSTITUTE FOR COMPARATIVE MODERNITIES

The Institute for Comparative Modernities (ICM) addresses a key problem in the study of modern culture and society: the transnational history of modernity and its global scope. A broad range of scholarship over the last few decades has contested and complicated the two primary dimensions of the received narrative of modernity: that it arose strictly within the confines of Europe, and that its extension outside Europe was a matter of simple diffusion and imitation. The Institute is dedicated to the emerging study of modernity as a global process in which deep and multifarious interconnections have created complementary cultural formations.

The Institute's primary emphasis falls on neglected or understudied articulations of modernity outside of the historically constituted hegemonic spaces of Europe and the United States, but it also gives serious attention to conflicts and complexities within the West. Inadequate understandings of the complex history of modernity have led to simplistic and untenable positions that unknowingly repeat colonialism's ideological juxtapositions of "us" and "them," with modernity (and all the positive connotations of historical progress that accrue to the term) on one side and inscrutable backwardness all on the other. This results in ghettoized scholarship that is damaging to all.

The standard equation of modernity with the West needs to be problematized and opened up to comparative examination. The Institute hopes to galvanize work in this direction by encouraging cross-disciplinary collaborative research that advances a genuinely global analysis of modernity that is also empirically faithful to geographical and historical specificity. By bringing attention to less frequently studied aesthetic and social practices from non-Western and immigrant communities, the Institute hopes to correct accounts of modernity as primarily Western in origin and dynamics.

To learn more about the ICM, please visit our website: http://www.icm.arts.cornell.edu/.

INDEX

"Passim" (literally "scattered") indicates intermittent discussion of a topic over a cluster of pages.

ABOUT PM PRESS

PM Press was founded at the end of 2007 by a small collection of folks with decades of publishing, media, and organizing experience. PM Press co-conspirators have published and distributed hundreds of books, pamphlets, CDs, and DVDs. Members of PM have founded enduring book fairs, spearheaded victorious tenant organizing campaigns, and worked closely with bookstores, academic conferences, and even rock bands to deliver political and challenging ideas to all walks of life. We're old enough to know what we're doing and young enough to know what's at stake.

We seek to create radical and stimulating fiction and non-fiction books, pamphlets, T-shirts, visual and audio materials to entertain, educate, and inspire you. We aim to distribute these through every available channel with every available technology—whether that means you are seeing anarchist classics at our bookfair stalls; reading our latest vegan cookbook at the café; downloading geeky fiction e-books; or digging new music and timely videos from our website.

PM Press is always on the lookout for talented and skilled volunteers, artists, activists, and writers to work with. If you have a great idea for a project or can contribute in some way, please get in touch.

PM Press
PO Box 23912
Oakland, CA 94623
www.pmpress.org

FRIENDS OF PM PRESS

These are indisputably momentous times—the financial system is melting down globally and the Empire is stumbling. Now more than ever there is a vital need for radical ideas.

In the seven years since its founding—and on a mere shoestring—PM Press has risen to the formidable challenge of publishing and distributing knowledge and entertainment for the struggles ahead. With over 300 releases to date, we have published an impressive and stimulating array of literature, art, music, politics, and culture. Using every available medium, we've succeeded in connecting those hungry for ideas and information to those putting them into practice.

Friends of PM allows you to directly help impact, amplify, and revitalize the discourse and actions of radical writers, filmmakers, and artists. It provides us with a stable foundation from which we can build upon our early successes and provides a much-needed subsidy for the materials that can't necessarily pay their own way. You can help make that happen—and receive every new title automatically delivered to your door once a month—by joining as a Friend of PM Press. And, we'll throw in a free T-shirt when you sign up.

Here are your options:

- **$30 a month** Get all books and pamphlets plus 50% discount on all webstore purchases
- **$40 a month** Get all PM Press releases (including CDs and DVDs) plus 50% discount on all webstore purchases
- **$100 a month** Superstar—Everything plus PM merchandise, free downloads, and 50% discount on all webstore purchases

For those who can't afford $30 or more a month, we're introducing **Sustainer Rates** at $15, $10 and $5. Sustainers get a free PM Press T-shirt and a 50% discount on all purchases from our website.

Your Visa or Mastercard will be billed once a month, until you tell us to stop. Or until our efforts succeed in bringing the revolution around. Or the financial meltdown of Capital makes plastic redundant. Whichever comes first.

Demanding the Impossible: A History of Anarchism

Peter Marshall

ISBN: 978-1-60486-064-1
$28.95 840 pages

Navigating the broad 'river of anarchy', from Taoism to Situationism, from Ranters to Punk rockers, from individualists to communists, from anarcho-syndicalists to anarcha-feminists, *Demanding the Impossible* is an authoritative and lively study of a widely misunderstood subject. It explores the key anarchist concepts of society and the state, freedom and equality, authority and power and investigates the successes and failure of the anarchist movements throughout the world. While remaining sympathetic to anarchism, it presents a balanced and critical account. It covers not only the classic anarchist thinkers, such as Godwin, Proudhon, Bakunin, Kropotkin, Reclus and Emma Goldman, but also other libertarian figures, such as Nietzsche, Camus, Gandhi, Foucault and Chomsky. No other book on anarchism covers so much so incisively.

In this updated edition, a new epilogue examines the most recent developments, including 'post-anarchism' and 'anarcho-primitivism' as well as the anarchist contribution to the peace, green and 'Global Justice' movements.

Demanding the Impossible is essential reading for anyone wishing to understand what anarchists stand for and what they have achieved. It will also appeal to those who want to discover how anarchism offers an inspiring and original body of ideas and practices which is more relevant than ever in the twenty-first century.

"Demanding the Impossible *is the book I always recommend when asked—as I often am—for something on the history and ideas of anarchism."*
—Noam Chomsky

"Attractively written and fully referenced… bound to be the standard history."
—Colin Ward, *Times Educational Supplement*

"Large, labyrinthine, tentative: for me these are all adjectives of praise when applied to works of history, and Demanding the Impossible *meets all of them."*
—George Woodcock, *Independent*

Stop, Thief!
The Commons, Enclosures, and Resistance

Peter Linebaugh

ISBN: 978-1-60486-747-3
$21.95 304 pages

In this majestic tour de force, celebrated historian Peter Linebaugh takes aim at the thieves of land, the polluters of the seas, the ravagers of the forests, the despoilers of rivers, and the removers of mountaintops. Scarcely a society has existed on the face of the earth that has not had commoning at its heart. "Neither the state nor the market," say the planetary commoners. These essays kindle the embers of memory to ignite our future commons.

From Thomas Paine to the Luddites, from Karl Marx—who concluded his great study of capitalism with the enclosure of commons—to the practical dreamer William Morris—who made communism into a verb and advocated communizing industry and agriculture—to the 20th-century communist historian E.P. Thompson, Linebaugh brings to life the vital commonist tradition. He traces the red thread from the great revolt of commoners in 1381 to the enclosures of Ireland, and the American commons, where European immigrants who had been expelled from their commons met the immense commons of the native peoples and the underground African-American urban commons. Illuminating these struggles in this indispensable collection, Linebaugh reignites the ancient cry, "STOP, THIEF!"

"There is not a more important historian living today. Period."
—Robin D.G. Kelley, author of *Freedom Dreams: The Black Radical Imagination*

"E.P. Thompson, you may rest now. Linebaugh restores the dignity of the despised luddites with a poetic grace worthy of the master… [A] commonist manifesto for the 21st century."
—Mike Davis, author of *Planet of Slums*

"Peter Linebaugh's great act of historical imagination… takes the cliché of 'globalization' and makes it live. The local and the global are once again shown to be inseparable—as they are, at present, for the machine-breakers of the new world crisis."
—T.J. Clark, author of *Farewell to an Idea*

Revolution at Point Zero: Housework, Reproduction, and Feminist Struggle

Silvia Federici

ISBN: 978-1-60486-333-8
$15.95 208 pages

Written between 1974 and the present, *Revolution at Point Zero* collects forty years of research and theorizing on the nature of housework, social reproduction, and women's struggles on this terrain—to escape it, to better its conditions, to reconstruct it in ways that provide an alternative to capitalist relations.

Indeed, as Federici reveals, behind the capitalist organization of work and the contradictions inherent in "alienated labor" is an explosive ground zero for revolutionary practice upon which are decided the daily realities of our collective reproduction.

Beginning with Federici's organizational work in the Wages for Housework movement, the essays collected here unravel the power and politics of wide but related issues including the international restructuring of reproductive work and its effects on the sexual division of labor, the globalization of care work and sex work, the crisis of elder care, the development of affective labor, and the politics of the commons.

"Finally we have a volume that collects the many essays that over a period of four decades Silvia Federici has written on the question of social reproduction and women's struggles on this terrain. While providing a powerful history of the changes in the organization of reproductive labor, Revolution at Point Zero *documents the development of Federici's thought on some of the most important questions of our time: globalization, gender relations, the construction of new commons."*
—Mariarosa Dalla Costa, coauthor of *The Power of Women and the Subversion of the Community* and *Our Mother Ocean*

"As the academy colonizes and tames women's studies, Silvia Federici speaks the experience of a generation of women for whom politics was raw, passionately lived, often in the shadow of an uncritical Marxism. She spells out the subtle violence of housework and sexual servicing, the futility of equating waged work with emancipation, and the ongoing invisibility of women's reproductive labors. Under neoliberal globalization women's exploitation intensifies—in land enclosures, in forced migration, in the crisis of elder care. With ecofeminist thinkers and activists, Federici argues that protecting the means of subsistence now becomes the key terrain of struggle, and she calls on women North and South to join hands in building new commons."
—Ariel Salleh, author of *Ecofeminism as Politics: Nature, Marx, and the Postmodern*

The Revolution of Everyday Life

Raoul Vaneigem
Translated by Donald Nicholson-Smith

ISBN: 978-1-60486-678-0
$20.00 288 pages

Originally published just months before the May 1968 upheavals in France, Raoul Vaneigem's *The Revolution of Everyday Life* offered a lyrical and aphoristic critique of the "society of the spectacle" from the point of view of individual experience. Whereas Debord's masterful analysis of the new historical conditions that triggered the uprisings of the 1960s armed the revolutionaries of the time with theory, Vaneigem's book described their feelings of desperation directly, and armed them with "formulations capable of firing point-blank on our enemies."

"I realise," writes Vaneigem in his introduction, "that I have given subjective will an easy time in this book, but let no one reproach me for this without first considering the extent to which the objective conditions of the contemporary world advance the cause of subjectivity day after day."

Vaneigem names and defines the alienating features of everyday life in consumer society: survival rather than life, the call to sacrifice, the cultivation of false needs, the dictatorship of the commodity, subjection to social roles, and above all the replacement of God by the Economy. And in the second part of his book, "Reversal of Perspective," he explores the countervailing impulses that, in true dialectical fashion, persist within the deepest alienation: creativity, spontaneity, poetry, and the path from isolation to communication and participation.

For "To desire a different life is already that life in the making." And "fulfillment is expressed in the singular but conjugated in the plural."

The present English translation was first published by Rebel Press of London in 1983. This new edition of *The Revolution of Everyday Life* has been reviewed and corrected by the translator and contains a new preface addressed to English-language readers by Raoul Vaneigem. The book is the first of several translations of works by Vaneigem that PM Press plans to publish in uniform volumes. Vaneigem's classic work is to be followed by *The Knight, the Lady, the Devil, and Death* (2003) and *The Inhumanity of Religion* (2000).